Visual Basic®
Instant Res

Visual Basic® 2005 Instant Results

Thearon Willis

John Wiley and Sons

Visual Basic® 2005 Instant Results

Published by
Wiley Publishing, Inc.
10475 Crosspoint Boulevard
Indianapolis, IN 46256
www.wiley.com

Copyright © 2007 by Wiley Publishing, Inc., Indianapolis, Indiana

Published simultaneously in Canada

ISBN: 978-0-470-11871-9

Manufactured in the United States of America

10 9 8 7 6 5 4 3 2 1

Library of Congress Cataloging-in-Publication Data is available from the Publisher

For general information on our other products and services please contact our Customer Care Department within the United States at (800) 762-2974, outside the United States at (317) 572-3993, or fax (317) 572-4002.

Wiley also publishes its books in a variety of electronic formats. Some content that appears in print may not be available in electronic books.

For my daughter, Stephanie, my most precious gift from God.

For Wendy, my love and friend in Christ.

About the Author

Thearon Willis is a senior consultant with over 25 years of programming experience. He started writing applications using the Basic language in 1980 and later moved on to Visual Basic and finally to Visual Basic .NET. He began working with databases in 1987 and has been hooked on writing database applications every since. He has experience with SQL Server, Oracle, and DB2 but works with SQL Server on a daily basis. Thearon has programmed in several other languages, some of which include C++, Assembler, Pascal, and COBOL. However, he enjoys Visual Basic .NET the best, as it provides the features needed to quickly build Windows and Web applications as well as components and Web Services. He currently develops intranet applications, Web Services, and server-side and client-side utilities using Visual Basic .NET. Most of these applications and utilities are database-driven and make use of XML and XSL.

Credits

Acquisitions Editor
Katie Mohr

Development Editor
Sydney Jones

Technical Editor
Andrew Parsons

Production Editor
William A. Barton

Copy Editor
Luann Rouff

Editorial Manager
Mary Beth Wakefield

Production Manager
Tim Tate

Vice President and Executive Group Publisher
Richard Swadley

Vice President and Executive Publisher
Joseph B. Wikert

Graphics and Production Specialists
Mike Park, Happenstance-Type-O-Rama
Craig Woods, Happenstance-Type-O-Rama

Proofreading
Ian Golder, Word One

Indexing
Johnna VanHoose Dinset

Anniversary Logo Design
Richard Pacifico

Acknowledgments

First and foremost I want to thank God for giving me the wisdom and knowledge to share with others. I would also like to thank Katie Mohr for giving me the opportunity to write this book, Sydney Jones for her hard work in editing it, and Andrew Parsons for his technical reviews. Also, thanks to all the other people at Wiley who worked so hard to bring this book to market after the writing was done.

Contents

Contents

Contents

INTRODUCTION

Visual Basic 2005 Instant Results is another title from the Wrox Instant Results series, which is designed for all levels of Visual Basic 2005 programmers who like a fast-track style of learning the Visual Basic .NET programming language. This book provides you with complete sample projects that are used in the real world. There are no step-by-step instructions for building the projects in this book. Instead, the compiled and source code for each project in this book is provided on the enclosed CD-ROM, and a discussion of the code in the projects is presented, enabling you to learn as little or as much about the code as you deem necessary.

What this book provides over most other titles is an instant source code repository, enabling you to use the classes in each of the projects throughout this book in your own applications. Another benefit of this book is that a code explanation is provided for the code in each class so that you can gain a better understanding of the more difficult code, enabling you to customize the code to meet your specific needs. The sample applications use the classes described, providing you with a complete understanding of how the classes fit together and work in an application.

Who This Book Is For

This book is ideal for any programmers with Visual Basic .NET experience who want to learn the new features of Visual Basic 2005 or any programmers who merely want to enhance their programming skills. It is also ideal for developers who have previous experience developing complete desktop Windows applications, but any developer with a desire to learn will find the material in this book useful. You should have a basic understanding of object-oriented programming to fully understand how classes are built and used in applications.

Because this book provides a fast-track learning style, each chapter is independent of the others. You can skim over the table of contents in this book to find a chapter that looks interesting to you and then simply dive into that chapter. This book is meant to be a quick reference guide, providing complete applications covering a specific topic. Some chapters may repeat a concept or topic for a thorough learning experience or may cover a concept or topic in more depth. Other chapters may refer to a concept or topic previously discussed, and a reference to the appropriate chapter will be provided so that you may look at that chapter for a full explanation of the concept or topic being covered.

What This Book Covers

This book contains 10 complete projects that demonstrate a wide variety of topics for desktop Windows applications, including how to access Web Services and how to make HTTP Web requests. Each project provides complete instructions on installing the compiled program so that you can run the sample applications as you read through the material. The goal of each chapter is to enable you to understand and quickly modify the complete source code that is included for each project so that you can experiment with enhancing the sample applications or use the classes in your own applications. Through the repeated design discussions and source code explanations, you'll gain a better understanding of the applications and how they work.

How This Book Is Structured

This book is similarly designed to other Wrox Press Instant Results titles in that it serves as a reference manual of usable and instructional source projects, rather than a traditional, linear book. This is because most programmers do not need to absorb all of the available information on a particular subject in a traditional fashion. Many times, programmers are looking for the answers within the code, and then read content or material on it as an afterthought. This book aims to satisfy this tendency, but not at the expense of providing quality information and useful instruction at the same time.

The structure of each chapter follows this general pattern:

- Overview — What does the application do?
- How to use the application
- Design
- Code and code explanation
- Setting up the application

Each application is designed with reusable components and classes. Components, classes, and noteworthy project files are highlighted and analyzed, with sufficient information in each chapter to make the research effort as easy as possible.

The chapters of the book, and consequently the source projects used within this book, are as follows:

- Chapter 1: Desktop Weather
- Chapter 2: Password Keeper
- Chapter 3: Application Registry Manager
- Chapter 4: Event Log and Trace Writing
- Chapter 5: Event Log Service
- Chapter 6: Multi-Threaded Notepad
- Chapter 7: Notepad Printing
- Chapter 8: Data Binding
- Chapter 9: Database Image Manager
- Chapter 10: Custom Controls

What You Need to Use This Book

The basic software that you need to use this book is Windows 2000 Professional or Windows XP Professional with Visual Studio 2005 Professional Edition. Chapters 6 and 7 require Microsoft Word

2003 and Chapter 9 requires SQL Server 2005 Express. Any additional specific software require-ments are listed at the beginning of each chapter. Because this book focuses on Visual Basic 2005, version 2.0 of the .NET Framework is required to run the applications.

Source Code

All of the source code used in this book is available on the companion CD-ROM and available for download at www.wrox.com. Once at the site, simply locate the book's title (either by using the Search box or by using one of the title lists) and click the Download Code link on the book's detail page to obtain all the source code for the book.

> *Because many books have similar titles, you may find it easier to search by the ISBN; this book's ISBN is 978-0-470-11871-9.*

Once you download the code, just decompress the file with your favorite compression tool. Alternatively, you can go to the main Wrox code download page at www.wrox.com/dynamic/ books/download.aspx to see the code available for this book and all other Wrox books.

Errata

We've made every effort to make sure that there are no errors in the text or in the code. However, no one is perfect and mistakes do occur. If you find an error in one of our books, such as a spelling mistake or a faulty piece of code, we would be very grateful to have your feedback. By sending in errata, you may save another reader from hours of frustration, and of course you will be helping us provide even higher quality information.

To find the errata page for this book, go to www.wrox.com, and locate the title using the Search box or one of the title lists. Then, on the book details page, click the Book Errata link. On this page you can view all errata that has been submitted for this book and posted by Wrox editors. A complete book list, including links to each book's errata, is also available at www.wrox.com/ misc-pages/booklist.shtml.

If you don't spot "your" error on the Book Errata page, go to www.wrox.com/contact/ techsupport.shtml and complete the form there to send us the error you have found. We'll check the information and, if appropriate, post a message to the book's errata page and fix the problem in subsequent editions of the book.

p2p.wrox.com

For author and peer discussion join the P2P forums at p2p.wrox.com. The forums are a Web-based system for you to post messages relating to Wrox books and related technologies and to interact with other readers and technology users. The forums offer a subscription feature to e-mail you topics of interest of your choosing when new posts are made to the forums. Wrox authors, editors, other indus-try experts, and your fellow readers are present on these forums.

Introduction

At p2p.wrox.com you will find a number of different forums that will help you, not only while you read this book, but also as you develop your own applications. To join the forums, just follow these steps:

1. Go to p2p.wrox.com and click the Register link.
2. Read the terms of use and click Agree.
3. Complete the required information to join as well as any optional information you wish to provide and click Submit.
4. Follow the instructions to subscribe and fill in your e-mail address and password.
5. You will receive an e-mail with information describing how to verify your account information and complete the joining process.

Once you join, you can post new messages and respond to messages other users post. You'll find this book's own forum under the Books category, which is available from the home page or by clicking View All Forums on the menu on the left. You can read messages at any time on the Web. If you would like to have messages from a particular forum e-mailed to you, click the Subscribe To This Forum icon by the forum name in the forum listing.

For more information about how to use the Wrox P2P forum, be sure to read the P2P FAQs for answers to questions about how the forum software works as well as many common questions specific to P2P and Wrox books. To read the FAQs, click the FAQ link on any P2P page.

1

Desktop Weather

Planning a trip to the beach, the mountains, or just a day of work in the yard? Most people want to know what the weather forecast will hold for the next several days so they can plan their outdoor activities accordingly. If you are at work, you may simply want to know what the current temperature is so you can plan that walk at lunchtime. Weather plays an important factor in most everything we do. How many people in a hurry turn on the evening news just to catch the weather forecast for the next several days?

The Desktop Weather program provides this information on your computer, where most of us spend our days working. Want to know what the current temperature is? With the Desktop Weather program you can simply look down at the temperature icon in the system tray. Want to know what Mother Nature holds in store for the next several days? Double-click the Desktop Weather's temperature icon in the system tray to display the Desktop Weather form showing the seven-day forecast.

In this chapter you will learn how to customize the Desktop Weather program, which uses a Web Service to retrieve the weather data for your area. This program uses the Web Service created by the National Weather Service in the United States to provide weather data for the United States. However, if you live in another country, you can adapt the Desktop Weather program to use a Web Service from anyone who provides weather information in your country.

Some of the technologies included in the Desktop Weather program are as follows:

- ❑ Accessing a Web Service
- ❑ Accessing a Web site programmatically
- ❑ Reading XML
- ❑ Using application and user settings in the `app.config` file
- ❑ Using the `NotifyIcon` class to create an icon in the system tray

Using the Desktop Weather Program

The Desktop Weather program can be started whenever you want or you can copy the program to your startup folder and have the program start when you log onto your computer. The section "Configuring the Application" at the end of this chapter describes how to add the program to your startup folder.

When the Desktop Weather program is started, it places a notification icon in the system tray with a temperature reading of 0° Fahrenheit. The program then checks to see whether a zip code has been saved in the application's user configuration file. If a zip code has not been saved in the user configuration file, the Desktop Weather form is displayed with the default label text and zeroes for the temperature, as shown in Figure 1-1.

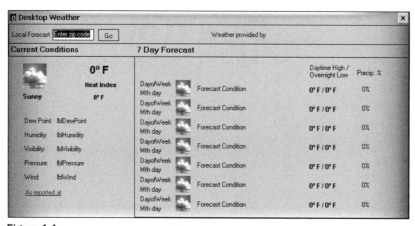

Figure 1-1

Once a zip code has been entered, the program will save it in the application's user configuration file and then make a call to the National Weather Service's Web site to retrieve the current forecast and then to the National Weather Service's Web Service to retrieve the seven-day forecast. This information is then updated on the form and the form's icon is updated with the current temperature, as shown in Figure 1-2.

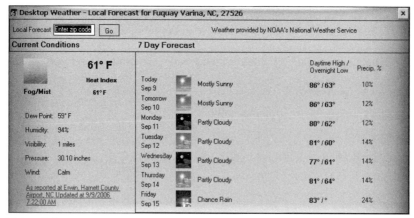

Figure 1-2

In addition to updating the form's icon, the notification icon displayed in the system tray is updated with the current temperature, as shown in Figure 1-3. When you hover your mouse over the notification icon in the system tray, a tool tip is displayed with the text `Desktop Weather`.

To display the Desktop Weather form, you can either double-click the notification icon or right-click the notification icon to view its context menu, shown in Figure 1-3. Note that clicking the X in the upper right-hand corner of the Desktop Weather form merely hides the form and does not stop the program. To stop the program, you must select Exit from the context menu (refer to Figure 1-3).

Figure 1-3

The Desktop Weather program will try to find the closest weather observation station for your zip code. It shows the source of the weather information in the lower left-hand corner of the Desktop Weather form shown in Figure 1-2. However, the weather observation station chosen may not be the closest observation station for your zip code.

Clicking the hyperlinked label on the form opens the Observation Stations dialog box shown in Figure 1-4. You can scroll through this list and choose the closest observation station for your zip code. After you click OK, the Desktop Weather program will retrieve the data from the observation station selected and update the current and seven-day forecast on the Desktop Weather form.

Figure 1-4

That covers the basics of how the Desktop Weather program works from a user's perspective. The next few sections describe the design of the Desktop Weather program and then we will dive into the details of how the code works.

Design of the Desktop Weather Program

The design of the Desktop Weather program is such that all of the heavy lifting of this program is done by classes that are distinct and separate from the Desktop Weather form that is considered the main program.

All of the classes used in this program have been consolidated into a Weather namespace, making it easier to use and locate the appropriate classes in the main program and in your own programs.

Additionally, the design allows for customization of the classes without affecting the main program. Thus, you can choose to use another Web Service to get your weather data and then just customize the WeatherData class that accesses and uses the Web Service data without affecting the main program.

Figure 1-5 shows the forms and classes used and how they relate to one another. The following sections go into the details of the main program and these classes.

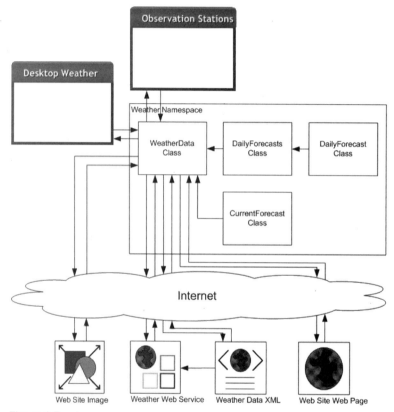

Figure 1-5

Main Program

The Desktop Weather program is the core of the application. This is the form that displays the weather data and the program that makes the calls to the WeatherData class to retrieve the current and seven-day forecast. This program also enables you to display the Observations Stations dialog box so you can select the weather observation station from which you want weather data. Not every zip code has an observation station so this form enables you to choose an observation station in a city close to your zip code. Observation stations report the current weather conditions and send this information to the National Weather Service.

The main program is also responsible for creating the notification icon in the system tray, creating the context menu used by the notification icon, and calling the methods in the WeatherData class every half hour to update the weather data.

The main program is as simple as that. It contains very few procedures, and provides the application with the basic user interface. All of the real work happens in the WeatherData class.

Classes

There are four classes in this program: WeatherData, CurrentForecast, DailyForecasts, and DailyForecast. The CurrentForecast class contains the current forecast data, while the DailyForecast class contains the forecast for a specific day. The DailyForecasts class contains a collection of DailyForecast classes that make up the seven-day forecast. The majority of the logic in this application lies in the WeatherData class, as indicated in Figure 1-5.

CurrentForecast Class

The CurrentForecast class merely contains a set of public properties that are set by the WeatherData class and read by the Desktop Weather form. Thus, the CurrentForecast class is more or less a repository for data. Table 1-1 details the public properties in this class.

Table 1-1: Public Properties of the CurrentForecast Class

Property	Return Type	Description
Conditions	String	The current weather conditions
DewpointCelsius	Integer	The current dew point in Celsius
DewpointCelsiusString	String	The dew point formatted as a string with the degree sign and the letter C
DewpointFahrenheit	Integer	The current dew point in Fahrenheit
DewpointFahrenheitString	String	The dew point formatted as a string with the degree sign and the letter F
HeatIndexCelsius	Integer	The current heat index in Celsius
HeatIndexCelsiusString	String	The heat index formatted as a string with the degree sign and the letter C
HeatIndexFahrenheit	Integer	The current heat index in Fahrenheit
HeatIndexFahrenheitString	String	The heat index formatted as a string with the degree sign and the letter F
LastUpdateDate	Date	The date and time that this data was last updated by the reporting weather station

Continued

Table 1-1: Public Properties of the CurrentForecast Class *(continued)*

Property	Return Type	Description
Location	String	The weather station that reported this data
PressureInches	Decimal	The current pressure in inches
PressureInchesString	String	The current pressure formatted as a string with the word inches
PressureMillibars	Decimal	The current pressure in millibars
PressureMillibarsString	String	The current pressure formatted as a string with the word millibars
RelativeHumidity	String	The current relative humidity formatted with the percent sign
TemperatureCelsius	Integer	The current temperature in Celsius
TemperatureCelsiusString	String	The current temperature formatted as a string with the degree sign and the letter C
TemperatureFahrenheit	Integer	The current temperature in Fahrenheit
TemperatureFahrenheitString	String	The current temperature formatted as a string with the degree sign and the letter F
Visibility	String	The current visibility in miles
WeatherSource	String	The source of the weather information
Wind	String	The current wind speed and direction

DailyForecast Class

The DailyForecast class contains a set of public properties that are set by the WeatherData class and read by the Desktop Weather form. Like the CurrentForecast class, this class is just a repository for data. A collection of these classes is added to the DailyForecasts class to represent the seven-day forecast. Therefore, each instance of the DailyForecast class contains the forecast for a given day. Table 1-2 details the public properties in this class.

Table 1-2: Public Properties of the DailyForecast Class

Property	Return Type	Description
ForecastDate	Date	The date that this forecast is for
ForecastDay	String	The day of the month that this forecast is for

Table 1-2: Public Properties of the DailyForecast Class *(continued)*

Property	Return Type	Description
ForecastDayName	String	The forecast day name (e.g., Today, Tomorrow, Monday, Tuesday)
ForecastHighLowTemp	String	The daytime high and nighttime low temperatures for the date of this forecast, formatted with degree signs and a forward slash separating the temperatures
ForecastImagePath	String	The Web URL of the forecast image
ForecastMonthName	String	The month that this forecast is for
ForecastPrecipitation	String	The precipitation that this forecast is for, formatted with the percent sign
ForecastSummary	String	The weather conditions for the forecasted date

DailyForecasts Class

The DailyForecasts class inherits the CollectionBase class in the .NET Framework and provides a collection of DailyForecast classes. This class contains the necessary methods to add, remove, and access DailyForecast classes within the collection. Table 1-3 details the methods and properties in this class.

Table 1-3: Methods and Properties of the DailyForecasts Class

Method/Property	Return Type	Description
Public Sub Add(ByVal dailyForecast As DailyForecast)	N/A	Adds a DailyForecast class to the collection
Public Overloads Sub RemoveAt(ByVal index As Integer)	N/A	Removes a DailyForecast class from the collection at the specified index
Public Sub Remove(ByVal dailyForecast As DailyForecast)	N/A	Removes the currently referenced DailyForecast class from the collection
Public ReadOnly Property Item(ByVal index As Integer) As DailyForecast	DailyForecast	Returns the DailyForecast class from the collection at the specified index
Public ReadOnly Property Item(ByVal dailyForecast As DailyForecast) As DailyForecast	DailyForecast	Returns the currently referenced DailyForecast class from the collection

WeatherData Class

The `WeatherData` class is the core of the Desktop Weather application. This class is where all the work takes place, calling the Web Service to get the current and seven-day forecast, and populating the classes for these forecasts with data. Table 1-4 details the methods and properties in this class.

The Weather Web Service provided by the National Weather Service uses longitude and latitude coordinates to retrieve the weather data. The Desktop Weather form merely asks for a zip code to retrieve weather data for. Therefore, the zip code provided must be translated into longitude and latitude coordinates.

There are two main functions in the `WeatherData` class: `GetCurrentForecast` and `Get7DayForecast`. As you may have surmised, the `GetCurrentForecast` function gets the current forecast for your zip code. This function has logic built into it to look up the zip code provided at the Geocoder Web site to retrieve the longitude and latitude coordinates.

It will also find the observation station that most closely matches the longitude and latitude coordinates found for the zip code. The observation stations are provided by the National Weather Service Web site as a unique URL. Each observation station provides its weather data to the National Weather Service. The National Weather Service in turn provides a specific RSS (Really Simple Syndication) feed of the current conditions reported by the observation stations.

This function then takes the data from the RSS feed and populates the `CurrentForecast` class and returns that data to the caller — in this case, the Desktop Weather form.

The other main function in this class is the `Get7DayForecast` function. This function calls the Weather Web Service to retrieve the seven-day forecast. The Weather Web Service returns a forecast for any number of days, but a seven-day forecast is typically adequate for most needs. Once the data is returned from the Weather Web Service, this function instantiates seven instances of the `DailyForecast` classes and adds them to the `DailyForecasts` class. It then populates each class with the appropriate data and returns the collection of forecasts to the caller.

Table 1-4: Methods and Properties of the WeatherData Class

Method	Return Type	Description
`Public Sub New()`	N/A	Reads all user settings from the application's `user.config` file
`Protected Overridable Sub Dispose(ByVal disposing As Boolean)`	N/A	Saves the user's settings in the application's `user.config` file
`Public Sub FindObservationStation()`	N/A	This procedure finds the closest observation station match for the longitude and latitude for the zip code specified. If no match can be ascertained, the Observation Stations form is displayed, which enables users to select the closest observation station for their zip code.

Continued

Table 1-4: Methods and Properties of the WeatherData Class *(continued)*

Method	Return Type	Description
`Public Function Get7DayForecast(ByVal zipCode As Integer)`	`DailyForecasts`	Calls the Web Service to retrieve the seven-day forecast, instantiates the `DailyForecasts` class, and adds a collection of `DailyForecast` classes to it. It then returns the collection as a `DailyForecasts` class.
`Public Function GetCurrentForecast (ByVal zipCode As Integer)`	`CurrentForecast`	Gets the current forecast XML file from the National Weather Service's Web site via an HTTP request. Instantiates the `CurrentForecast` class, sets its properties, and returns the `CurrentForecast` class.
`Private Function Http(ByVal url As String)`	`String`	Makes a call to a Web site and returns the data as a string
`Public Function StreamBitmap(ByVal url As String)`	`Stream`	Retrieves an image from the Web and returns it as an IO Stream
`Public Sub ZipCodeLookup(ByVal zipCode As Integer)`	`N/A`	Gets the longitude and latitude for a given zip code as well as the city and state. It saves this information in local variables that are saved to the application's `user.config` file.
`Public ReadOnly Property Latitude()`	`Decimal`	Returns the latitude for the current zip code
`Public ReadOnly Property Longitude()`	`Decimal`	Returns the longitude for the current zip code
`Public ReadOnly Property Location()`	`String`	Returns the location for the current zip code
`Public ReadOnly Property State()`	`String`	Returns the state abbreviation for the current zip code
`Public ReadOnly Property RawCurrentForecast()`	`String`	Returns the raw XML used to generate the current forecast
`Public ReadOnly Property Raw7DayForecast()`	`String`	Returns the raw XML used to generate the seven-day forecast

Code and Code Explanation

This section describes the application details and how all the pieces fit together. Because there is not enough room to explain all of the code, only the major procedures and functions are covered. The bulk of the work of this application is performed in the `WeatherData` class, so this is where the majority of your time will be spent.

Resource Files

The Desktop Weather application displays the current temperature in the system tray, so you must have icons created for the temperature range in your area. The program currently has icons in the range of 0 to 110, which represents the temperatures most likely to occur in my local area.

It is highly probable that you may live in an area where temperatures exceed the low or high range currently provided by the program. If that is the case, you'll need to create the appropriate temperature icons and add them to the application. All icons are stored in the resource file for the application that is compiled in the executable program. After adding new icons to the resource file, you need to recompile the application.

You can use your favorite icon editor to create new temperature icons or you can create new temperature icons directly in the Visual Studio IDE. The Visual Studio IDE provides a very basic icon editor but it does provide a font tool, so creating the basic temperature icons displayed in the system tray is relatively easy.

Settings

This application uses one application setting and seven user settings. The application setting cannot be changed by any user and contains the URL of the Weather Web Service. The user settings are read and saved by the application based on what the user enters and does. Table 1-5 lists the various user and application settings.

Table 1-5: User and Application Settings

Name	Type	Scope
Latitude	Decimal	User
Longitude	Decimal	User
State	String	User
ZipCode	Integer	User
CurrentForecastUrl	String	User
FormLocation	System.Drawing.Point	User
Location	String	User
Desktop_Weather_NationalWeatherService _ndfdXML	Web Service URL	Application

The `Latitude`, `Longitude`, `State`, and `ZipCode` settings are self-explanatory. The `CurrentForecastUrl` setting is used to store the URL of the RSS feed for the current forecast. The `Location` setting is used to store the city, state, and zip code string displayed at the top of the Desktop Weather form. Finally, the `FormLocation` setting is used to store the position on the screen to which the user moves the Desktop Weather form. This location is then used to position the form the next time the form is displayed or the next time the program starts.

The `Desktop_Weather_NationalWeatherService_ndfdXML` setting is generated by Visual Studio 2005. When the Web reference was set, this setting was automatically generated. To change the Weather Web Service to your preferred Weather Web Service, open the solution in Visual Studio 2005, expand the Web References folder in the Solution Explorer, and then click `NationalWeatherService`. In the Properties window, change the `Web Reference` property, replacing the URL with the URL of your Weather Web Service.

DesktopWeather Form

There are three main procedures in the DesktopWeather form: `DesktopWeather_Load`, `btnGo_Click`, and `GetWeatherData`. The logical place to start is the `DesktopWeather_Load` procedure.

The `DesktopWeather_Load` procedure is executed when the application first starts. The first part of this code sets up the context menu that is used by the `NotifyIcon` in the system tray. It instantiates the `ContextMenu` class and the `MenuItem` class to create and add the menu items to the context menu.

A `Menu` and `ContextMenu` contain a collection of `MenuItem` classes. A `MenuItem` is the menu item that you see. For example, in the Visual Studio IDE, the File menu would be represented by a `Menu` class, and the menu items Open and New Project would be represented by the `MenuItem` class.

In the following code, the `objContextMenu` object is a context menu that contains two menu items: `objShowWeather` and `objExit`. These two objects are defined as a `MenuItem` class and one of the constructors for the `MenuItem` class enables you to pass the caption of the menu item as it is displayed to the user. Here, the `objShowWeather` object will have a menu item that is displayed as Show Weather, while the `objExit` object will have a menu item that is displayed as Exit.

You can also add menu items directly to the `Menu` or `ContextMenu` classes if you do not need to handle any events for the menu item. This is the case with the menu item separator, which is specified as a single dash. When the context menu is built and displayed, the single dash becomes a solid line separating the two menu items. Here is the code:

```
Private Sub DesktopWeather_Load(ByVal sender As Object, _
    ByVal e As System.EventArgs) Handles Me.Load

    'Setup the context menu
    objContextMenu = New ContextMenu
    objShowWeather = New MenuItem("&Show Weather")
    objContextMenu.MenuItems.Add(objShowWeather)
    objContextMenu.MenuItems.Add("-")
    objExit = New MenuItem("E&xit")
    objContextMenu.MenuItems.Add(objExit)
```

The `NotifyIcon` object is instantiated next and the icon with the number 0 is loaded from the resource file and set in the `objNotifyIcon` object. This is the icon that will be displayed in the system tray, and a zero temperature is an indication to the user that a zip code must be entered.

When you add resources, such as icons and images, to the resource file that begin with a number instead of a letter, Visual Studio prefixes these names with an underscore. The reason behind this is that Visual Studio implements read-only properties with the resource name. As you are undoubtedly aware, property names cannot begin with a number but can begin with an underscore. Thus, Visual Studio has implemented the icon name `0.ico` as a property named `_0`.

The tooltip text is set next in the `Text` property. This is the text that is displayed when you hover your mouse over the temperature icon in the system tray. The last line of code here sets the context menu to be associated with the icon:

```
'Setup the NotifyIcon object
objNotifyIcon = New NotifyIcon
objNotifyIcon.Icon = My.Resources._0
objNotifyIcon.Text = "Desktop Weather"
objNotifyIcon.Visible = True
objNotifyIcon.ContextMenu = objContextMenu
```

The necessary event handlers are set up next, identifying the objects and events and the procedures to be executed by those objects when the specified event occurs. The `AddHandler` statement accepts two parameters: the event to handle and the procedure to be executed when the event occurs. To specify the event, you specify the object name, type a period, and then select the appropriate event associated with the object as it is displayed in the IntelliSense drop-down menu. To specify the procedure to be executed, type the `AddressOf` keyword and then the procedure name that will handle the event. Note that the procedure you specify must implement the same input parameters that are passed from the event delegate.

```
'Setup event handlers
AddHandler objNotifyIcon.DoubleClick, AddressOf NotifyIcon_DoubleClick
AddHandler objShowWeather.Click, AddressOf ShowWeather_Click
AddHandler objExit.Click, AddressOf Exit_Click
```

Now you set the icons on the form. The first icon is the icon associated with the actual `DesktopWeather` form. This is the icon that is displayed in the taskbar in Windows when the form is displayed. The next icon is the icon that is displayed in the upper-left corner of the `DesktopWeather` form. The `DesktopWeather` form is a borderless form, so it has a `PictureBox` control in the upper-left corner of the form where the icon would normally be displayed if the form had a title bar.

The next line of code positions the form in Windows according to the form location stored in the application's `user.config` file using the user setting `FormLocation`. The last line of code sets the interval for the timer. When the timer's interval has elapsed, it makes a call to the `GetWeatherData` procedure to get the current and seven-day forecasts:

```
'Setup the icons for the program
Me.Icon = My.Resources._0
imgIcon.Image = My.Resources._0.ToBitmap

'Position the form
Me.Location = New Point(My.Settings.FormLocation)
```

```
'Setup the timer
objTimer.Interval = 1800000 '30 minutes
```

The last part of code in the `DesktopWeather_Load` procedure checks whether a zip code has been stored in the `ZipCode` user setting in the `user.config` file. If a zip code has been stored, it is retrieved and a call is made to the `GetWeatherData` procedure to get the current and seven-day forecasts and the timer is started. Then the `blnShow` variable is set to `False`, indicating that the form should not be shown.

If no zip code is found, the `blnShow` variable is set to `True` and the `DesktopWeather` form is displayed and waits for a zip code to be entered:

```
'Get weather if location is available
If My.Settings.ZipCode <> 0 Then
    GetWeatherData()
    objTimer.Start()
    blnShow = False
Else
    blnShow = True
End If
End Sub
```

The next procedure that needs to be discussed is the `btnGo_Click` procedure. This procedure is executed when the user clicks the Go button on the `DesktopWeather` form. The code in this procedure is wrapped in a `Try...Catch...Finally` block. This provides the necessary error handling for this procedure, as a call is made to the `ZipCodeLookup` procedure in the `WeatherData` class.

The first thing that happens in this procedure is validation of the zip code data. This first section of code validates that the zip code entered is a numeric value. If it is not, then the appropriate message is displayed in a `MessageBox` dialog box.

If you are adapting this program for a country that allows alphanumeric postal codes, then you need to change the logic in this section to properly validate postal codes in your area. A separate function could be created that performs the validation and returns a `True/False` value indicating a whether a valid postal code was entered.

```
Private Sub btnGo_Click(ByVal sender As Object, ByVal e As System.EventArgs) _
    Handles btnGo.Click

    Try
        'Validate the zip code
        If Not IsNumeric(txtZipCode.Text) Then
            MessageBox.Show("Zip Code must be a numeric value.", _
            My.Application.Info.Title, MessageBoxButtons.OK, _
            MessageBoxIcon.Warning)
            txtZipCode.Focus()
            Exit Sub
        End If
```

Because looking up the zip code and retrieving the weather data can take some time (5–10 seconds), the Go button is disabled and the application's cursor is changed to a wait cursor, indicating the application is busy doing some work.

13

Next, the `WeatherData` class is instantiated in a `Using...End Using` block and the `ZipCodeLookup` procedure is called. This procedure, which you'll see in detail when the `WeatherData` class is discussed, calls the Geocoder Web site and retrieves the longitude, latitude, city, and state for the zip code provided. It sets this data in local variables in the `WeatherData` class, which in turn saves these values to the appropriate user settings in the `user.config` file:

```
'Disable the Go button and make the mouse cursor busy
btnGo.Enabled = False
Me.Cursor = Cursors.WaitCursor

'Instantiate a new WeatherData object
Using objWeather As New Weather.WeatherData
    'Lookup the zip code provided
    objWeather.ZipCodeLookup(CType(txtZipCode.Text, Integer))
End Using
```

Once the zip code has been processed and the relevant data has been saved to the appropriate user settings in the `user.config` file, a call is made to the `GetWeatherData` procedure. This procedure, discussed next, makes two calls to the `WeatherData` class to get the current and seven-day forecast. The next two lines of code reset the text in the zip code text box on the form and select the text. Finally, the timer is started so that the weather data is updated every half hour:

```
'Get the weather forecasts
GetWeatherData()

'Reset the text
txtZipCode.Text = "Enter Zip Code"
txtZipCode.SelectAll()

'Turn the timer on
objTimer.Start()
```

The last section of code in this procedure provides the error handling should an error occur in any of the calls made to other procedures and functions. Here, you simply display a `MessageBox` dialog box with the appropriate error that has been returned.

The `Finally` block in the following code enables the Go button on the form and sets the application's cursor back to the default cursor. The code in the `Finally` block is always executed, even when an error occurs. The code shown here is housekeeping code to reset the UI:

```
Catch ExceptionErr As Exception
    MessageBox.Show("DesktopWeather.btnGo_Click: " & _
        ExceptionErr.Message, My.Application.Info.Title, _
        MessageBoxButtons.OK, MessageBoxIcon.Error)
Finally
    'Enable the Go button and make the mouse cursor ready
    btnGo.Enabled = True
    Me.Cursor = Cursors.Default
End Try
End Sub
```

The GetWeatherData procedure gets the weather data from the WeatherData class and loads the details of the forecast in the DesktopWeather form. This procedure starts by declaring a couple of local variables that are used to enumerate through the collection of DailyForecast classes and to retrieve and set the current temperature icons.

The code in this procedure is wrapped in a Try...Catch block to handle any errors that might be thrown in the WeatherData class. Inside the Try statement, you declare and instantiate a new instance of the WeatherData class in a Using...End Using statement block. Then you declare the objCurrentForecast object as a CurrentForecast class and call the GetCurrentForecast method on this object to retrieve the current forecast for your area by passing it the zip code from the user settings in the app.config file:

```
Private Sub GetWeatherData()
    'Declare local variables
    Dim intIndex As Integer = 0
    Dim strIconName As String

    Try
        'Instantiate a new WeatherData object for the local forecast
        Using objWeather As New Weather.WeatherData
            'Get the current forecast
            Dim objCurrentForecast As Weather.CurrentForecast
            objCurrentForecast = _
                objWeather.GetCurrentForecast(My.Settings.ZipCode)
```

Next, set the Text property of the form and the Text property of the caption label to the TitleText constant and the location as specified in the Location property of the WeatherData class. You also set the Text property of the credits label near the top of the form using the WeatherSource property. This will tell you who provided the weather data.

The icon name is retrieved from the TemperatureFahrenheit property and set in the strIconName variable. This variable is then used to set the icon in the system tray, the icon for the form, and the icon that is displayed in the upper left-hand corner of the form. The reason why the icon name was set in the local strIconName variable is because we only want to read the TemperatureFahrenheit property once, thereby reducing the amount of code to be executed and increasing the performance of the application.

After the temperature icons have been set, the current conditions image is loaded and then the rest of the current forecast is loaded into the Text properties of the current forecast labels. The current forecast is the forecast displayed on the left-hand side of the DesktopWeather form.

```
            'Set the current forecast labels and images on the form
            Me.Text = TitleText & objWeather.Location
            lblCaption.Text = TitleText & objWeather.Location
            lblCredits.Text = "Weather provided by " & _
                objCurrentForecast.WeatherSource
            strIconName = objCurrentForecast.TemperatureFahrenheit
            objNotifyIcon.Icon = My.Resources.GetIconByName(strIconName)
            Me.Icon = My.Resources.GetIconByName(strIconName)
            imgIcon.Image = My.Resources.GetIconByName(strIconName).ToBitmap
            imgCurrentConditions.Image = New Bitmap(objWeather.StreamBitmap( _
                objCurrentForecast.ForecastImagePath))
            lblCurrentConditions.Text = objCurrentForecast.Conditions
            lblTemperature.Text = _
```

```
                       objCurrentForecast.TemperatureFahrenheitString
            lblHeatIndex.Text = objCurrentForecast.HeatIndexFahrenheitString
            lblDewPoint.Text = objCurrentForecast.DewpointFahrenheitString
            lblHumidity.Text = objCurrentForecast.RelativeHumidity
            lblVisibility.Text = objCurrentForecast.Visibility
            lblPressure.Text = objCurrentForecast.PressureInchesString
            lblWind.Text = objCurrentForecast.Wind
            lblStation.Text = "As reported at " & _
                objCurrentForecast.Location & " Updated at " & _
                objCurrentForecast.LastUpdateDate.ToString
        End Using
```

Now you want to set up another `Using...End Using` statement block to declare and instantiate the `WeatherData` class. You then declare the `objDailyForecasts` object as a `DailyForecasts` class and then call the `Get7DayForecast` method in the `WeatherData` class, again passing the zip code for your area.

Remember that the `DailyForecasts` class actually contains a collection of seven `DailyForecast` classes. To that end, you set up a `For Each...Next` loop to process each `DailyForecast` class in the `objDailyForecasts` object. The `intIndex` variable is used inside this loop to keep track of the current day number so you can properly access the labels and `PictureBox` controls on the form:

```
'Instantiate a new WeatherData object for the local forecast
Using objWeather As New Weather.WeatherData
    'Get the 7 day forecast
    Dim objDailyForecasts As Weather.DailyForecasts
    objDailyForecasts = objWeather.Get7DayForecast(My.Settings.ZipCode)

    'Set the 7 day forecast labels and images on the form
    For Each objDailyForecast As Weather.DailyForecast _
        In objDailyForecasts

        'Increment the index for the days
        intIndex += 1
```

Now you want to loop through the labels on the `Panel` control, which has been named `pnl7DayForecast`, and set their `Text` properties to the appropriate seven-day forecast. You do this in a `For Each...Next` loop accessing the `Controls` collection of the panel. Inside the loop, you check the type of control that you have and compare it against the `Label` control using the `TypeOf` operator. If the control that you have a reference to in the `objControl` object is a `Label` control, you use a `Select...Case` statement to query the `Name` property of the control. Once you find the correct name of the label, you set the `Text` property of that label using the appropriate property from the `objDailyForecast` object:

```
'Loop through the controls on the 7 day forecast panel
For Each objControl As Control In pnl7DayForecast.Controls
    'If the control is a label...
    If TypeOf objControl Is Label Then
        'Find the correct label and set its Text property
        Select Case objControl.Name
            Case "lbl7DayDay" & intIndex.ToString
                objControl.Text = _
                    objDailyForecast.ForecastDayName
            Case "lbl7DayDate" & intIndex.ToString
                objControl.Text = _
```

```
                        objDailyForecast.ForecastMonthName & _
                        " " & objDailyForecast.ForecastDay
                Case "lbl7DayForecastCondition" & intIndex.ToString
                    objControl.Text = _
                        objDailyForecast.ForecastSummary
                Case "lbl7DayHighLow" & intIndex.ToString
                    objControl.Text = _
                        objDailyForecast.ForecastHighLowTemp
                Case "lbl7DayPrecipitation" & intIndex.ToString
                    objControl.Text = _
                        objDailyForecast.ForecastPrecipitation
            End Select
```

If the control that you have is not a `Label` control, you check the control against a `PictureBox` control in the `ElseIf` statement that follows. If the control is a `PictureBox` control, you again use a `Select...Case` statement to find the appropriate `PictureBox` control and set its `Image` property to the image of the forecast.

Notice that you are using the `StreamBitmap` method in the `WeatherData` class to get the image specified in the `ForecastImagePath` and load it in the `Image` property of the `PictureBox` control. The `ForecastImagePath` property merely contains the URL of the image, not the actual image itself. The `StreamBitmap` method will read the image from the URL specified in the `ForecastImagePath` property and return that image as a `Stream` class. Then you can load the image in the `PictureBox` control using the `Stream` provided by the `StreamBitmap` method:

```
                    'Else If the control is a picture box...
            ElseIf TypeOf objControl Is PictureBox Then
                    'Find the correct picture box and
                    'set its Image property
                Select Case objControl.Name
                    Case "img7DayCondition" & intIndex.ToString
                        'The Object class does not provide an Image
                        'property so we must cast the object into the
                        'correct class, in this case a PictureBox
                        DirectCast(objControl, PictureBox).Image = _
                            New Bitmap(objWeather.StreamBitmap( _
                            objDailyForecast.ForecastImagePath))
                End Select
            End If
        Next
    Next
End Using
```

The last part of this procedure contains the `Catch` block, which simply handles any errors that might have occurred and displays a `MessageBox` dialog box indicating the error that occurred:

```
    Catch ExceptionErr As Exception
        MessageBox.Show("DesktopWeather.GetWeatherData: " & _
            ExceptionErr.Message, My.Application.Info.Title, _
            MessageBoxButtons.OK, MessageBoxIcon.Error)
    End Try
End Sub
```

WeatherData Class

The WeatherData class implements the IDisposable interface and therefore has a constructor called New and a destructor called Dispose. This enables you to use this class in the Using...End Using block in the DesktopWeather form. Any class used in the Using...End Using block must implement the IDisposable interface, as the Using...End Using block calls the New constructor when it instantiates the class, and calls the Dispose destructor when it disposes of the class.

When the Desktop Weather application first starts, the user settings in the user.config file are read and stored in cache. Because these values can and do change during the execution of the application, these settings must be reloaded in cache to get the latest changes. The New constructor procedure first reloads the user settings into cache and then uses these settings to set the values in the local variables defined in this class:

```
Public Sub New()
    'Reload the user settings
    My.Settings.Reload()

    'Set default local values from user settings
    If My.Settings.Latitude <> 0 Then
        decLatitude = My.Settings.Latitude
    End If
    If My.Settings.Longitude <> 0 Then
        decLongitude = My.Settings.Longitude
    End If
    If My.Settings.ZipCode <> 0 Then
        intZipCode = My.Settings.ZipCode
    End If
    If My.Settings.State.Trim.Length > 0 Then
        strState = My.Settings.State
    End If
    If My.Settings.Location.Trim.Length > 0 Then
        strLocation = My.Settings.Location
    End If
    If My.Settings.CurrentForecastUrl.Trim.Length > 0 Then
        strCurrentForecastUrl = My.Settings.CurrentForecastUrl
    End If
End Sub
```

The majority of the code in the Dispose procedure is automatically generated when the IDisposable interface is declared in the class. The code to persist the user settings has been added to this procedure to save the changes made in this class to the user settings in the user.config file:

```
Protected Overridable Sub Dispose(ByVal disposing As Boolean)
    If Not Me.disposedValue Then
        If disposing Then
            'Persist the user settings
            My.Settings.Latitude = decLatitude
            My.Settings.Longitude = decLongitude
            My.Settings.ZipCode = intZipCode
            My.Settings.State = strState
            My.Settings.Location = strLocation
            My.Settings.CurrentForecastUrl = strCurrentForecastUrl
```

```
                    My.Settings.Save()
                End If

            End If
            Me.disposedValue = True
        End Sub
```

Http Function

The next piece of code that you'll want to take a look at is the `Http` function. This function is used throughout the `WeatherData` class to retrieve RSS data feeds and Web pages. Basically, this function accepts a URL as input, makes the appropriate Web request, and returns the output of the Web response as a string to the caller of this procedure. This function has the same effect as if you opened a browser, entered a URL, and viewed the Web page for the URL entered.

First, this function declares the local variables needed. Then the `WebRequest` class is used to make a Web request using a URL. The `WebResponse` class is used to receive the response from the `WebRequest` class when calling the `GetResponse` method. The other classes listed in the following code are used to provide the proper encoding, read the response, and return it as a string:

```
        Private Function Http(ByVal url As String) As String
            'Declare variables
            Dim objWebRequest As WebRequest
            Dim objWebResponse As WebResponse
            Dim objResponseStream As Stream
            Dim objEncoding As Encoding
            Dim objStreamReader As StreamReader
            Dim strResponse As String
```

A `Try...Catch...Finally` block is used in this function to properly handle any error that may occur. The first line of code in the `Try` block creates the `objWebRequest` object by calling the `Create` method of the `WebRequest` class, passing it the URL provided as input to this function.

Next, you post the request by calling the `GetResponse` method of the `objWebRequest` object, and get the response back in the `objWebResponse` object. Then you need to read the response, which is done by calling the `GetResponseStream` method on the `objWebResponse` object. You set the results of this stream to the `objResponseStream` object.

The `Stream` class supports reading and writing bytes of data, but you want to read the entire contents of the stream into a `String` variable. To that end, you use the `objStreamReader` object, which is instantiated from the `StreamReader` class. Part of the constructor for the `StreamReader` class is the encoding to be used when reading the data. Here you specify the `objEncoding` object, which has been set to a value of `utf-8` (Unicode Transformation Format 8), the most common Unicode Transformation Format, supporting most Unicode characters. Then you read the entire contents of the stream into the `strResponse` variable:

```
        Try
            'Setup the web request
            objWebRequest = WebRequest.Create(url)

            'Post the request and get the response
            objWebResponse = objWebRequest.GetResponse()
            'Read the response into a stream object
            objResponseStream = objWebResponse.GetResponseStream()
```

```
objEncoding = System.Text.Encoding.GetEncoding("utf-8")
'Read the response stream object
objStreamReader = New StreamReader(objResponseStream, objEncoding)
'Place the response into a string
strResponse = objStreamReader.ReadToEnd()
```

The `Catch` block handles any exception thrown from any of the objects used in this function and sets them in the `strReponse` variable, which is returned to the caller of this function.

The `Finally` block closes the `objWebResponse` object by calling the `Close` method, which effectively closes the stream.

The results of the `strResponse` variable are returned from this function in the last line of code, shown here:

```
Catch ExceptionErr As Exception
    strResponse = ExceptionErr.Message
Finally
    If Not IsNothing(objWebResponse) Then
        objWebResponse.Close()
    End If
End Try

'Return the response
Return strResponse
End Function
```

ZipCodeLookUp Procedure

The `ZipCodeLookup` procedure is used internally in the `WeatherData` class, and it is also called from the code in the `DesktopWeather` form. This procedure uses the `Http` function just discussed to call the Geocoder Web site to get the longitude, latitude, city, and state, which is done in the first line of code in this procedure:

```
Public Sub ZipCodeLookup(ByVal zipCode As Integer)
    'Get the zip code coordinates
    strZipCodeCoordinates = _
        Http("http://geocoder.us/service/csv/geocode?zip=" & _
        zipCode.ToString)
```

Once the data has been retrieved, you check for the error message indicating that the zip code was not found and throw an exception indicating such, which is returned to the caller.

If the zip code was found, you need to parse out the longitude and latitude, which is what the next two lines of code do. The variables used to store the longitude and latitude are defined as decimal, so the values that are parsed out of the string need to be cast as decimal values, which is what the `CType` function does. The `CType` function accepts the expression to be converted followed by the data type to which it should convert the expression:

```
If strZipCodeCoordinates.IndexOf("sorry") <> -1 Then
    Throw New Exception("Zip Code not found.")
End If

'Parse out the latitude and longitude
```

```
decLatitude = CType(strZipCodeCoordinates.Substring( _
    0, strZipCodeCoordinates.IndexOf(",")), Decimal)
decLongitude = CType(strZipCodeCoordinates.Substring( _
    strZipCodeCoordinates.IndexOf(",") + 2, _
    strZipCodeCoordinates.IndexOf(",", _
    strZipCodeCoordinates.IndexOf(",") - _
    strZipCodeCoordinates.IndexOf(","))), Decimal)
```

Next, you want to parse out the state abbreviation and save it in the `strState` variable and then parse out the full location, which includes city, state, and zip code. This value is stored and displayed at the top of the `DesktopWeather` form. Finally, you save the zip code in the `intZipCode` variable:

```
'Parse out the state
strState = strZipCodeCoordinates.Substring( _
    strZipCodeCoordinates.LastIndexOf(",") - 2, 2)

'Parse out the full location
strLocation = strZipCodeCoordinates.Substring( _
    (strZipCodeCoordinates.IndexOf(",", _
    strZipCodeCoordinates.IndexOf(",") + 2)) + 2)

'Set the zip code in the local variable so it can be saved
intZipCode = zipCode
End Sub
```

FindObservationStation Procedure

The `FindObservationStation` procedure requires a little more logic than the previous two procedures. This procedure will retrieve a list of observation stations from the National Weather Service, returned in XML format for all 50 states in the U.S. This procedure must filter that data to just the state you are looking for and then try to find the closest match using the longitude and latitude provided in the XML to the longitude and latitude returned for the zip code specified.

The `FindObservationStation` procedure gets a list of observation stations, which is returned in XML format. Remember that a `DataSet` in the .NET Framework is nothing more than XML behind the scenes, so you use a `StringReader` to read the string and then read the XML into the `objDataSet` object using the `ReadXML` method, passing it to the `objStringReader` object:

```
Public Sub FindObservationStation()
    'Get the observation XML and load it into a StringReader
    strObservationXML = _
        Http("http://www.weather.gov/data/current_obs/index.xml")
    Dim objStringReader As New StringReader(strObservationXML)

    'Load the XML into a DataSet
    objDataSet = New DataSet
    objDataSet.ReadXml(objStringReader)
```

With the XML data now loaded in a `DataSet` object, you need to filter the information to include the data for only the state that your zip code is in. This is done by using a `DataView` object and setting the `RowFilter` property to only include the state you want to work with. Next, you sort the data based on latitude, which is listed in the XML before longitude:

```
'Load and filter the data in a DataView
objDataView = New DataView(objDataSet.Tables("station"))
With objDataView
    .RowFilter = "state = '" & strState & "'"
    .Sort = "latitude asc"
End With
```

Because this procedure is called from other procedures within the WeatherData class and from the DesktopWeather form, a Boolean variable is set internally within this class when an auto lookup is to be performed. This next section of code is executed only if this procedure was called from another procedure in this class for which this Boolean variable has been set to True.

The longitude and latitude listed in the XML data is broken into three parts, with each part separated by a decimal and followed by one character indicating North, South, East, and West. If the longitude and latitude are not available, the characters NA are displayed.

Given all the complexities of the longitude and latitude lookup, this section of logic will look at only the first part of the longitude and latitude preceding the first decimal. Therefore, the first order of business is to extract the first part of the longitude and latitude preceding the decimal from the variables decLatitude and decLongitude and set them in the string variables strLatitude and strLongitude:

```
If blnAutoLookup Then
    strLatitude = decLatitude.ToString.Substring( _
        0, decLatitude.ToString.IndexOf("."))
    strLongitude = decLongitude.ToString.Substring( _
        0, decLongitude.ToString.IndexOf("."))
```

Now you want to loop through the DataView trying to find the closest match for longitude and latitude. If the latitude does not equal the character string NA, you want to get the latitude from the DataView and set it in the strLatitudeLookup variable. However, you only want to get the first part of this value that precedes the decimal. Next, you want to ensure that the value you retrieved can be converted to an Integer value, so this is what the next line of code does. This is just a safety measure to ensure you have a valid number:

```
'Now loop through the records for the state and find the closest
'match for latitude and longitude
For intIndex = 0 To objDataView.Count - 1
    If objDataView.Item(intIndex).Item("latitude") <> "NA" Then
        'Get the whole number part of the latitude
        strLatitudeLookup = objDataView.Item(intIndex).Item( _
            "latitude").ToString.Substring( _
            0, objDataView.Item(intIndex).Item( _
            "latitude").ToString.IndexOf("."))
        'Ensure the latitude number is formated as a proper integer
        strLatitudeLookup = _
            CType(strLatitudeLookup, Integer).ToString
```

Now compare the value in the strLatitudeLookup variable to the value in the strLatitude variable. If these values are equal, then you proceed and try to find a matching longitude value.

Once inside the If...Then statement, perform the extraction as you did for the latitude, only extracting the value preceding the decimal. You then set that value in the strLongitudeLookup variable and again ensure that the number can be converted to an Integer data type:

```
                        'Compare the whole number part of the latitudes
                    If strLatitudeLookup = strLatitude Then
                        'Get the longitude
                        strLongitudeLookup = objDataView.Item(intIndex).Item( _
                            "longitude").ToString.Substring( _
                            0, objDataView.Item(intIndex).Item( _
                            "longitude").ToString.IndexOf("."))
                        'Ensure the longitude number is formated
                        'as a proper integer
                        strLongitudeLookup = "-" & _
                            CType(strLongitudeLookup, Integer).ToString
```

Now you compare the `strLongitudeLookup` value to the `strLongitude` value; if they are equal, you consider this a close match. The `DesktopWeather` form displays the observation station as a hyperlink in the lower-left corner of the form and allows users to view and change the observation station if the match found is not close to their zip code.

You'll get the current forecast URL from the `DataView` and save it in the `strCurrentForecastUrl` variable, which will be saved and used to retrieve the current weather conditions. Then you exit the procedure, as you are done:

```
                        'Compare the whole number part of the latitudes
                    If strLongitudeLookup = strLongitude Then
                            'We'll consider this a close match
                            strCurrentForecastUrl = _
                                objDataView.Item(intIndex).Item("xml_url")
                            'We are all done so exit
                            Exit Sub
                        End If
                    End If
                End If
            Next
        End If
```

If you made it this far in the code, then a match was not found. In that case, you'll want to display the `ObservationStations` form and allow the user to select the appropriate observation station. Because the user will be viewing a list of observation stations, it only makes sense to display the list in alphabetical order by observation station name. This is accomplished by sorting the `DataView` by `station_name`.

Next, display the `ObservationStations` form as a modal dialog using the `ShowDialog` method of the `ObservationStations` form and passing to this method the name of the parent form, `DesktopWeather`. If the user clicks the OK button in the `ObservationStations` form, you set the `strCurrentForecastUrl` variable to the station selected. Then you immediately save the current forecast URL in the `user.config` file in case this procedure was called from the `DesktopWeather` form:

```
            'If we made it this far then no match was found
            'Display a dialog and let the user choose
            objDataView.Sort = "station_name asc"
            Dim objStations As New ObservationStations(objDataView)
            If objStations.ShowDialog(DesktopWeather) = DialogResult.OK Then
```

```
              strCurrentForecastUrl = objStations.lstStations.SelectedValue
          End If
          objStations.Dispose()
          'Save the current forecast url
          My.Settings.CurrentForecastUrl = strCurrentForecastUrl
          My.Settings.Save()
      End Sub
```

GetCurrentForecast Function

The GetCurrentForecast function is fairly straightforward. It is the function that is called to get the current weather conditions for a specified zip code. This function accepts the zip code as the one and only input parameter and returns the current forecast as a CurrentForecast class.

The first line of code in this function validates the zip code. If the zip code passed equals 0 or is not equal to the zip code stored in the user.config file, then a zip code lookup must take place and a call to the ZipCodeLookup procedure is performed to get the longitude and latitude for the zip code passed.

If the strCurrentForecastUrl variable does not contain any data, then a call to the FindObservationStation procedure must be made to find the appropriate URL for the current forecast for the zip code passed. Notice that before this call is made, the blnAutoLookup variable is set to True so that the FindObservationStation procedure will automatically try to find a matching observation station.

The next line of code makes a call to the National Weather Service's Web site to retrieve the current forecast in XML, returning that data in the strRawCurrentForecast variable. There is a property in this class called RawCurrentForecast that will return the raw XML data set in this variable. This enables you to customize this class and save this data if so desired:

```
      Public Function GetCurrentForecast(ByVal zipCode As Integer) _
          As Weather.CurrentForecast

          If intZipCode = 0 Or intZipCode <> zipCode Then
              'Perform the zip code lookup
              ZipCodeLookup(zipCode)
          End If

          'Find the observation station url
          If strCurrentForecastUrl.Trim.Length = 0 Then
              blnAutoLookup = True
              FindObservationStation()
          End If

          'Get the current forecast
          strRawCurrentForecast = Http(strCurrentForecastUrl)
```

Now that you have the current forecast XML data in a string variable, you instantiate an XmlDocument object and load the XML by calling the LoadXml method, which loads XML data from a string. Then you instantiate a new instance of the CurrentForecast class using this function's name, as it returns this type of data:

```
      'Instantiate the XMLDocument object and load the XML
      objXMLDocument = New XmlDocument
```

```
objXMLDocument.LoadXml(strRawCurrentForecast)

'Instatiate a new instance of the CurrentForecast class
GetCurrentForecast = New Weather.CurrentForecast
```

Now you can go about setting the properties of the `CurrentForecast` class using the XML data. The `observation_time_rfc822` element in the XML is specified as a date and time followed by a hyphen and then the number of hours from GMT (Greenwich Mean Time). In order to correctly set the `LastUpdateDate` property in the `CurrentForecast` class, you must extract just the date and time portion of this text and then cast that value to a `Date` value.

The remaining properties in the `CurrentForecast` class are set by reading and converting data as necessary from the XML document:

```
'Set the properties of the of the CurrentForecast class
GetCurrentForecast.WeatherSource = _
    objXMLDocument.SelectSingleNode("//credit").InnerText
GetCurrentForecast.Location = _
    objXMLDocument.SelectSingleNode("//location").InnerText
strData = _
    objXMLDocument.SelectSingleNode( _
    "//observation_time_rfc822").InnerText
GetCurrentForecast.LastUpdateDate = _
    CType(strData.Substring(0, strData.IndexOf("-") - 1), Date)
GetCurrentForecast.Conditions = _
    objXMLDocument.SelectSingleNode("//weather").InnerText
GetCurrentForecast.TemperatureFahrenheit = _
    CType(objXMLDocument.SelectSingleNode("//temp_f").InnerText, _
    Integer)
GetCurrentForecast.TemperatureCelsius = _
    CType(objXMLDocument.SelectSingleNode("//temp_c").InnerText, _
    Integer)
GetCurrentForecast.RelativeHumidity = _
    objXMLDocument.SelectSingleNode("//relative_humidity").InnerText
GetCurrentForecast.Wind = _
    objXMLDocument.SelectSingleNode("//wind_string").InnerText
GetCurrentForecast.PressureInches = _
    CType(objXMLDocument.SelectSingleNode("//pressure_in").InnerText, _
    Decimal)
```

The `pressure_mb` element in the XML could have a value of `NA` so this must be checked, and then the `PressureMillibars` property is set using a value of `0`. The same check holds true for the `heat_index_f` element as well as the `heat_index_c` element:

```
If objXMLDocument.SelectSingleNode("//pressure_mb").InnerText = _
    "NA" Then
    GetCurrentForecast.PressureMillibars = 0
Else
    GetCurrentForecast.PressureMillibars = _
        CType(objXMLDocument.SelectSingleNode( _
        "//pressure_mb").InnerText, Decimal)
End If
GetCurrentForecast.DewpointFahrenheit = _
    CType(objXMLDocument.SelectSingleNode( _
```

```
                "//dewpoint_f").InnerText, Integer)
            GetCurrentForecast.DewpointCelsius = _
                CType(objXMLDocument.SelectSingleNode( _
                "//dewpoint_c").InnerText, Integer)
            If objXMLDocument.SelectSingleNode("//heat_index_f").InnerText = _
                "NA" Then
                GetCurrentForecast.HeatIndexFahrenheit = _
                    CType(objXMLDocument.SelectSingleNode( _
                    "//temp_f").InnerText, Integer)
            Else
                GetCurrentForecast.HeatIndexFahrenheit = _
                    CType(objXMLDocument.SelectSingleNode( _
                    "//heat_index_f").InnerText, Integer)
            End If
            If objXMLDocument.SelectSingleNode("//heat_index_c").InnerText = _
                "NA" Then
                GetCurrentForecast.HeatIndexCelsius = _
                    CType(objXMLDocument.SelectSingleNode( _
                    "//temp_c").InnerText, Integer)
            Else
                GetCurrentForecast.HeatIndexCelsius = _
                    CType(objXMLDocument.SelectSingleNode( _
                    "//heat_index_c").InnerText, Integer)
            End If
            GetCurrentForecast.Visibility = _
                CType(objXMLDocument.SelectSingleNode( _
                "//visibility_mi").InnerText, Integer).ToString
            GetCurrentForecast.ForecastImagePath = _
                objXMLDocument.SelectSingleNode("//icon_url_base").InnerText & _
                objXMLDocument.SelectSingleNode("//icon_url_name").InnerText

            'Cleanup
            objXMLDocument = Nothing
        End Function
```

Get7DayForecast Function

The next function to be discussed is the Get7DayForecast function. This is the function that calls the Weather Web Service to get the seven-day forecast. Like its predecessor, this function also accepts the zip code as the one and only input parameter and returns its results in the DailyForecasts class. Remember that this class contains a collection of DailyForecast classes.

The first thing you do in this function is declare the XmlNodeList objects that will be used to get a collection of XML nodes:

```
        Public Function Get7DayForecast(ByVal zipCode As Integer) _
            As Weather.DailyForecasts

            'Declare local variables
            Dim objLayoutKeyList As XmlNodeList
            Dim objStartTimeList As XmlNodeList
            Dim objTemperatureList As XmlNodeList
            Dim objPrecipitationList As XmlNodeList
```

```
Dim objForecastSummaryList As XmlNodeList
Dim objImageList As XmlNodeList
```

The code in this function is wrapped in a `Try...Catch` block and returns any errors to the caller. The first thing that you do in the `Try...Catch` block is declare the `objWebService` object as the `NationalWeatherService` Web Service. If you customize this application to use a Weather Web Service of your choosing, this is the function that you need to modify to call the methods defined in your Weather Web Service.

Now you call the `NDFDgenByDay` method, passing it the required parameters. This method expects the latitude, the longitude, the date to start reporting from, the number of forecasted days to return, and the forecast format. The Weather Web Service will return the XML in the `strRaw7DayForecast` variable. Then you dispose of the `objWebService` object and set it to `Nothing`:

```
Try
    'Declare and instantiate a new instance of the
    'National Weather Service Web Service
    Dim objWebService As New NationalWeatherService.ndfdXML

    'Call the web service
    strRaw7DayForecast = objWebService.NDFDgenByDay( _
        decLatitude, decLongitude, Date.Today, 7, "12 hourly")

    'Clean up
    objWebService.Dispose()
    objWebService = Nothing
```

The `WeatherData` class also contains the `Raw7DayForecast` property, which returns the raw seven-day forecast XML data as a string. You can use this property to save the forecast data to a file if so desired.

The next step is to instantiate an `XmlDocument` object and to load the XML from the `strRaw7DayForecast` variable using the `LoadXml` method.

Because this function returns the forecast data as a `DailyForecasts` class, it instantiates a new instance of this class. Then it adds seven new instances of the `DailyForecast` class to its collection. This sets up the entire collection of classes, enabling you to loop through the collection and set the various properties of each class:

```
'Instantiate the XMLDocument object and load the XML
objXMLDocument = New XmlDocument
objXMLDocument.LoadXml(strRaw7DayForecast)

'Instantiate a collection of Daily Forecast objects
Get7DayForecast = New DailyForecasts
For intIndex = 0 To 6
    Get7DayForecast.Add(New DailyForecast)
Next
```

Now you want to get a collection of `time-layout` and `start-valid-time` nodes from the XML. Once you have a collection of nodes for each of these, you loop through the collection of `DailyForecast` classes and set the `ForecastDayName` and `ForecastDate` properties using the `InnerText` property of the XML nodes.

This is accomplished by accessing the Item property of the XmlNodeList and specifying the index of the item. The Item property contains a collection of XmlNode objects:

```
'Get a collection of layouts and times
objLayoutKeyList = _
    objXMLDocument.SelectNodes("//time-layout")
objStartTimeList = _
    objLayoutKeyList.Item(0).SelectNodes("start-valid-time")

'Add the day names and dates
For intIndex = 0 To 6
    Get7DayForecast.Item(intIndex).ForecastDayName = _
        objStartTimeList.Item(intIndex).Attributes( _
        "period-name").Value
    Get7DayForecast.Item(intIndex).ForecastDate = _
        CType(objStartTimeList.Item(intIndex).InnerText, Date)
Next
```

You repeat the preceding process by getting a collection of high and low temperatures from the XML and adding them to an XmlNodeList object. Then you again loop through the collection of DailyForecast classes and set the ForecastHighLowTemp property:

```
'Get a collection of high and low temperatures
objTemperatureList = _
    objXMLDocument.SelectNodes("//parameters/temperature/value")

'Add the high and low temperatures
For intIndex = 0 To 6
    Get7DayForecast.Item(intIndex).ForecastHighLowTemp = _
        objTemperatureList.Item(intIndex).InnerText & "° / " & _
        objTemperatureList.Item(intIndex + 7).InnerText & "°"
Next
```

The next collection of values that you want to retrieve from the XML data are the precipitation values. Again, you get this data in an XmlNodeList collection and then loop through the DailyForecast classes, this time setting the ForecastPrecipitation property:

```
'Get a collection of precipitation values
objPrecipitationList = _
    objXMLDocument.SelectNodes( _
    "//parameters/probability-of-precipitation/value")

'Add the precipitation percentages
For intIndex = 0 To 6
    If intIndex = 0 Then
        Get7DayForecast.Item(intIndex).ForecastPrecipitation = _
            objPrecipitationList.Item(intIndex).InnerText & "%"
    Else
        Get7DayForecast.Item(intIndex).ForecastPrecipitation = _
            objPrecipitationList.Item(intIndex + 1).InnerText & "%"
    End If
Next
```

You get a collection of forecast summaries next. This is the text value describing the upcoming forecasts. Again, you get the data in an XmlNodeList object and set the ForecastSummary property in the DailyForecast classes:

```
'Get a collection of forecast summaries
objForecastSummaryList = _
    objXMLDocument.SelectNodes("//weather/weather-conditions")

'Add the forecast summaries
For intIndex = 0 To 6
    If intIndex = 0 Then
        If Not IsNothing( _
            objForecastSummaryList.Item(intIndex).Attributes( _
            "weather-summary")) Then
            Get7DayForecast.Item(intIndex).ForecastSummary = _
                objForecastSummaryList.Item(intIndex).Attributes( _
                "weather-summary").Value
        Else
            Get7DayForecast.Item(intIndex).ForecastSummary = _
                objForecastSummaryList.Item( _
                intIndex + 1).Attributes( _
                "weather-summary").Value
        End If
    Else
        Get7DayForecast.Item(intIndex).ForecastSummary = _
            objForecastSummaryList.Item(intIndex + 1).Attributes( _
            "weather-summary").Value
    End If
Next
```

The final collection that you want to retrieve is the collection of image paths. This will be the URL of the forecast icon images. You set the collection in an XmlNodeList object and then set the ForecastImagePath property of the DailyForecast classes:

```
'Get a collection of image paths
objImageList = _
    objXMLDocument.SelectNodes("//conditions-icon/icon-link")

'Add the image paths
For intIndex = 0 To 6
    If intIndex = 0 Then
        If objImageList.Item(0).InnerText <> String.Empty Then
            Get7DayForecast.Item(intIndex).ForecastImagePath = _
                objImageList.Item(0).InnerText
        Else
            Get7DayForecast.Item(intIndex).ForecastImagePath = _
                objImageList.Item(1).InnerText
        End If
    Else
        Get7DayForecast.Item(intIndex).ForecastImagePath = _
            objImageList.Item(intIndex + 1).InnerText
    End If
Next
```

The final step is to return the data to the caller. The `Catch` block following the `Return` statement simply returns any errors to the caller of this function if any should occur:

```
                Return Get7DayForecast
        Catch ExceptionErr As Exception
            Throw New Exception("WeatherData.Get7DayForecast: " & _
                ExceptionErr.Message)
        End Try
    End Function
```

StreamBitmap Function

The `StreamBitmap` function is used to retrieve the images specified in the `ForecastImagePath` property of the `DailyForecast` class. The image specified in this property is set in the Desktop Weather form. In order to get the images from the URL specified in the `ForecastImagePath` property into the `Image` property of a `PictureBox` control in the Desktop Weather form, you make a call to this procedure, passing it the URL of the image to be retrieved.

This function takes that URL and creates a `WebRequest` object, passing the `Create` method the URL of the image to retrieve. The `GetResponse` method of the `objWebRequest` object returns the response of the Web request as a `WebResponse` class set in the `objWebResponse` object.

Then you need to get a stream of the image, which can be read by the `Image` property of the `PictureBox` control. This is done by calling the `GetResponseStream` method on the `objWebResponse` object, which is returned from this function.

When the `Image` property is set on a `PictureBox` control in the Desktop Weather form, the `Image` property creates the image from the stream provided by this function. Thus, the images displayed on the Desktop Weather form are never saved on your hard drive but are actually read directly from the URL specified and set directly in the `Image` property of the `PictureBox` control:

```
        Public Function StreamBitmap(ByVal url As String) As Stream
            Dim objWebRequest As WebRequest = WebRequest.Create(url)
            Dim objWebResponse As WebResponse = objWebRequest.GetResponse()
            Return objWebResponse.GetResponseStream()
        End Function
```

Setting Up the Desktop Weather Program

Each chapter in this book provides you with two options for setting up the program discussed: using the installer to install the program or manual setup, whereby you copy the required files to your computer. The latter option provides more control over setup and does not register the program in the Add Or Remove Programs dialog box in the Control Panel.

Using the Installer

This and the rest of the programs in this book use the ClickOnce technology introduced with Visual Studio 2005. This technology not only enables you to publish programs for deployment over the Web, it also enables you to publish programs from a file share of removable media such as a CD-ROM.

To install the Desktop Weather Program, locate the `Chapter 01 - Desktop Weather\Installer` folder on the CD-ROM that came with this book and double-click the `setup.exe` program. You will be prompted with the Application Install dialog, and clicking the Install button will install and launch the application.

Manual Installation

To manually install the Desktop Weather program, first create a folder on your computer where you want to place the program executable files. Then locate the `Chapter 01 - Desktop Weather\Source` folder on the CD-ROM that came with this book and navigate to the `bin\Release` folder. Copy the following files from the `Release` folder to the folder that you created on your computer:

- ❑ `Desktop Weather.exe`
- ❑ `Desktop Weather.exe.config`
- ❑ `Desktop Weather.xml`
- ❑ `Desktop Weather.XmlSerializers.dll`

To run the Desktop Weather program, double-click the `Desktop Weather.exe` file.

Configuring the Application

There is no special configuration required for the Desktop Weather program. Once the application has launched, you are prompted to enter your zip code in order for the program to retrieve the current and seven-day forecast for your area. See the section "Using the Desktop Weather Program" at the beginning of this chapter for details about how to use this program.

If you used the installer to install the program, it was installed in your `Local Settings\App\2.0` folder by default. For example, the complete path to my `Local Settings\App\2.0` folder is `C:\Documents and Settings\Thearon\Local Settings\Apps\2.0`. This is where the actual program was installed. The shortcut to the program was installed in your personal `Start Menu\Programs\Wiley Publishing, Inc` folder. Again, the complete path to my `Start Menu\Programs\Wiley Publishing, Inc` folder is `C:\Documents and Settings\Thearon\Start Menu\Programs\Wiley Publishing, Inc`.

If you want the application to automatically start when you log into your computer, you can copy the shortcut in the `Start Menu\Programs\Wiley Publishing, Inc` folder if you installed the program using the setup program to the `Start Menu\Programs\Startup` folder. If you performed a manual installation, create a shortcut in the previously described folder to the `Desktop Weather.exe` program.

Summary

This chapter has reviewed several useful technologies provided by the .NET Framework. First, you learned how to programmatically create a notification icon in the system tray and programmatically create a context menu and attach it to the notification icon. You learned how to read and write user data in the application's `user.config` file.

You also learned how to create your own classes and even a collection of classes as provided by the `DailyForecast` and `DailyForecasts` classes. The `WeatherData` class provided simple code that enabled you to load and read XML data from a string variable.

However, without a doubt, the most useful topics covered in this chapter were how to programmatically call a Web Service and how to programmatically make and receive an HTTP request to and from a Web site. These topics and the included sample code will serve you well in your future endeavors.

The automated installation of the Desktop Weather program was provided using ClickOnce technology. If you chose this option to install the program on your computer, you saw firsthand how simple it is to use this technology for deploying applications. This technology is built into every Windows project that you create, making it an ideal way to distribute your applications.

2

Password Keeper

Have you done any online shopping lately? Have you visited a Web site to read an article only to have to register and enter yet another login and password? It seems that just about every Web site you visit and want to interact with wants you to register, entering a login name and password. Some Web sites are good about requiring strongly typed passwords: passwords that contain uppercase and lowercase letters, numbers, and special characters. Some Web sites don't support special characters in their passwords. Each Web site has its own special set of rules about password strength and length.

Trying to keep up with your login names and passwords for the various Web sites that you frequent can become tiresome. This is especially true for Web sites that you visit less frequently because you are prone to forgetting your login and password.

This is where the Password Keeper application can assist you. This application keeps track of the Web site URL you visit and your login and password associated with that Web site. The best part of this application is that it keeps all of this information in an encrypted format so that your personal data is not compromised in the event that someone gains access to your computer. In this chapter you will learn how the Password Keeper is put together and how to use the technologies employed in this application.

The main technologies used in this application are as follows:

❑ Reading and writing XML data

❑ Encrypting and decrypting data

❑ Hashing data

Using the Password Keeper Program

The Password Keeper program provides a secure application for storing and managing your Web site logins and passwords. Not only does this program store this information for you, it also enables you to copy a password to the Clipboard and then paste that password into the password field of a Web site.

To use the program, you must first log into the program using a login name and password that you choose. When you first start the program you are presented with the Login screen shown in Figure 2-1. You should enter a login name and password that you are not likely to forget. There are no restrictions on the length of the password or rules requiring a strongly typed password. However, you should use a password that is both strongly typed and easily remembered.

Figure 2-1

After you have entered a login name and password, the program will create the `WebSites.xml` file, which is used to store all of your Web sites, logins, and passwords. All of this information is contained in this file in an encrypted format. The file stores the login and password that you choose to use to validate your credentials the next time you log in. This information is stored in a hashed format that is unrecognizable as login credentials to the casual observer.

After successfully logging in, the Password Keeper's main screen is displayed, as shown in Figure 2-2. Once you have entered one or more Web sites, logins, and passwords, you can simply right-click on a Web site to view the context menu shown in Figure 2-2 to copy a password to the Clipboard. This feature facilitates entering a password in the Web site you are trying to log into.

Additionally, the status bar displays the number of Web sites that you have stored in this program, just as a quick reference. To visit a Web site that you have entered, simply double-click the Web site to have your default browser launched with the URL entered in the Web Site Url column.

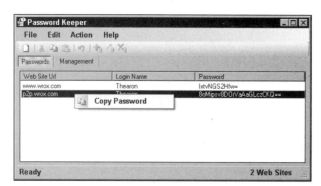

Figure 2-2

To enter a new Web site, login, and password, you need to click the Management tab. The fields on this screen, shown in Figure 2-3, enable you to manage your Web site information. You can use the buttons on the toolbar to add, update, and delete this information.

When you click on a Web site on the Passwords tab and then click the Management tab, details about the entry selected on the Passwords tab are populated in the text fields, as shown in Figure 2-3. This enables you to edit the existing data and then update that data by clicking the Update button on the toolbar. You can also delete the entry by clicking the Delete button on the toolbar.

To enter a new Web site, login, and password, you can overtype the existing data or click the New button on the toolbar to clear the edit fields. Then you can enter the appropriate data and click the Add button on the toolbar to add the new entry.

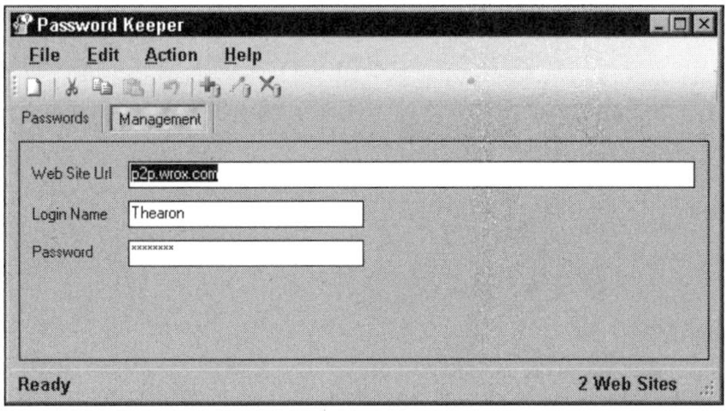

Figure 2-3

As mentioned previously, the Web site data that you enter along with your login credentials are stored in the `WebSites.xml` file. Figure 2-4 shows what the data for the Web sites shown in Figure 2-2 looks like. Your login credentials are hashed and then joined together in such a way that the result looks like a GUID (Globally Unique Identifier) to the casual observer. It is stored in the `ID` attribute of the `WebSites` element.

```
<?xml version="1.0" encoding="utf-8" ?>
- <WebSites ID="aeafc971-feca-159f-a5fb-f0c51259343f">
  - <WebSite ID="a9a190e2-5816-4999-8687-849b0727353c">
      <Url>bEqr2dKXUAaymyDrSYDJuQ==</Url>
      <Login>RtrAnK+2JEE=</Login>
      <Password>IxtvNGS2Hfw=</Password>
    </WebSite>
  - <WebSite ID="c2d68a3a-a4d3-4f40-b9cc-7f76b49492ff">
      <Url>jzBCRdLUpwI8VcuIg2XGPw==</Url>
      <Login>RtrAnK+2JEE=</Login>
      <Password>8oMipsv8DOrVaAaGLczCKQ==</Password>
    </WebSite>
</WebSites>
```

Figure 2-4

Design of the Password Keeper Program

The design of the Password Keeper program is simple and kept to four main components: the `MainEntry` class, the Login Form, the Passwords form, and the `Crytpo` class. Figure 2-5 shows the classes and forms used in this program and how they relate to one another.

The workflow is simple and starts with the `MainEntry` class, which is the main entry into the program. From here the Login form is displayed, and then, optionally, the Passwords form. The `Crypto` class is used by both the Login and Passwords forms.

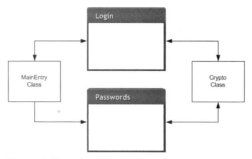

Figure 2-5

MainEntry Class

The `MainEntry` class, as its name suggests, is the main entry into the program. This class contains only one procedure: `Main`. The details of this class and the `Main` procedure are discussed in detail in the section "Code and Code Explanation" later in this chapter.

Login Form

The Login form contains the logic to create the GUID stored in the `WebSites.xml` file, using a combination of characters from your hashed login name and password. It also creates the `WebSites.xml` file if it does not exist or will validate your credentials in this file against the credentials entered in the Login form if the `WebSites.xml` does exist.

The Login form contains the three main methods, not associated with any form controls, as described in Table 2-1.

Table 2-1: Login Form Methods Not Associated with any Form Controls

Method	Return Type	Description
`Public Function GenerateID()`	`String`	Hashes the login name and password and generates a GUID based on the hashed values
`Private Sub CreateCredentials()`	N/A	Creates the `WebSites.xml` file and writes the `ID` attribute in the `WebSites` element using the GUID from the `GenerateID` function
`Private Function IsValidCredentials()`	`Boolean`	Reads the `ID` attribute in the `WebSites` element from the `WebSites.xml` file and compares it against the credentials entered

Passwords Form

The Passwords form is responsible for adding, updating, and deleting Web site URLs and associated data from the `WebSites.xml` file. It is also loads and displays the Web site URLs in this form, as well as launches the selected Web site in a browser.

Outside of the code associated with the form controls, there are two main methods in this form, as described in Table 2-2.

Table 2-2: Password Form Methods

Method	Return Type	Description
`Private Function IsValidFields(ByVal action As String)`	`Boolean`	Validates the fields on the Management tab of this form
`Private Sub LoadList`	N/A	Loads the Web sites, login names, and passwords from the `WebSites.xml` file

Crypto Class

The `Crypto` class is a simple yet powerful class that contains five main methods, as shown in Table 2-3. This class implements the `IDisposable` interface and has two overloaded constructors, also shown in Table 2-3. This class hashes data and encrypts and decrypts data.

Table 2-3: Overloaded Constructors of the Crypto Class

Method	Return Type	Description
`Public Sub New()`	N/A	Default constructor for the class
`Public Sub New(ByVal key() As Byte, ByVal iv() As Byte)`	N/A	Overload constructor that will initialize the security key and initialization vector used to encrypt and decrypt data
`Public Function Decrypt(ByVal value As String)`	`String`	Decrypts the data passed to this function and returns the decrypted string
`Public Function Encrypt(ByVal value As String)`	`String`	Encrypts the data passed to this function and returns the encrypted string
`Public Function Hash(ByVal value As String)`	`String`	Hashes the data passed to this function and returns the hashed result as a string

Code and Code Explanation

Now that you know what the main components are and what they are used for, it's time to dive into the details of each component to see how they work and to gain a better understanding of how the pieces fit together. This section explains the code details for each of the forms and classes used in this application.

MainEntry Class

The `MainEntry` class is the main entry into the program. It contains only one procedure: `Main`. In order to have your Windows application use a `Main` procedure as the entry point instead of a form, you must disable the application framework for your application. This is accomplished by double-clicking on the `My Project` file in the Solution Explorer and then clicking the Application tab. You then need to uncheck the Enable Application Framework check box in order to have `Sub Main` appear in the `Startup form` combo box. Once you have unchecked the check box, you can select `Sub Main` in the `Startup form` combo box.

The `Main` procedure declares and instantiates the `objLogin` object in a `Using...End Using` block. It then shows the Login form and checks for the `DialogResult` returned from the Login form. If the `DialogResult` is equal to `Cancel`, the code exits the `Main` procedure and the program ends:

```
Public Shared Sub Main()
    'Show the Login form
    Using objLogin As New Login
        If objLogin.ShowDialog = DialogResult.Cancel Then
            Exit Sub
        End If
    End Using
```

If the `DialogResult` returned from the Login form was not `Cancel`, then the next section of code is executed. Here you declare and instantiate the `objPasswords` object in a `Using...End Using` block and show the Passwords form. When the user closes the Passwords form, control returns here and the program ends:

```
    'Show the Passwords form
    Using objPasswords As New Passwords
        objPasswords.ShowDialog()
    End Using
End Sub
```

Login Form

Because the Login form is responsible for verifying the existence of the `WebSites.xml` file and for creating this file as well as reading and writing XML data, the Login form needs to import two namespaces to support these operations, as shown in the following code:

```
Imports System.IO
Imports System.Xml
```

The Login form has logic built into it to automatically close after three unsuccessful attempts at logging in. Therefore, in order to keep track of these attempts and to prevent the form from closing prematurely, the following variables are declared at the start of the form's class definition. Additionally, the last variable shown in the following code is used to keep track of the user's ID, which is generated based on the hashed values of the login name and password:

```
'Private variables
Private blnAllowClosing As Boolean = False
Private intAttemptCount As Integer = 0
Private strID As String
```

The Login form has an OK button and a Cancel button (refer to Figure 2-1). These buttons have been set to return a `DialogResult` of `OK` and `Cancel`, respectively. To that end, you need to add code to the `FormClosing` event of the Login form to detect whether the form is closing prematurely as a result of the user having clicked the `X` in the upper right-hand corner of the form.

The `FormClosing` event is fired whenever the form is closing. If the user has clicked the `X` in the upper right-hand corner of the form, the `blnAllowClosing` variable is `False` and the `intAttemptCount` variable will be less than three. You do not want to allow the form to close, as you want the user to click either the OK button or the Cancel button to return the appropriate `DialogResult`. Therefore, at this point, you cancel the `FormClosing` event and set the `Cancel` property of the form to `True`, which cancels this event and keeps the Login form open:

```
Private Sub Login_FormClosing(ByVal sender As Object, _
    ByVal e As System.Windows.Forms.FormClosingEventArgs) _
    Handles Me.FormClosing

    If Not blnAllowClosing Then
        If intAttemptCount < 3 Then
            e.Cancel = True
        End If
    End If
End Sub
```

The `Load` event for the form contains the necessary logic to extract the user's login name using the `My.User` object. This object will return the login name of the user logged in if the user is logged into a network domain. The typical implementation of Windows authentication returns the domain name followed by the user login name. Therefore, the appropriate logic exists to extract just the username if the domain name is also provided.

The last line of code in this procedure sets the focus to the password field so users can just enter their password:

```
Private Sub Login_Load(ByVal sender As System.Object, _
    ByVal e As System.EventArgs) Handles MyBase.Load

    'Set the default login name based on the login name in Windows
    If My.User.Name.IndexOf("\") = -1 Then
        txtLoginName.Text = My.User.Name
    Else
        txtLoginName.Text = _
            My.User.Name.Substring(My.User.Name.IndexOf("\") + 1)
    End If
```

```
                    'Set the focus to the password field
                    txtPassword.Focus()
              End Sub
```

If the user clicks the Cancel button on the form, you want to allow the form to close. Therefore, set the blnAllowClosing variable to True and then call the Close method on the form:

```
              Private Sub btnCancel_Click(ByVal sender As Object, _
                    ByVal e As System.EventArgs) Handles btnCancel.Click

                    blnAllowClosing = True
                    Me.Close()
              End Sub
```

The Click event for the OK button contains the necessary logic to validate the user's credentials if the WebSites.xml file already exists or to create the WebSites.xml file if it does not exist. The first step is to validate that the user has entered the appropriate information. Therefore, the first section of logic in this procedure validates the txtLoginName text field on the form. If the user did not enter a login name, then a MessageBox dialog box is displayed, indicating that the login name field is a required field and setting focus to that field:

```
              Private Sub btnOK_Click(ByVal sender As Object, _
                    ByVal e As System.EventArgs) Handles btnOK.Click

                    'Validate user input
                    If txtLoginName.Text.Trim.Length = 0 Then
                        MessageBox.Show("Login Name is a required field.", _
                            My.Application.Info.Title, MessageBoxButtons.OK, _
                            MessageBoxIcon.Information)
                        txtLoginName.Focus()
                        Exit Sub
                    End If
```

The next validation that occurs is the check for the txtPassword field on the form. As before, this logic validates that the user has entered a password. If not, it displays a MessageBox dialog box indicating that the user must enter a password. It then sets the focus to that field on the form:

```
                    If txtPassword.Text.Trim.Length = 0 Then
                        MessageBox.Show("Password is a required field.", _
                            My.Application.Info.Title, MessageBoxButtons.OK, _
                            MessageBoxIcon.Information)
                        txtPassword.Focus()
                        Exit Sub
                    End If
```

After all validations have occurred, a call is made to the GenerateID function to generate the ID based on the user's credentials. You'll examine this function in more detail shortly.

The next step is a check to determine whether the WebSites.xml file already exists. If the file exists, you'll want to confirm that the credentials entered by the user are valid by calling the IsValidCrendentials function. If the credentials are valid, then you set the blnAllowClosing variable to True and then set the DialogResult property of the form to a DialogResult of OK.

If the credentials were not valid, you increment the `intAttemptCount` variable and then check it to see whether this was the third attempt at logging on. If this was the third attempt, you set the `DialogResult` property of the form to a `DialogResult` of `Cancel` and then call the `btnCancel_Click` event, passing a value of `Nothing` for the parameters of this event:

```
'Get the user's ID
strID = GenerateID()

'Check to see if the WebSites.xml file exists
If File.Exists("WebSites.xml") Then
    'The file exists so we need to validate the login name and password
    If IsValidCredentials() Then
        'If valid credentials then allow the form to close and return
        'a DialogResult of OK
        blnAllowClosing = True
        Me.DialogResult = Windows.Forms.DialogResult.OK
    Else
        'Increment attempt count
        intAttemptCount += 1
        If intAttemptCount = 3 Then
            'If three attempts were made, set the DialogResult to Cancel
            'and close the form
            Me.DialogResult = Windows.Forms.DialogResult.Cancel
            Call btnCancel_Click(Nothing, Nothing)
        End If
    End If
```

If the `WebSites.xml` file does not exist, you make a call to the `CreateCredentials` procedure to have the `WebSites.xml` file created and to generate and write the root of the XML document to the file. You'll examine this procedure shortly. Then you set the `blnAllowClosing` variable to `True` and set the `DialogResult` property of the form to a `DialogResult` of `OK`:

```
Else
    'The file does not exist so we need to create the file
    CreateCredentials()
    'Allow the form to close and return a DialogResult of OK
    blnAllowClosing = True
    Me.DialogResult = Windows.Forms.DialogResult.OK
End If
End Sub
```

The `IsValidCredentials` function validates the user's login credentials and returns a `Boolean` value indicating whether or not the credentials are valid. The first thing that happens in this procedure is the declaration of the local variables used in this function.

The `strXmlId` variable is used to hold the ID value read from the `WebSites.xml` file, and the `objXmlTextReader` object is set to an instance of the `XmlTextReader` class. Notice that the `WebSites.xml` file is passed to the constructor of the `XmlTextReader` class. The `XmlTextReader` class provides a fast, non-cached, forward-only reader of XML data. This class provides the most efficient access when reading XML data from top to bottom.

The next line of code positions the objXmlTextReader object to the first node in the XML file, which is the WebSites element. Once you are at the correct position in the XML file, you want to get the value in the ID attribute of this element, which is done by using the GetAttribute method of the objXmlTextReader object:

```
Private Function IsValidCredentials() As Boolean
    'Declare local variables and objects
    Dim strXmlId As String
    Dim objXmlTextReader As New XmlTextReader("WebSites.xml")

    'Move to the content and get the ID
    objXmlTextReader.MoveToContent()
    strXmlId = objXmlTextReader.GetAttribute("ID")
```

The next step is to clean up the objXmlTextReader object by closing it and setting it to Nothing. Then you compare the value read from the ID attribute in the WebSites.xml file, placed in the strXmlId variable, to the strID variable. If the values are equal, then you return a value of True; if they are not equal, then you return a value of False:

```
    'Cleanup
    objXmlTextReader.Close()
    objXmlTextReader = Nothing

    'Return the appropriate Boolean value based on the values
    If strXmlId = strID Then
        Return True
    Else
        Return False
    End If
End Function
```

The CreateCredentials procedure creates the WebSites.xml file and writes the WebSites element as well as the ID attribute, using the generated ID of the user's credentials. The start of this procedure declares the objXmlTextWriter object using the XmlTextWriter class. The XmlTextWriter class provides a fast, non-cached, forward-only way to generate XML files. This is by far the most efficient means of generating an XML file from top to bottom.

The next line of code actually creates the WebSites.xml file using utf-8 (Unicode Transformation Format 8) encoding. To keep the XML file readable in Notepad or a browser, the Formatting property of the objXmlTextWriter object is set to Indented. This causes each element in the XML file to be properly indented:

```
Private Sub CreateCredentials()
    'Declare local variables and objects
    Dim objXmlTextWriter As XmlTextWriter

    'Create the WebSites.xml document
    objXmlTextWriter = New _
        XmlTextWriter("WebSites.xml", System.Text.Encoding.UTF8)

    'Use indenting for readability
    objXmlTextWriter.Formatting = Formatting.Indented
```

After the XML file has been created, you call the `WriteStartDocument` method to write the XML declaration of `<?xml version="1.0" encoding="utf-8" ?>`. Then, by calling the `WriteStartElement` method, you write the `WebSites` element; and calling the `WriteAttributeString` method, you write the `ID` attribute on the `WebSites` element with the value contained in the `strID` variable.

Because the `WebSites` element is all that is contained in the XML document at this point, you want to close the `WebSites` element by calling the `WriteEndElement` method, which writes the closing tag for this element. Then you close the XML document by calling the `WriteEndDocument` method:

```
'Write the XML delcaration
objXmlTextWriter.WriteStartDocument()

'Write a root element
objXmlTextWriter.WriteStartElement("WebSites")

'Write the ID attribute
objXmlTextWriter.WriteAttributeString("ID", strID)

'Write the close tag for the root element
objXmlTextWriter.WriteEndElement()

'Write the ending element of the document
objXmlTextWriter.WriteEndDocument()
```

Now you flush the buffer and underlying stream to actually write the data to the file by calling the `Flush` method. Then close the XML document by calling the `Close` method. Finally, you clean up by setting the `objXmlTextWriter` object to `Nothing`:

```
'Write the XML to file and close the writer
objXmlTextWriter.Flush()
objXmlTextWriter.Close()

'Cleanup
objXmlTextWriter = Nothing
End Sub
```

The final function to look at in the Login form is the `GenerateID` function. This function is called to generate an ID value based on the combined hashed values of the login name and password that the user has entered. Remember that this function generates an ID value that is stored in the `WebSites.xml` file and has the appearance of a standard GUID to the casual observer.

The first thing that you do in this function is declare the local variables that will be used. The `strNameGuid` and `strPasswordGuid` variables have been set to valid standard GUIDs minus the dashes. These will be used later in this function to pad the hashed login and password values if necessary.

```
Public Function GenerateID() As String
    'Declare local variables
    Dim intIndex As Integer
    Dim strHashName As String
    Dim strHashPassword As String
    Dim strNameGuid As String = _
        "aeaf7cab560345fabacf878405a16e5f"
    Dim strPasswordGuid As String = _
        "c2712c35cc0c462c8195c1d66ab7f4b0"
```

Now generate a hashed string of the login name and password values. This is accomplished by calling the `Hash` method of the `Crypto` class and passing it the appropriate values.

In order to reduce the amount of code required for declaring, instantiating, and disposing of the `Crypto` class, it has implemented the `IDisposable` interface, which enables this class to be used in a `Using...End Using` statement block. The `Using...End Using` statement block enables you to declare and instantiate the class in the `Using` part of the `Using...End Using` statement, and when the `End Using` statement is executed it will automatically call the `Dispose` method in the class. A class must implement the `IDisposable` interface in order to be used in a `Using...End Using` statement block:

```
'Hash the login name and password and save in the global variables
Using objCrypto As New Crypto()
    strLoginName = objCrypto.Hash(txtLoginName.Text)
    strLoginPassword = objCrypto.Hash(txtPassword.Text)
End Using
```

A valid GUID contains 32 characters minus the dashes and can only contain the numbers 0 through 9 and the letters A through F. You'll use the first 16 characters of the login name and the first 16 characters of the password to create the ID. However, the `strLoginName` and `strPassword` variables are also used in the Passwords form and need to be 24 bytes in length for that code. Therefore, ensure that the login name and password contain at least 24 characters of data.

If the hashed login name stored in the `strLoginName` variable is less than 24 characters, pad the string with the necessary number of characters from the `strNameGuid` variable. Next, you perform the same operation on the hashed password stored in the `strLoginPassword` variable using characters from the `strPasswordGuid` string to pad the `strLoginPassword` variable:

```
'Pad the hash name if necessary
If strLoginName.Length < 24 Then
    strLoginName = _
        strNameGuid.Substring(0, 24 - strLoginName.Length)
End If

'Pad the hash password if necessary
If strLoginPassword.Length < 24 Then
    strLoginPassword = _
        strPasswordGuid.Substring(0, 24 - _
            strLoginPassword.Length)
End If
```

Set the `strHashName` and `strHashPassword` variables using the `strLoginName` and `strLoginPassword` variables and convert the characters to all lowercase letters.

Next, replace all nonvalid characters in the `strHashName` variable with valid variables from the `strNameGuid` variable. Nonvalid characters in a GUID are any letters greater than the letter f:

```
'Get a local lower case representation of the
'hashed name and password to work with
strHashName = strLoginName.ToLower
strHashPassword = strLoginPassword.ToLower
```

```
'Now loop through the first 16 characters of the
'hash name replacing any letter greater than f
For intIndex = 0 To 15
    If strHashName.Chars(intIndex) > "f"c Then
        strHashName = _
            strHashName.Replace( _
            strHashName.Chars(intIndex), _
            strNameGuid.Chars(intIndex))
    End If
Next
```

Now perform the same procedure on the strHashPassword, replacing any nonvalid characters using characters from the strPasswordGuid variable:

```
'Now loop through the first 16 characters of the
'hash password replacing any letter greater than f
For intIndex = 0 To 15
    If strHashPassword.Chars(intIndex) > "f"c Then
        strHashPassword = _
            strHashPassword.Replace( _
            strHashPassword.Chars(intIndex), _
            strPasswordGuid.Chars(intIndex))
    End If
Next
```

Finally, generate a GUID string using parts of the strHashName and strHashPassword variables. This generates a string that looks like a GUID to the casual observer, which is in turn stored in the ID attribute of the WebSites element in the WebSites.xml file:

```
'Generate a GUID string based on a combination of the
'hashed login name and password
GenerateID = strHashName.Substring(0, 4) & _
    strHashPassword.Substring(0, 4) & "-" & _
    strHashName.Substring(3, 4) & "-" & _
    strHashPassword.Substring(3, 4) & "-" & _
    strHashName.Substring(7, 2) & _
    strHashPassword.Substring(7, 2) & "-" & _
    strHashPassword.Substring(9, 6) & _
    strHashName.Substring(9, 6)
End Function
```

Passwords Form

The Passwords form handles reading and writing XML data to and from the WebSites.xml file. To that end, there are two namespaces used in this form to support these operations, as shown in the following code:

```
Imports System.IO
Imports System.Xml
```

Several variables are used in this form. They are declared after the Passwords class declaration:

```
'Private variables and objects
Private blnKeyInitialized As Boolean = False

Private strID As String
Private strKey As String
Private strProcess As String

Private objXMLDocument As XmlDocument
Private objXMLRoot As XmlNode
Private objXMLNode As XmlNode
Private objXMLChildNode As XmlNode
Private objXMLNodeList As XmlNodeList
Private objXMLAttribute As XmlAttribute

Private objControl As Control
Private objTextBox As TextBox
Private objTimerTextBox As TextBox
Private objListViewItem As ListViewItem
```

The second overloaded constructor of the Crypto class requires the security key and initialization vector as input. These are 24-byte Byte arrays that are declared in the Passwords form. These bytes are extracted from the login name and password that the user entered on the Login form, thus making the encryption and decryption of data unique to the user's security credentials:

```
Private objCrypto As Crypto

'The crypto algorithm supports a key length of
'192 bits (192 bits / 8) = 24 bytes
Private bytCryptoKey() As Byte = _
    System.Text.Encoding.UTF8.GetBytes( _
    strLoginName.Substring(0, 24))
Private bytCryptoIV() As Byte = _
    System.Text.Encoding.UTF8.GetBytes( _
    strLoginPassword.Substring(0, 24))
```

The Load event for the Passwords form instantiates the objCrypto object using a new instance of the Crypto class, passing it the Byte arrays for the key and initialization vector. Then it makes a call to the LoadList procedure, which is discussed next.

```
Private Sub Passwords_Load(ByVal sender As Object, _
    ByVal e As System.EventArgs) Handles Me.Load

    'Instantiate the Crypto object
    objCrypto = New Crypto(bytCryptoKey, bytCryptoIV)

    'Load the Web Sites list
    LoadList()
End Sub
```

LoadList Procedure

The `LoadList` procedure reads all of the data from the `WebSites.xml` file into an `XmlDocument` class. The `XmlDocument` class represents an XML document loaded into memory. The first step in this procedure is to instantiate a new instance of the `XmlDocument` class in the `objXMLDocument` object. Then it loads the XML from the `WebSites.xml` document by calling the `Load` method of the `objXMLDoucment` object. Next, you get the root element in the XML document and set it in the `objXMLRoot` object.

The next step is to clear the list of Web sites in the `ListView` control on the form, as this procedure will be called whenever you add, update, or delete a Web site in order to refresh the Web sites list:

```
Private Sub LoadList()
    objXMLDocument = New XmlDocument
    objXMLDocument.Load("Websites.xml")
    objXMLRoot = objXMLDocument.DocumentElement


    'Clear the list
    lvwWebSites.Items.Clear()
```

You want to get a collection of XML nodes for the `WebSite` elements in the XML document. This is performed using the `SelectNodes` method of the `objXMLRoot` object. Once you have a collection of `WebSite` nodes in the `objXMLNodeList` object, loop through the collection and populate the `ListView` control on the form.

The first order of business inside the loop is to instantiate a new instance of the `ListViewItem` in the `objListViewItem` object. The `ListViewItem` class represents a single row of data in the `ListView` control. This includes the data in the first column, which is referred to as the `Item`, and every subsequent column in the row, which is referred to as the `SubItem`.

Set the `Text` property of this object using the `URL` element for the XML node that you are working with. Because all of the data in the `WebSites.xml` file is encrypted, you have to make a call to the `Decrypt` method in the `objCrypto` object to decrypt the data. The `Tag` property of the `objListViewItem` object is set using the `ID` attribute of the node, and this will be the value used to locate an element in the `WebSites.xml` file when updating or deleting a Web site.

The next two lines of code set the values in the `Login Name` and `Password` columns in the `ListView` control. These values are considered sub-items of the `ListViewItem` and as such are added to the `SubItems` collection of the `objListViewItem` object. Again, the values read from the XML node must be decrypted, so a call is made to the `Decrypt` method of the `Crypto` class.

The last line of code in this loop actually adds the `ListViewItem` represented in the `objListViewItem` object to the `ListView` control on the form:

```
objXMLNodeList = objXMLRoot.SelectNodes("//WebSite")
For Each objXMLNode In objXMLNodeList
    'Create a new listview item
    objListViewItem = New ListViewItem

    'Add the data to the listview item
    objListViewItem.Text = _
        objCrypto.Decrypt(objXMLNode.Item("Url").InnerText)
```

```
              objListViewItem.Tag = objXMLNode.Attributes("ID").Value

              'Add the sub items to the listview item
              objListViewItem.SubItems.Add( _
                  objCrypto.Decrypt(objXMLNode.Item("Login").InnerText))
              objListViewItem.SubItems.Add( _
                  objXMLNode.Item("Password").InnerText)

              'Add the listview item to the listview control
              lvwWebSites.Items.Add(objListViewItem)
          Next
```

The last line of code in this procedure updates the Web site count in the status bar. The Count property of the objXMLNodeList contains the number of XML nodes that were read. This is the number of WebSite elements in the WebSites.xml file:

```
          'Display the total number of web sites in the list
          WebSitesToolStripStatusLabel.Text = _
              objXMLNodeList.Count.ToString & " Web Sites"
      End Sub
```

lvwWebSites_DoubleClick Procedure

The next procedure to consider is the DoubleClick event procedure for the lvwWebSites control. This is the ListView control that contains a list of Web sites on the Passwords form. When you double-click an item in the list, this procedure is fired.

The first thing that you want to do in this procedure is read the Text property of the selected item and set it in the strProcess variable; this will be the Web site URL.

Next, you want to determine whether the URL starts with http, https, or www. If the URL does not start with any of these prefixes, you add the prefix of http://. This is needed so that the Start method of the Process class knows that this is a URL and that it needs to launch the default browser with this URL.

The last line of code here calls the Start method on the Process class to launch the default browser:

```
      Private Sub lvwWebSites_DoubleClick(ByVal sender As Object, _
          ByVal e As System.EventArgs) Handles lvwWebSites.DoubleClick

          'Set the process string
          strProcess = lvwWebSites.SelectedItems(0).Text.ToLower

          'If the process string does not begin with
          'http, https, or wwww then add http
          If Not strProcess.StartsWith("http") _
              And Not strProcess.StartsWith("https") _
              And Not strProcess.StartsWith("www") Then
              strProcess = strProcess.Insert(0, "http://")
          End If

          'Open the web site
          Process.Start(strProcess)
      End Sub
```

CopyToolStripMenuItem_Click Procedure

When you select `Copy Password` on the context menu or click the Copy menu item or button on the toolbar, the `CopyToolStripMenuItem_Click` procedure is executed. This procedure has an `If...Then...ElseIf` statement to determine whether you want to copy text from a `TextBox` control or copy the password from the `ListView` control.

The first part of the `If...Then...ElseIf` statement uses the `TypeOf` operator to compare an object reference variable to a data type. In this case, the object reference variable is the `ActiveControl` on the form and the data type is a `TextBox` control. If this comparison is equal, then the code following the `If` statement is executed. Here, you get a reference to the `ActiveControl` in the `objTextBox` object and then copy the text in that object to the Clipboard using the `Copy` method of the `objTextBox` object.

The `ElseIf` statement also uses a `TypeOf` operator to compare an object reference variable, and again uses the `ActiveControl` of the form. However, this time you compare the `ActiveControl` of the form to a `ListView` control. If the comparison is equal, then you decrypt the password for the selected item in the `ListView` control and set that text on the Clipboard using the `SetText` method of the `My.Computer.Clipboard` object:

```
Private Sub CopyToolStripMenuItem_Click(ByVal sender As Object, _
    ByVal e As System.EventArgs) Handles CopyToolStripMenuItem.Click

    'Ensure this is a TextBox control
    If TypeOf Me.ActiveControl Is TextBox Then
        'Get a reference to the active TextBox control
        Dim objTextBox As TextBox = Me.ActiveControl
        'Copy the text and place it on the clipboard
        objTextBox.Copy()
    ElseIf TypeOf Me.ActiveControl Is ListView Then
        My.Computer.Clipboard.SetText( _
            objCrypto.Decrypt(lvwWebSites.Items( _
            lvwWebSites.SelectedIndices.Item(0)).SubItems(2).Text))
    End If
End Sub
```

lvwWebSites_SelectedIndexChanged Procedure

The next procedure in the Passwords form that you'll want to take a look at is the `SelectedIndexChanged` event of the `lvwWebSites ListView` control. This procedure is executed whenever you select a new item in the `ListView` control. It is used to populate the edit fields on the Management tab of the Passwords form.

Because this event is fired as the control is being loaded, you first want to check whether anything was selected. You do this by querying the `Count` property of the `SelectedIndices` property of the `lvwWebSites` object. If the `Count` property returns a value of `0`, then no item has been selected and you exit this procedure.

If an item has been selected, then you want to populate the text fields on the Management tab using the `Text` properties of the `Item` and `SubItems` property of the `lvwWebSites` object. Because the Web site URL and login name are displayed in an unencrypted format, you can use the value from the `Text` property directly. However, the password is always encrypted so it must be decrypted before being placed in the `txtPassword` text box:

```
Private Sub lvwWebSites_SelectedIndexChanged( _
    ByVal sender As Object, ByVal e As System.EventArgs) _
    Handles lvwWebSites.SelectedIndexChanged

    'If nothing was selected then exit the procedure
    If lvwWebSites.SelectedIndices.Count = 0 Then
        Exit Sub
    End If

    'Populate the edit fields
    txtWebSiteUrl.Text = _
        lvwWebSites.Items( _
        lvwWebSites.SelectedIndices.Item(0)).Text
    txtLoginName.Text = _
        lvwWebSites.Items( _
        lvwWebSites.SelectedIndices.Item(0)).SubItems(1).Text
    txtPassword.Text = _
        objCrypto.Decrypt( _
        lvwWebSites.Items( _
        lvwWebSites.SelectedIndices.Item(0)).SubItems(2).Text)
End Sub
```

AddToolStripMenuItem_Click Procedure

The `AddToolStripMenuItem_Click` procedure is executed when you click the Add Web Site button on the toolbar or click on the Action menu and select the Add Web Site menu item. This procedure adds a new Web site to the `WebSites.xml` file.

This procedure starts off by validating the input fields via a call to the `IsValidFields` function, passing it the action that it is to perform. The `IsValidFields` function is a simple function to validate that all fields contain data. The `action` parameter is used in the error message should the validation fail.

```
Private Sub AddToolStripMenuItem_Click(ByVal sender As Object, _
    ByVal e As System.EventArgs) Handles AddToolStripMenuItem.Click

    'Validate fields
    If Not IsValidFields("adding") Then
        Exit Sub
    End If
```

In order to add a new Web site to the `WebSites.xml` file, you must create a new XML node and then add the XML node to the XML document. This section begins by creating the `WebSite` node and then adding the `ID` attribute to the node. Then a new `Guid` is generated and set in the `ID` attribute. This will uniquely identify this XML node within the XML document. Once the XML node has been created, you add it to the XML document by calling the `AppendChild` method, passing it the new XML node:

```
'Create a new WeSite node
objXMLNode = objXMLDocument.CreateNode( _
    XmlNodeType.Element, "WebSite", Nothing)
objXMLAttribute = objXMLDocument.CreateAttribute("ID")
```

```
objXMLAttribute.Value = Guid.NewGuid.ToString
objXMLNode.Attributes.SetNamedItem(objXMLAttribute)
objXMLRoot.AppendChild(objXMLNode)
```

You now want to refresh the objXMLNodeList object by selecting all nodes that equal the text WebSite. Then you get the last one in the list by setting it in your objXMLNode object. Remember that you must use Count - 1, as the Count property indicates the total number of nodes but the nodes are accessed using a zero-based index:

```
'Select the WebSite nodes and get the last one
objXMLNodeList = objXMLRoot.SelectNodes("//WebSite")
objXMLNode = objXMLNodeList.Item(objXMLNodeList.Count - 1)
```

Once you have the new XML node that you just created in the objXMLNode object, you create the child nodes beneath that. The child nodes will include the URL, Login, and Password nodes. Each of these nodes will have their InnerText property set to encrypted values. After each child node has been created in the objXMLChildNode object, it is added to the WebSite node contained in the objXMLNode object using the AppendChild method:

```
'Create the WebSite/Url sub node and set its value
objXMLChildNode = objXMLDocument.CreateNode( _
    XmlNodeType.Element, "Url", Nothing)
objXMLChildNode.InnerText = objCrypto.Encrypt(txtWebSiteUrl.Text)
objXMLNode.AppendChild(objXMLChildNode)

'Create the WebSite/Login sub node and set its value
objXMLChildNode = objXMLDocument.CreateNode( _
    XmlNodeType.Element, "Login", Nothing)
objXMLChildNode.InnerText = objCrypto.Encrypt(txtLoginName.Text)
objXMLNode.AppendChild(objXMLChildNode)

'Create the Wesite/Password sub node and set its value
objXMLChildNode = objXMLDocument.CreateNode( _
    XmlNodeType.Element, "Password", Nothing)
objXMLChildNode.InnerText = objCrypto.Encrypt(txtPassword.Text)
objXMLNode.AppendChild(objXMLChildNode)
```

Once the entire WebSite node has been constructed, save the XML data to the WebSites.xml file. Then a call is made to the LoadList procedure to rebuild the Web site list. A call is also made to the NewToolStripMenuItem_Click procedure to clear the edit field, and a message is displayed in the status bar:

```
'Save the changes
objXMLDocument.Save("WebSites.xml")

'Reload the list
LoadList()

'Display message
NewToolStripMenuItem_Click(Nothing, Nothing)
ToolStripStatusLabel.Text = "Record added"
End Sub
```

UpdateToolStripMenuItem_Click Procedure

The `UpdateToolStripMenuItem_Click` procedure is executed when you click the Update Web Site button on the toolbar or click on the Action menu and select the Update Web Site menu item.

This procedure starts off by first validating the input fields via a call to the `IsValidFields` function, passing it an action parameter of `updating`. Again, this action parameter is used in the error message should the fields fail to be validated:

```
Private Sub UpdateToolStripMenuItem_Click(ByVal sender As Object, _
    ByVal e As System.EventArgs) Handles UpdateToolStripMenuItem.Click

    'Validate fields
    If Not IsValidFields("updating") Then
        Exit Sub
    End If
```

Updating a `WebSite` node presents a different challenge from adding a new `WebSite` node. Here you must find the correct `WebSite` node in the XML document. To find the `WebSite` node that you are looking for, you use the `SelectSingleNode` method of the `XmlDocument` class contained in your `objXMLDocument` object. You pass the `SelectSingleNode` method an XPath expression that contains the `WebSite` node name along with the `ID` attribute and the value of the attribute that you are trying to find. The `ID` attribute value must be enclosed in double quotes, which is why you specified them using the `Quote` field from the `ControlChars` class. The XML node that is found as a result of the `SelectSingleNode` method is placed in the `objXMLNode` object:

```
'Get the selected node
objXMLNode = objXMLDocument.SelectSingleNode("//WebSite[@ID=" & _
    ControlChars.Quote & lvwWebSites.SelectedItems.Item(0).Tag() & _
    ControlChars.Quote & "]")
```

Once you have the correct XML node in your `objXMLNode` object, you set the `InnerText` property of the appropriate child nodes, encrypting the values from the form. You access the child nodes in the `objXMLNode` object by specifying the `Item` property and the child node names (i.e., `URL`, `Login`, and `Password`):

```
'Update the values
objXMLNode.Item("Url").InnerText = objCrypto.Encrypt(txtWebSiteUrl.Text)
objXMLNode.Item("Login").InnerText = objCrypto.Encrypt(txtLoginName.Text)
objXMLNode.Item("Password").InnerText = objCrypto.Encrypt(txtPassword.Text)
```

Save the changes to the XML data in the `WebSites.xml` file and call the `LoadList` procedure to rebuild the Web site list. Next, call the `NewToolStripMenuItem_Click` procedure to clear the edit field and display a message in the status bar indicating that this Web site was updated:

```
'Save the changes
objXMLDocument.Save("WebSites.xml")

'Reload the list
LoadList()

'Display message
NewToolStripMenuItem_Click(Nothing, Nothing)
ToolStripStatusLabel.Text = "Record updated"
End Sub
```

DeleteToolStripMenuItem_Click Procedure

The `DeleteToolStripMenuItem_Click` procedure deletes an existing Web site from the `WebSites.xml` file. Because you are not adding or updating any nodes, there is no validation to be performed in this procedure. The `Tag` property of the selected item in the `lvwWebSites ListView` control contains the value of the node you want to delete.

Notice that once again you are using the `SelectSingleNode` method of the `objXMLDocument` object to select the node in question. You are also using the same XPath expression that you used when updating the node to find the appropriate node.

The node returned this time, however, is set in the `objXMLChildNode` object. Then you get the parent node for this node by calling the `ParentNode` property and set that node in the `objXMLNode` object. Next, you call the `RemoveChild` method of the parent node contained in the `objXMLNode`.

You can save the XML document in the `WebSites.xml` file, rebuild the Web site list, clear the edit fields, and display a message indicating that the Web site was deleted:

```
Private Sub DeleteToolStripMenuItem_Click(ByVal sender As Object, _
    ByVal e As System.EventArgs) Handles DeleteToolStripMenuItem.Click

    'Get the selected node
    objXMLChildNode = objXMLDocument.SelectSingleNode("//WebSite[@ID=" & _
        ControlChars.Quote & lvwWebSites.SelectedItems.Item(0).Tag() & _
        ControlChars.Quote & "]")

    'Get the parent
    objXMLNode = objXMLChildNode.ParentNode

    'Remove it from the document
    objXMLNode.RemoveChild(objXMLChildNode)

    'Save the changes
    objXMLDocument.Save("WebSites.xml")

    'Reload the list
    LoadList()

    'Display message
    NewToolStripMenuItem_Click(Nothing, Nothing)
    ToolStripStatusLabel.Text = "Record deleted"
End Sub
```

Cryptography Sidebar

Before diving into the code in the `Crypto` class, I want to briefly talk about cryptography as it relates to the .NET Framework. Cryptography enables you to encrypt, decrypt, and hash data to make it secure. This can be data stored in your application (e.g., stored in files or the database) and data that is transmitted between applications, whether it is internally or across the Internet.

Continued

Cryptography Sidebar (*continued*)

The .NET Framework implements cryptography in several different classes that enable you to use secret keys or public keys to encrypt and decrypt data. It also provides classes that enable you to use digital signatures with encrypted or raw data.

Secret keys are keys that only your application knows about and with which your data can be encrypted and decrypted by your application. The same key is used to encrypt and decrypt the data in your application.

Public keys enable you to use a public key and a private key pair to encrypt and decrypt data. A public key can be sent to those applications that need to encrypt and send data. The private key is held only by the application receiving the encrypted data. Data encrypted with the public key can only be decrypted with the private key. Thus, an unauthorized person who might have gotten hold of a public key cannot decrypt the data.

Digitial signatures can be used to authenticate the identity of the data's sender and to protect the integrity of the data. Digital signatures also make use of a private and public key. However, in this instance, the public key is common knowledge and is available to anyone. The application sending the data uses a private key to sign the data and the receiving application uses the public key to verify the digital signature. Verification of the signature ensures that the data stream associated with the digital signature has not changed during transmission.

Hashing is one way of converting data. Once data has been hashed, it cannot be unhashed. Hashing is typically used with passwords, whereby you initially hash a password and then store that hashed value. Then, when you need to validate a password that has been entered, you hash the password entered and compare the hash values to see if they are equal.

The .NET Framework provides many classes that implement various encryption algorithms. The one that I find the easiest to use and which provides a very good level of security is the `TripleDESCryptoServiceProvider` class. This class provides a wrapper for the `TripleDES` class, which implements the Triple Data Encryption Standard algorithms and supports 192-bit security keys.

In addition to the security key, this class also requires an initialization vector (IV), which is used in concert with the security key to encrypt and decrypt data. This provides an extra level of security because the initialization vector is used in the symmetric algorithm, which performs *cipher block chaining* on the data being encrypted. Basically, cipher block chaining is the process of taking information from the previous block of encrypted text and mixing it into the process of encrypting the next block of data.

The key and IV used in the `TripleDESCryptoServiceProvider` class must be the same length, although you want to ensure that the values are different. The key and IV length used in this class can be from 128 bits to 192 bits, in increments of 64 bits.

Recall the basics of computer programming: 8 bits equals a byte and a single alphanumeric character equals one byte. However, when using Unicode characters, a single Unicode character equals two bytes. Single-byte alphanumeric characters are those characters located on a standard U.S. keyboard.

Therefore, when using a 192-bit encryption key and IV, the number of standard alphanumeric characters that can be used is 24. If you are using all Unicode characters, this number would be reduced by half, to 12. You can use a mix of standard alphanumeric and Unicode characters in your security key and IV.

Crypto Class

The `Crypto` class encrypts and decrypts data using the cryptography services in the .NET Framework. To that end, three namespaces are required in this class, as illustrated by the following code:

```
Imports System.IO
Imports System.Text
Imports System.Security.Cryptography
```

Also used throughout this class are several variables, which have been defined to be global to the class. The first three variables are defined as `Byte` arrays and are used in encrypting and decrypting data.

The Triple Data Encryption Standard (TripleDES) algorithm was chosen as the algorithm to be used for encryption and decryption of data due to its ease of use and strong security key and initialization vector. Thus, the `objTripleDES` object is declared as an instance of the `TripleDESCryptoServiceProvider` class. A memory stream is required for encrypting and decrypting data, so the `objOutputStream` object has been declared using the `MemoryStream` class:

```
'Private variables and objects
Private bytKey() As Byte
Private bytIV() As Byte
Private bytInput() As Byte

Private objTripleDES As TripleDESCryptoServiceProvider
Private objOutputStream As MemoryStream
```

The `Crypto` class contains two constructors, as shown in the following code. The first constructor is the default constructor for this class and contains no code. This is the constructor used when instantiating this class in order to call the `Hash` method.

The second constructor accepts the key and initialization vector `Byte` arrays as input and instantiates a new instance of the `TripleDESCryptoServiceProvider` class. This is the constructor that is called when this class is used to encrypt and decrypt data.

```
Public Sub New()

End Sub

Public Sub New(ByVal key() As Byte, ByVal iv() As Byte)
    'Initialize the security key and initialization vector
    bytKey = key
    bytIV = iv

    'Instantiate a new instance of the
    'TripleDESCryptoServiceProvider class
    objTripleDES = New TripleDESCryptoServiceProvider
End Sub
```

The `Encrypt` function accepts the string value to be encrypted and returns the encrypted string as output. A `Try...Catch` block handles any errors that might occur when attempting to encrypt data.

The first thing that you need to do in this function is convert the input string into a `Byte` array, which is done using the `Encoding` class. The `Encoding` class is used to encode data in the various character formats.

The UTF8 property of this class represents data encoding in the Unicode Transformation Format 8-bit (UTF-8) format, which is the most widely used method of encoding data. This format handles Unicode characters, so it can be used on any language to provide international support in your applications. The GetBytes method encodes the string supplied as input into a Byte array of UTF-8 characters.

```
Public Function Encrypt(ByVal value As String) As String
    Try
        'Convert the input string to a byte array
        Dim bytInput() As Byte = Encoding.UTF8.GetBytes(value)
```

The CryptoStream class performs the actual encryption using the cryptographic algorithm that you specified; in this case, it is the TripleDES algorithm. The constructor for the CryptoStream class expects an output stream to write the encrypted results to, the cryptographic transformation algorithm to be used, and the mode that should be used.

The output from the CryptoStream class is written to a MemoryStream object, so you initialize the objOutputStream object in a Using...End Using block. Then you declare and initialize an object for the CryptoStream class, passing the constructor the required parameters.

Notice the cryptographic transformation parameter to the CryptoStream class. You are calling the CreateEncryptor method on the objTripleDes object, passing it the key and initialization vector. This returns a TripleDes encryptor object to be used for the cryptographic transformation.

```
'Instantiate a new instance of the MemoryStream class
Using objOutputStream As New MemoryStream
    'Encrypt the byte array
    Dim objCryptoStream As New CryptoStream(objOutputStream, _
        objTripleDES.CreateEncryptor(bytKey, bytIV), _
        CryptoStreamMode.Write)
```

Now you can write the encrypted output to the objOutputStream object. Use the Write method from the CryptoStream class. Here you are specifying the Byte array that contains the input, the offset within that Byte array, and the number of bytes to be written. Because you want to write the entire contents to the output buffer, you use the Length property of the Byte array to determine how many bytes should be written. Next, you flush the buffer, signifying that the write operation is complete.

```
objCryptoStream.Write(bytInput, 0, bytInput.Length)
objCryptoStream.FlushFinalBlock()
```

You need to transform the Byte array back into a complete string to be returned by this function. The Convert class converts one base data type into another. The following code uses the ToBase64String method to convert an array of bytes into a complete string. The input to this method is a Byte array, so you use the ToArray function to convert the individual bytes in the objOutputStream object to a byte array. Converting the encrypted data into a Base64 string enables you to work with this data safely in XML documents because all the special characters that are not allowed in an XML document have been removed and replaced with characters that are allowed in an XML document.

```
'Return the byte array as a Base64 string
Encrypt = Convert.ToBase64String(objOutputStream.ToArray())
End Using
```

The `Catch` block handles an exception if thrown and then throws a new exception to the caller when an error occurs:

```
        Catch ExceptionErr As Exception
            Throw New System.Exception(ExceptionErr.Message, _
                ExceptionErr.InnerException)
        End Try
    End Function
```

The `Decrypt` function works in the same manner as the `Encrypt` function except in reverse. You convert your encrypted string into a `Byte` array. Notice that you are using the `Convert` function for this and the `FromBase64String` method:

```
    Public Function Decrypt(ByVal value As String) As String
        Try
            'Convert the input string to a byte array
            Dim inputByteArray() As Byte = Convert.FromBase64String(value)
```

Next, you initialize a new instance of the `MemoryStream` class followed by the `CryptoStream` class, passing it the required parameters to decrypt the string. Using the `Write` method of the `objCryptoStream` object, you write the decrypted value into a `Byte` array and then flush the memory stream:

```
            'Instantiate a new instance of the MemoryStream class
            Using objOutputStream As New MemoryStream
                'Decrypt the byte array
                Dim objCryptoStream As New CryptoStream(objOutputStream, _
                    objTripleDES.CreateDecryptor(bytKey, bytIV), _
                    CryptoStreamMode.Write)
                objCryptoStream.Write(inputByteArray, 0, inputByteArray.Length)
                objCryptoStream.FlushFinalBlock()
```

You want to return the decrypted string back to the caller in UTF-8 format, so you use the `Encoding` class with the `UTF8` property to get the decrypted string from the `Byte` array.

The `Catch` block handles any errors that occur and throws a new exception that will be returned to the caller:

```
                'Return the byte array as a string
                Decrypt = Encoding.UTF8.GetString(objOutputStream.ToArray())
            End Using

        Catch ExceptionErr As Exception
            Throw New System.Exception(ExceptionErr.Message, _
                ExceptionErr.InnerException)
        End Try
    End Function
```

The final method in the `Crypto` class is the `Hash` function. This function starts by declaring a couple of `Byte` arrays that are used to store both the input value to be hashed and the hashed value to be returned.

Then you instantiate a new instance of the `SHA1CryptoServiceProvider` class in a `Using...End Using` block. This class is used to compute an SHA1 hash value.

You must convert the value passed to this function into a Byte array, so you use the GetBytes method of the UTF8 property of the Encoding class. This is the same code that you saw when encrypting data in the Encrypt method.

After the value has been converted into a Byte array, you call the ComputeHash method to hash the value. The output from this method is a Byte array containing the hashed value. You need to convert the Byte array back into a string before returning it to the caller, so you use the ToBase64String method of the Convert class. This is the same code that you used in the Encrypt method.

All of the code is in a Try...Catch block to handle any errors that may occur, and the Catch block simply throws the error that it receives so the error is returned to the caller of this function.

```
Public Function Hash(ByVal value As String) As String
    Try
        'Declare local variables
        Dim bytValueIn() As Byte
        Dim bytValueOut() As Byte

        Using objHashAlgorithm As New SHA1CryptoServiceProvider
            'Convert the input value to an array of bytes
            bytValueIn = Encoding.UTF8.GetBytes(value)

            'Compute the Hash (returns an array of bytes)
            bytValueOut = objHashAlgorithm.ComputeHash(bytValueIn)

            'Return a base 64 encoded string of the hashed value
            Hash = Convert.ToBase64String(bytValueOut)
        End Using
    Catch ExceptionErr As Exception
        Throw New System.Exception(ExceptionErr.Message, _
            ExceptionErr.InnerException)
    End Try
End Function
```

Setting Up the Password Keeper Program

You have two options for setting up the Password Keeper program: use the installer or manually copy the required files to your computer. The first option provides an easy, fast approach to installing the program, whereas the second method provides more control over where the program is placed.

Using the Installer

To install the Password Keeper Program, locate the Chapter 02 - Password Keeper\Installer folder on the CD-ROM that came with this book and double-click the setup.exe program. You will be prompted with the Application Install dialog. Clicking the Install button will install and launch the application.

Manual Installation

To manually install the Password Keeper program, first create a folder on your computer where you want to place the program executable file. Then locate the Chapter 02 - Password Keeper\Source folder on the CD-ROM that came with this book and navigate to the `bin\Release` folder. Copy the `Password Keeper.exe` file from the `Release` folder to the folder that you created on your computer.

To run the Password Keeper program, double-click on the `Password Keeper.exe` file.

Configuring the Application

No special configuration is required for the Password Keeper program. Once the application has launched, you are prompted to enter your security credentials in the Login form. See the section "Using the Password Keeper Program" at the beginning of this chapter for details about using this program.

Summary

This chapter has reviewed several technologies available in the .NET Framework, including data encryption and data hashing. These are two very important technologies that you can use to secure the data in your applications. The `Crypto` class provided in this application can be easily used in your own applications to provide data security.

You also learned how to read and write XML data using a forward-only, non-cached XML text reader and text writer. When simply reading XML data from top to bottom, the `XmlTextReader` class is the most efficient method of reading XML data. When generating XML data from top to bottom, the `XmlTextWriter` class is the most efficient method of writing XML data.

Also covered in this chapter is the `XmlDocument` class, which provides a method of reading and writing XML data in any order. This class was used in the `Passwords` class to not only read all of the XML data, but also to search for specific elements within the XML data to update and delete. It was also used to search for specific elements in the XML data to read.

3

Application
Registry Manager

When writing software applications that run on a server, you typically place the required configuration values for that application in the system registry. This placement makes your application more secure than it would be if you put those values in an application configuration file. The system registry is typically restricted to only those users who have permissions to view it, whereas it is most likely that anyone could browse to the folder where your application is installed and view the application configuration file.

One challenge of using the registry in your applications is knowing how to create registry keys programmatically from your application and setting and reading key values stored in the registry. The Application Registry Manager program demonstrated in this chapter should help you to gain a better understanding of how to perform these tasks within your own applications. This application demonstrates creating and deleting registry keys for an application, as well as setting and deleting the values for those keys.

The main technologies used in this application are as follows:

❑   Using the `RegistryKey` class in the .NET Framework

❑   Using a `TreeView` control

❑   Using a `ListView` control

❑   Recursively calling a procedure to enumerate values

Using the Application Registry Manager Program

The registry is a repository for data. It controls how your operating system, services, and applications work. You should never modify registry values that you have not created unless you know what you are doing, as it could cause your operating system to stop working. Before modifying the registry, you should know how to back up and restore the registry in case a problem occurs. See the Microsoft Knowledge Base article 256986 for a description of the registry and for links on how to back up and restore the registry. This article can be located at http://support.microsoft.com/kb/256986/en-us.

Given that editing the registry could cause your operating system to stop working, this program restricts the user to the current user hive and local machine hive of the registry and to the Software node in the registry. You can still cause plenty of damage to the operating system and other services and programs if you edit registry keys that you have not created, so use extreme caution if you choose to proceed.

When you first start the Application Registry Manager program, it will create a set of demonstration keys and key values in the current user hive of the registry and automatically display that information in the program, as shown in Figure 3-1. This provides a quick start for seeing what functionality the program provides. It also provides a place for you to practice creating and deleting registry keys and setting and deleting key values.

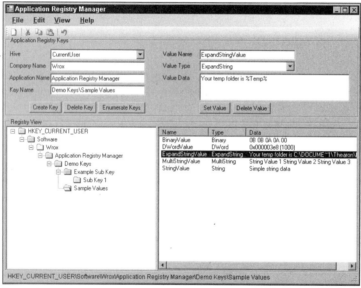

Figure 3-1

The current user hive of the registry applies only to the user currently logged on, while the local machine hive of the registry applies to all users. If you are creating registry keys such as user preferences, you will want to create those keys in the current user hive of the registry. If you are creating registry keys such as program defaults or file locations for the program, you will want to create those keys in the local machine hive of the registry so that they apply to any user who uses the program.

The upper-left portion of Figure 3-1 shows the registry key that you are working with and provides fields and buttons for entering and creating new registry keys. You must first select the hive of the registry where you want the registry key created, current user or local machine, and then enter the company name and application name. The Key Name field is where you enter the key name to be created. If you are creating subkeys under an existing key, you must enter both key names separated by a backslash, as demonstrated in Figure 3-1.

Using the Create Key button you can create a new registry key, and using the Delete Key button you can delete an existing key. The Enumerate Keys button will enumerate the existing keys for the company name and application name that you enter. This causes the program to read the registry for the information that you have entered and display that information in the Registry View section of the program, also shown in Figure 3-1.

The upper-right section of Figure 3-1 shows where you can set the values for a registry key. A registry key can contain multiple values, as demonstrated in Figure 3-1. This program enables you to create binary values, double-word values, expanding string values, multiple-string values, and simple string values.

A binary value is self-explanatory in that it stores raw binary data. The double-word value stores a number that is four bytes long. The expanding string value stores system variables that expand when the data is read, as shown in the highlighted entry in Figure 3-1. This example uses the `%Temp%` system variable, which points to the temporary directory for the current user. The multiple-string value stores multiple data values that are typically separated by a carriage return linefeed character. The string value stores simple string values of any length.

To create a value, you must first click a key name in the Registry View section of the program and then enter the value name, select a value type, and enter the value data. Click the Set Value button to have the value created. The Delete Value button in this section will delete a key value.

As you add and delete keys and values, the Registry View section of this program displays the information that you create or removes the information that you delete, respectively. This section provides a view of the data as it exists in the registry.

When working with expanding string values, the default for reading the values is to expand the system variable used. You can turn off this default behavior by clicking the View menu and selecting the Expand Multi String Values menu item. This menu item is checked when this option is turned on, and is unchecked when this option is turned off.

The View menu also contains the Demo Registry Keys menu item, which provides a quick way to view the demonstration keys shown in Figure 3-1. If you clear the current values or are viewing another application's registry key, you can select this menu item to view the demonstration keys that are built when the program starts.

Design of the Application Registry Manager Program

The design of the Application Registry Manager program is simple and includes only one class, `RegistryHelper`, that encapsulates the main functionality needed to create, delete, and enumerate keys, and to set and delete key values, as shown in Figure 3-2.

This design enables you to drop the `RegistryHelper` class into your own applications and the code in the `RegistryManager` form provides the sample code necessary to read and write keys and values in the registry.

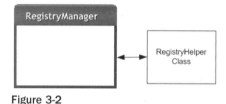

Figure 3-2

RegistryManager Form

The `RegistryManager` form provides the UI (User Interface) for this program, and all major functionality in this form is derived from the data provided by the `RegistryHelper` class. When you click a button, a call is made to a method in the `RegistryHelper` class, and whenever you click the `TreeView` control or the `ListView` control, a call is made to a method in the `RegistryHelper` class. The `RegistryManager` form is merely the UI component of this program, with the `RegistryHelper` class providing the data displayed in this form.

The top portion of the form contains the edit fields and buttons to create and delete keys, as well as to set and delete key values, while the bottom portion of the form contains the data that has been created, giving you a snapshot of what the data looks like in the registry (refer to Figure 3-1).

RegistryHelper Class

The `RegistryHelper` class contains all the methods necessary to read, create, and delete registry keys, as well as methods to read, set, and delete key values. All the functionality required to interact with the system registry is contained in this class.

To make this class easy to use in your UI, it implements the `IDisposable` interface. This enables you to use this class in a `Using...End Using` block, saving you the trouble of instantiating and disposing of the class each time you want to use it.

This class has several overloaded methods to provide the data needed in various circumstances, such as the overloaded `GetValue` method, which can return expanding string value data in either expanded or non-expanded form.

Table 3-1 lists the methods available in this class and provides a brief description of their functions. You'll see more details about these methods in the next section, "Code and Code Explanation."

Table 3-1: Methods in the RegistryHelper Class

Method	Return Type	Description
`Public Sub New()`	N/A	Provides an empty constructor for the class
`Protected Overridable Sub Dispose()`	N/A	Cleans up registry resources used in this class

Table 3-1: Methods in the RegistryHelper Class *(continued)*

Method	Return Type	Description
`Public Function CreateKey(ByVal hive As RegistryHive, ByVal companyName As String, ByVal applicationName As String, ByVal keyName As String)`	Boolean	Creates a new registry key
`Public Function DeleteKey(ByVal hive As RegistryHive, ByVal companyName As String, ByVal applicationName As String, ByVal keyName As String`	Boolean	Deletes a registry key
`Public Function DeleteValue(ByVal hive As RegistryHive, ByVal companyName As String, ByVal applicationName As String, ByVal keyName As String, ByVal valueName As String)`	Boolean	Deletes a key value
`Public Function GetKeyNames(ByVal hive As RegistryHive, ByVal companyName As String, ByVal applicationName As String, ByVal keyName As String)`	String Array	Returns a string array of subkey names for the specified key
`Public Function GetValue(ByVal hive As RegistryHive, ByVal companyName As String, ByVal applicationName As String, ByVal keyName As String, ByVal name As String)`	Object	Returns the key value for the specified value name without expanding the paths specified in the expanding string value
`Public Function GetValue(ByVal name As String)`	Object	Returns the key value for the specified value name, expanding the paths specified in the expanding string value
`Public Function GetValue(ByVal name As String, ByVal defaultValue As String, ByVal options As RegistryValueOptions)`	Object	Returns the key value for the specified value name and gives you the option to expand the path in expanding string values
`Public Function GetValueKind(ByVal name As String)`	RegistryValueKind	Returns the registry value kind (e.g., data type) of the value name

Continued

Table 3-1: Methods in the RegistryHelper Class *(continued)*

Method	Return Type	Description
`Public Function GetValueNames(ByVal hive As RegistryHive, ByVal companyName As String, ByVal applicationName As String, ByVal keyName As String)`	`String Array`	Returns a string array of all value names for the specified key
`Private Function IsValidInput(ByVal validateKeyName As Boolean)`	`Boolean`	A private function used internally to validate input
`Private Sub OpenRegistryKey(ByVal hive As RegistryHive, ByVal writeable As Boolean)`	N/A	A private procedure used internally to open a registry key for reading or writing
`Private Sub OpenRegistryKey(ByVal hive As RegistryHive, ByVal name As String)`	N/A	A private procedure used internally to open a registry key

Code and Code Explanation

This section explains how the two pieces of the application fit together, helping you to gain a better understanding of how both the RegistryManager form and RegistryHelper class work. You'll also dive into the details of the code to gain insight into how to manipulate the registry and how you can use the RegistryHelper class in your own applications.

RegistryHelper Class

There are just over a dozen methods in this class but most are very simple. All but three of these methods are called from the code in the RegistryManager form. The other three methods are used internally by this class, as you'll see next.

Internal Functions and Procedures

The IsValidInput function is used to validate user input to the methods in this class. At this point, you may well be wondering about a key design issue: Why not simply pass the company name, application name, and key name to this method instead of setting them in global class variables? The reason is that those variables are used in other methods in this class, so it made more sense to set them in global class variables, rather than pass them to this method.

This method validates the input for company name, application name, and (optionally) key name. Notice the validateKeyName Boolean input parameter, which specifies whether this procedure should validate the key name. This function also returns a Boolean value indicating success or failure.

The validations in this method are simple: trim the strings and then check the length of the trimmed strings. If the length of the string is zero, then this method returns a value of `False`:

```
Private Function IsValidInput(ByVal validateKeyName As Boolean) _
    As Boolean

    'Validate input
    If strCompanyName.Trim.Length = 0 Then
        Return False
    End If
    If strApplicationName.Trim.Length = 0 Then
        Return False
    End If
    If validateKeyName Then
        If strKeyName.Trim.Length = 0 Then
            Return False
        End If
    End If

    'All validations passed
    Return True
End Function
```

The `OpenRegistryKey` method is another overloaded method in this class with two overloads. This first overloaded method has two input parameters: `hive` and `writeable`. The `hive` parameter is specified as a constant from the `RegistryHive` enumeration and is used to determine the hive of the registry in which the registry key should be opened. The `writeable` parameter is specified as a `Boolean` value and determines whether the registry key should be opened as writeable or for reading only.

This procedure starts off by first checking the `strKeyName` global class variable to determine whether the variable contains any data. This is done by checking the length of this variable. If this variable contains data, then another check is made to determine whether this variable starts with a backslash character. If it does not, then this variable is prefixed with a backslash character.

```
Private Sub OpenRegistryKey(ByVal hive As RegistryHive, _
    ByVal writeable As Boolean)

    'Add a path separator if necessary
    If strKeyName.Trim.Length > 0 Then
        If Not strKeyName.StartsWith("\") Then
            strKeyName = "\" & strKeyName
        End If
    End If
```

A `Select Case` statement is used to determine which hive of the registry should be opened. Again, a `Select Case` statement is used to allow for future expansion by you if you desire to read or write to the other hives in the registry.

This overloaded `OpenSubKey` method of the `Registry` class accepts two parameters: the full path of the registry key to open and a `Boolean` value indicating whether the registry key should be opened for writing or for reading only. This method returns an opened `RegistryKey` class, which is set in the `objRegistryKey` object.

```
        'Open the appropriate key
        Select Case hive
            Case RegistryHive.CurrentUser
                objRegistryKey = Registry.CurrentUser.OpenSubKey( _
                    "Software\" & strCompanyName & "\" & _
                    strApplicationName & strKeyName, writeable)
            Case RegistryHive.LocalMachine
                objRegistryKey = Registry.LocalMachine.OpenSubKey( _
                    "Software\" & strCompanyName & "\" & _
                    strApplicationName & strKeyName, writeable)
        End Select
```

If the `OpenSubKey` method failed to open the specified registry key, the `objRegistryKey` object will have a value of `Nothing`. The next statement checks for this condition and throws an error that is returned to the caller:

```
        If IsNothing(objRegistryKey) Then
            'Return the error to the caller
            Throw New Exception("RegistryHelper.OpenRegistryKey " & _
                "Registry key not found.")
        End If
    End Sub
```

The other overloaded `OpenRegistryKey` method accepts two input parameters: `hive` and `name`. There is no validation of the inputs because this method is `Private` and is only called internally within this class.

A `Select Case` statement is used again to determine in which hive of the registry the key should be opened, and then opens the appropriate key as specified in the `name` parameter. Even though this method is called internally, as a good coding practice you still want to check the `objRegistryKey` object to ensure that it is not `Nothing`, and throw an error if it is:

```
    Private Sub OpenRegistryKey(ByVal hive As RegistryHive, ByVal name As String)
        'Open the appropriate key
        Select Case hive
            Case RegistryHive.CurrentUser
                objRegistryKey = Registry.CurrentUser.OpenSubKey(name, True)
            Case RegistryHive.LocalMachine
                objRegistryKey = Registry.LocalMachine.OpenSubKey(name, True)
        End Select

        If IsNothing(objRegistryKey) Then
            'Return the error to the caller
            Throw New Exception("RegistryHelper.OpenRegistryKey " & _
                "Registry key not found.")
        End If
    End Sub
```

SetValue Method

Now we can examine the public methods in the `RegistryHelper` class, starting with the `SetValue` method. This method sets the value for a value name. As you'll notice, it includes the usual input parameters that you've seen in the `CreateKey`, `DeleteKey`, and `GetKeyNames` methods.

In addition to these usual input parameters, there are three others: `valueName`, `valueData`, and `valueType`. Notice that `valueName` is a `String` data type, as you would expect, and that `valueData` is an `Object` data type. Because a value can be one of multiple registry value kinds, this parameter is defined as an `Object`. The `valueType` parameter is defined as a constant from the `RegistryValueKind` enumeration.

```
Public Function SetValue(ByVal hive As RegistryHive, _
    ByVal companyName As String, ByVal applicationName As String, _
    ByVal keyName As String, ByVal valueName As String, _
    ByVal valueData As Object, ByVal valueType As RegistryValueKind) _
    As Boolean
```

The usual parameters are set in the global class variables and then the standard validation is performed through the `IsValidInput` method. Now you need to validate the `valueName` parameter to ensure that it contains some data. This is done by calling the `Trim` method of the `String` class and then checking the length using the `Length` property of the `String` class. An error is thrown if the length of this parameter is zero, and the error is returned to the caller.

The next validation that is performed is the validation of the `valueData` parameter. Because this parameter is defined as an `Object` data type, you merely check to confirm that it is not set to a value of `Nothing` using the `IsNothing` function. If this parameter has a value of `Nothing`, then you throw an error, which is returned to the caller:

```
Try
    'Set class variables
    strCompanyName = companyName
    strApplicationName = applicationName
    strKeyName = keyName

    'Validate input
    If Not IsValidInput(True) Then
        Throw New Exception("RegistryHelper.SetValue " & _
            strValidationMessage2)
    End If

    'Validate value data
    If valueName.Trim.Length = 0 Then
        Throw New Exception("RegistryHelper.SetValue " & _
            "Value Name is a required input parameter.")
    End If

    If IsNothing(valueData) Then
        Throw New Exception("RegistryHelper.SetValue " & _
            "Value Data is a required input parameter.")
    End If
```

Open the appropriate registry key by calling the `OpenRegistryKey` method and then set the value by calling the `SetValue` method in the `RegistryKey` class. Notice that this method needs three parameters: `valueName`, `valueData`, and `valueType`. After the value has been set, you return a value of `True` from this method.

The `Catch` block handles any errors that occur and the error is returned to the caller of this method:

```
        'Open the registry key
        OpenRegistryKey(hive, True)

        'Set the value
        objRegistryKey.SetValue(valueName, valueData, valueType)

        Return True

    Catch ExceptionErr As Exception
        'Return the error to the caller
        Throw New Exception("RegistryHelper.SetValue " & ExceptionErr.Message)
    End Try
End Function
```

CreateKey Method

The `CreateKey` method creates a new registry key for an application. There are four input parameters to this method: `hive`, `companyName`, `applicationName`, and `keyName`. The `hive` parameter is specified as a value from the `RegistryHive` enumeration. This enables you to create a key in any hive of the registry, although the `RegistryManager` form restricts this to either the `CurrentUser` or `LocalMachine` hive.

Next is the `companyName` parameter. This is a `String` value that specifies the company name for the application. Following the `companyName` parameter is the `applicationName` parameter, which is a `String` value specifying the application name to be created.

The `keyName` parameter is last and specifies the key name to be created for the company and application. The key name is a single key to be created. If you are creating a subkey under an existing key, you must specify both keys followed by a backslash. This is handled in the UI but is worth noting here.

The code in this method is wrapped in a `Try...Catch` block and will simply return any errors to the caller of this method. This method starts out by setting the global `String` variables in this class, `strCompanyName`, `strApplicationName`, and `strKeyName`, using the input parameters passed to this method. These global variables are used in the private procedures in the class.

Next, a call to the `IsValidInput` method is made and the results of this call are checked. The `IsValidInput` method returns a `Boolean` variable indicating whether the input is valid. You'll see this method later in this section. If the input is not valid, then a new exception is thrown, which causes the code path to branch into the `Catch` block and in turn returns the error to the caller.

```
    Public Function CreateKey(ByVal hive As RegistryHive, _
        ByVal companyName As String, ByVal applicationName As String, _
        ByVal keyName As String) As Boolean

        Try
```

```
'Set class variables
strCompanyName = companyName
strApplicationName = applicationName
strKeyName = keyName

'Validate input
If Not IsValidInput(True) Then
    Throw New Exception("RegistryHelper.CreateKey " & _
        strValidationMessage2)
End If
```

If the `strKeyName` variable does not begin with a backslash (\), then one is prefixed to the variable in the first line of code shown here. Next, using the `hive` input parameter, a `Select Case` statement is used to execute the appropriate code to create the new key in the correct hive of the registry. A call to the `CreateSubKey` method is made in the `Registry` class in the appropriate hive to create the key.

Notice that the key being created is fully qualified in the call to the `CreateSubKey` method. The value of `Software` is hard-coded to prevent the user from creating keys in other parts of the `CurrentUser` or `LocalMachine` hive of the registry. Additionally, the company name, application name, and key name are all concatenated and separated with a backslash:

```
'Add a path separator if necessary
If Not strKeyName.StartsWith("\") Then
    strKeyName = "\" & strKeyName
End If

'Create the key in the appropriate hive
Select Case hive
    Case RegistryHive.CurrentUser
        objRegistryKey = Registry.CurrentUser.CreateSubKey( _
            "Software\" & strCompanyName & "\" & _
            strApplicationName & strKeyName)
    Case RegistryHive.LocalMachine
        objRegistryKey = Registry.LocalMachine.CreateSubKey( _
            "Software\" & strCompanyName & "\" & _
            strApplicationName & strKeyName)
End Select
```

The `CreateSubKey` method returns a reference to the newly created key as a `RegistryKey` class, which has been defined globally in this class as `objRegistryKey`. In this next line of code you check to ensure that the `objRegistryKey` object does not have a value of `Nothing` by using the `IsNothing` function. The `IsNothing` function returns a `Boolean` variable indicating whether or not the object passed to it has a value of `Nothing`.

If the `objRegistryKey` object was not set to an instance of the `RegistryKey` class, then the call to the `CreateSubKey` method failed and you want to raise an error, which causes the code path to branch to the `Catch` block. If the `objRegistryKey` object does contain an instance of the `RegistryKey` class with the newly created key, then you simply return a value of `True` from this method.

The `Catch` block simply throws a new exception and returns the error to the caller of this method. In an effort to help identify where the error is coming from, the first part of the error message contains the class name and method separated by a period. Then the actual error message is appended to this string and is returned.

```
If IsNothing(objRegistryKey) Then
    'Return the error to the caller
    Throw New Exception( _
        "RegistryHelper.CreateKey Registry key not created.")
End If

Return True

Catch ExceptionErr As Exception
    'Return the error to the caller
    Throw New Exception("RegistryHelper.CreateKey " & ExceptionErr.Message)
End Try
End Function
```

DeleteKey Method

As its name suggests, the DeleteKey method deletes a registry key. This method accepts the same input parameters as the CreateKey method and begins the same as the CreateKey method by wrapping the code in a Try...Catch block to return any errors that may occur to the caller of this method.

Next, two local variables are declared in this method: strSubKey and strKeys(). The strSubKey variable is a String variable used to extract the subkey to be deleted. The strKeys() variable is a String array variable used to determine whether any other keys exist for this application.

Again, the global class variables are set using the input parameters to this method and then a call is made to the IsValidInput method to determine whether the input to this method is valid. If the input parameters are not valid, then an exception is thrown and then returned to the caller.

```
Public Function DeleteKey(ByVal hive As RegistryHive, _
    ByVal companyName As String, ByVal applicationName As String, _
    ByVal keyName As String) As Boolean

    Try
        'Declare local variables
        Dim strSubKey As String
        Dim strKeys() As String

        'Set class variables
        strCompanyName = companyName
        strApplicationName = applicationName
        strKeyName = keyName

        'Validate input
        If Not IsValidInput(True) Then
            Throw New Exception("RegistryHelper.DeleteKey " & _
                strValidationMessage2)
        End If
```

Now you need to extract the actual key to be deleted and set it in the strSubKey variable and the remaining value in the strKeyName variable. This is done because you have to open the registry key for the application in order to delete a key but you cannot open the actual key to be deleted; you must open the registry at one level above the key to be deleted. Remember that the `keyName` input parameter to this method may contain one or more key names, each separated by a backslash.

To set the last key in the `strKeyName` variable, you use the `LastIndexOf` method, checking for a backslash. If this method does not find a match, then it returns a value of –1. Otherwise, this method returns the index of the backslash in the string.

If the value returned by the `LastIndexOf` method is not equal to –1, then you extract the key name to be deleted from the `strKeyName` variable and set it in the `strSubKey` variable. Then you set the remaining key name in the `strKeyName` variable, effectively removing the key name to be deleted.

The code in the `Else` statement is executed if the `strKeyName` variable does not contain any backslashes. It simply sets the `strSubKey` variable to the value contained in the `strKeyName` variable and then sets the `strKeyName` variable to an empty string.

```
'Extract the sub key to be deleted
If strKeyName.LastIndexOf("\") <> -1 Then
    strSubKey = strKeyName.Substring(strKeyName.LastIndexOf("\") + 1)
    strKeyName = strKeyName.Substring(0, strKeyName.LastIndexOf("\"))
Else
    strSubKey = strKeyName
    strKeyName = String.Empty
End If
```

A call is made to the `OpenRegistryKey` method next. This is an overloaded method that you'll be examining shortly. The overloaded method that you are using here accepts a value from the `RegistryHive` enumeration and a `Boolean` value indicating whether to open the registry as writeable.

Once the registry key has been opened, the `objRegistryKey` object will have been set to the instance of the key that was specified in the `strKeyName` variable. Remember that this key is one level above the actual key to be deleted. Then a call is made to the `DeleteSubKey` method, passing it the key name in the `strSubKey` variable to be deleted.

```
'Open the registry key
OpenRegistryKey(hive, True)

'Delete the key name
objRegistryKey.DeleteSubKey(strSubKey)
```

After deleting the specified key, you need to determine whether the `strKeyName` variable contains an empty string. If it does, then this indicates that you may have deleted the last key for the application, in which case you want to go ahead and delete the application name and company name if appropriate.

The code inside the `If...Then` statement makes a call to a different overloaded method of `OpenRegistryKey`, passing it the `RegistryHive` and the key to open, consisting of the string constant `Software` concatenated with the company and application name. Then a call is made to the `GetSubKeyNames` method of the `RegistryKey` class to get a list of key names if any remain.

Next, check the length of the `strKeys String` array to see whether any key names were returned from the call to the `GetSubKeyNames` method. If the length is greater than zero, then other keys still exist for this application, so you return a value of `True` because this method has now completed its task.

```
'If this was the last key specified then check for other keys
If strKeyName = String.Empty Then

    'Open the registry key
    OpenRegistryKey(hive, "Software\" & strCompanyName & _
        "\" & strApplicationName)

    'See if the company has any other applications
    strKeys = objRegistryKey.GetSubKeyNames

    If strKeys.Length > 0 Then
        'Other application keys exist to return
        Return True
    End If
```

If no key names were returned, delete the application name by again making a call to the `OpenRegistryKey` method, passing it the `RegistryHive` and the key to open, consisting of the string constant `Software` concatenated with the company name. Remember that this is one level above the key you want to delete. Then a call is made to the `DeleteSubKey` method to delete the application name.

Next, make another call to the `GetSubKeyNames` method to return any keys for the company name. A company name in the Software node of the registry may contain other applications. For example, the Microsoft company name node under the Software node for either the `CurrentUser` or `LocalMachine` hive of the registry contains many different applications.

Again, check whether any keys exist. If no further keys exist for the company, delete the company node from the registry. Here you make another call to the `OpenRegistryKey` method, passing it the `RegistryHive` and the key to open, consisting of only the string constant `Software`. Then you call the `DeleteSubKey` method to delete the company name.

```
'Open the registry key
OpenRegistryKey(hive, "Software\" & strCompanyName)

'Delete the application
objRegistryKey.DeleteSubKey(strApplicationName)

'See if the company has any other applications
strKeys = objRegistryKey.GetSubKeyNames

If strKeys.Length = 0 Then

    'Open the registry key
    OpenRegistryKey(hive, "Software")

    'Delete the application
    objRegistryKey.DeleteSubKey(strCompanyName)

End If

End If
```

At this point you have completed the task required by the `DeleteKey` method and returned a value of `True`, indicating success of this method. If any errors occurred in this method, then the code in the `Catch` block would be invoked and would return the error to the caller.

```
        Return True

    Catch ExceptionErr As Exception
        'Return the error to the caller
        Throw New Exception("RegistryHelper.DeleteKey " & ExceptionErr.Message)
    End Try
End Function
```

DeleteValue Method

The next method, and notice these are being covered in alphabetical order, is the `DeleteValue` method. This method will delete a key value in the registry for the specified key name. This method accepts the same input parameters as the `CreateKey` and `DeleteKey` methods, with one additional parameter: `valueName`. The `valueName` parameter contains the value name for the key to be deleted.

The code is wrapped in a `Try...Catch` block to handle any errors that may occur. The first thing that happens in this method is setting the global variables in this class to the company name, application name, and key name passed to this method:

```
Public Function DeleteValue(ByVal hive As RegistryHive, _
    ByVal companyName As String, ByVal applicationName As String, _
    ByVal keyName As String, ByVal valueName As String) As Boolean

    Try
        'Set class variables
        strCompanyName = companyName
        strApplicationName = applicationName
        strKeyName = keyName
```

Next, you need to validate the input parameters, so again a call is made to the `IsValidInput` method and an error is thrown if the input is not valid. Then the `valueName` parameter is validated.

Here you simply check the length of the parameter to ensure that it does contain data by first calling the `Trim` method of the `String` class and then checking the `Length` property of the `String` class. Because the `valueName` parameter is a `String` variable, these methods and properties are automatically inherited with this parameter. If the length of this input parameter is zero, then you throw a new exception, which in turn is returned to the caller:

```
        'Validate input
        If Not IsValidInput(True) Then
            Throw New Exception("RegistryHelper.SetValue " & _
                strValidationMessage2)
        End If

        'Validate value data
        If valueName.Trim.Length = 0 Then
            Throw New Exception("RegistryHelper.SetValue " & _
                "Value Name is a required input parameter.")
        End If
```

If all of the input parameters were validated successfully, you'll find yourself here, and you make a call to the `OpenRegistryKey` method to open the registry key whose value name you want to delete. Then you call the `DeleteValue` method of the `RegistryKey` class to delete the value name. If all was successful, you return a value of `True` indicating success of this method.

The `Catch` block simply returns the error to the caller, as shown in the previous two methods.

```
        'Open the registry key
        OpenRegistryKey(hive, True)

        objRegistryKey.DeleteValue(valueName)

        Return True

    Catch ExceptionErr As Exception
        'Return the error to the caller
        Throw New Exception("RegistryHelper.CreateKey " & _
            ExceptionErr.Message)
    End Try
End Function
```

GetKeyNames Method

The `GetKeyNames` method is very simple. It returns a `String` array of key names under the specified key. This method accepts the same input parameters as the `CreateKey` and `DeleteKey` methods, and once again the code is wrapped in a `Try...Catch` block to handle any errors that may occur.

The input parameters to this method are set in the global class variables and then a call is made to the `IsValidInput` method to validate the input. If the input is not valid, then an exception is thrown and the error is returned to the caller via the `Catch` block in this method.

```
    Public Function GetKeyNames(ByVal hive As RegistryHive, _
        ByVal companyName As String, ByVal applicationName As String, _
        ByVal keyName As String) As String()

        Try
            'Set class variables
            strCompanyName = companyName
            strApplicationName = applicationName
            strKeyName = keyName

            'Validate input
            If Not IsValidInput(False) Then
                Throw New Exception("RegistryHelper.GetKeyNames " & _
                    strValidationMessage1)
            End If
```

Now a call is made to the `OpenRegistryKey` method to open the appropriate registry key. Notice that this time a `Boolean` value of `False` is passed to this method, as you are simply reading values from the registry, so there is no need to open the registry as writeable.

Next, a call is made to the GetSubKeyNames method of the RegistryKey class and the results are set in the return variable of this method. When doing this, you simply specify the method name as the variable name because this method returns a String array.

The Catch block handles any exceptions and returns the error to the caller.

```
            'Open the registry key
            OpenRegistryKey(hive, False)

            'Get the key names
            GetKeyNames = objRegistryKey.GetSubKeyNames

        Catch ExceptionErr As Exception
            'Return the error to the caller
            Throw New Exception("RegistryHelper.GetKeyNames " & _
                ExceptionErr.Message)
        End Try
    End Function
```

GetValue Methods

The GetValue method is an overloaded method with three overloads. The first overloaded method that you'll want to examine is the method that is called when you click on an item in the ListView control on the RegistryManager form. This method has five input parameters: RegistryHive, companyName, applicationName, keyName, and name.

You've already seen the first four input parameters in the previous methods that you've examined for this class; only the name parameter is new. The name parameter specifies the value name for the registry key. The return type from this function is an Object data type, as this function could return any of the different value types that the registry supports (e.g., Binary, DWord, MultiString, String). The caller of this method is responsible for determining the correct data type returned.

```
    Public Function GetValue(ByVal hive As RegistryHive, _
        ByVal companyName As String, ByVal applicationName As String, _
        ByVal keyName As String, ByVal name As String) As Object
```

The code in this method is wrapped in a Try...Catch block and the first part of this code sets the global class variables and then validates the input. You've seen this code in the previous methods.

```
        Try
            'Set class variables
            strCompanyName = companyName
            strApplicationName = applicationName
            strKeyName = keyName

            'Validate input
            If Not IsValidInput(True) Then
                Throw New Exception("RegistryHelper.GetValueNames " & _
                    strValidationMessage2)
            End If
```

The registry key is opened by way of a call to the OpenRegistryKey method. Then the GetValue method of the RegistryKey class is called to get the value of the value name specified. The GetValue method used here expects three input parameters: value name, default value, and registry value options.

The value name is self-explanatory and is the same value as the name parameter for this method. The default value parameter is used to return a default value in case the value name specified does not exist. In this case, you are passing an empty string. The registry value options parameter is a constant from the RegistryValueOptions enumeration, and, in this particular case, the DoNotExpandEnvironmentNames constant. This tells the GetValue method not to expand any environment variable names when returning the value.

The Catch block is the standard Catch block that you've seen in the other methods in this class and simply returns any errors to the caller of this method.

```
        'Open the registry key
        OpenRegistryKey(hive, False)

        Return objRegistryKey.GetValue(name, String.Empty, _
            RegistryValueOptions.DoNotExpandEnvironmentNames)
    Catch ExceptionErr As Exception
        'Return the error to the caller
        Throw New Exception("RegistryHelper.GetValue " & ExceptionErr.Message)
    End Try
End Function
```

The next overloaded GetValue method is quite simple and has only one input parameter: name. The name parameter is the value name to be read. This method is called from the LoadKeyValues procedure in the RegistryManager form. When this method is called from the RegistryManager form, the appropriate registry key is already open so there is no need to pass the parameters for the registry key or open the registry key.

This method simply reads and returns the value for the value name specified. The code is wrapped in a Try...Catch block and returns any errors to the caller.

```
    Public Function GetValue(ByVal name As String) As Object
        Try
            Return objRegistryKey.GetValue(name)
        Catch ExceptionErr As Exception
            'Return the error to the caller
            Throw New Exception("RegistryHelper.GetValue " & _
                ExceptionErr.Message)
        End Try
    End Function
```

The last overloaded GetValue method accepts three input parameters: name, defaultValue, and options. These are the parameters that the GetValue method in the RegistryKey class uses, which you've already examined in the first overloaded GetValue method.

This method is also called from the LoadKeyValues procedure in the RegistryManager form. If the ExpandMultiStringValuesToolStripMenuItem menu item is checked, then a call is made to this method to expand the environment variables; if it is not checked, then a call is made to this method to not expand the environment variables.

Again, the appropriate registry key is already open so there is no need to pass the parameters for the registry key or to open the registry key. Thus, the code in this method is simple and contains the appropriate error handling that you've already seen:

```
Public Function GetValue(ByVal name As String, _
    ByVal defaultValue As String, ByVal options As RegistryValueOptions) _
    As Object

    Try
        Return objRegistryKey.GetValue(name, defaultValue, options)
    Catch ExceptionErr As Exception
        'Return the error to the caller
        Throw New Exception("RegistryHelper.GetValue " & _
            ExceptionErr.Message)
    End Try
End Function
```

GetValueKind Method

The next method to be examined is the GetValueKind method. This method returns the registry value kind (e.g., data type) of the value specified in the name input parameter. Notice that this method returns the registry value kind as a constant from the RegistryValueKind enumeration.

The code in this method is simple and wrapped in a Try...Catch block. When this method is called, the appropriate registry key is already open so there is only one line of code in this method: a call to the GetValueKind method in the RegistryKey class:

```
Public Function GetValueKind(ByVal name As String) As RegistryValueKind
    Try
        Return objRegistryKey.GetValueKind(name)
    Catch ExceptionErr As Exception
        'Return the error to the caller
        Throw New Exception("RegistryHelper.GetValueNames " & _
        ExceptionErr.Message)
    End Try
End Function
```

GetValueNames Method

The GetValueNames method returns a String array of value names for the specified registry key. Notice that the input parameters for this method match those of the CreateKey, DeleteKey, and GetKeyNames methods. Because these input parameters are the same as those for other methods you have already examined, there is no need to cover them again.

This method also starts the same as the previously mentioned methods by setting the values in the global class variables and then validating the input:

```
Public Function GetValueNames(ByVal hive As RegistryHive, _
    ByVal companyName As String, ByVal applicationName As String, _
```

```
            ByVal keyName As String) As String()

    Try
        'Set class variables
        strCompanyName = companyName
        strApplicationName = applicationName
        strKeyName = keyName

        'Validate input
        If Not IsValidInput(True) Then
            Throw New Exception("RegistryHelper.GetValueNames " & _
                strValidationMessage2)
        End If
```

The appropriate registry key is opened via a call to the `OpenRegistryKey` method. Then a call is made to the `GetValueNames` method in the `RegistryKey` class and set in the name of this method. Because this method returns a `String` array and the `GetValueNames` method in the `RegistryKey` class returns a `String` array, you can set the results of this call to the name of this method.

The `Catch` block returns to the caller any errors that may occur.

```
        'Open the registry key
        OpenRegistryKey(hive, False)

        'Get the key names
        GetValueNames = objRegistryKey.GetValueNames

    Catch ExceptionErr As Exception
        'Return the error to the caller
        Throw New Exception("RegistryHelper.GetValueNames " & _
            ExceptionErr.Message)
    End Try
End Function
```

RegistryManager Form

There are many procedures and functions in the `RegistryManager` form, but six main procedures warrant close examination:

- ❑ `AddTreeNode`
- ❑ `AddApplicationKeys`
- ❑ `btnEnumerateKeys_Click`
- ❑ `LoadKeyValues`
- ❑ `tvwRegistry_AfterSelect`
- ❑ `lvwRegistryValues_Click`

These six main procedures perform the core processing in the `RegistryManager` form, while the other procedures and functions provide ancillary support for the UI.

AddTreeNode Procedure

Let's start by examining the `AddTreeNode` procedure, which adds nodes to the `TreeView` control. This control is loaded with the data that represents how your registry keys look in the registry. There are two input parameters to this procedure: `treeNode` and `subKey`.

The `treeNode` parameter contains a reference to the current `TreeNode` in the `TreeView` control and is used to add a child node to the `TreeNode`. The `subKey` parameter is a string value of the registry key representing the text that is displayed for the `TreeNode`.

The first thing that this procedure does is declare a new `TreeNode` object using the `subKey` input parameter. The value `0` represents the image index in the `TreeView`'s image list that will be displayed for this node, and the value `1` represents the image index in the image list that will be used to indicate the selected image for this node.

Next, the child node is added to the `TreeView` using the input parameter `treeNode`. The `Nodes` collection of the `treeNode` contains a collection of child nodes for this node. The `Add` method is used to add the child node.

```
Private Sub AddTreeNode(ByVal treeNode As TreeNode, ByVal subKey As String)
    'Declare a child TreeNode using the subKey passed
    Dim objChildNode As New TreeNode(subKey, 0, 1)

    'Add the new child node to the parent TreeNode
    treeNode.Nodes.Add(objChildNode)
End Sub
```

AddApplicationKeys Procedure

The next procedure to be examined is the `AddApplicationKeys` procedure. This procedure is called to enumerate the registry keys for an application and will call itself recursively until all registry subkeys have been listed. Like the preceding procedure, this procedure also accepts the `treeNode` and `subKey` parameters as input parameters.

The first thing that happens in this procedure is the declaration of the local variables needed in this procedure. Remember from the previous table that the `GetKeyNames` method in the `RegistryHelper` class returns a `String` array of key names, so the `strKeys` variable is declared as a `String` array. Next, the `strKey` variable is declared as a `String` and is used to enumerate the `strKeys` String array:

```
Private Sub AddApplicationKeys(ByVal treeNode As TreeNode, _
    ByVal subKey As String)

    'Declare local variables
    Dim strKeys() As String
    Dim strKey As String
```

The `RegistryHelper` class is used in a `Using...End Using` block because the `Using` statement takes care of declaring and instantiating the `RegistryHelper` class, and the `End Using` statement takes care of calling the `Dispose` method in the `RegistryHelper` class. This is another reason why this class implemented the `IDisposable` interface. In fact, any class that you want to use in a `Using...End Using` statement block must implement the `IDisposable` interface.

The code inside the `Using...End Using` block is wrapped in a `Try...Catch` block to handle any errors that may occur from calling the methods in the `RegistryHelper` class.

```
'Declare and instantiate the RegistryHelper class
Using objRegistry As New RegistryHelper

    Try
```

The first thing to do inside the `Try...Catch` block is to get a list of key names from the registry for the specified application. The `GetKeyNames` method expects the registry hive to read this, and it is passed by using the `SelectedIndex` property of the `cboHive` combo box. Next, the company name is passed from the `txtCompanyName` text box, and the application name is passed from the `txtApplicationName` text box. The `subKey` parameter is initially an empty string when this procedure is called but when this procedure calls itself recursively, it passes the current key contained in the `strKey` variable.

```
'Get a list of registry keys
strKeys = objRegistry.GetKeyNames( _
    cboHive.SelectedIndex, txtCompanyName.Text, _
    txtApplicationName.Text, subKey)
```

Using a `For...Each...Next` block, you iterate through the list of key names that are contained in the `strKeys` String array, adding each one to the `TreeView` control. Here, you make a call to the `AddTreeNode` procedure, passing it the current `TreeNode` that was passed to this procedure and the key name contained in the `strKey` variable.

```
'Loop through the list of keys
For Each strKey In strKeys

    'Add the key to the parent TreeNode
    AddTreeNode(treeNode, strKey)
```

Next, you want to concatenate the key name contained in the `strKey` variable to the key name contained in the `subKey` input parameter. First, you need to determine whether the `subKey` parameter contains any data by checking the length to determine whether it is greater than zero. If it is greater than zero, then you set the `strKey` variable using the `subKey` parameter, followed by a backslash, and then use the `strKey` variable.

Next, make a recursive call to this procedure, passing it the last node in the `treeNode` input parameter and the `strKey`, which contains the key and/or subkey to be read.

```
'Concatenate the key to the parent key if necessary
If subKey.Trim.Length > 0 Then
    strKey = subKey & "\" & strKey
End If

'Get and add the subkeys of this key if they exist
AddApplicationKeys(treeNode.LastNode, strKey)

Next
```

The last part of this procedure contains the error handling code in the Catch block. Here, you merely display a MessageBox dialog box with the error that was handled in the ExceptionErr variable:

```
      Catch ExceptionErr As Exception
          MessageBox.Show(ExceptionErr.Message, My.Application.Info.Title, _
              MessageBoxButtons.OK, MessageBoxIcon.Warning)
      End Try

    End Using
  End Sub
```

btnEnumerateKeys_Click Event Handler Procedure

The next procedure that you'll want to examine is the btnEnumerateKeys_Click procedure. This procedure is executed when you click the Enumerate Keys button. It will read the registry for the application that you have specified and load all keys in the TreeView control.

The first thing that happens in this procedure is the validation of the input fields. The IsValidInput function returns a Boolean value indicating whether the input fields are valid. It also accepts a Boolean parameter indicating whether it should validate the txtKeyName field, which in this case you do not want to validate.

```
    Private Sub btnEnumerateKeys_Click(ByVal sender As System.Object, _
      ByVal e As System.EventArgs) Handles btnEnumerateKeys.Click

      'Validate input
      If Not IsValidInput(False) Then
          Exit Sub
      End If
```

Next, you declare a TreeNode object that will be used to build the nodes in the TreeView control. In order to reduce flickering and enhance performance while the TreeView control is being built, you call the BeginUpdate method of the TreeView control. This prevents the control from repainting itself when a new node is added until you call the EndUpdate method.

Now you want to clear any existing nodes in the tree, so you call the Clear method on the Nodes collection in the TreeView control:

```
      'Declare local variables
      Dim objTreeNode As TreeNode

      'Suppress repainting the TreeView control until
      'all nodes have been created
      tvwRegistry.BeginUpdate()

      'Clear the TreeView control
      tvwRegistry.Nodes.Clear()
```

You need to determine whether the user has chosen the current user hive or local machine hive of the registry. To do so, use a Select Case statement. This enables you to expand this section in the future if you want to add other hives in the registry to this program. Once you determine which hive the user has chosen, you add the appropriate text to the TreeView control by calling the Add method of the Nodes collection.

Now get a reference to the last node added in the `TreeView` control in the `objTreeNode` object and then call the `AddTreeNode` procedure to add the next child node:

```
'Add a root TreeNode
Select Case cboHive.SelectedIndex
    Case 0
        tvwRegistry.Nodes.Add(New TreeNode("HKEY_CURRENT_USER"))
    Case 1
        tvwRegistry.Nodes.Add(New TreeNode("HKEY_LOCAL_MACHINE"))
End Select

'Get the root node
objTreeNode = tvwRegistry.Nodes(0)
'Add the Software node
AddTreeNode(objTreeNode, "Software")
```

You continue the process by getting a reference to the last node added and calling the `AddTreeNode` procedure, adding each node in turn that the user has specified for company and application. This starts building the hierarchy in the `TreeView` control that matches the registry.

```
'Get the Software node
objTreeNode = tvwRegistry.Nodes(0).FirstNode
'Add the company node
AddTreeNode(objTreeNode, txtCompanyName.Text)

'Get the company node
objTreeNode = tvwRegistry.Nodes(0).FirstNode.FirstNode
'Add the application node
AddTreeNode(objTreeNode, txtApplicationName.Text)
```

Once again you get a reference to the last node added in the `TreeView` control and then call the `AddApplicationKeys` procedure. Remember that this procedure will call itself recursively, adding all the key names for the application specified.

Finally, you call the `EndUpdate` method on the `TreeView` control to have it repaint itself, and then expand all the nodes in the `TreeView` control by calling the `ExpandAll` method:

```
'Get the application node
objTreeNode = tvwRegistry.Nodes(0).FirstNode.FirstNode.FirstNode
'Now add all the keys and subkeys of the application
AddApplicationKeys(objTreeNode, String.Empty)

'Repaint the TreeView control
tvwRegistry.EndUpdate()

'Expand all nodes
tvwRegistry.ExpandAll()
End Sub
```

LoadKeyValues Procedure

The next procedure that needs to be examined is the `LoadKeyValues` procedure. This procedure is called from various other procedures in the form. It will load the `ListView` control with the key values for the selected key in the `TreeView` control.

The first thing that happens in this procedure is the declaration of the local variables that are needed in this procedure. Then the list of items in the `ListView` control is cleared by calling the `Clear` method on the `Items` collection:

```
Private Sub LoadKeyValues()
    'Declare local variables
    Dim strValueNames() As String
    Dim strValueName As String
    Dim objListViewItem As ListViewItem

    'Clear the list
    lvwRegistryValues.Items.Clear()
```

Next, instantiate an instance of the `RegistryHelper` class in a `Using...End Using` block, as you'll be making numerous calls to this class to get a list of value names, getting the value data for each value name. After instantiating the `RegistryHelper` class, you make a call to the `GetValueNames` method, passing it the required parameters in order for it to return a `String` array of value names:

```
'Declare and instantiate the RegistryHelper class
Using objRegistry As New RegistryHelper

    'Get a list of registry value names
    strValueNames = objRegistry.GetValueNames( _
        cboHive.SelectedIndex, txtCompanyName.Text, _
        txtApplicationName.Text, txtKeyName.Text)
```

Enumerate through the list of value names with a `For Each...Next` statement. The first thing that happens inside this loop is the instantiation of a new instance of the `ListViewItem` class in the `objListViewItem` object. Then you add the value name contained in the `strValueName` variable to the `Text` and `Tag` property.

The `Text` property is the text that is displayed in the first column of the `ListView` control, and the `Tag` property provides a method of associating a key with the item. In a database application, the `Text` property would be set to the text to be displayed, and the `Tag` property would be set to the primary key of the item, which is typically a number or GUID (globally unique identifier).

```
'Loop through the list of keys
For Each strValueName In strValueNames

    'Create a new listview item
    objListViewItem = New ListViewItem

    'Add the data to the listview item
    objListViewItem.Text = strValueName
    objListViewItem.Tag = strValueName
```

To determine the value type for the value name, use a `Select Case` statement by making a call to the `GetValueKind` method in the `RegistryHelper` class. The first `Case` statement checks for a `Binary` value type in the `RegistryValueKind` enumeration. The first statement in this `Case` statement adds the value kind from the `RegistryValueKind` enumeration to the `SubItems` collection of the `ListViewItem` using the `Add` method.

Because you are dealing with binary data, you need to convert it to a displayable format for the user. The first step in this process is to convert the data into a Byte array. The GetValue method in the RegistryHelper class returns the data as an Object, which has to be converted to a Byte array. This is done using the CType method, which accepts the value to be converted and the data type to which the data should be converted.

Once the data is in the bytBinary variable, you want to clear the strData variable by setting it to an empty string. Then you loop through the bytBinary array and add the data to the strData variable. Part of this process includes formatting the data using the Format method of the String class.

The Format method in this code accepts two parameters: a string containing the format item and the object to be formatted. The format item is specified as {alignment:formatstring}. The alignment part of this format item specifies the minimum length of the formatted item and will pad the item to the left with spaces if it does not meet the minimum length specified. Here, a value of 0 is specified, indicating that no minimum length is needed. The formatstring part of this format item specifies the data format that you want. The x specifies that the data should be formatted in hex, and the 2 specifies the length of the hexadecimal (hex) value.

Once the data string has been built with the binary value converted to hex, it is added to the ListViewItem again using the Add method of the SubItems collection:

```
'Get the value type and value data
'and add the sub items to the listview item
Select Case objRegistry.GetValueKind(strValueName)

    Case RegistryValueKind.Binary
        objListViewItem.SubItems.Add( _
            RegistryValueKind.Binary.ToString)

        'Cast the return value to a byte array
        bytBinary = CType(objRegistry.GetValue(strValueName), _
            Byte())
        strData = String.Empty

        'Build a string of the binary data
        For intIndex = 0 To bytBinary.Length - 1
            strData &= String.Format("{0:x2} ", _
                bytBinary(intIndex))
        Next

    objListViewItem.SubItems.Add(strData)
```

The next Case statement checks for a value type of DWord. The first code statement here adds the string DWord to the SubItems collection by calling the Add method. Then you get the value in the strValue String variable. The next line of code formats the value in both hex and decimal. The format string places the text 0x at the beginning and then uses the format text of {0:x8} to indicate that the number should be formatted in hex using eight digits. Then the decimal number is appended to the end of the string unformatted. Finally, the formatted string containing the hex and decimal value is added to the SubItems collection of the ListViewItem:

```
Case RegistryValueKind.DWord
    objListViewItem.SubItems.Add( _
        RegistryValueKind.DWord.ToString)
```

```
'Get the value and build a data string with the value in
'hex and decimal
strValue = objRegistry.GetValue(strValueName).ToString
strData = String.Format("0x{0:x8}", _
    CType(strValue, Integer)) & " (" & strValue & ")"

objListViewItem.SubItems.Add(strData)
```

A value type of `ExpandString` is checked in the next `Case` statement. Again, the first line of code adds the string `ExpandString` to the `SubItems` collection. Then you need to determine whether the `ExpandMultiStringValuesToolStripMenuItem` menu item is checked. If `ExpandMultiStringValuesToolStripMenuItem` is checked, you want to read the key value with the path variable expanded, which is done in the first part of the `If...Then...Else` statement. This line of code simply reads the key value, expanding the path variable, and places that value in the `SubItems` collection of the `ListViewItem`.

The line of code in the `Else` part of the `If...Then...Else` statement reads the key value without having the path variable expanded using an overloaded `GetValue` method. This value is placed in the `SubItems` collection of the `ListViewItem`.

```
Case RegistryValueKind.ExpandString
    objListViewItem.SubItems.Add( _
        RegistryValueKind.ExpandString.ToString)

    If ExpandMultiStringValuesToolStripMenuItem.Checked Then
        objListViewItem.SubItems.Add( _
            objRegistry.GetValue(strValueName).ToString)
    Else
        objListViewItem.SubItems.Add( _
            objRegistry.GetValue(strValueName, String.Empty, _
            RegistryValueOptions.DoNotExpandEnvironmentNames _
            ).ToString)
    End If
```

The next `Case` statement checks for a value type of `MultiString`. The first line of code adds the text `MultiString` to the `SubItems` collection and then the next line of code converts the value into a `String` array using the `CType` function. Clear any previous value in the `strData` variable by setting it to an empty string.

Now you need to loop through the values in the `strValues` `String` array and append each one to the `strData` variable, separating each value with a blank space. Finally, add the data in the `strData` variable to the `SubItems` collection:

```
Case RegistryValueKind.MultiString
    objListViewItem.SubItems.Add( _
        RegistryValueKind.MultiString.ToString)

    'Cast the return value to a string array
    strValues = CType(objRegistry.GetValue(strValueName), _
        String())
```

```
                      strData = String.Empty

                      'Build a string of the values
                      For Each strValue In strValues
                          strData &= strValue & " "
                      Next
                      objListViewItem.SubItems.Add(strData)
```

The last `Case` statement here checks for a value type of `String`. This is the simplest data type; you merely add the text `String` to the `SubItems` collection and then add the actual `String` value to the `SubItems` collection:

```
                  Case RegistryValueKind.String
                      objListViewItem.SubItems.Add( _
                          RegistryValueKind.String.ToString)
                      objListViewItem.SubItems.Add( _
                          objRegistry.GetValue(strValueName).ToString)

              End Select
```

To wrap things up in this procedure, add the `ListViewItem` to the `ListView Items` collection using the `Add` method. The last line of code in this procedure simply sorts the data in the `ListView` control using the default sort order, which sorts the data in the Name column:

```
              'Add the listview item to the listview control
              lvwRegistryValues.Items.Add(objListViewItem)

          Next

      End Using

      'Sort the ListView control by Name
      lvwRegistryValues.Sorting = SortOrder.Ascending
  End Sub
```

tvwRegsitry_AfterSelect Event Handler Procedure

The next procedure to examine is the `tvwRegistry_AfterSelect` procedure. This procedure is the event handler for the `TreeView` control and handles the `AfterSelect` event. After you click on a node in the `TreeView` control, this event will be fired.

The code in this procedure is very simple; the main work is done in the procedures that you've already examined. You start this procedure by adding the full path of the selected node to the status bar using the `FullPath` property of the selected node.

Next, examine the length of the application node, the node that contains the application name, against the selected node. If the length of the full path of the application node is greater than the length of the full path of the selected node, this indicates that a node above the application node has been selected. In this case, you want to clear the `txtKeyName` field on the form and clear the items in the `ListView` control. This is handled through the first two lines of code in the `If...Then...Else` statement:

```
      Private Sub tvwRegistry_AfterSelect(ByVal sender As Object, _
          ByVal e As System.Windows.Forms.TreeViewEventArgs) _
```

```
Handles tvwRegistry.AfterSelect

'Display the full path to the selected node in the status bar
StatusToolStripStatusLabel.Text = e.Node.FullPath

If tvwRegistry.Nodes(0).FirstNode.FirstNode.FirstNode.FullPath.Length + 1 _
    > e.Node.FullPath.Length Then
    'Clear the key name field and value list
    txtKeyName.Text = String.Empty
    lvwRegistryValues.Items.Clear()
```

The code in the `Else` statement of the `If...Then...Else` statement sets the text in the `txtKeyName` field to the key or keys of the selected node. Because the `FullPath` property of the `Node` item returns the entire path from the top, remove everything from the first node through the application name node, leaving just the key or keys selected. This is done using the `Substring` method of the `String` class. The `FullPath` property of the `Node` item returns a `String` value, so it automatically exposes the properties and methods of the `String` class.

After setting the `txtKeyName` field to the key or keys selected, make a call to the `LoadKeyValues` method to load any values that the selected key may have. The last line of code in this procedure clears the value fields in the top-right corner of the form:

```
Else
    'Set the key name field to the key selected
    txtKeyName.Text = e.Node.FullPath.Substring( _
        tvwRegistry.Nodes(0).FirstNode.FirstNode.FirstNode.FullPath. _
        Length + 1)

    'Load the list of registry values
    LoadKeyValues()
End If

'Clear the value fields
ClearValueFields()
End Sub
```

lvwRegsitryValues_Click Event Handler Procedure

The last main procedure in the `RegistryManager` form that you need to take a look at is the `lvwRegistryValues_Click` procedure. This is the event handler for the `Click` event of the `ListView` control. Whenever you click on an item in the `ListView` control, this procedure is executed.

This first thing that happens in this procedure is the declaration and setting of the `strValueType` variable. This variable is declared as a `String` and is set to the value type contained in the first item of the `SubItems` collection. Interestingly enough, most collections in the .NET Framework are zero-based, meaning that the first item is item 0. The `SubItems` collection is the exception to this rule, so the first item in the `SubItems` collection is item 1.

Next, set the `txtValueName` field on the form using the value in the `Name` column of the `ListView` by accessing the `Text` property of the `Item` collection of the `SelectedItems` collection of the `ListView`. Select the appropriate entry in the `cboValueType` combo box by looping through the items in the combo box looking for an item that matches the value in the `strValueType` variable. Once you have a match,

set the `SelectedIndex` property of the combo box using the `intIndex` variable and then exit the
`For...Next` loop:

```
Private Sub lvwRegistryValues_Click(ByVal sender As Object, _
    ByVal e As System.EventArgs) Handles lvwRegistryValues.Click

    'Declare local variables
    Dim strValueType As String = _
        lvwRegistryValues.SelectedItems.Item(0).SubItems(1).Text

    'Set the value fields
    txtValueName.Text = lvwRegistryValues.SelectedItems.Item(0).Text

    For intIndex = 0 To cboValueType.Items.Count - 1
        If cboValueType.Items(intIndex).ToString = strValueType Then
            cboValueType.SelectedIndex = intIndex
            Exit For
        End If
    Next
```

You now want to get the actual key value from the registry, as the values displayed in the `ListView` control have been formatted for display there. You want to get the raw value and put it in the `txtValueData`
field on the form. You do this by declaring and instantiating the `RegistryHelper` class in a `Using...End`
`Using` block.

Using the `strValueType` variable in a `Select...Case` statement, determine the value type that has
been selected. The first `Case` statement is for a `Binary` value type, and there you get the binary value
from the registry and convert it into a `Byte` array in the first line of code in this `Case` statement.

Next, clear the `strData` variable by setting it to an empty `String`. Loop through the `Byte` array converting the bytes to a string and separating each byte with a space. Each byte is separated with a space
so that you can properly convert the bytes back into a binary number when you set the value. Finally,
trim the trailing space from the `strData` variable:

```
'Declare and instantiate the RegistryHelper class
Using objRegistry As New RegistryHelper
    Select Case strValueType
        Case "Binary"
            'Cast the return value to a byte array
            bytBinary = CType(objRegistry.GetValue( _
                cboHive.SelectedIndex, txtCompanyName.Text, _
                txtApplicationName.Text, txtKeyName.Text, _
                txtValueName.Text), Byte())
            strData = String.Empty

            'Build a string of the binary data
            For intIndex = 0 To bytBinary.Length - 1
                strData &= bytBinary(intIndex).ToString & " "
            Next

            'Trim the trailing space
            strData = strData.Remove(strData.Length - 1, 1)
```

The next `Case` statement checks for a `MultiString` value type. The first line of code in this `Case` statement gets the value from the registry and converts it to a `String` array. Then the `strData` variable is again set to an empty `String`.

A `MultiString` value in the registry can be separated by spaces, commas, or carriage return linefeed characters. However, to properly display the values in the `txtValueData` field, each entry in the `String` array will be separated with a carriage return linefeed character using the `CrLf` constant from the `ControlChars` module. This ensures that each entry in the `MultiString` value is on a separate line in the text field on the form.

This is achieved by looping through each entry in the `strValues String` array and adding the data to the `strData` variable, followed by a carriage return linefeed character from the `ControlChars` module:

```
Case "MultiString"
    'Cast the return value to a string array
    strValues = CType(objRegistry.GetValue( _
        cboHive.SelectedIndex, txtCompanyName.Text, _
        txtApplicationName.Text, txtKeyName.Text, _
        txtValueName.Text), String())
    strData = String.Empty

    'Build a string of the values
    For Each strValue In strValues
        strData &= strValue & ControlChars.CrLf
    Next
```

The last `Case` statement here is the `Case Else` statement. The code in the `Case Else` statement will be executed if none of the conditions for the prior `Case` statements were met. Here you simply get the data from the registry and set the data in the `strData` variable. No special conversions are needed for value types of `DWord`, `ExpandString`, and `String`. You simply get the raw data and use it without conversion.

The last line of code in this procedure takes the value contained in the `strData` variable and sets it in the `Text` property of the `txtValueData` field on the form:

```
        Case Else
            strData = objRegistry.GetValue( _
                cboHive.SelectedIndex, txtCompanyName.Text, _
                txtApplicationName.Text, txtKeyName.Text, _
                txtValueName.Text).ToString
        End Select

        txtValueData.Text = strData
    End Using
End Sub
```

CreateDisplayDemo Procedure

While this procedure was not listed as a major procedure in the RegistryManager form, it is interesting to see. This procedure is called from the form's `Load` event and will create the demo keys and key values that were shown in Figure 3-1.

This procedure starts off by declaring the local `strKeys` variable as a `String` array. This variable will be used to hold all the key names for the demo keys, which are retrieved next. Set the `SelectedIndex` of the `cboHive` ComboBox to select the current user hive of the registry. Then set the company name and application name.

In a `Using...End Using` statement block, you declare and instantiate the `RegistryHelper` class. Notice that it is inside this `Using...End Using` block that you set up a `Try...Catch` block.

What's going to happen here is that you are going to try to read the demo keys from the registry in the `Try` statement block. If the demo keys do not exist, then an exception will be thrown and handled in the `Catch` block. The `Catch` block will then create the demo keys.

The only line of code in the `Try` block is the code to get the key names for the company and application that were previously set. When the keys are not found, an exception will be thrown. If the keys were found, then processing resumes after the `Try...Catch` block:

```
Private Sub CreateDisplayDemo()
    'Declare local variables
    Dim strKeys() As String

    'Set the form values
    cboHive.SelectedIndex = 0
    txtCompanyName.Text = "Wrox"
    txtApplicationName.Text = "Application Registry Manager"

    'Declare and instantiate the RegistryHelper class
    Using objRegistry As New RegistryHelper

        Try

            'Get a list of registry keys
            strKeys = objRegistry.GetKeyNames( _
                cboHive.SelectedIndex, txtCompanyName.Text, _
                txtApplicationName.Text, String.Empty)
```

The `Catch` block contains all of the code necessary to create the appropriate registry keys, as shown in the first part of this code. The second part of this code sets the demo values for the `Sample Values` key. One demo value for each value type supported in the registry is created.

The code shown inside the `Catch` block provides a good demonstration of how to create keys and set their key values. While this code is also demonstrated in other sections of this form, the values that are supplied are retrieved from the form fields. Here, you can get an idea of what the code looks like with the values filled in:

```
        Catch ExceptionErr As Exception

            'No keys found so create the demo keys
            objRegistry.CreateKey( _
                cboHive.SelectedIndex, txtCompanyName.Text, _
                txtApplicationName.Text, "Demo Keys")
            objRegistry.CreateKey( _
                cboHive.SelectedIndex, txtCompanyName.Text, _
```

```
                        txtApplicationName.Text, "Demo Keys\Sample Values")
                    objRegistry.CreateKey( _
                        cboHive.SelectedIndex, txtCompanyName.Text, _
                        txtApplicationName.Text, "Demo Keys\Example Sub Key")
                    objRegistry.CreateKey( _
                        cboHive.SelectedIndex, txtCompanyName.Text, _
                        txtApplicationName.Text, "Demo Keys\Example Sub Key\Sub Key 1")

                    'Create the demo values
                    objRegistry.SetValue(cboHive.SelectedIndex, txtCompanyName.Text, _
                        txtApplicationName.Text, "Demo Keys\Sample Values", _
                        "BinaryValue", New Byte() {11, 11, 10, 10, 0}, _
                        RegistryValueKind.Binary)
                    objRegistry.SetValue(cboHive.SelectedIndex, txtCompanyName.Text, _
                        txtApplicationName.Text, "Demo Keys\Sample Values", _
                        "DWordValue", 1000, RegistryValueKind.DWord)
                    objRegistry.SetValue(cboHive.SelectedIndex, txtCompanyName.Text, _
                        txtApplicationName.Text, "Demo Keys\Sample Values", _
                        "ExpandStringValue", "Your temp folder is %Temp%", _
                        RegistryValueKind.ExpandString)
                    objRegistry.SetValue(cboHive.SelectedIndex, txtCompanyName.Text, _
                        txtApplicationName.Text, "Demo Keys\Sample Values", _
                        "MultiStringValue", _
                        New String() {"String Value 1", "String Value 2", _
                        "String Value 3"}, _
                        RegistryValueKind.MultiString)
                    objRegistry.SetValue(cboHive.SelectedIndex, txtCompanyName.Text, _
                        txtApplicationName.Text, "Demo Keys\Sample Values", _
                        "StringValue", "Simple string data", RegistryValueKind.String)

                End Try

            End Using
```

The last part of this procedure calls `btnEnumerateKeys_Click` to get a list of the registry keys and loads them in the `tvwRegistry TreeView` control. Then the last node of the `TreeView` control is selected to display the key values for the `Sample Values` registry key:

```
            'List the keys
            btnEnumerateKeys_Click(Nothing, Nothing)

            'Select the Sample Vlaues key
            tvwRegistry.SelectedNode = _
                tvwRegistry.Nodes(0).FirstNode.FirstNode.FirstNode.FirstNode.LastNode
        End Sub
```

Setting Up the Application Registry Manager

You have two options for setting up the Application Registry Manager program: use the installer or manually copy the required files to your computer. The first option provides an easy, fast approach to installing the program, whereas the second method provides more control over where the program is placed.

Using the Installer

To install the Application Registry Manager program, locate the `Chapter 03 - Application Registry Manager\Installer` folder on the CD-ROM that came with this book and double-click the `setup.exe` program. You will be prompted with the Application Install dialog, and clicking the Install button will install and launch the application.

Manual Installation

To manually install the Application Registry Manager program, first create a folder on your computer where you want to place the program executable file. Then locate the `Chapter 03 - Application Registry Manager\Source` folder on the CD-ROM that came with this book and navigate to the `bin\Release` folder. Copy the `Application Registry Manager.exe` file from the `Release` folder to the folder that you created on your computer.

To run the Application Registry Manager program, double-click on the `Application Registry Manager.exe` file.

Configuring the Application

No special configuration is required for the Application Registry Manager program. Once the application has launched, the demonstration keys and key values are created as shown in Figure 3-1. See the section "Using the Application Registry Manager Program" at the beginning of this chapter for details about how to use this program.

Summary

This chapter has covered the `RegistryHelper` class, which encapsulates most of the functionality in the registry and `RegistryKey` classes, making the methods in those classes easier to use. It has also provided you with a working example of how to create, delete, and read registry keys in your own applications, as well as how to set, delete, and read key values.

As an added bonus, you may have learned a little more about the `TreeView` and `ListView` controls and how they can be used in your applications to provide a friendly user interface. The `TreeView` control provided a hierarchical view of the registry keys for an application, and the `ListView` control provided a multicolumn display of value names, types, and values.

After reviewing this chapter in detail and examining how the Application Registry Manager program operates, you should feel comfortable dropping the `RegistryHelper` class into your own projects to read and write registry values.

The registry is a very powerful tool that can provide configuration values for your applications. It can also be a very dangerous tool to the unskilled user who edits registry keys without knowing what they do or how they might affect programs or the operating system itself. Again, I urge you to use caution and know how to back up and restore the registry before editing keys and values that you did not create.

Event Log and Trace Writing

How do you know whether your application is doing its job? If you have a Web application or Windows application, you can visually see what is being done by the application. You can enter data, click through some screens, and then view the data that was entered. This is a visual indication that the application is doing the job it was designed to do.

However, if you have written a Web Service or Windows Service, you have no visual indicators that the service is doing the job that it was designed to do, as it has no user interface (UI). This is where *event logging* comes into play. Built into the operating system, the event log exposes three pre-built logs: application, security, and system. The application log can be written to by any application; and using the Event Viewer that comes with the operating system, you can view the various events in the application log.

Now suppose your service is not behaving as expected and no events are being written to the application log. How are you going to determine what is happening inside the service? This is where *trace writing* comes into play. Trace writing enables you to monitor the health of your application by having your application write trace events at different levels: error, warning, informational, and verbose. The first section of this chapter explains these different levels in detail.

This chapter also shows you how to write events to the application log and how to write trace events to a custom event log — all of which are viewable using the Event Viewer. You'll also learn how to control the level of trace writing so that you are getting the level of information needed without hampering the performance of your application.

Instead of writing a brand-new application just to write event log and trace messages, the Application Registry Manager program has been enhanced to provide this functionality. This serves two purposes. One, it provides a useful and functional application that can benefit from these technologies. Two, it provides an application that can be run in debug mode, which enables you to see how these technologies are used step by step.

The main technologies used in this chapter are as follows:

❑　Creating an application-specific event resource DLL

❑　Creating an event source

❑　Writing events to the application log

❑　Creating and configuring a trace switch

❑　Writing various levels of trace information to a custom event log

Using the Application Registry Manger Program

The last chapter covered how the Application Registry Manager program works, so I won't cover those details again. I do, however, want to point out the functions of the application that cause events to be written to the application event log, and trace events to be written to the custom event log.

If you recall from the last chapter, when the Application Registry Manager program starts, it creates and displays a set of demonstration keys and key values, as shown in Figure 4-1. This demonstration application in the current user hive of the registry provides an ideal place for you to practice creating and deleting keys and key values in order to see the various application events and trace events being written to the event log.

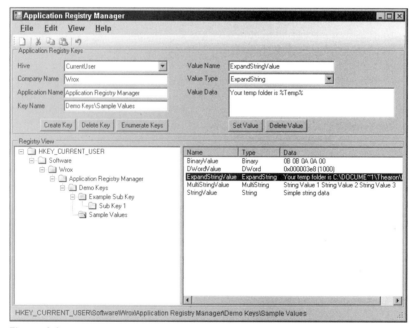

Figure 4-1

Trace events fall into four categories: error, warning, informational, and verbose. These categories are numbered sequentially starting with error, with a value of 1; warning, with a value of 2; and so on. Figure 4-2 shows how the TraceSwitch is configured in the app.config file in your application and controls the level of tracing that your application performs. The higher the number, the more trace information written.

```
<?xml version="1.0" encoding="utf-8" ?>
<configuration>
    <system.diagnostics>
        <switches>
            <!-- Set value property of the TraceSwitch switch to:
                1(error), 2(warning), 3(info), 4(verbose) -->
            <add name="TraceSwitch" value="4" />
        </switches>
    </system.diagnostics>
</configuration>
```

Figure 4-2

For example, when the TraceSwitch is set to a value of 1, only error events are written. When the TraceSwitch is set to a value of 2, error and warning events are written. When the TraceSwitch is set to a value of 3, error, warning, and informational events are written. A value of 4 causes all events to be written. Finally, a value of 0 causes no trace events to be written and provides a way to turn off trace writing.

When the Application Registry Manager program starts, a verbose trace event is written to the custom event log for the application in the application's Load event. The custom event log for this application is named WroxTraces and is viewable in the Event Viewer.

When the application's FormClosing event is fired, a warning trace event is written, and when the FormClosed event is fired an informational trace event is written. These different levels demonstrate the various levels of events that can be generated by setting the TraceSwitch in the app.config file to different values.

The Click event for the Create Key button causes an informational event to be written to the application event log when a registry key is successfully created. An informational trace event is also written to the custom event log if the TraceSwitch is configured for informational messages. Should an error occur and the registry key is not created, an error event is written to the application event log and an error trace event is written to the custom event log if the TraceSwitch is so configured.

The Click event for the Delete Key, Set Value, and Delete Value buttons all work in the same manner regarding event logging and trace logging.

Event Logs and Messages

Now that you know what functions cause events to be written to the application event log, and trace events to be written to the custom event log, you'll want to get a feel for what these events look like first-hand. Before that, however, take a look at a sample of the events that have been written to the application event log, as shown in Figure 4-3.

This window shows several informational messages and one error message in the application event log. Also notice that the events are organized into different categories and have different event numbers. These are values that you can set when you write your application.

Double-clicking on a message displays the Event Properties dialog box, also shown in Figure 4-3. This dialog box provides the same overview information as the Event Viewer in addition to the actual event message. In this instance, the details of the message indicate that a registry key was created, and provide the details about this key.

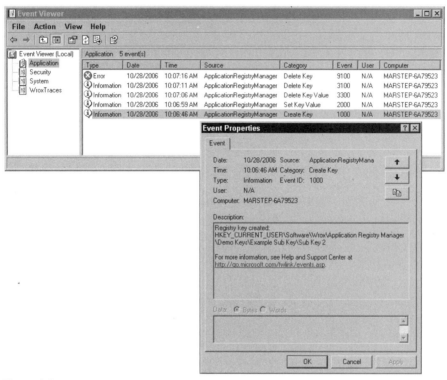

Figure 4-3

One of the nice benefits of writing events to the application event log is that the tools for viewing these events have already been created and are part of your operating system. Another benefit is that the Event Properties dialog box provides the Copy button, which enables you to copy the details of an event to the Clipboard and paste those details into any text editor. An example of the event details shown in the Event Properties dialog box in Figure 4-3 were copied to the Clipboard using the Copy button and pasted below unformatted. As you can see, this information has already been nicely formatted by the Event Properties dialog box and can be pasted into an e-mail message or Word document and sent to the appropriate persons as needed:

```
Event Type:       Information
Event Source:     ApplicationRegistryManager
Event Category:   Create Key
Event ID:         1000
Date:             10/28/2006
Time:             10:06:46 AM
User:             N/A
```

```
Computer:        MARSTEP-6A79523
Description:
Registry key created:
HKEY_CURRENT_USER\Software\Wrox\Application Registry Manager\Demo Keys\Example Sub
Key\Sub Key 2

For more information, see Help and Support Center at
http://go.microsoft.com/fwlink/events.asp.
```

The events in the application event log are displayed by three different types, as shown in the Type column in Figure 4-3. Figure 4-3 shows Information and Error types along with their appropriate icon. A Warning type is also displayed in this column with its icon, although this type is not shown in Figure 4-3.

The application's custom event log, called WroxTraces, is shown in Figure 4-4. There are a few things to note about this event log. First, all event types are listed as Information in the Type column because the WriteLine method of the Trace class does not support writing different types of events.

The Write method does support writing an event using a specific category but the category is not displayed in the Category column but as the first part of the description, as shown in the Event Properties dialog box shown in Figure 4-4. Additionally, the source listed in the Source column takes on the name of the custom event log instead of the event source specified in code.

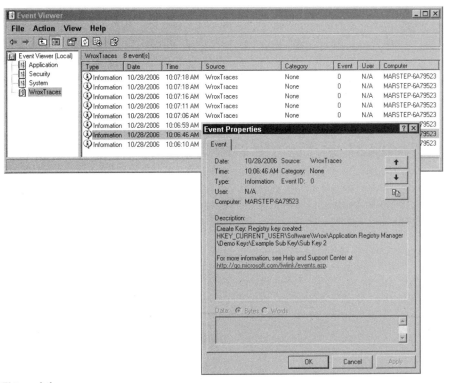

Figure 4-4

The upside of all of this is that you do get your trace events written in a custom event log complete with date and timestamp information. This information is not natively available when using a text file for a trace event log. You also get a tool that enables you to view and sort the information, as the column headers in the Event Viewer are sortable.

Changing Trace Levels

As mentioned earlier, the level of trace events that are written is controlled through the `TraceSwitch` in the `app.config` file for your application. In the IDE (Integrated Development Environment) this file has the name of `app.config`, but in the `bin` folder (debug or release) it takes on the name of your application suffixed with the `.config` extension. Therefore, for this application, the `.config` file in the `bin\debug` folder is named `Application Registry Manager.exe.config`.

The following `app.config` file shows the `TraceSwitch` set to a value of 4, which will display all trace events between 1 and 4. You can set the `TraceSwitch` to a value of 0 to disable all trace events, or any level between 1 and 4 for the various trace events that you want to see in the custom event log. This flexibility enables you to monitor the health of your applications by only writing the levels of information that you need. Moreover, they can be changed without requiring your application to be recompiled.

```xml
<?xml version="1.0" encoding="utf-8" ?>
<configuration>
    <system.diagnostics>
      <switches>
        <!-- Set value property of the TraceSwitch switch to:
             1(error), 2(warning), 3(info), 4(verbose) -->
        <add name="TraceSwitch" value="4" />
      </switches>
    </system.diagnostics>
  </configuration>
```

Testing Application Events and Trace Events

Before you run the Application Registry Manager program, edit the config file and set the `TraceSwitch` to a value of 1 so that only errors display. Now start your program. When the demo registry keys are displayed, click the Example Sub Key registry key and then click the Delete Key button. You'll receive an error indicating that this key has subkeys and that recursive removes are not allowed, as shown in Figure 4-5.

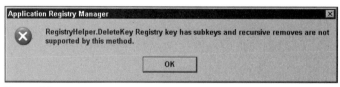

Figure 4-5

Now stop your program and open the Event Viewer. The Event Viewer is located under the Administrative Tools program group. When the Event Viewer is displayed, click the Application log to view the one event message written, which is an error. Double-click this event message to view the details in the Event Properties dialog box. Click the OK button to close the Event Properties dialog box when you have finished viewing the details of the event.

Now click the WroxTraces custom event log. You'll see only one message there with the same error details. You can view the details by double-clicking the event.

Edit the config file again by setting the TraceSwitch to a value of 2, which will write trace events for errors and warnings. Start your program and perform the same steps as you did before. When you are done, stop your program.

If the Event Viewer is still open, you'll need to right-click the application event log and choose Refresh from the context menu to refresh the event messages. Perform the same procedure for the WroxTraces custom event log.

The application event log will still display only one error event for this test. However, the WroxTraces custom event log will display two trace events for this test. The first event, in chronological time order, displays the trace event error message; and the second trace event, which is a warning trace event, informs you that the Application Registry Manager is closing.

Edit your config file again by setting the TraceSwitch to a value of 3, which will cause error, warning, and informational trace events to be written to the event log. Try to delete the same registry key as you did in the previous two tests. In addition, create a new key using any name that you like. When you are done, stop your program.

In the Event Viewer, refresh the application event log and the WroxTraces custom event log. This time, the application event log will display two messages for this test: one error and one informational.

The WroxTraces custom event log, however, will display four trace event messages for this test: one error message indicating that the key could not be deleted, one informational message indicating that a key was created, one warning message indicating that the application is closing, and one informational message indicating that the application has closed.

The final test to be performed is for the verbose trace event message. Edit the config file and set the value for the TraceSwitch to a value of 4. Then run your program and run the same test that you just ran.

In the Event Viewer, refresh the WroxTraces custom event log. Note that there are five trace events for this test. The first trace event is a verbose trace event message indicating that the application has started. The remaining four you just saw in your last test.

These tests have demonstrated how the TraceSwitch can affect the number and types of trace events that are generated from your application. Now that you have run these tests and looked at the messages, you should have a good feel for how this might benefit your own applications.

Design of the Application Registry Manager Program

The design of the Application Registry Manager program was covered in the last chapter when we looked at the `RegistryManager` form and the `RegistryHelper` class. This chapter enhances that design with the addition of the `app.config` file and the `EventLog`, `EventSourceCreationData`, and `Trace` classes. These are classes in the .NET Framework and are available to all applications. They have been included in the diagram shown in Figure 4-6 because they play an integral part in writing application events and trace events.

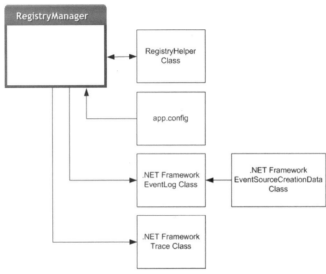

Figure 4-6

RegistryManager Form

The design of the `RegistryManager` form remains the same because the only changes made to the form were in code, enhancing the functionality to write to the application and trace log. These code enhancements will be covered shortly.

RegistryHelper Class

There were no enhancements made to the `RegistryHelper` class because the functionality to write events to the application and trace log are contained in the `RegistryManager` form.

EventSourceCreationData Class

Even though this is a .NET Framework class, it deserves to be listed in the design shown in Figure 4-6 and mentioned here because it plays a critical part in the functionality introduced in this chapter. However, many properties and methods in this class are not covered in this chapter, so Table 4-1 lists only the properties and methods used in the Application Registry Manager program.

Table 4-1: Properties and Methods in the EventSourceCreationData Class

Property/Method	Return Type	Description
`Public Sub New(ByVal source As <String>, ByVal logName As <String>)`	N/A	Constructor for this class
`Public Property CategoryResourceFile`	String	Gets or sets the path of the resource file that contains category strings for the source
`Public Property CategoryCount`	Integer	Gets or sets the number of categories in the category resource file

EventLog Class

The `EventLog` class is also a .NET Framework class and is included here because it also plays a critical part in the functionality introduced in this chapter. Only the methods used in the Application Registry Manager program are listed in Table 4-2.

Table 4-2: Methods of the EventLog Class

Method	Return Type	Description
`Public Shared Function SourceExists(ByVal source As <String>)`	Boolean	Determines whether an event source is registered on the local computer
`Public Shared Sub CreateEventSource(ByVal sourceData As EventSourceCreationData)`	N/A	Establishes an application as a valid event source for writing localized event messages, using the specified configuration properties for the event source and the corresponding event log
`Public Shared Sub CreateEventSource(ByVal source As <String>, ByVal logName As <String>)`	N/A	Establishes an application, using the specified source, as a valid event source for writing entries to a log on the local computer
`Public Shared Sub WriteEntry (ByVal source As <String>, ByVal message As <String>, ByVal type As EventLogEntryType, ByVal eventID As <Integer>, ByVal category As <Short>)`	N/A	Writes an entry with the given message text, application-defined event identifier, and application-defined category to the event log, using the specified registered event source

Trace Class

The Trace class uses the TraceSwitch class to determine whether trace events should be written. The core functionality of the TraceSwitch class is contained in the app.config file, so it has not been included in the diagram shown in Figure 4-6. The Trace class, also a .NET Framework class, is listed in the design shown in Figure 4-6 because it plays a critical part in the functionality introduced in this chapter. Table 4-3 lists only the properties and methods used in the Application Registry Manager program.

Table 4-3: Methods of the Trace Class

Method	Return Type	Description
Public Function Listeners.Add (ByVal listener As TraceListener)	Integer	Adds a TraceListener to the TraceListenerCollection
Public Shared Sub Write(ByVal message As <String>, ByVal category As <String>)	N/A	Writes a category name and a message to the trace listeners in the Listeners collection

Code and Code Explanation

In this section of the chapter you'll learn how the new classes fit into the Application Registry Manager program and gain a better understanding of how these classes work to write events to the application and trace logs. I'll begin with the .NET Framework classes mentioned previously before moving on to how they are used in the RegistryManager form.

EventSourceCreationData Class

The EventSourceCreationData class represents the settings required to create an event log source. This class is used by the CreateEventSource method in the EventLog class to enable an application to write event messages to an event log.

The EventSourceCreationData class contains required information such as the source name for the application, the event log to write to (e.g., Application, System, or Custom log), and a resource DLL if one is to be included for your application.

An event source only needs to be registered once, and the code in the form's Load event handles this as shown in the following code. The event source name for the application is defined in the EventSource constant with a string value of ApplicationRegistryManager.

As you can see, the SourceExists method of the EventLog class accepts the event source name as its input and returns a Boolean value indicating whether or not the source name exists. Therefore, the code inside this If...End If statement will be executed only the first time the application runs and is bypassed on every subsequent execution.

If the event source name has not been registered, then the first thing that happens inside this `If...End If` block is the declaration of an object for the `EventSourceCreationData` class. The constructor for this class accepts the event source name and the name of the log to which the application wants to write.

Once the `objEventSourceCreationData` object has been declared and instantiated, a `With...End With` block is used to set the properties of this object. Here you specify the category resource DLL to be associated with the event source, and indicate how many category names are specified in the resource file.

> *The* `EventLogCategories.dll` *is a resource file for your application that contains the categories displayed in the Event Log, as shown previously in Figure 4-3. Instructions for customizing and compiling the* `EventLogCategories.dll` *are contained in the section "Configuring the Application" at the end of this chapter.*

Finally, you call the `CreateEventSource` method of the `EventLog` class to create this event source and associate it with the application:

```
Private Sub RegistryManager_Load(ByVal sender As System.Object, _
    ByVal e As System.EventArgs) Handles MyBase.Load

    'Create the source if it does not already exist
    'for writing to the application event log
    If Not EventLog.SourceExists(EventSource) Then
        Dim objEventSourceCreationData As New _
            EventSourceCreationData(EventSource, "Application")
        With objEventSourceCreationData
            .CategoryResourceFile = "EventLogCategories.dll"
            .CategoryCount = 4
        End With
        EventLog.CreateEventSource(objEventSourceCreationData)
    End If
```

EventLog Class

Many properties and methods are available in the `EventLog` class but you will only use a handful in this application. The first two of these, `SourceExists` and `CreateEventSource`, were just covered in the preceding section as they related to the `EventSourceCreationData` class.

The last method that needs to be covered is the `WriteEntry` method. This method contains several overloaded versions, but the version that is used throughout this application provides plenty of details about the event being written to the event log.

To recap, the overloaded version that is used in this application is shown in the syntax that follows. The `source` parameter specifies the event source name for the application, which is defined in the `EventSource` constant. The `message` parameter is the actual message text that should be written to the event log. The `EventLogEntryType` enumeration provides the input for the `type` parameter, and the `eventID` parameter is specified as any `Integer` value that you want. Finally, the `category` parameter is a `Short` data type that relates to one of the categories defined in the application's category resource DLL.

```
Public Shared Sub WriteEntry (ByVal source As String, ByVal message As String, _
    ByVal type As EventLogEntryType, ByVal eventID As Integer, _
    ByVal category As Short)
```

So what does this actually look like in practice? The code snippet that follows is taken from the code in the `RegistryManager` form. It writes an event message to the application event log when a registry key is created. Notice that the actual message is broken up into several lines, as shown earlier in Figure 4-3.

You can also see that the category name has been displayed in the application event log, while the category number for this category has been specified in the `WriteEntry` method.

```
'Log the creation of the registry key
EventLog.WriteEntry(EventSource, "Registry key created:" & _
    ControlChars.CrLf & strRegistryKey, _
    EventLogEntryType.Information, 1000, 1)
```

TraceSwitch Class

The `TraceSwitch` class consists of two parts: an object defined in code as a `TraceSwitch` class and the `TraceSwitch` values set in the `app.config` file, as shown earlier in Figure 4-2 and described in the section "Changing Trace Levels" covered earlier.

The actual `TraceSwitch` object defined in code is configured from the values in the `app.config` file through the constructor of the `TraceSwitch` class, as shown in the following code. The first parameter of the constructor is the display name that correlates to the name of the switch in the `app.config` file. The second parameter is the description of the trace switch, which can be any free-form text that you like. In the code that follows, a value of `TraceSwitch` is used for both parameters, which keeps the name and description short and to the point.

The `value` property in the `app.config` file specifies the level of trace writing to be performed, and the `TraceSwitch` object defined in code controls whether a trace event is written.

```
'Instantiate the TraceSwitch object based on the level
'from the app.config file
objTraceSwitch = New TraceSwitch("TraceSwitch", "TraceSwitch")
```

Trace Class

The last .NET Framework class to be covered is the `Trace` class. The `Trace` class provides many properties and methods but only two are used in this application. The first of these is the `Add` method of the `Listeners` property. Before you can write trace events, you must first register a `TraceListener` in the `TraceListenerCollection`. A `TraceListener` listens for output from the `Trace` class and directs the output to the registered listener.

The following code shows how a new `TraceListener` is added to the `TraceListenerCollection`. The constructor for the `EventLogTraceListener` class accepts the name of the event log source and is specified here using the constant `TraceLog`, which is defined in code as a `String` constant with a value of `WroxTraces`:

```
'Instantiate a new trace listener and output it to a
'custom event log and add the trace listener
Trace.Listeners.Add(New EventLogTraceListener(TraceLog))
```

Once the listener has been added, you can use the `Trace` class to write new events to the trace log, as shown in the next code fragment. Notice that the `objTraceSwitch` object is used to determine whether the trace event should be written.

The `Write` method of the `Trace` class accepts the trace event message to be written and the category name for the event message. The messages outputted from the `Write` method were shown earlier in Figure 4-4.

```
'Write a verbose trace message
If objTraceSwitch.TraceVerbose Then
    Trace.Write("Application Registry Manager started.", _
        "Start Up")
End If
```

Notice that the `TraceVerbose` property of the `TraceSwitch` class was used to determine whether a trace event should be written. You must decide which messages to write and how critical those messages are. The `TraceSwitch` class provides the `TraceError`, `TraceInfo`, `TraceVerbose`, and `TraceWarning` properties for use in determining when the appropriate trace event should be written.

This trace message is categorized as a verbose trace message and will be written only when the `value` property in the `app.config` file is set to a value of 4, specifying a level of verbose. As you can see from the message shown in the preceding code, you are merely indicating that the application is starting. Obviously this message is not very important, but it is useful in its own right.

RegistryManager Form

Now that you've examined all the little components, its time to see how they fit together and work in unison to control writing events to the event and trace logs. I want to start with some form-level declarations. The first of these is the `objTraceSwitch` object defined as a `TraceSwitch`. You saw this object in use earlier in the discussion of the `TraceSwitch` class.

Next are three constants defined as strings. The first constant, `EventSource`, defines the event source name for the application, as shown in the Source column of the Event Viewer (refer to Figure 4-3). Because this event source name is used throughout the application when writing events to the event log, and given the fact that this name never changes, it only makes sense to define this as a constant.

Next is the `TraceEventSource` constant. This constant defines the event source name used to write to the trace log. Although the name never appears in the custom log, it is used to register the application to write trace events to the trace log.

The final constant is the `TraceLog` constant. This constant defines the name of the trace log, which is nothing more than a custom event log. You saw the `WroxTraces` custom application log in the Event Viewer shown in Figure 4-4.

```
Private objTraceSwitch As TraceSwitch

Private Const EventSource As String = "ApplicationRegistryManager"
Private Const TraceEventSource As String = "ApplicationRegistryManagerTrace"
Private Const TraceLog As String = "WroxTraces"
```

RegistryManager_Load Event Handler Procedure

When the form loads, the `Load` event is executed and a check is made to determine whether an event source has been registered for this application. This is the same code that you saw earlier during the discussion of the `EventSourceCreationData` class. You declare an object using the `EventSourceCreationData` class, passing it the event source name and the event log that the application will write to — in this case, the application event log.

Next, you specify the category resource DLL and the number of categories contained in the resource DLL. Finally, you register the event source using the `CreateEventSource` method of the `EventLog` class. As mentioned earlier, this code is executed only once on a machine, thus registering your application to be able to write events to the event log. Once registered, you do not have to register the application again.

```vb
Private Sub RegistryManager_Load(ByVal sender As System.Object, _
    ByVal e As System.EventArgs) Handles MyBase.Load

    'Create the source if it does not already exist
    'for writing to the application event log
    If Not EventLog.SourceExists(EventSource) Then
        Dim objEventSourceCreationData As New _
            EventSourceCreationData(EventSource, "Application")
        With objEventSourceCreationData
            .CategoryResourceFile = "EventLogCategories.dll"
            .CategoryCount = 4
        End With
        EventLog.CreateEventSource(objEventSourceCreationData)
    End If
```

Next, check whether the event source for writing to the custom event log has been registered. This is where you will be writing your trace events, and again you need to register this application only once.

After this check, you want to read the `TraceSwitch` value from the `app.config` file and set the `objTraceSwitch` object. This will control the level of trace events that are written to the custom application log.

Finally, you add a listener to the `TraceListenerCollection`. This enables the `Trace` class to listen for trace events being written and directs the output to the appropriate listener. This was covered in detail earlier in the chapter in the section "Trace Class."

```vb
    'Create the source if it does not already exist for
    'writing to a custom event log
    If Not EventLog.SourceExists(TraceEventSource) Then
        EventLog.CreateEventSource(TraceEventSource, TraceLog)
    End If

    'Instantiate the TraceSwitch object based on the level
    'from the app.config file
    objTraceSwitch = New TraceSwitch("TraceSwitch", "TraceSwitch")

    'Instantiate a new trace listener and output it to a
    'custom event log and add the trace listener
    Trace.Listeners.Add(New EventLogTraceListener(TraceLog))
```

The next bit of code in the `Load` event checks whether the `TraceSwitch` has been set to verbose by querying the `TraceVerbose` property. If the `TraceSwitch` has been set to verbose, then a trace event is written using the `Write` method of the `Trace` class. The `Write` method accepts the message to be written and the category for the trace event.

```
'Write a verbose trace message
If objTraceSwitch.TraceVerbose Then
    Trace.Write("Application Registry Manager started.", _
        "Start Up")
End If
```

RegistryManager_FormClosing Event Handler Procedure

You need to determine the number of trace events to be written by your application and at what level these events should be written. This will depend on the amount of information that you believe you'll need to properly monitor and debug your application in a production environment.

I've included a trace event in the `FormClosing` event for the form to demonstrate the use of the `TraceWarning` property and the different values that can be set in the `app.config` file for the `TraceSwitch` class. Again, you call the `Write` method on the `Trace` class, passing it the message to be written and the category for this message.

```
Private Sub RegistryManager_FormClosing(ByVal sender As Object, _
    ByVal e As System.Windows.Forms.FormClosingEventArgs) _
    Handles Me.FormClosing

    'Write a warning trace message
    If objTraceSwitch.TraceWarning Then
        Trace.Write("Application Registry Manager closing.", _
            "Shut Down")
    End If
End Sub
```

RegistryManager_FormClosed Event Handler Procedure

Following is the `FormClosed` event to demonstrate the use of the `TraceInfo` property of the `TraceSwitch` class:

```
Private Sub RegistryManager_FormClosed(ByVal sender As Object, _
    ByVal e As System.Windows.Forms.FormClosedEventArgs) _
    Handles Me.FormClosed

    'Write an informational trace message
    If objTraceSwitch.TraceInfo Then
        Trace.Write("Application Registry Manager closed.", _
            "Shut Down")
    End If
End Sub
```

btnCreateKey_Click Event Handler Procedure

Now you come to the decision-making process for determining where you want to write events to the event log, and trace events to the trace log. You do not want to flood the application event log with useless messages; you only want to write messages that are relevant and will help you to monitor your application. The `btnCreateKey_Click` procedure is an ideal place to write events to the event log — one event when a registry key is created or one event when the program fails to create a registry key.

This will provide the appropriate information in the application event log for registry keys that are created. This information can be useful to determine when your application is working and what information was specified when an error occurred, as you'll see shortly.

Now that you know where you want to write an event, you need to determine how much information should be included in the event message. You want to provide enough information to make the event message meaningful and worthwhile but you don't want to provide an abundance of information that will be used to debug your program. Remember that the Application log can be a wonderful tool for monitoring your application but it is not a place to store all of the debug information from your program. Please do not write out the stack trace from the exception that your program throws.

You can write out the stack trace of the exception from your program in the trace event because you are writing to your own custom application log. However, this is really not advisable unless deemed absolutely necessary. Write out enough information in your custom application log as necessary to monitor and debug your application in a production environment.

The following code fragment demonstrates writing an event to the event log and writing a trace event to the trace log after a registry key has been created. Notice the string constant `Registry key created:` followed by a carriage return linefeed character and then the `strRegistryKey` variable. This variable contains the fully qualified registry key that was created. This will provide enough meaningful information in not only in the event log, but also the trace log.

In the code that follows, an event ID of `1000` has been specified in the `WriteEntry` method of the `EventLog` class. The event ID is application specific and you can use any value that you want. I like to group the event ID into groups of 1000 that relate to specific tasks that the application is performing. This was evident in the Event column shown in Figure 4-3, and you can choose any event ID that you want for your application.

The code that writes a trace event to the trace log will write this trace event message only if the info value is set in the `TraceSwitch` in the `app.config` file. This enables you to look for errors or warnings in your trace log without having to weed through a bunch of informational messages.

```
'Add the key
objRegistry.CreateKey( _
    cboHive.SelectedIndex, txtCompanyName.Text, _
    txtApplicationName.Text, txtKeyName.Text)

'Log the creation of the registry key
EventLog.WriteEntry(EventSource, "Registry key created:" & _
    ControlChars.CrLf & strRegistryKey, _
    EventLogEntryType.Information, 1000, 1)

'Write an informational trace message
If objTraceSwitch.TraceInfo Then
    Trace.Write("Registry key created:" & _
        ControlChars.CrLf & strRegistryKey, "Create Key")
End If
```

Should an error occur in the `btnCreateKey_Click` procedure, the `Catch` block will write an event to the event log, and a trace event to the trace log. Again, you are providing the registry key that you were trying to create, along with the message from the exception. The `Message` property of the `Exception` class should provide you with enough information about the error to properly debug it.

```
Catch ExceptionErr As Exception
    MessageBox.Show(ExceptionErr.Message, _
        My.Application.Info.Title, MessageBoxButtons.OK, _
        MessageBoxIcon.Error)

    'Log the failure to create the registry key
    EventLog.WriteEntry(EventSource, _
        "Error attempting to create the registry key:" & _
        ControlChars.CrLf & strRegistryKey & _
        ControlChars.CrLf & ExceptionErr.Message, _
        EventLogEntryType.Error, 9100, 1)

    'Write an error trace message
    If objTraceSwitch.TraceError Then
        Trace.Write("Error attempting to create the " & _
            "registry key:" & ControlChars.CrLf & _
            strRegistryKey & ControlChars.CrLf & _
            ExceptionErr.Message, "Create Key")
    End If
End Try
```

btnDeleteKey_Click Event Handler Procedure

The `btnDeleteKey_Click` event handler also contains code to write an event to the event log after a registry key has been deleted as follows. After the event has been written to the event log, an informational trace message is written to the trace log if the info value has been set in the `TraceSwitch` in the `app.config` file.

```
'Delete the key
objRegistry.DeleteKey( _
    cboHive.SelectedIndex, txtCompanyName.Text, _
    txtApplicationName.Text, txtKeyName.Text)

'Log the deletion of the registry key
EventLog.WriteEntry(EventSource, "Registry key deleted:" & _
    ControlChars.CrLf & strRegistryKey, _
    EventLogEntryType.Information, 3100, 2)

'Write an informational trace message
If objTraceSwitch.TraceInfo Then
    Trace.Write("Registry key deleted:" & _
        ControlChars.CrLf & strRegistryKey, "Delete Key")
End If
```

The `Catch` block for this procedure also contains code to write an event to the event log, and an error to the trace log:

```
Catch ExceptionErr As Exception
    MessageBox.Show(ExceptionErr.Message, _
        My.Application.Info.Title, MessageBoxButtons.OK, _
```

```
                    MessageBoxIcon.Error)

            'Log the failure to delete the registry key
            EventLog.WriteEntry(EventSource, "Error attempting to " & _
                "delete the registry key:" & ControlChars.CrLf & _
                strRegistryKey & ControlChars.CrLf & ExceptionErr.Message, _
                EventLogEntryType.Error, 9100, 2)

            'Write an error trace message
            If objTraceSwitch.TraceError Then
                Trace.Write("Error attempting to delete the " & _
                    "registry key:" & ControlChars.CrLf & _
                    strRegistryKey & ControlChars.CrLf & _
                    ExceptionErr.Message, "Delete Key")
            End If
    End Try
```

btnDeleteValue_Click Event Handler Procedure

Deleting a registry key value is just as important as deleting a registry key and thus the
btnDeleteValue_Click procedure has code added to log an event to the event log and to
write an informational trace message.

The following code is capturing the key value that is being deleted in both the application event log
and in the application's trace log. This enables you to reset the deleted value for the registry key in the
unlikely event that this key value was mistakenly deleted.

```
            'Delete the value
            objRegistry.DeleteValue( _
                cboHive.SelectedIndex, txtCompanyName.Text, _
                txtApplicationName.Text, txtKeyName.Text, _
                txtValueName.Text)

            'Log the deletion of the registry key value
            EventLog.WriteEntry(EventSource, "Registry key value deleted:" & _
                ControlChars.CrLf & strRegistryKey & ControlChars.CrLf & _
                "Value Name: " & txtValueName.Text, _
                EventLogEntryType.Information, 3300, 4)

            'Write an informational trace message
            If objTraceSwitch.TraceInfo Then
                Trace.Write("Registry key value deleted:" & _
                    ControlChars.CrLf & strRegistryKey & ControlChars.CrLf & _
                    "Value Name: " & txtValueName.Text, "Delete Key Value")
            End If
```

Again, code has been also added to the Catch block to log the error that occurred in the event log and
trace log:

```
        Catch ExceptionErr As Exception
            MessageBox.Show(ExceptionErr.Message, _
                My.Application.Info.Title, MessageBoxButtons.OK, _
                MessageBoxIcon.Error)
```

```
                    'Log the failure to delete the registry key value
                    EventLog.WriteEntry(EventSource, "Error attempting to " & _
                        "delete the registry key value:" & ControlChars.CrLf & _
                        strRegistryKey & ControlChars.CrLf & _
                        "Value Name: " & txtValueName.Text & ControlChars.CrLf & _
                        ExceptionErr.Message, EventLogEntryType.Error, 9300, 4)

                    'Write an error trace message
                    If objTraceSwitch.TraceError Then
                        Trace.Write("Error attempting to delete the " & _
                            "registry key value:" & ControlChars.CrLf & _
                            strRegistryKey & ControlChars.CrLf & _
                            "Value Name: " & txtValueName.Text & ControlChars.CrLf & _
                            ExceptionErr.Message, "Delete Key Value")
                    End If
            End Try
```

btnSetValue_Click Event Handler Procedure

The `btnSetValue_Click` procedure has code added after the `End Select` statement that sets the key value for a registry key. This code will write an event to the event log and write an informational message to the trace log.

Again, these log statements are capturing pertinent information that is necessary for you to troubleshoot the application in the unlikely event that something has gone wrong.

```
            End Select

            'Log the set value of the registry key
            EventLog.WriteEntry(EventSource, "Registry key value set:" & _
                ControlChars.CrLf & "Key: " & strRegistryKey & _
                ControlChars.CrLf & "Value Name: " & txtValueName.Text & _
                ", Value Type: " & cboValueType.SelectedItem.ToString & _
                ", Value Data: " & txtValueData.Text, _
                EventLogEntryType.Information, 2000, 3)

            'Write an informational trace message
            If objTraceSwitch.TraceInfo Then
                Trace.Write("Registry key value set:" & ControlChars.CrLf & _
                    "Key: " & strRegistryKey & ControlChars.CrLf & _
                    "Value Name: " & txtValueName.Text & ", Value Type: " & _
                    cboValueType.SelectedItem.ToString & ", Value Data: " & _
                    txtValueData.Text, "Set Key Value")
            End If
```

This `Catch` block also writes an event to the event log and trace log, capturing the required information to properly troubleshoot the application:

```
        Catch ExceptionErr As Exception
            MessageBox.Show(ExceptionErr.Message, My.Application.Info.Title, _
                MessageBoxButtons.OK, MessageBoxIcon.Error)

            'Log the failure to set the registry key value
            EventLog.WriteEntry(EventSource, "Error attempting to set the " & _
```

113

```
                    "registry key value:" & ControlChars.CrLf & _
                    "Key: " & strRegistryKey & ControlChars.CrLf & _
                    "Value Name: " & txtValueName.Text & ", Value Type: " & _
                    cboValueType.SelectedItem.ToString & ", Value Data: " & _
                    txtValueData.Text & ControlChars.CrLf & ExceptionErr.Message, _
                    EventLogEntryType.Error, 9200, 3)

                'Write an error trace message
                If objTraceSwitch.TraceError Then
                    Trace.Write("Error attempting to set the registry " & _
                        "key value:" & ControlChars.CrLf & _
                        "Key: " & strRegistryKey & ControlChars.CrLf & _
                        "Value Name: " & txtValueName.Text & ", Value Type: " & _
                        cboValueType.SelectedItem.ToString & ", Value Data: " & _
                        txtValueData.Text & ControlChars.CrLf & _
                        ExceptionErr.Message, "Set Key Value")
                End If
        End Try
```

As you can see, writing events to the event log, and trace events to the trace log, provides a way for you to monitor your application. The trace log also provides a way for you to monitor your application at various levels by setting the appropriate value in the `app.config` file.

Setting Up the Application Registry Manager

You have two options for setting up the Application Registry Manager program: use the installer or manually copy the required files to your computer. The first option provides an easy, fast approach to installing the program, whereas the second method provides more control over where the program is placed.

Using the Installer

To install the Application Registry Manager program, locate the `Chapter 04 - Application Registry Manager\Installer` folder on the CD-ROM that came with this book and double-click the `setup.exe` program. You will be prompted with the Application Install dialog. Clicking the Install button will install and launch the application.

Manual Installation

To manually install the Application Registry Manager program, first create a folder on your computer where you want to place the program executable file. Then locate the `Chapter 04 - Application Registry Manager\Source` folder on the CD-ROM that came with this book and navigate to the `bin\Release` folder. Copy the following files from the `Release` folder to the folder that you created on your computer:

- ❏ `Application Registry Manager.exe`
- ❏ `Application Registry Manager.exe.config`
- ❏ `EventLogCategories.dll`

To run the Application Registry Manager program, double-click the `Application Registry Manager.exe` file.

Configuring the Application

No special configuration is required for the Application Registry Manager program for normal use. However, to control the level of trace events being written to the trace log, you need to edit the `Application Registry Manager.exe.config` file in the `bin` folder, setting the `value` property of the `TraceSwitch` to the level of messages desired.

When writing events to the event log, you can choose whether to specify a category for the events. However, when you group your events into categories, it is easier to associate the events at a later time to specific areas of your application.

Note one drawback to specifying a category when writing events: The category must be specified as a `Short` data type, which means that the category names must be specified in a resource DLL somewhere. Because you are typically creating an application with a specific purpose, the default system categories are of no use. Therefore, you must create and compile your own event source resource DLL and register this resource DLL with the event log. Then, when you view the events for your application using the Event Viewer, the category numbers that you specified when you wrote the events are replaced with the category names from your resource DLL.

A category resource DLL has already been compiled for this application and resides in the `bin` folder so that the resource DLL is distributed with the application and the application automatically registers this DLL with the event log. However, should you choose to customize the category names, or create your own categories for own application, you'll need to know how to create and compile this resource DLL.

The `EventLogCategories.txt` source file is included in the project for this application, as listed below for reference. As you can see in the listing, the instructions for compiling this file are included in the descriptive header. Before entering the commands, you need to open the Visual Studio 2005 Command Prompt window by navigating to Start ➪ All Programs ➪ Microsoft Visual Studio 2005 ➪ Visual Studio Tools and then clicking the Visual Studio 2005 Command Prompt icon.

Once the window opens, you can navigate to the directory where this file is located and then enter the three commands to create the resource DLL. The `mc` command is the message compiler, which creates the messages in binary format, and the header file and resource script files that are input to the resource compiler. The `rc` command is the resource compiler, which takes these files and creates a compiled resource script that is then linked into a DLL by the `link` command.

Once you have the compiled resource file in the form of a DLL, you must either copy the DLL to the `bin` folder of your application or put the file in a specific folder on your computer and specify the full path to the file in your code. The first method is easier and less error prone, especially when distributing your application to other computers.

```
; // EventLogCategories.txt
; // ********************************************************************

; // Use the following commands to build this file:
```

```
; //    mc -s EventLogCategories.txt
; //    rc EventLogCategories.rc
; //    link /DLL /SUBSYSTEM:WINDOWS /NOENTRY /MACHINE:x86 EventLogCategories.Res
; // ****************************************************************************
```

Now that you know how to compile this file, let's take a look at the definition of the event categories in it. As you can see by the next comment in this file, the categories must be numbered sequentially, starting with 1, in the `MessageId` statement. The `Severity` statement can be set to one of four possible values: `Success`, `Informational`, `Warning`, and `Error`.

The `SymbolicName` statement is used to specify the C++ symbolic constant associated with this category. The `Language` statement is fairly obvious and specifies the language associated with this file. Finally, the category name is specified in free-form text. A complete category is terminated with a period on a new line after the category name.

```
; // - Event categories -
; // Categories must be numbered consecutively starting at 1.
; // ********************************************************
MessageId=0x1
Severity=Success
SymbolicName=CREATE_KEY
Language=English
Create Key
.

MessageId=0x2
Severity=Success
SymbolicName=DELETE_KEY
Language=English
Delete Key
.

MessageId=0x3
Severity=Success
SymbolicName=SET_VALUE
Language=English
Set Key Value
.

MessageId=0x4
Severity=Success
SymbolicName=DELETE_KEY_VALUE
Language=English
Delete Key Value
.
```

Summary

This chapter has expanded on the Application Registry Manager program introduced in the last chapter, enhancing it to include writing events to the application event log, and writing trace events to a custom trace log. You learned how to create and compile your own resource DLL that contains the categories required by your application, and Figure 4-2 displayed these categories in the Event Viewer.

You also learned how you can register your application to be able to write events to the application event log and how to write events to the event log. Figure 4-1 demonstrated what these event messages look like and how they are displayed in the application event log in the Event Viewer. Write events to the event log sparingly, as your application is not the only application that writes events to the application event log.

The `TraceSwitch` class is a very powerful tool that enables you to not only to turn trace event writing on and off, but also to control the level of trace output, as demonstrated earlier. You also had the opportunity to see how your application can register itself to write to a custom event log that can be used for writing trace output.

You should now have a better understanding of the `TraceSwitch` class and how this powerful tool enables you to monitor and debug your application in a production environment.

Getting messages in the custom trace log is easy, but how do you view them in a production environment? The next chapter provides a method to automatically read the event logs and e-mail messages to the persons responsible for supporting the application.

5

Event Log Service

In the last chapter you explored writing events to the application event log and writing trace events to a custom event log. Writing events from your application provides important information about what your application is doing, and writing trace events provides important information about how your application is performing.

Now suppose that your application has been deployed to a production environment to which developers are not granted access. How are you to determine how your application is performing and how are you to view the events that your application is writing?

This is where the Wrox Event Log Service program comes into the picture. This Windows Service can be installed on the same production machine as your application, and can be configured to process several times a day to read the application event log and custom trace log and e-mail those events to you that were logged by your application. This enables you to monitor the health of your application and to see what events your application is writing.

In this chapter you will learn how to read events from the application event log and custom trace log on a timed schedule, how to process those events, and how to e-mail the events to a variety of people. All of the information that the Wrox Event Log Service needs could be supplied in an application configuration file but will be supplied in the registry using the Application Registry Manager program.

The main topics covered in this chapter are as follows:

- ❑ Reading values from the registry
- ❑ Using a system timer to execute code on a timed event
- ❑ Reading events from the application event log and custom trace log
- ❑ Creating and e-mailing event log messages

Using the Event Log Service

The Wrox Event Log Service runs as a Windows Service, as shown in Figure 5-1, and therefore provides no user interface for interaction. The service will run according to the schedule that you provide in the registry, so once the registry values have been created and the service has been installed and started, you do not need to do anything but wait for the e-mails to start coming in.

The Services Microsoft Management Console (MMC) can be located in the Administrative Tools group, which can be accessed by clicking Start ➪ Administrative Tools ➪ Services. Once the Services console is displayed, locate the Wrox Event Log Service and click on it.

Four buttons are provided on the toolbar for controlling the service: Start, Stop, Pause, and Restart. These buttons are self-explanatory, with the Start Service button starting the service, the Stop Service button stopping the service, and so on. The Pause Service button will pause a service, causing the tooltip text on the Start Service button to read Resume Service. The Restart Service button performs the same functions as the Stop Service and Start Service buttons in one step. In other words, the service will be stopped and then restarted immediately.

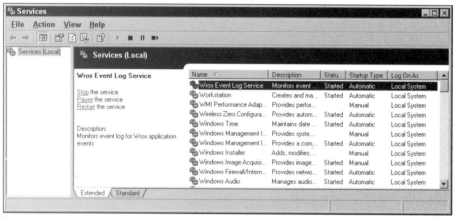

Figure 5-1

The registry values required by the Wrox Event Log Service are detailed in Table 5-1. When you change a value in the registry, you must restart the Wrox Event Log Service in order to have the service read the new values from the registry.

When the Wrox Event Log Service starts it reads the values from the registry and sets them in local variables, so restarting the Wrox Event Log Service will cause the service to be stopped and started automatically, thus reading the new values from the registry.

Table 5-1: Registry Values Required by the Wrox Event Log Service

Value Name	Value Type	Description
Application Log	String	The name of the application event log
Application Source	String	The application name as recorded in the application event log to be processed
Email Addresses	MultiString	A list of e-mail addresses that should receive the e-mail of events
Process Times	MultiString	A list of times that you want the service to read the event log. Times are specified in 24-hour format (e.g., 08:00, 16:00)
Schedule	Binary	Four bytes representing the days of the week. For example, Sunday and Monday would be the first byte, Tuesday and Wednesday would be the second byte, and so on. A value of 1 indicates that the service should process on this day, and a value of 0 indicates the service should not process.
SMTP Server	String	The Domain Name System (DNS) name or Internet Protocol (IP) address of your outbound mail server
Trace Log	String	The name of the trace event log
Trace Source	String	The application trace name as recorded in the trace event log to be processed

Design of the Wrox Event Log Service

The design of the Wrox Event Log Service is very simple. The EventLogService class inherits from the .NET Framework ServiceBase class, so this class has been included in the diagram shown in Figure 5-2. All of the methods that the EventLogService class needs to operate as a service are inherited from the ServiceBase class and include the OnStart, OnStop, OnPause, OnContinue, and OnShutdown methods.

The ProjectInstaller class is used to install the service, thereby registering the service with the operating system, which causes it to be displayed in the Services console. A ProjectInstaller class is required for each service that you write and provides the means to register and unregister your service with the various Windows operating systems.

In addition, notice that the RegistryHelper class created in Chapter 3 has again been reused in this program to read values from the registry. You should get a good feel for how easy it will be to drop this class in your own applications after reviewing the code in the EventLogService class that makes use of the methods in the RegistryHelper class.

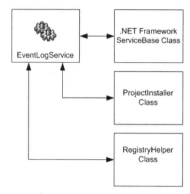

Figure 5-2

EventLogService Class

The EventLogService class is the main class in this service and is where the majority of the processing takes place. Because this class inherits from the .NET Framework ServiceBase class, it must override several methods from that class. They are detailed in Table 5-2, so the ServiceBase class is not discussed separately here. Two additional methods outlined in the table are unique to this class. They perform the main processing of this service: reading and processing events from the application and trace event logs.

Table 5-2: Properties and Methods of the EventLog Class

Property/Method	Return Type	Description
Protected Overrides Sub OnStart(ByVal args() As String)	N/A	Contains code that needs to be executed when the service starts
Protected Overrides Sub OnStop()	N/A	Contains code that needs to execute when the service is stopped
Protected Overrides Sub OnPause()	N/A	Contains code that needs to execute when the service is paused
Protected Overrides Sub OnContinue()	N/A	Contains code that needs to execute when the service is continued
Protected Overrides Sub OnShutdown()	N/A	Contains code that needs to execute when the service is stopped and the system is shutting down
Private Sub EventLogTimer_Elapsed(ByVal sender As Object, ByVal e As System.Timers.ElapsedEventArgs)	N/A	A procedure to check the schedule, current date and time, and process times to determine whether processing of the event log should be performed

Table 5-2: Properties and Methods of the EventLog Class *(continued)*

Property/Method	Return Type	Description
`Private Sub ProcessEventLog(ByVal logName As String, ByVal applicationSource As String)`	N/A	Processes events from the application or trace event log, builds an e-mail of events found, and mails the message to the appropriate recipients

ProjectInstaller Class

This is another .NET Framework class (refer to Figure 5-2). This class is added from the Properties window of the `EventLogService` designer. This class doesn't contain any code that is modified, but it contains two very important components: `ServiceProcessInstaller` and `ServiceInstaller`.

The `ServiceProcessInstaller` interacts with the installation utility to install an executable program containing classes that extend the .NET `ServiceBase` class. It also writes registry entries associated with the service being installed. The Properties window contains properties that can be set, but the main property that is typically set for this component is the `Account` property, as shown in Figure 5-3. This property determines the account type that a service will run under and is typically set to `Local System` so that the service runs under the Windows local system account.

The `ServiceInstaller` class also interacts with the installation utility to install an executable program containing classes that extend the .NET `ServiceBase` class and to write entries to the registry. The Properties window for this component contains many properties that you'll want to customize for your service. Table 5-3 details the properties that you are most likely to customize.

Table 5-3: Customizable Properties and Methods

Property/Method	Return Type	Description
`Description`	`String`	The description of the service that is displayed in the Description column of the Services console
`DisplayName`	`String`	The name of the service as it should be displayed in the Name column of the Services console
`ServiceName`	`String`	The name used by the system to identify this service
`ServicesDependedOn`	`String()`	A `String` array of other services that must be running before this service can be started
`StartType`	`ServiceStartMode`	A `ServiceStartMode` enumeration that indicates how this service is started

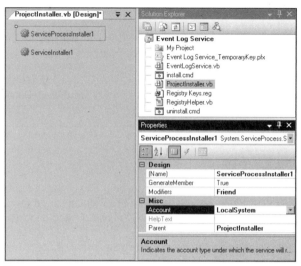

Figure 5-3

RegistryHelper Class

The `RegistryHelper` class was covered in Chapter 3. Please refer to the section "RegistryHelper Class" in Chapter 3 for details on this class.

Code and Code Explanation

This section of the chapter covers all the methods in the `EventLogService` class. Because no custom code was written in the `ProjectInstaller` class, it is not covered here; and the `RegistryHelper` class was covered in detail in Chapter 3.

EventLogService Class

This class contains five overridden methods, shown in Table 5-2, that override the methods in the .NET `ServiceBase` class. These are all very simple methods that control the starting and stopping of the service. Before getting to those methods and the other methods in this class, I want to start with the variables and objects that are defined at the class level and used throughout the program.

The `Process Times` registry entry shown in Table 5-1 is a `MultiString` value type, meaning that you could have one or more times that the service should process the events in the event log. To keep track of when data has been processed, the `blnTimeEntryProcessed` variable has been declared as a `Boolean` array. This array will contain one entry for each of the process times and will keep track of when a particular time entry has been processed.

The `bytSchedule` variable is defined as a `Byte` array and is used to hold the `Schedule` value read from the registry. Remember that the `Schedule` value in the registry is defined as a `Binary` value type and is converted into a `Byte` array.

The `intIndex` variable is simply used as an index for accessing the values in the various arrays:

```
'Declare private variables and objects
Private blnTimeEntryProcessed() As Boolean

Private bytSchedule() As Byte

Private intIndex As Integer
```

The next set of variables are defined as `String` and `String` array variables. These variables are used to hold the various `String` value types read from the registry, to process the values in the `String` arrays, and to hold the distribution list that a mail message is sent to and to hold the actual mail message:

```
Private strApplicationLog As String
Private strApplicationSource As String
Private strTraceLog As String
Private strTraceSource As String
Private strProcessTimes() As String
Private strProcessTime As String
Private strEmailAddresses() As String
Private strEmailAddress As String
Private strSchedule As String = String.Empty
Private strMailTo As String = String.Empty
Private strMailBody As String = String.Empty
Private strSmtpServer As String
```

The next set of variables are defined as constants, as their values never change. The first three constants are used to define the company, application, and key in the registry where the values for this application are stored. The last constant in this list is used to hold the `from` string that is used when sending a mail message:

```
Private Const Company As String = "Wrox"
Private Const Application As String = "Event Log Service"
Private Const Key As String = "Parameters"
Private Const From As String = "EventLogService@marstep.com"
```

The following `DateTime` variables are used to set the start date and time and end date and time to be used when reading the application and trace event logs. You only want to process events that fall within the range of the start and end dates and times.

The `EventLogTimer` object is defined as a `System.Timer` and is used to control the processing of the service. The `Interval` property of this timer is set in the `OnStart` method, and the timer is started at that point.

```
Private dteStart As DateTime
Private dteEnd As DateTime

Private WithEvents EventLogTimer As Timer
```

OnStart Procedure

When you create a Service application, the OnStart and OnStop methods are automatically inserted in the code with comments to add your start and stop code. The args String array is specified as an input parameter to the OnStart method as a way to pass arguments to the OnStart method, but it is rarely used.

The code in the OnStart method is wrapped in a Try...Catch block to handle any errors that might occur. This method starts out by reading the values for this service from the registry via the RegistryHelper class, setting them in the class-level variables just discussed:

```
Protected Overrides Sub OnStart(ByVal args() As String)
    Try
        'Get the values from the registry
        Using objRegistry As New RegistryHelper
            strApplicationLog = CType(objRegistry.GetValue( _
                RegistryHelper.RegistryHive.LocalMachine, Company, _
                Application, Key, "Application Log"), String)
            strApplicationSource = CType(objRegistry.GetValue( _
                RegistryHelper.RegistryHive.LocalMachine, Company, _
                Application, Key, "Application Source"), String)
            strTraceLog = CType(objRegistry.GetValue( _
                RegistryHelper.RegistryHive.LocalMachine, Company, _
                Application, Key, "Trace Log"), String)
            strTraceSource = CType(objRegistry.GetValue( _
                RegistryHelper.RegistryHive.LocalMachine, Company, _
                Application, Key, "Trace Source"), String)
            bytSchedule = CType(objRegistry.GetValue( _
                RegistryHelper.RegistryHive.LocalMachine, Company, _
                Application, Key, "Schedule"), Byte())
            strProcessTimes = CType(objRegistry.GetValue( _
                RegistryHelper.RegistryHive.LocalMachine, Company, _
                Application, Key, "Process Times"), String())
            strEmailAddresses = CType(objRegistry.GetValue( _
                RegistryHelper.RegistryHive.LocalMachine, Company, _
                Application, Key, "Email Addresses"), String())
            strSmtpServer = CType(objRegistry.GetValue( _
                RegistryHelper.RegistryHive.LocalMachine, Company, _
                Application, Key, "SMTP Server"), String)
        End Using
```

The next step in the OnStart method is to take the values in the bytData array that represent the processing schedule for the days of the week and to concatenate them in the strSchedule variable as 1s and 0s. A value of 1 indicates that the service should process, and a value of 0 indicates that the service should not process. This is performed using the String Format method discussed in Chapter 3, converting the data in the Byte array into a two-digit hexadecimal number:

```
'Convert the schedule to a string
For Each bytData As Byte In bytSchedule
    strSchedule &= String.Format("{0:X2}", bytData)
Next
```

Now you need to redimension the `blnTimeEntryProcessed` array to the appropriate size based on the number of entries on the `strProcessTimes` array. This is accomplished using the `Length` property of the `strProcessTimes` array:

```
'Redimension the variable to the appropriate number of entries
ReDim blnTimeEntryProcessed(strProcessTimes.Length)

'Build the To line of the email message
For Each strEmailAddress In strEmailAddresses
    strMailTo &= strEmailAddress & ","
Next
```

At this point, the `EventLogTimer` is initialized, the `Interval` property is set, and the timer is started via the `Start` method. The `Interval` property is specified in milliseconds, with 1,000 milliseconds representing one second; therefore, the value in the following code represents one minute.

The `Catch` block writes any exceptions thrown by this service to the application event log. Notice that the `EventLog` class in the `Catch` block has been prefixed with the `Diagnostics` namespace. This is required in a service because the `ServiceBase` class, which your service class inherits, implements a read-only property named `EventLog`. To distinguish between the two, the `Diagnostics` namespace has been prefixed on the `EventLog` class name:

```
'Initialize the timer object
EventLogTimer = New Timer
With EventLogTimer
    .Interval = 60000
    .Start()
End With
Catch ExceptionErr As Exception
    Diagnostics.EventLog.WriteEntry(Application, ExceptionErr.Message, _
        EventLogEntryType.Error, 1000)
End Try
End Sub
```

OnStop, OnPause, OnContinue, and OnShutdown Procedures

The `OnStop` method contains the code to stop and dispose of the timer as follows. Any other objects in your service, such as database connections, would be disposed of here and then reinitialized in the `OnStart` method:

```
Protected Overrides Sub OnStop()
    'Clean up
    EventLogTimer.Stop()
    EventLogTimer.Dispose()
End Sub
```

The `OnPause` and `OnShutdown` methods that follow simply call the `OnStop` method to stop and dispose of the timer. The `OnContinue` method calls the `OnStart` method, passing a value of `Nothing` as the arguments. Remember that the `OnStart` method contains all of the necessary code to initialize the variables used in this service.

```
        Protected Overrides Sub OnPause()
            Call OnStop()
        End Sub

        Protected Overrides Sub OnContinue()
            Call OnStart(Nothing)
        End Sub

        Protected Overrides Sub OnShutdown()
            Call OnStop()
        End Sub
```

EventLogTimer_Elapsed Procedure

The `Elapsed` event for the timer is where the main processing occurs to determine whether the service should process the event logs. This is where the schedule is checked, the process times are checked, and the start and end date and times are calculated.

The `EventLogTimer_Elapsed` procedure has only two local variables: `intHour` and `intMinute`. Both of these variables are defined as `Integer` data types and are used in determining the start and end hours and minutes:

```
        Private Sub EventLogTimer_Elapsed(ByVal sender As Object, _
            ByVal e As System.Timers.ElapsedEventArgs) Handles EventLogTimer.Elapsed

            'Declare local variables and objects
            Dim intHour As Integer
            Dim intMinute As Integer
```

The code in this procedure is wrapped in a `Try...Catch...Finally` block. A `Finally` block is included in this `Try...Catch` block to restart the timer that is stopped in this procedure. Whether the code completes in the `Try` block or an error occurs and control is passed to the `Catch` block, the code in the `Finally` block is always executed.

The first check in the `Try` block is a check to determine whether you should be processing on this day according to the schedule that was read from the registry. The `strSchedule` variable contains a value of `1` or `0` for each day in the week. For example, a schedule that would only be processed Monday through Friday would be represented in the `strSchedule` variable as `01111100`. Notice the extra zero at the end. This is just an extra digit from the last byte of the binary value that was read from the registry, and it is always ignored.

The `DayOfWeek` enumeration contains the actual days of the week, with `Sunday` having an `Integer` value of `0` and `Saturday` having an `Integer` value of `6`. This enables you to use the day of week value in this enumeration as an index into the `strSchedule` variable to get to the byte of data in the string that enables you to determine whether processing should occur on a given day. The value that is read is converted to a `Boolean` value for use in the `If...Then` statement. Remember that a value of `0` in a `Boolean` variable means `false` and any other value means `true`, which also corresponds to the values in the `strSchedule` variable.

```
            Try
                'Is this day of the week on the schedule to be processed...
                'DayOfWeek enumeration returns Sunday - Saturday with values of 0 - 6
```

```
'Characters 0 - 6 in the strSchedule variable match the
'days of the week
If CType(strSchedule.Substring((DateTime.Now.DayOfWeek), 1), _
    Boolean) Then
```

If you should be processing on this day of the week, the next step is to initialize the intIndex variable to a value of -1 and then process each time in the strProcessTimes variable in a For Each...Next loop. The strProcessTimes variable is a String array containing the times of day, in 24-hour format, that the service should process. The first line of code inside the loop increments the intIndex variable:

```
'Reset the index counter
intIndex = -1

'Is the current time within the range of a minute of the
'process times...
For Each strProcessTime In strProcessTimes
    'Increment the index counter
    intIndex += 1
```

You want to compare the current system time to the scheduled process time. The Compare method of the DateTime structure compares two dates or times and returns an indication of the relative values. A value of 0 indicates that the times are equal, and a value greater than 0 indicates that the current system time is greater than the scheduled process time. A value less than 0 indicates that the system time is less than the scheduled process time.

The following If...Then statement contains the And clause to ensure that the current system time is equal to or greater than the scheduled process time, but also that it is less than the scheduled process time plus one minute. Adding one minute to the process time accommodates any inaccuracies in the system timer ticks, thus causing you to miss the scheduled process time.

```
If DateTime.Compare(DateTime.Now.ToShortTimeString, _
    CType(strProcessTime, DateTime).ToShortTimeString) >= 0 _
    And DateTime.Compare(DateTime.Now.ToShortTimeString, _
    CType(strProcessTime, DateTime).AddMinutes(1). _
    ToShortTimeString) <= 0 _
    Then
```

If it is determined that you should be processing, then the next check will be to determine whether you have already processed this scheduled time. You do this by checking the blnTimeEntryProcessed Boolean variable. Remember that this variable is a Boolean array containing one entry for each scheduled process time, and you use the intIndex variable to access the appropriate entry in the array for testing.

If it is determined that you have not processed this particular scheduled time, then you want to stop the timer. This prevents this procedure from starting again while you are currently executing it, which would cause duplicate e-mails to be sent with the same data.

```
'Has this time entry already been processed...
If Not blnTimeEntryProcessed(intIndex) Then

    'Stop the timer
    EventLogTimer.Stop()
```

Now you want to calculate the start and end date and times for processing events from the event logs. The intHour variable is set using the hour from the strProcessTime variable, and the intMinute is set using the minutes from the strProcessTime variable.

The start date is set in the dteStart variable to the previous day's date. This is done by using the Now property of the DateTime structure, which returns the current date and time, and then by using the AddDays method passes it a value of -1, which subtracts one day from the date. The end date is set in the dteEnd variable using the current date and time.

Now you want to refine the current time in the dteEnd variable to the hour and minute that you just set in the intHour and intMinute variables. This is done by calling the New constructor on the DateTime structure and passing it the year, month, day, hour, minute, and seconds:

```
'Calculate the start and end date/times
intHour = CType(strProcessTime.Substring(0, _
    strProcessTime.IndexOf(":")), Integer)
intMinute = strProcessTime.Substring( _
    strProcessTime.IndexOf(":") + 1, 2)

dteStart = DateTime.Now.AddDays(-1)
dteEnd = DateTime.Now

'The end date/time is always the same
dteEnd = New DateTime(dteEnd.Year, dteEnd.Month, _
    dteEnd.Day, intHour, intMinute, 0)
```

The next check is a check to determine whether there is only one scheduled process time. If that is the case, you want to process all events from yesterday at the scheduled time through today at the scheduled time. The Length property of the strProcessTimes String array will tell you how many entries are in the String array.

If there is only one entry in the String array, then you set the start date and time using the date that was already set in the dteStart variable, and the hour and minutes set in the intHour and intMinute variables:

```
If strProcessTimes.Length = 1 Then
    'The start date is yesterday at the same time
    dteStart = New DateTime(dteStart.Year, _
        dteStart.Month, dteStart.Day, intHour, _
        intMinute, 0)
Else
```

If there is more than one scheduled process time, then you want to see whether you are using the first scheduled process time in the String array. If that is the case, set the intHour and intMinute variable to the last scheduled process time in the strProcessTimes array. Then you set the new hour and minute in the dteStart variable that already contains the previous day's date:

```
Select Case intIndex
    Case 0
        'The start date/time is yesterday's date
        'and the last time in the array
```

```
                                intHour = CType(strProcessTimes( _
                                    strProcessTimes.Length - 1). _
                                    Substring(0, strProcessTimes( _
                                    strProcessTimes.Length - 1). _
                                    IndexOf(":")), Integer)
                                intMinute = strProcessTimes( _
                                    strProcessTimes.Length - 1). _
                                    Substring(strProcessTimes( _
                                    strProcessTimes.Length - 1). _
                                    IndexOf(":") + 1, 2)
                                dteStart = New DateTime(dteStart.Year, _
                                    dteStart.Month, dteStart.Day, _
                                    intHour, intMinute, 0)
```

If this is not the first entry in the strProcessTimes String array, you set the intHour and intMinute variable to the previous entry in the String array and then set the dteStart variable using the new hour and minute. Next, add one day to the start date so that you are processing events only for the current day's date and processing events between the previous scheduled process time and the current scheduled process time:

```
                        Case Else
                            'The start date/time is today's date
                            'and the previous time in the array
                            intHour = CType(strProcessTimes( _
                                intIndex - 1).Substring(0, _
                                strProcessTimes(intIndex - 1). _
                                IndexOf(":")), Integer)
                            intMinute = strProcessTimes( _
                                intIndex - 1).Substring( _
                                strProcessTimes(intIndex - 1). _
                                IndexOf(":") + 1, 2)
                            dteStart = New DateTime(dteStart.Year, _
                                dteStart.Month, dteStart.Day, _
                                intHour, intMinute, 0)
                            dteStart = dteStart.AddDays(1)
                    End Select
                End If
```

Now that the dteStart and dteEnd dates and times have been set, you call the ProcessEventLog procedure to process the application event log, and then call it to process the trace event log. Finally, you set the current entry in the blnTimeEntryProcessed Boolean array to True, indicating that you have already processed this scheduled process time:

```
                'Process Application log
                ProcessEventLog(strApplicationLog, _
                    strApplicationSource)

                'Process Trace log
                ProcessEventLog(strTraceLog, strTraceSource)

                'Set the processed flag to True
                blnTimeEntryProcessed(intIndex) = True
```

```
                              End If

               End If
```

The next If...Then statement compares the current time to the scheduled process time. If it is
greater than zero, the current time is greater than the scheduled process time, so you set the entry in
the blnTimeEntryProcessed Boolean array to False, indicating that this scheduled time has not been
processed. This allows it to be processed on the next day:

```
               'If the current time is greater than the process time
               'then reset the processed flag
               If DateTime.Compare(DateTime.Now.ToShortTimeString, _
                   CType(strProcessTime, DateTime).ToShortTimeString) > 0 _
                   Then
                   blnTimeEntryProcessed(intIndex) = False
               End If

           Next

       End If
```

The Catch block handles any errors that might occur and writes them to the application event log. The
Finally block will start the timer regardless of whether an error occurred. Once the timer is started, it
will not process another Elapsed event until the interval has passed, which means it will not process for
another minute:

```
       Catch ExceptionErr As Exception
           Diagnostics.EventLog.WriteEntry(Application, ExceptionErr.Message, _
               EventLogEntryType.Error, 1000)
       Finally
           'Start the timer
           EventLogTimer.Start()
       End Try
   End Sub
```

ProcessEventLog Procedure

The last procedure in this class is the ProcessEventLog procedure. This procedure actually reads the
events from the event logs. It has two parameters: logName and applicationSource. The logName parameter specifies the name of the application log or trace log to read from and the applicationSource
parameter specifies the application source that you are looking for within the event log.

Three local objects are defined in this procedure: objEventLog, objLogEntry, and objStringBuilder.
The objEventLog object is set to the event log to be read, and the objLogEntry object is used to contain
a single event entry from the event log. The objStringBuilder object is used to build a string of the
mail message body and is more efficient than appending text to a String variable:

```
       Private Sub ProcessEventLog(ByVal logName As String, _
           ByVal applicationSource As String)
```

```
'Declare local variables and objects
Dim objEventLog As EventLog
Dim objLogEntry As EventLogEntry
Dim objStringBuilder As New StringBuilder
```

The code in this procedure is wrapped in a `Try...Catch` block to handle any errors that might occur. The first thing that happens inside the `Try` block is that the `objEventLog` object is instantiated to the event log that you want to read. The constructor for the `EventLog` class accepts the log name to be processed, and here you specify the value contained in the `logName` input parameter to this procedure.

Next, you start building an HTML mail message, appending the message text to the `objStringBuilder` object. You are creating a table in the mail message, and the column headers in the first row of the table include the column names. This is a very simple HTML mail message, but you can enhance it by using cascading style sheets if you want.

```
Try
    'Instantiate an instance of the event log
    objEventLog = New EventLog(logName)

    'Start building the message body
    objStringBuilder.Append("<table border=""0"">")
    objStringBuilder.Append("<tr>")
    objStringBuilder.Append("<th nowrap align=""left"">Type</th>")
    objStringBuilder.Append("<th width=""10""> </th>")
    objStringBuilder.Append("<th nowrap align=""left"">Date/Time</th>")
    objStringBuilder.Append("<th width=""10""> </th>")
    objStringBuilder.Append("<th nowrap align=""left"">Category</th>")
    objStringBuilder.Append("<th width=""10""> </th>")
    objStringBuilder.Append("<th align=""left"">Message</th>")
    objStringBuilder.Append("</tr>")
```

Now you process each event in the event log using a `For Each...Next` loop. The `objLogEntry` object is set to the `Entries` property of the `EventLog` class contained in the `objEventLog` object. This sets the `objLogEntry` to a single entry in the event log.

Next, you check the date and time that this event entry was written by comparing the `TimeWritten` property of the `objLogEntry` object to see whether it falls within the range of the date and time contained in the `dteStart` and `dteEnd` variables. If it does, then you perform another check on this log entry.

```
'Process all event entries
For Each objLogEntry In objEventLog.Entries

    'Was the event written in the time frame we are looking for...
    If DateTime.Compare(objLogEntry.TimeWritten, dteStart) >= 0 _
        And DateTime.Compare(objLogEntry.TimeWritten, dteEnd) <= 0 _
        Then
```

The next check you perform determines whether the value in the `Source` property of the `objLogEntry` object matches the value in the `applicationSource` input parameter. If the values match, then this is a log entry that you want to process.

You add a new row to the mail message specifying the entry type using the `EntryType` property of the `objLogEntry` object, the time written and category using the `TimeWritten` and `Category` properties, and finally the log entry message contained in the `Message` property:

```
                        'Is this event from the source we are looking for...
                        If objLogEntry.Source = applicationSource Then

                            'Add the event to the message body
                            objStringBuilder.Append("<tr>")
                            objStringBuilder.Append("<td nowrap valign=""top"">" & _
                                objLogEntry.EntryType.ToString & "</td>")
                            objStringBuilder.Append("<td> </td>")
                            objStringBuilder.Append("<td nowrap valign=""top"">" & _
                                objLogEntry.TimeWritten & "</td>")
                            objStringBuilder.Append("<td> </td>")
                            objStringBuilder.Append("<td nowrap valign=""top"">" & _
                                objLogEntry.Category & "</td>")
                            objStringBuilder.Append("<td> </td>")
                            objStringBuilder.Append("<td>" & objLogEntry.Message & _
                                "</td>")
                            objStringBuilder.Append("</tr>")

                        End If
```

After all log entries in the event log have been processed, close the table and then set the string contained in the `objStringBuilder` object in the `strMailBody` variable. If you want to include any other text in your mail message, it would be added after the table was closed.

```
                    End If

                Next

                'Close the table in the message
                objStringBuilder.Append("</table>")

                'Set the mail message body variable
                strMailBody = objStringBuilder.ToString
```

Because the start of the HTML table was built in the mail message body before any log entries were processed, it is possible that no log entries existed for the date and time range specified. Therefore, you need to query the `Length` property of the `strMailBody` variable to see if it is greater than 120 characters, indicating that at least one log entry was processed.

If the `strMailBody` variable contains more than 120 characters, then you instantiate a new `MailMessage` class in a `Using...End Using` block. The constructor for the `MailMessage` class accepts the from address, to address, subject, and message text as input parameters. After the `objMailMessage` object has been instantiated to a new `MailMessage` class, you set the `IsBodyHTML` property to `True` to indicate that this mail message contains HTML.

Next, declare and instantiate a new instance of the `SmtpClient` class in the `objSmtpClient` object, passing the constructor for this class the DNS name or IP address of the outbound mail server that will be sending this mail message. Then you call the `Send` method on this class, passing it the `objMailMessage` object so that it can send the mail message. Finally, set the `objSmtpClient` object to `Nothing`, as you are done with this object:

```
'If the mail message body contains text...
If strMailBody.Length > 120 Then

    'Construct and mail the message
    Using objMailMessage As New MailMessage(From, strMailTo, _
        applicationSource & " Log Events", strMailBody)
        objMailMessage.IsBodyHtml = True
        Dim objSmtpClient As New SmtpClient(strSmtpServer)
        objSmtpClient.Send(objMailMessage)
        objSmtpClient = Nothing
    End Using

End If
```

The `Catch` block writes any errors that may have occurred to the application event log:

```
Catch ExceptionErr As Exception
    Diagnostics.EventLog.WriteEntry(Application, ExceptionErr.Message, _
        EventLogEntryType.Error, 1000)
    End Try
End Sub
```

There's one thing that should be considered before using this service. The machine on which this service runs needs to be able to communicate to the Simple Mail Transfer Protocol (SMTP) server that you specify in the preceding code. The SMTP server can be an outbound mail server on your network or it can be your Internet Service Provider's outbound mail server.

Setting Up the Event Log Service

While the normal means exist for setting up the Event Log Service, this is one time that you'll want to perform a manual installation. Because this is a Windows Service, extra steps are required to install the service that do not exist using the installer. The installer will simply install the program on your computer and write the appropriate registry entries so that the program is displayed in the Add Or Remove Programs dialog box in the Control Panel. It will not physically install the service in the Services console.

Using the Installer

To install the Event Log Service, locate the `Chapter 05 - Event Log Service\Installer` folder on the CD-ROM that came with this book and double-click the `setup.exe` program. You will be prompted with the Application Install dialog. Clicking the Install button will install and launch the application. Once the installer has installed your program, read and follow the instructions in the "Configuring the Application" section of this chapter.

Manual Installation

To manually install the Event Log Service, first create a folder on your computer where you want to place the program executable file. Then locate the `Chapter 05 - Event Log Service\Source` folder on the CD-ROM that came with this book and navigate to the `bin\Release` folder. Copy the following files from the `Release` folder to the folder that you created on your computer:

- ❑ `Event Log Service.exe`
- ❑ `install.cmd`
- ❑ `uninstall.cmd`
- ❑ `Registry Keys.reg`

Read and follow the instructions in the next section in order to complete the installation.

Configuring the Application

Before installing and starting the Event Log Service in the Services console, you need to both create the registry keys required by the service and edit the `install.cmd` and `uninstall.cmd` files. The `Registry Keys.reg` file located in the `bin\Release` folder contains a set of sample registry keys.

To merge this registry file into the registry, you can simply double-click it in Windows Explorer. You will be prompted with the Registry Editor dialog box, shown in Figure 5-3. Click the Yes button to create the keys in the registry.

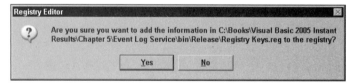

Figure 5-4

After the registry keys have been created, you can use the Application Registry Manager program from Chapters 3 or 4 to edit the registry and provide valid values for your testing, as shown in Figure 5-5. This would include providing one or more valid e-mail addresses and a valid SMTP Server name or Internet Protocol (IP) address. You can also update the other values to suit your needs.

You'll need to edit the `install.cmd` and `uninstall.cmd` files next using Notepad or some other text editor. Verify the Windows directory name in these files. On some Windows installations it is called Windows, and on some other installations it is called WINNT. Look on the C drive of the target computer to see what the Windows directory name is and edit these files accordingly.

To install the Event Log Service, double-click the `install.cmd` file. When the service has been successfully installed in the Services console, you must start the service by clicking Start ➪ Administrative Tools ➪ Services. When the Services console is displayed, locate the Wrox Event Log Service and click it and then click the Start button at the top of the Services console (refer to Figure 5-1).

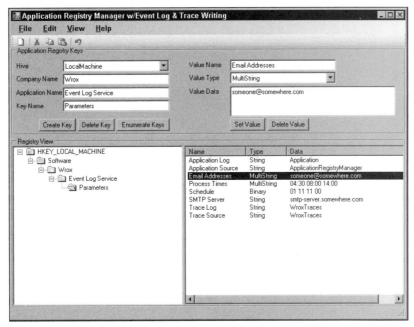

Figure 5-5

At this point your service should be running and there is nothing further that you need to do. The service will automatically start when the computer is started and will run even when you are not logged on. If you change the registry keys, you'll need to restart the service in order to have it pick up the new key values.

Tips on Creating Windows Services

The real trick to creating code for a Windows Service is to create code that is simple, to the point, and as bulletproof as you can possibly make it. A Windows Service has to be installed and started before being run; thus, the Visual Studio IDE (Integrated Development Environment) provides no method for debugging a Windows Service project.

A method that has worked well for me when creating code for a Windows Service is to first write the code in a Windows application that simulates the methods available in a Windows Service and that makes use of the classes that will be provided in your service.

Figure 5-6 shows the test application that I created when writing the code for this service. This test application enabled me to view the registry keys that were read and to stop, start, and restart the service code at will, as well as to step through the code for debugging purposes. This enables you to simulate the actions available in your Windows Service.

Figure 5-6

This test application is included on the CD that came with this book as an example of writing Service code in a test application. The project can be located on the CD at `Chapter 05 - Event Log Service Test Application`.

The following steps provide a quick reference for creating a Windows Service:

1. Write and test your service code in a Windows application.

2. Create a new Windows Service project.

3. Rename the default `Service1` class in the Solution Explorer to a name of your choosing.

4. Add your code to the service class that you just renamed.

5. Open and click on the Service designer of the service class that you renamed and set the following properties in the Properties window:

   ❑ `CanPauseAndContinue`

   ❑ `CanShutdown`

   ❑ `ServiceName`

6. At the bottom of the Properties window, click the Add Installer link.

7. Click the `ServiceProcessInstaller1` component in the ProjectInstaller designer and set the following properties in the Properties window:

   ❑ `Account` — Typically set to `LocalSystem`

8. Click on the `ServiceInstaller1` component in the ProjectInstaller designer and set the following properties in the Properties window:

   ❑ `Description` — This is the description that will be displayed in the Services console.

   ❑ `DisplayName` — This is the name that will be displayed in the Services console.

   ❑ `ServiceName` — This should match the `ServiceName` property set in Step 5.

   ❑ `StartType` — Typically set to Automatic so the service is started when Windows starts.

9. Optionally, add `install.cmd` and `uninstall.cmd` files to the project and add code to install your service and uninstall your service. See the section "Configuring the Application" for details.

10. Optionally, add a registry file to the project with the required registry keys needed by your service.

11. Build your solution, install the service, and start it.

Summary

This chapter has introduced you to a few important topics that every good developer should understand: how to create a Windows Service, how to read events from the event log, how to use system timers, and how to create and send mail messages using the `System.Net` namespace. Along the way, you also saw how important code reuse is by reusing the `RegistryHelper` class that was initially created in Chapter 3.

The basic steps for creating a Windows Service were outlined in the "Tips on Creating Windows Services" section, along with some helpful tips on writing and testing your service code. The steps outlined there will provide a quick reference guide for you in the future.

Reading events from the event log is something that will be useful to you in the future as you write other applications and services. Developers benefit from applications that write useful events to the event log and from applications that can read those events, as this data can provide a wealth of information about what an application is doing and how it is performing.

Using system timers is very straightforward and involves a minimal amount of code. Moreover, the benefits that they provide are enormous. Using system timers enables you to have code in your programs execute at timed intervals, thereby reducing the amount of system resources required by your applications.

You had the opportunity to see firsthand how the `MailMessage` and `SmtpClient` classes in the `System.Net` namespace work when an HTML mail message is created and sent. There is much more functionality available in these classes, but for the most part the code demonstrated in this chapter will provide for the majority of your e-mailing needs in a Windows application.

6

Multi-Threaded Notepad

Have you ever used the Notepad application that comes with Windows? Did you ever wish that it had a toolbar that provided the icons for cut, copy, and paste? Did you ever wish that it had a spell checker? Have you ever wondered how Microsoft Word automatically corrects text as you type? Have you ever wanted to create a multi-threaded application but weren't quite sure how to go about it?

This chapter answers all of these questions and more as you examine a multi-threaded Notepad application that includes an auto-correct feature that automatically corrects words as you type and provides a spell checker that can be invoked via an icon on the toolbar.

The Notepad Plus application uses the Component Object Model (COM) exposed by Microsoft Word 2003 to access the spell checker features included in that application, as well as the method used to extract the list of auto-correct words and their replacements.

While this may not be desirable for some readers, it demonstrates a couple of important points. First and foremost, it demonstrates how to tap into the rich features of Microsoft Word 2003 using the COM interfaces. It also demonstrates how to create a multi-threaded application.

Therefore, running the application in this chapter requires that Microsoft Word 2003 is installed on your computer, as well as the Microsoft Office Primary Interop Assemblies. When the design of the application is discussed, I'll explain how to update the COM reference to use other versions of Microsoft Word. The "Configuring the Application" section at the end of this chapter discusses the Microsoft Office Primary Interop Assemblies that are also required.

The main technologies used in this chapter are as follows:

- ❑ Accessing the public methods exposed by the Microsoft Word 2003 COM interface
- ❑ Using the `BackgroundWorker` class to create a multi-threaded application
- ❑ Extending an existing control in the .NET Framework
- ❑ Using the `BinaryFormatter` class to serialize objects to and from the disk

Using the Notepad Plus Application

Using the Notepad Plus application is just like using any other text editor; you start it up and begin typing. Figure 6-1 shows what the application looks like when you first start it up. You have the option to either start typing or open an existing file. If there is text on the Clipboard, the Paste icon on the toolbar is enabled, allowing you to paste the text into the application.

The File menu contains the standard menus items such as New, Open, Save, Print, and so on. Note, however, that Print functionality has not been implemented in this chapter. It will be implemented in the next chapter.

The Edit and Format menus contain the same functionality that exists in the Microsoft Notepad application, enabling you to perform the standard editing tasks. In addition, you can turn word wrapping on and off in the Format menu.

The View menu not only allows you to show and hide the status bar, it also allows you to show and hide the toolbar as well. The Help menu contains the standard help menu items, although only the About menu item has been implemented.

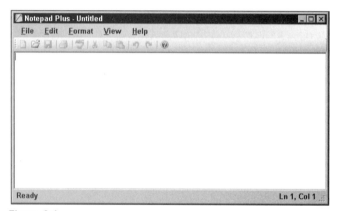

Figure 6-1

When the application first starts, it loads an auto-correct list from disk and uses that list when checking for words that can be automatically corrected as you type. The application will also check the date and time of the existing list on disk and get a new list of words from Microsoft Word 2003 if the existing list is over two hours old. The new list will be saved to disk and used the next time the application starts.

Depending on the speed of your computer and the number of additional entries that you have added to the AutoCorrect list in Microsoft Word, loading a new list of words can take as long as 15 seconds, which is why the list is saved to disk and loaded when the application starts. Loading a new list happens on a separate thread from the main user interface (UI), so it does not impede the user experience.

A second thread is also used as you type words in the application. When you type a word and the next character that you type is a space, the second thread is started to look up the word just typed in the auto-correct list. If a matching entry is found, then the application replaces the word just typed with the replacement word from the auto-correct list.

When you have finished typing, you can invoke the Spell Checker via the Spell Check icon on the toolbar. The Spelling dialog box, shown in Figure 6-2, calls the public methods in Microsoft Word 2003 to check a word for correct spelling. If a word is misspelled, another call is made to Microsoft Word to retrieve a list of suggested words for the misspelled word.

Using the COM interface for Microsoft Word enables you to avoid maintaining a dictionary of your own for this application and having to introduce complex logic to determine a list of suggested words for a misspelled word.

When the Spelling dialog box is displayed, it copies the text from the Notepad Plus application into the dialog box and performs a check on each and every word. When a misspelled word is found, it highlights that word in a bold red font and retrieves a list of suggested words (refer to Figure 6-2).

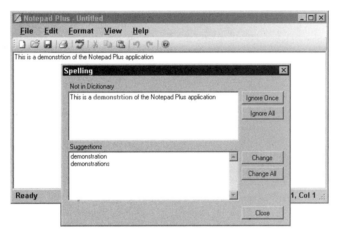

Figure 6-2

You have the option to ignore the misspelled word one time or every time it is encountered. You also have the option to change the word or to change all the words like it. Additionally, you have the option to cancel additional spell checking by clicking the Close button in the Spelling dialog box.

Any changes made through the Spelling dialog box will automatically be applied in the Notepad Plus application. Therefore, if one word is corrected and you close the Spelling dialog box, the updates are applied in the Notepad Plus application.

Design of the Notepad Plus Application

The design of the Notepad Plus application revolves around two main parts: extending the RichTextBox class and interacting with the Microsoft Word application. Figure 6-3 illustrates how the application interacts with both the .NET Framework RichTextBox class and the Microsoft Word application through the Microsoft.Office.Interop namespace.

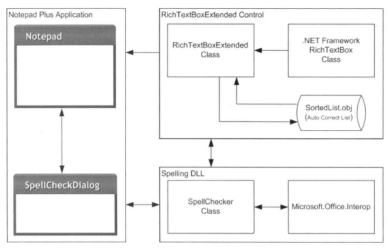

Figure 6-3

Notepad Form

The Notepad form is the main form in the Notepad Plus application. This is the user interface for the application and is where most of the simple logic for this application is implemented. The Notepad form uses the RichTextBoxExtended control, which contains the RichTextBoxExtended class and the logic to extend the .NET Framework RichTextBox class, as you'll see shortly. The Notepad form also displays the SpellCheckDialog form when invoking the spell checking functionality for this application.

The design of the Notepad form is very simple and basically mimics the Microsoft Notepad application. However, the Notepad Plus application implements a toolbar, which the Microsoft Notepad application lacks. This application also implements the word auto-correct feature and spell checking functionality.

RichTextBoxExtended Control

This RichTextBoxExtended class inherits the RichTextBox class from the .NET Framework in order to extend the functionality provided in that class. The RichTextBox class was chosen over the TextBox class in order to provide the Notepad Plus application with a UI that supports rich text, such as text in various fonts and colors.

This class contains a property to return the current cursor position within the RichTextBoxExtended control. An Application Programming Interface (API) call is made to the Windows operating system via the SendMessage API to retrieve the current line and column of the cursor in the RichTextBoxExtended control.

This class also implements multiple threads. One thread loads the saved auto-correct list from disk via the SortedList.obj object and will also retrieve and save an updated auto-correct list from Microsoft Word. The second thread handles checking words typed in the RichTextBoxExtended control against the auto-correct list, automatically correcting them if found in the list.

Table 6-1 details the properties, methods, and event handlers implemented in this class. Details about these properties and methods are covered in the section "Code and Code Explanation" later in the chapter.

Table 6-1: Properties and Methods of the RichTextBoxExtended Class

Property/Method	Return Type	Description
`Public Sub New()`	N/A	Starts the background thread to load the auto-correct list and to get an updated list if necessary
`Public ReadOnly Property CursorPosition()`	`Point`	Returns the cursor's current row and column position in the control
`Private Sub RichTextBoxExtended_TextChanged(ByVal sender As Object, ByVal e As System.EventArgs)`	N/A	Resets the start index variable for the text entered
`Private Sub RichTextBoxExtended_KeyUp(ByVal sender As Object, ByVal e As System .Windows.Forms.KeyEventArgs)`	N/A	Invokes the background thread to check the word just typed
`Private Sub LoadSortedList_DoWork(ByVal sender As Object, ByVal e As System .ComponentModel.DoWorkEventArgs)`	N/A	Procedure for the background thread that loads the auto-correct list
`Private Sub AutoCorrect_DoWork(ByVal sender As Object, ByVal e As System .ComponentModel.DoWorkEventArgs)`	N/A	Procedure for the background thread that checks a word against the auto-correct list
`Private Sub AutoCorrect_RunWorkerCompleted(ByVal sender As Object, ByVal e As System .ComponentModel .RunWorkerCompletedEventArgs)`	N/A	Procedure that handles the `RunWorkerCompleted` event from the background thread that checks words and updates the word in the `RichTextBox` control

SpellCheckDialog Form

This is the Spelling dialog box shown in Figure 6-2. This form interacts with the `SpellChecker` class in the Spelling DLL to check each word for correct spelling, retrieving a list of suggested words if a word has been misspelled.

This dialog box enables the user to change one or more words that are misspelled or to ignore one or more words if they are spelled correctly but not in the dictionary. This dialog box contains the entire text from the Notepad form and highlights each word in a bold, red font when it is presented to the user for spelling correction.

The major procedures in this form are listed in Table 6-2 and are explained in detail in the section "Code and Code Explanation" coming up next.

Table 6-2: Major Procedures in SpellCheckerDialog Form

Method	Return Type	Description
`Private Sub SpellCheck()`	N/A	Iterates over the words in the Notepad form and checks their spelling. Also retrieves a list of suggested words if the word being checked is misspelled.
`Private Function FindEndOfWord()`	Integer	Finds the end of the current word
`Private Sub RevertWord()`	N/A	Reverts the current misspelled word back to its original font and color
`Private Sub btnIgnoreOnce_Click(ByVal sender As System.Object, ByVal e As System.EventArgs)`	N/A	Ignores the current misspelled word
`Private Sub btnIgnoreAll_Click(ByVal sender As System.Object, ByVal e As System.EventArgs)`	N/A	Adds the misspelled word to a list of words to ignore when checking for spelling errors
`Private Sub ChangeWord()`	N/A	Changes the misspelled word using the selected entry from the list of suggested words
`Private Sub btnChange_Click(ByVal sender As System.Object, ByVal e As System.EventArgs)`	N/A	Changes the current misspelled word
`Private Sub btnChangeAll_Click(ByVal sender As System.Object, ByVal e As System.EventArgs)`	N/A	Changes all words like the currently misspelled word
`Private Sub txtData_KeyUp(ByVal sender As Object, ByVal e As System.Windows.Forms.KeyEventArgs)`	N/A	Finds the end of the current word and reverts the word back to its original font and color

Spelling DLL

The SpellChecker class in the Spelling DLL is the main and only class that directly interacts with the Microsoft Word application via the Microsoft.Office.Interop namespace. The main purpose of this class is to perform spell checking of words, but it also implements a function to retrieve and return a list of auto-correct words from Microsoft Word's AutoCorrect list.

The design of this class has been kept simple and its functionality specific, to interact with Microsoft Word. This is the class that you would extend if you wanted to implement other features of Microsoft Word in your applications.

Table 6-3 details the properties and methods in this class.

Table 6-3: Methods and Properties of the Spelling DLL

Property/Method	Return Type	Description
Public Sub New()	N/A	Instantiates the Microsoft Word application in an object defined at the class level
Protected Overridable Sub Dispose(ByVal disposing As Boolean)	N/A	Closes the Microsoft Word application and cleans up
Public ReadOnly Property AutoCorrectList()	SortedList	Retrieves a list of auto-correct words from Microsoft Word and returns them in a SortedList object
Public Function IsWordMisspelled(ByVal wordToCheck As String)	Boolean	Calls Microsoft Word's SpellingErrors property to determine whether a word is misspelled
Public Function SpellingSuggestions(ByVal wordToCheck As String)	String()	Calls Microsoft Word's GetSpellingSuggestions property to retrieve a list of suggested words for the misspelled word

To change the COM reference to another version of Microsoft Word, right-click the Spelling project in the Solution Explorer and choose Add Reference from the context menu. Then, in the Add Reference dialog box, click the COM tab and locate the appropriate version of the Microsoft Word Object Library in the list, select it, and then click OK to have the reference added to the project.

After a new reference has been set, you need to verify the code in the SpellChecker class to ensure that all methods and properties of Microsoft Word that are used in the code are supported by the version that you have set a reference to.

Code and Code Explanation

This section provides the details of the properties and methods shown earlier in the chapter and demonstrates an example of the code in use. This enables you to see how all the pieces work and fit together to form the complete application.

As you gain a better understanding of the code and components in use in this application, you should begin to realize how you might use the components and classes in this application in your own applications. You'll also start to see how you might want to extend the functionality of these components and classes to implement other rich features from Microsoft Word into your own applications.

SpellChecker Class

I want to start this section with the `SpellChecker` class in the Spelling DLL because it is at the core of the functionality provided in this application. This class starts by importing the `Microsoft.Office.Interop` namespace. Before you can import this namespace in a new application, you need to add a reference to the Microsoft Word Object Library using the current version of Microsoft Office that you have installed. You'll have access to this namespace only after installing the Microsoft Office Primary Interop Assemblies, which is discussed in the "Configuring the Application" section at the end of this chapter.

```
Imports Microsoft.Office.Interop
```

Because of the way this class is used in the other classes in this application, this class implements the `IDisposable` interface. This enables the class to be used in a `Using...End Using` block. Therefore, you can declare, use, and dispose of this class all within the `Using...End Using` block of code.

```
Public Class SpellChecker
    Implements IDisposable
```

This class has one object defined at the class level, `objWord`. As you can see in the following code, this object is defined as a `Word.Application`, thus enabling you to create a Word document in your code and providing access to all of the interfaces, classes, properties, and methods that Microsoft Word exposes through its COM interface.

```
    Private objWord As Word.Application
```

New and Dispose Procedures

When you implement the `IDisposable` interface, the `Dispose` procedure is automatically inserted into the class. All you have to do is add a constructor to the class in the form of a `New` procedure. The constructor for this class instantiates a new instance of the `Word.Application` object, as shown in the following code:

```
    Public Sub New()
        'Start Microsoft Word and add a document
        objWord = New Word.Application
    End Sub
```

Because you instantiated the `Word.Application` class in the `objWord` object, you need to dispose of it when the class is disposed of. The following `Dispose` procedure is automatically inserted into your class when you implement the `IDisposable` interface, and the highlighted code in this procedure has been added to quit the Microsoft Word application and set the `objWord` object to `Nothing`:

```
Protected Overridable Sub Dispose(ByVal disposing As Boolean)
    If Not Me.disposedValue Then
        If disposing Then

        End If

        'Quit Word without saving changes
        objWord.Quit(False)
        objWord = Nothing
    End If
    Me.disposedValue = True
End Sub
```

AutoCorrectList Property

The `AutoCorrectList` property gets a list of auto-correct entries from Microsoft Word and adds them to a `SortedList` object. The auto-correct entries are contained in a name-value pair. The name contains the name of the word that is typically mistyped, and the value contains the replacement word for the mistyped word. A `SortedList` is used to sort the entries by name; it provides the `ContainsKey` method, allowing for quick access when looking up a word.

This property starts out by instantiating a new instance of the `SortedList` class. Because this property returns a `SortedList`, the name of the property is used to instantiate a new `SortedList`. Next, you get a count of the number of entries in Word's AutoCorrect list.

Once you have the number of entries, you start iterating through the list of entries and adding them to the `SortedList` in the `AutoCorrectList` property. Notice that the `For...Next` loop starts with a value of 1 and ends with the number of entries contained in the `intCount` variable. This is not typically how the .NET Framework works but the `Word.Application` is implemented through a COM interface and not a .NET Framework class.

```
Public ReadOnly Property AutoCorrectList() As SortedList
    Get
        'Instantiate the SortedList
        AutoCorrectList = New SortedList

        'Get the total number of autocorrect entries
        Dim intCount As Integer = objWord.Application.AutoCorrect.Entries.Count

        'Process the list
        For intIndex As Integer = 1 To intCount
            AutoCorrectList.Add( _
                objWord.Application.AutoCorrect.Entries(intIndex).Name, _
                objWord.Application.AutoCorrect.Entries(intIndex).Value)
        Next
    End Get
End Property
```

IsWordMisspelled Function

The IsWordMisspelled function accepts the word to check for misspelling as its input parameter and returns a Boolean value indicating whether the word is misspelled. The first thing that happens in this function is the declaration of two objects: objRange and objSpellingErrors. Note that these objects are Word objects and are necessary for interacting with Microsoft Word.

You have to add a new document to the Documents collection, which you do in the following line of code. Next, you instantiate the Range object within the document, which you do as shown in the following code. Microsoft Word operates on documents and ranges. A document is self-explanatory and the range is a range of words within the document:

```
Public Function IsWordMisspelled(ByVal wordToCheck As String) As Boolean
    'Declare local objects
    Dim objRange As Word.Range
    Dim objSpellingErrors As Word.ProofreadingErrors

    'Add a document to Word
    objWord.Documents.Add()

    'Instantiate the document range
    objRange = objWord.ActiveDocument.Range
```

Once the range has been instantiated, you need to add the word to be checked to the range, using the InsertAfter method. This method inserts the word after the start of the range.

Next, you check to see whether the word is misspelled by calling the SpellingErrors method. This method returns a list of misspelled words in the range in the objSpellingErrors object. A range in a Word document typically contains multiple words, sentences, or even paragraphs. However, in this implementation it contains only a single word: the word to check for misspelling:

```
    'Add the word to the range
    objRange.InsertAfter(wordToCheck)

    'Get the spelling errors
    objSpellingErrors = objRange.SpellingErrors
```

A quick check of the Count property tells you whether a word has been misspelled. If the Count property is greater than 0, then the word is misspelled and you return a value of True from this function. Otherwise, you return a value of False:

```
    'Is word misspelled...
    If objSpellingErrors.Count > 0 Then
        Return True
    Else
        Return False
    End If
End Function
```

SpellingSuggestions Function

The `SpellingSuggestions` function accepts the word to check as its only input parameter and returns a `String` array of suggested replacement words. This function starts with the declaration of some local variables and objects.

The `intIndex` variable is used to enumerate through the list of suggested words returned from Microsoft Word, and the `strWords()` variable is used to hold a `String` array of suggested words. Finally, the `objSpellingSuggestions` object is used to implement the `SpellingSuggestions` interface from Word.

The first line of code in this function instantiates the `objSpellingSuggestions` object with a list of words returned by calling the `GetSpellingSuggestions` method on the `objWord` object. The `GetSpellingSuggestions` method has many optional parameters but only one required parameter: the word for which spelling suggestions should be returned.

```
Public Function SpellingSuggestions(ByVal wordToCheck As String) As String()
    'Declare local variables and objects
    Dim intIndex As Integer
    Dim strWords() As String
    Dim objSpellingSuggestions As Word.SpellingSuggestions

    'Get a list of suggested words
    objSpellingSuggestions = objWord.GetSpellingSuggestions(wordToCheck)
```

After calling the `GetSpellingSuggestions` method, you need to see whether a list of suggested words has been returned. This is done by checking the `Count` property of the `objSpellingSuggestions` object and then processing the list of suggested words if present.

The first thing that happens inside this `If...Then...Else` statement is the re-dimensioning of the `strWords` `String` array. You need to re-dimension this `String` array to the size of the list of suggested words returned from the `GetSpellingSuggestions` method.

The `For...Next` loop enumerates through the list of words in the `objSpellingSuggestions` object and adds them to the `strWords` `String` array. The starting index of the list of words in the `objSpellingSuggestions` object starts at 1, while the starting index of the `strWords` `String` array starts at 0. This is why you see `intIndex - 1` when adding a word to the `strWords` `String` array.

The `Else` statement in the `If...Then...Else` statement block of code contains the logic to re-dimension the `strWords` `String` array to a size of one dimension and adds the text of `"No Suggestions"`. Finally, the `String` array is returned to the caller in the last line of code in this function:

```
'Build the list of suggested words
If objSpellingSuggestions.Count > 0 Then
    ReDim strWords(objSpellingSuggestions.Count - 1)
    For intIndex = 1 To objSpellingSuggestions.Count
        strWords(intIndex - 1) = objSpellingSuggestions.Item(intIndex).Name
    Next
Else
    ReDim strWords(0)
```

```
                strWords(0) = "No Suggestions"
        End If

        'Return the list of words
        Return strWords
    End Function
```

RichTextBoxExtended Class

The `RichTextBoxExtended` class in the `RichTextBoxExtended` control provides an extended `RichTextBox` control with enhanced functionality. As previously mentioned, this class implements multiple threads through the use of the .NET Framework `BackgroundWorker` class to load and retrieve a list of auto-correct words and to check typed words against the list of auto-correct words. It also makes an API call to the Windows operating system to return the current cursor position in the `RichTextBox`.

Because this class extends an existing class in the .NET Framework, the control has no visual interface that you would normally have in a user control. When creating your own user controls, you have a designer available to create your control. When extending an existing control, you inherit the class of that control and simply provide additional functionality to the code.

This class has a lot going on and thus includes a lot of `Imports` statements, as shown later in this section. The `System.Windows.Forms` namespace is imported so that this class can function as a control and thus have access to the classes in this namespace. The `System.Drawing` namespace is imported to gain access to the `Point` class, which is used in the `CursorPosition` property.

The `System.IO` namespace is used to access the necessary classes for reading and writing the `SortedList.obj` to and from disk. The `System.ComponentModel` namespace is used to access the `BackgroundWorker` class for multi-threaded operations.

The `System.Runtime.Serialization` and `System.Runtime.Serialization.Formatters.Binary` namespaces are used to both serialize an `ArrayList` object to disk as `SortedList.obj` and to de-serialize `SortedList.obj` back into an `ArrayList` object.

The `System.Runtime.InteropServices` namespace is used to access the `DllImportAttribute` class, which is used to declare a shared function in the Windows `user32.dll`, thereby providing access to the Windows APIs exposed by this DLL.

Finally, the `Spelling` namespace is imported to expose the methods in the `SpellChecker` class. The `SpellChecker` class is used to retrieve a current auto-correct list from Microsoft Word.

```
Imports System.Windows.Forms
Imports System.Drawing
Imports System.IO
Imports System.ComponentModel
Imports System.Runtime.Serialization
Imports System.Runtime.Serialization.Formatters.Binary
Imports System.Runtime.InteropServices
Imports Spelling
```

Because this class extends the `RichTextBox` class, it must inherit the `RichTextBox` class in order to gain access to its properties and methods. This is done through the `Inherits` statement, as shown in the code that follows.

Several variables and objects are defined at the class level so that they are accessible to all procedures and functions in this class. The first of these are the `intX` and `intY` variables. These variables are set to the *X* and *Y* coordinates of the cursor within the `RichTextBox` control. The `intStartIndex` and `intEndIndex` are used to keep track of the starting and ending index of the current word to be checked against the auto-correct list.

Finally, the `arrAutoCorrectList` object is used to contain a list of commonly misspelled words and their replacements. This is the list that is loaded from disk from the `SortedList.obj` object and is used to check words typed by the user:

```
Public Class RichTextBoxExtended
    Inherits RichTextBox

    'Private variables and objects
    Private intX As Integer
    Private intY As Integer
    Private intStartIndex As Integer = 0
    Private intEndIndex As Integer

    Private arrAutoCorrectList As SortedList
```

Two background worker threads are defined in the `LoadSortedList` and `AutoCorrect` objects. Notice that these objects are defined using the `BackgroundWorker` class and are defined with the `WithEvents` keywords. This exposes the events of the `BackgroundWorker` class in the Method Name combo box in the Visual Studio IDE:

```
    Private WithEvents LoadSortedList As New BackgroundWorker
    Private WithEvents AutoCorrect As New BackgroundWorker
```

The `SendMessage` function, defined in the last part of this next block of code, requires a numeric identifier of the message being sent to a Window. These identifiers are defined in the two constants shown in the next block of code.

To access the `SendMessage` function defined in the Windows `user32.dll`, you must import the DLL and define the function within the DLL that you want to use. Because the `user32.dll` is a Windows DLL and not managed code within the .NET Framework, you must use the `DllImportAttribute` class to define the function.

Here you specify the `DllImportAttribute` class as `DllImport` and then specify the DLL name as a `String` in parentheses. Next, you define the function that you want to call within the DLL that you are importing, along with its parameters and return value. This is defined in a `Private Shared Function` along with the `End Function` keywords:

```
    'Declare WIN32 Constants
    Private Const EM_LINEINDEX As Integer = &HBB
    Private Const EM_LINEFROMCHAR As Integer = &HC9
```

153

```
'Declare WIN32 API Calls
<DllImport("user32.dll")> _
Private Shared Function SendMessage(ByVal hWnd As IntPtr, _
    ByVal wMsg As Integer, ByVal wParam As Integer, _
    ByVal lParam As IntPtr) As Integer
End Function
```

New Constructor and LoadSortedList_DoWork Event Handler Procedure

The constructor for this class starts a thread by calling the RunWorkerAsync method on the LoadSortedList object. This causes a new thread to be started in your application, and the code in the DoWork event for the LoadSortedList object to be executed in the background independently of your UI.

The LoadSortedList_DoWork procedure starts off with the declaration of a few objects needed in this procedure. The objFileInfo object is declared using the FileInfo class, and you use it to get the file information about the SortedList.obj object. The arrSortedList object is declared using the SortedList class and is populated with a new auto-correct list from Word if deemed necessary.

The objBinaryFormatter object is declared using the BinaryFormatter class, and the objFileStream is declared using the FileStream class. The objBinaryFormatter object is used to serialize and de-serialize the SortedList.obj object to and from disk. The objFileStream object is used to read and write the binary data from and to disk.

```
Public Sub New()
    'Start the background thread to load the list
    LoadSortedList.RunWorkerAsync()
End Sub

Private Sub LoadSortedList_DoWork(ByVal sender As Object, _
    ByVal e As System.ComponentModel.DoWorkEventArgs) _
    Handles LoadSortedList.DoWork

    'Declare local variables and objects
    Dim objFileInfo As FileInfo
    Dim arrSortedList As SortedList
    Dim objBinaryFormatter As BinaryFormatter
    Dim objFileStream As FileStream
```

The BinaryFormatter class has two extremely useful methods: Serialize and Deserialize. The Serialize method takes a binary object and serializes it to a Stream class, enabling you to write the binary object to disk, while the Deserialize method reads the binary data from a Stream and returns an Object class. This enables you to take a SortedList object, write it to disk in binary format, and then read that binary data back from disk and cast it back to an object defined using the SortedList class.

This next block of code starts by instantiating the objBinaryFormatter object using the BinaryFormatter class. Then the objFileStream object is instantiated using the FileStream class, passing it the required parameters for the constructor. This overloaded method of the constructor expects the file path and name of the file to read, the file mode to be used to access the file, the access method to be used to access the file, and the file share, which is used to determine how the file will shared by this process.

In the constructor, you pass the filename to be read: `SortedList.obj`. Because you expect this file to be in the same directory as this component, a file path has not been specified. You need to read from this file, so a file mode of `Open` has been specified from the `FileMode` enumeration. Next, you simply want to read data from the file, so the `Read` constant has been specified from the `FileAccess` enumeration and the `FileShare` enumeration.

At this point, the `SortedList.obj` file is open, so all you need to do now is read the data from the file and load it into the appropriate object. The `objBinaryFormatter` object is used, calling the `Deserialize` method, and you pass it the `objFileStream` object as its input. The results of the `Deserialize` method return an object, which you cast into the appropriate class by using the `CType` function. This casts the object into a `SortedList` class, which is set in the `arrAutoCorrectList`.

Now that you have read the binary data from disk and it is loaded into the appropriate object, you simply perform a little cleanup. Close the `objFileStream` object by calling the `Close` method. Then dispose of the object by calling the `Dispose` method.

At this point, the list of auto-correct words has been loaded into the `arrAutoCorrectList` object and is ready to be used by the application as the user types words in the `RichTextBoxExtended` control. All of this has happened in the background and takes less than a second to complete. In fact, the auto-correct list will probably be loaded before the user has typed the first character.

```
'Load the AutoCorrect list from disk
objBinaryFormatter = New BinaryFormatter
objFileStream = New FileStream("SortedList.obj", FileMode.Open, _
    FileAccess.Read, FileShare.Read)
arrAutoCorrectList = CType(objBinaryFormatter.Deserialize( _
    objFileStream), SortedList)
objFileStream.Close()
objFileStream.Dispose()
```

The next step in this process is to get the file information from the `SortedList.obj`. You do so using the `GetFileInfo` method of the `My.Computer.FileSystem` object. The `GetFileInfo` method reads file information from a file and returns the results in a `FileInfo` class, which the `objFileInfo` object has been declared as.

Once you have the file information, compare the date and time when the file was last written to with the current date and time. You are looking for a difference greater than two hours, so add two hours to the date and time of the file time.

All of this is done in an `If...Then` statement using the `Compare` method of the `DateTime` structure. If you recall from the previous chapter, the `Compare` method of the `DateTime` structure compares two dates or times and returns an indication of the relative values.

Using the `LastWriteTime` property of the `objFileInfo` object, you retrieve the last time the file was written to and add two hours to it using the `AddHours` method. Then you compare that date and time to the current date and time. If the results of that comparison are less than zero, the file date and time are more than two hours old and you want to get a new auto-correct list from Word and save it to disk.

Once inside the `If...Then` block of code, you get a new list of auto-correct words from the Spelling DLL. This is done in a `Using...End Using` block whereby you declare, instantiate, use, and dispose of the class. The list of auto-correct words is retrieved and set in the `arrSortedList` object by calling the `AutoCorrectList` method in the `SpellChecker` class contained in the Spelling DLL.

The process of retrieving this list of auto-correct words may take up to 15 seconds or more depending on the speed of your computer and the size of the auto-correct list contained in Microsoft Word. However, this is not a problem because this process is running on a separate thread from the main UI and will in no way interfere with the UI or the user experience of the application.

```
'Get the file information
objFileInfo = My.Computer.FileSystem.GetFileInfo("SortedList.obj")

'If the file is more than 2 hours old, get and save a new version
If DateTime.Compare(objFileInfo.LastWriteTime.AddHours(2), _
    DateTime.Now) < 0 Then

    'Get a new version of the AutoCorrect list from Word
    Using objSpellChecker As New SpellChecker
        arrSortedList = objSpellChecker.AutoCorrectList
    End Using
```

Now instantiate a new instance of the `BinaryFormatter` class in the `objBinaryFormatter` object and then instantiate a new instance of the `FileStream` class in the `objFileStream` object. This time the parameters for the constructor of the `FileStream` class are a little different because you now want to write data to a file. Here you specify a file mode of *create* and a file access method of *write*. Because you are writing to a file, you do not want to share this file with any other process, so specify no sharing using the `None` constant from the `FileShare` enumeration.

Using the `Serialize` method of the `objBinaryFormatter` object, write the binary data from the `arrSortedList` object to the file. Then close the file stream by calling the `Close` method on the `objFileStream` object and dispose of it by calling the `Dispose` method.

```
        'Save the AutoCorrect list to disk
        objBinaryFormatter = New BinaryFormatter
        objFileStream = New FileStream("SortedList.obj", FileMode.Create, _
            FileAccess.Write, FileShare.None)
        objBinaryFormatter.Serialize(objFileStream, arrSortedList)
        objFileStream.Close()
        objFileStream.Dispose()

    End If
End Sub
```

CursorPosition Property

The `CursorPosition` property is a public, read-only property that is used by the consumer of this component. This property returns the current line and column number of the cursor in the `RichTextBox` control. The results of this property are returned as a `Drawing.Point`, which is why the `System.Drawing` namespace was imported at the top of this class.

The first thing that happens in this property is determining the current character position on a given line by calling the `SendMessage` function, which sends a message to the window that is the `RichTextBoxExtended` control. You pass the handle of this control, which is a pointer contained in the `Handle` property.

The next parameter of the `SendMessage` function is the identifier of the message to be sent. The `EM_LINEINDEX` constant contains the numeric identifier of the message, indicating that you want to determine the character position of the cursor from the start of the current line. The next parameter is the `message` parameter, and a value of `-1` indicates to start from the beginning of the current line. The last parameter is not used and thus a value of `0` is passed.

The character index returned is always the beginning of any selected text, so the value returned from the `SendMessage` function is subtracted from the `SelectionStart` property of the `RichTextBoxExtended` control and a value of `1` is added to the entire results, as the number returned is a zero-based character position.

To retrieve the current line number in the `RichTextBoxExtended` control, another call is made using the `SendMessage` function. This time the `EM_LINEFROMCHAR` constant is used. This message returns the line number where the cursor is positioned. Again you specify a value of `-1` for the message parameter to indicate that the value returned should be from the start of the `RichTextBoxExtended` control. The last parameter is not used and a value of `0` is passed for it. The value returned from this call is a zero-based index, so you add a value of `1` to the results returned.

Finally, you return a new `Point`, passing the constructor of this class the X and Y coordinates of the cursor contained in the `intX` and `intY` variables.

```
Public ReadOnly Property CursorPosition() As Point
    Get
        'Get the column position
        intX = Me.SelectionStart - SendMessage(Me.Handle, EM_LINEINDEX, _
            -1, 0) + 1
        'Get the line number
        intY = SendMessage(Me.Handle, EM_LINEFROMCHAR, -1, 0) + 1
        'Return the results as a new Point
        Return New Point(intX, intY)
    End Get
End Property
```

RichTextBoxExtended_TextChanged Event Handler Procedure

When you extend an existing class that exposes events such as the `TextChanged` event shown in the next procedure and you add code to that procedure in your extended class, the code in the extended class is executed before the code for the same event in the form that is hosting that control.

In other words, the Notepad Plus application uses the `RichTextBoxExtended` control and implements code for the `TextChanged` event. However, the code for this event is executed in this class before it is executed in the Notepad form.

The `TextChanged` event is used to reset the `intStartIndex` variable if the text in the `RichTextBox` control has been cleared. This is the variable that keeps track of the starting index of the word being typed.

```
Private Sub RichTextBoxExtended_TextChanged(ByVal sender As Object, _
    ByVal e As System.EventArgs) Handles Me.TextChanged

    'Reset the starting index if the text was cleared
    If Me.Text.Length = 0 Then
```

```
                intStartIndex = 0
        End If
    End Sub
```

RichTextBoxExtended_KeyUp Event Handler Procedure

The KeyUp event is used to determine whether the key just pressed and released was a space key. This procedure also checks the Length property of the Text property to determine whether the existing text was cleared. If so, it resets the intStartIndex variable to a value of 0.

The next thing that happens in this procedure is a check of the KeyData property of the KeyEventArgs class. This property returns the key constant from the Keys enumeration of the key just released. A comparison is made against the Space constant from the Keys enumeration and if a match is made, then the code in the If...Then statement is executed.

The first thing that you do here is capture the ending index of the current word using the SelectionStart property minus 1, which accounts for the space that was just entered. Next, you want to recalculate the starting index of the word just typed if the intStartIndex variable is greater than the SelectionStart property. This accounts for the user clicking in different areas of the text and typing.

The starting index is recalculated by getting the position of the last space in the text, + 1, from the start of the Text property up to the SelectionStart property. The SelectionStart property returns the starting point of selected text in the RichTextBoxExtended control or the insertion point for text if no text has been selected.

If the starting index has to be recalculated, then the ending index of the last word also must be recalculated and is set to the SelectionStart property minus 1 to account for the space just typed.

Once the intStartIndex and intEndIndex are verified to be valid or have been recalculated, a new thread is started by a call to the RunWorkerAsync method of the AutoCorrect object. The RunWorkerAsync method of the BackgroundWorker class is an overloaded method that either accepts no parameters or accepts an Object as a parameter, meaning that it will accept anything that you pass it. In this case, you are passing this method the actual word to be checked against the auto-correct list:

```vb
    Private Sub RichTextBoxExtended_KeyUp(ByVal sender As Object, _
        ByVal e As System.Windows.Forms.KeyEventArgs) Handles Me.KeyUp

        'Reset the starting index if the text was cleared
        If Me.Text.Length = 0 Then
            intStartIndex = 0
        End If

        'If the key pressed was the space key...
        If e.KeyData = Keys.Space Then
            'Set the ending index
            intEndIndex = Me.SelectionStart - 1
            'Recalculate the starting index if necessary
            If intStartIndex > Me.SelectionStart Then
                intStartIndex = Me.Text.Substring(0, _
                    Me.SelectionStart - 1).LastIndexOf(" "c) + 1
                intEndIndex = Me.SelectionStart - 1
```

```
                End If
                'Check the word that was typed
                AutoCorrect.RunWorkerAsync(Me.Text.Substring( _
                    intStartIndex, intEndIndex - intStartIndex))
            End If
        End Sub
```

AutoCorrect_DoWork Event Handler Procedure

When you call the RunWorkerAsync method of the BackgroundWorker class, it raises the DoWork event. The AutoCorrect_DoWork procedure is the event handler procedure for this event. The first thing that happens in this procedure is the declaration of the strWords String array.

Next, the first item in this String array is set to the word passed to this procedure via the Argument property of the DoWorkEventArgs class. Then the second item in this String array is set to an empty string.

```
        Private Sub AutoCorrect_DoWork(ByVal sender As Object, _
            ByVal e As System.ComponentModel.DoWorkEventArgs) _
            Handles AutoCorrect.DoWork

            'Declare local variable
            Dim strWords(2) As String

            'Get the word to check
            strWords(0) = e.Argument

            'Set the replacement word to an empty string
            strWords(1) = String.Empty
```

Using the ContainsKey method of the SortedList class, you can quickly determine whether the word you are looking for is in the auto-correct list. The ContainsKey method returns a Boolean value indicating whether the key is found. If it is, then you set the second item in the strWords String array using the Item property of the arrAutoCorrectList. You access a specific item in the SortedList by using its key, which is the word being checked.

Finally, you set the Result property of the DoWorkEventArgs class to the strWords String array:

```
            'Get the replacement word if one exists
            If arrAutoCorrectList.ContainsKey(strWords(0)) Then
                strWords(1) = arrAutoCorrectList.Item(strWords(0))
            End If

            'Return the result
            e.Result = strWords
        End Sub
```

AutoCorrect_RunWorkerCompleted Event Handler Procedure

The RunWorkerCompleted event is raised when the background thread has completed its work. Just as a side note here, the Result property of the RunWorkerCompletedEventArgs class is set to the Result property of the DoWorkEventArgs class, so it's important that you set the Result property in the DoWork event handler if you want to pass the results of that operation to this event handler.

In the `AutoCorrect_RunWorkerCompleted` procedure, you start by declaring a `String` array, just as in the previous event handler. Then you set this `String` array to the `Result` property of the `RunWorkerCompletedEventArgs` class, which contains the results from the `DoWork` event handler.

If the `Length` property of the second word in the `String` array is greater than zero, you replace the word in the `RichTextBoxExtended` control with the word contained in the `String` array. You do so by first selecting the current word in the `RichTextBoxExtended` control by calling the `Select` method of the `RichTextBoxExtended` control, passing it the starting index of the word and the length of the word.

Next, replace the selected text with the word from the `strWords` `String` array. Set the `SelectionLength` property to a value of `0` so no text is selected, and then set the `SelectionStart` property to the `intEndIndex` + `1` so that the user can continue typing.

Finally, you need to set the `intStartIndex` to the end of the word just replaced or the end of the current word. This is done by finding the index of the next space in the text starting at the beginning of the last word + `1` to account for the actual space.

If the `intStartIndex` variable equals a value of `-1` it means that no space was found. It's possible the user just stopped typing, so the `intStartIndex` is set to the length of the text contained in the `RichTextBoxExtended` control.

```
Private Sub AutoCorrect_RunWorkerCompleted(ByVal sender As Object, _
    ByVal e As System.ComponentModel.RunWorkerCompletedEventArgs) _
    Handles AutoCorrect.RunWorkerCompleted

    'Declare local variable
    Dim strWords(2) As String

    'Get the results passed
    strWords = CType(e.Result, String())

    'Replace the word if a replacement exists
    If strWords(1).Length > 0 Then
        Me.Select(intStartIndex, strWords(0).Length)
        Me.SelectedText = strWords(1)
        Me.SelectionLength = 0
        Me.SelectionStart = intEndIndex + 1
    End If

    'Find the end of the word
    intStartIndex = Me.Text.IndexOf(" "c, intStartIndex + 1) + 1
    If intStartIndex = -1 Then
        intStartIndex = Me.Text.Length
    End If
End Sub
```

That wraps up the code in the `RichTextBoxExtended` class. There are very few procedures in this class, but what has been implemented has extended the functionality of the `RichTextBox` control significantly.

Notepad Form

The Notepad form implements the `RichTextBoxExtended` control, so all of the code in this form is simple, to-the-point code that supports the UI (e.g., cut, copy, paste, open, save, etc.). Therefore, because there is no significant code that needs to be explained, I'll move on to the code for the last part of the application: the SpellCheckDialog form.

SpellCheckDialog Form

The SpellCheckDialog form contains several functions and procedures. However, most of the functions and procedures are simple and merely call other functions and procedures or implement basic code. Covered here are details of the major procedures listed in Table 6-2.

SpellCheck Procedure

The main procedure in the SpellCheckDialog form is the `SpellCheck` procedure, so I'll start there. This procedure begins by declaring a couple of variables and objects that are local to this procedure. The `blnProcess` variable is used to determine whether a word should be processed for spelling errors. Any word that has been chosen to be ignored throughout the spell check process is added to an `ArrayList`. The `objEnumerator` object is used to enumerate through the list of ignored words, comparing them to the current word being processed:

```
Private Sub SpellCheck()
    'Declare local variables and objects
    Dim blnProcess As Boolean = True
    Dim objEnumerator As IEnumerator = arrIgnoredWords.GetEnumerator
```

An initial check of the `inStartIndex` variable against the `Length` property of the `Text` property in the `RichTextBoxExtended` control quickly lets you know whether you have reached the end of the data. If so, a call to the `SpellCheckComplete` procedure is made and then you exit this procedure.

The next line of code calls the `FindEndOfWord` procedure to find the end of the current word, setting that value in the `intEndIndex` variable. Finally, you extract the word to be checked from the `RichTextBoxExtended` control:

```
    'If the start index is equal to or greater then the length...
    If intStartIndex >= txtData.Text.Length Then
        SpellCheckComplete()
        Exit Sub
    End If

    'Find the end of the word
    intEndIndex = FindEndOfWord()

    'Get the word
    strWord = txtData.Text.Substring(intStartIndex, _
        intEndIndex - intStartIndex)
```

The next check compares the word to check for spelling against the list of words to be ignored. This list is built when the user clicks the Ignore All button in the `SpellCheckDialog` form. You enumerate through the list of words in the `arrIgnoredWords` ArrayList, comparing them against the `strWord` variable. If a match is found, then you set the `blnProcess` variable to `False` and exit the `While...End While` loop:

```
'If this a word to ignore
While objEnumerator.MoveNext
    If objEnumerator.Current = strWord Then
        blnProcess = False
        'A match was found, look no further
        Exit While
    End If
End While
```

A call is made to the `IsWordMisspelled` function to process the current word and check it for spelling errors. If that function returns a value of `True`, indicating the word is misspelled, you turn on the error flag in the `blnErrors` variable and then get a list of suggested replacement words via a call to the `SpellingSuggestions` method. The error flag is used in the `SpellCheckComplete` procedure to determine whether the SpellCheckDialog form can be closed automatically.

```
If blnProcess Then
    'Check the word for spelling
    If objSpellChecker.IsWordMisspelled(strWord) Then

        'Turn on the error flag
        blnErrors = True

        'Get a list of suggested words
        strSuggestions = objSpellChecker.SpellingSuggestions(strWord)
```

After you have a list of suggested words, you need to clear the previous list of words from the `lstSuggestions` ListBox by calling the `Clear` method on the `Items` property. Then you enumerate through the new list of suggested words and add them to the `lstSuggestions` ListBox.

You always want to ensure that the word being checked is in view in the SpellCheckDialog form, so you select the word and then call the `ScrollToCaret` method, which automatically scrolls the data in the `RichTextBoxExtended` into view:

```
'Add the suggested words to the list
lstSuggestions.Items.Clear()
For Each strSuggestion In strSuggestions
    lstSuggestions.Items.Add(strSuggestion)
Next

'Select the word and scroll the word into view
txtData.Select(intStartIndex, intEndIndex - intStartIndex)
txtData.ScrollToCaret()
```

Because you are using a `RichTextBoxExtended` control, and words in the control might have been set to various fonts and colors, you want to preserve those attributes before changing the color and setting the font to bold. You do this in the next few lines of code.

Once the original color and font of the word have been saved, set the color of the word to red and set the font style to bold so that the word is readily identifiable as the word being checked and misspelled (refer to Figure 6-2).

At this point, the word has been identified as being misspelled, the list of suggested words has been populated, the misspelled word has been scrolled into view, and it has been appropriately bolded and the font color set to red. Now you need to wait for user input about what to do next so you exit this procedure.

```
'Save the original color and font
objOriginalColor = New Color
objOriginalColor = txtData.SelectionColor
objOriginalFont = New Font(txtData.SelectionFont.FontFamily, _
    txtData.SelectionFont.Size, FontStyle.Regular)

'Highlight the misspelled word in bold red color
txtData.SelectionColor = Color.Red
txtData.SelectionFont = New Font( _
    txtData.SelectionFont.FontFamily, _
    txtData.SelectionFont.Size, FontStyle.Bold)
txtData.SelectionStart = intEndIndex
txtData.SelectionLength = 0

'Exit the procedure and wait for the user
Exit Sub
End If
End If
```

If the word being checked was not misspelled or was a word to be ignored, you need to update the `intStartIndex` variable to the beginning of the next word. This is done by setting the `intStartIndex` to the `intEndIndex + 1` to account for a space character.

Next, perform another check to determine whether you are at the end of the data. If you are not, then perform a recursive call to this procedure. If you are at the end of the data, then you call the `SpellCheckComplete` procedure.

The `SpellCheckComplete` procedure is not covered here but it simply displays a dialog box indicating that the spell check is complete and closes the SpellCheckDialog form.

```
'Increment the start index
intStartIndex = intEndIndex + 1

'If we are not at the end of data...
If intStartIndex < txtData.Text.Length Then
    'Perform a recursive call to this procedure
    SpellCheck()
Else
    SpellCheckComplete()
End If

End Sub
```

FindEndOfWord Function

The `FindEndOfWord` function finds the end of the current word to be checked. The `intStartIndex` variable points to the beginning of the current word and this function finds the space character following the word and returns that position in the `intIndex` variable.

Next, a quick check of the `intIndex` variable determines whether a space was found. A value of `-1` indicates that no space was found, so the `Length` property of the `Text` property of the `RichTextBoxExtended` control is then set in the `intIndex` variable, indicating that this is the last word to be checked. Finally, the `intIndex` variable is returned from this function, indicating the end of the current word:

```
Private Function FindEndOfWord() As Integer
    'Find the end of the word
    intIndex = txtData.Text.IndexOf(" "c, intStartIndex)
    If intIndex = -1 Then
        intIndex = txtData.Text.Length
    End If
    Return intIndex
End Function
```

RevertWord Procedure

The `RevertWord` procedure reverts the current word being checked back to its original color and font style. First, select the current word by calling the `Select` method on the `RichTextBoxExtended` control and set the `SelectionColor` property to the saved color. Then set the `SelectionFont` to the saved font. Next, set the `SelectionStart` property using the `intEndIndex` variable and then set the `SelectionLength` property to `0`, which effectively deselects the word:

```
Private Sub RevertWord()
    'Revert the word back to it's original state
    txtData.Select(intStartIndex, intEndIndex - intStartIndex)
    txtData.SelectionColor = objOriginalColor
    txtData.SelectionFont = objOriginalFont
    txtData.SelectionStart = intEndIndex
    txtData.SelectionLength = 0
End Sub
```

btnIgnoreOnce_Click Event Handler Procedure

The code for the Ignore Once button is shown next. The first thing that you want to do here is check the `Text` property of this button. If the `Text` property equals `Resume`, then change the `Text` property back to `Ignore Once` and then call the `SpellCheck` procedure to continue checking the rest of the text.

If the `Text` property is already set to Ignore Once, then revert the word back to its original state and then increment the starting index. After that, a quick call to the `Refresh` method of the `RichTextBoxExtended` control is in order so that the word that was bold and red can be seen in its original state. Then the `SpellCheck` procedure is called to check the next word.

Because the `SpellCheck` procedure can call itself recursively, it will consume all of the processing time for this thread. Therefore, the data in the `RichTextBoxExtended` control will not be refreshed until the

SpellCheck procedure stops. This is why a call to the Refresh method of the RichTextBoxExtended control is made: to refresh the display of data before the SpellCheck procedure starts again.

```
Private Sub btnIgnoreOnce_Click(ByVal sender As System.Object, _
    ByVal e As System.EventArgs) Handles btnIgnoreOnce.Click

    If btnIgnoreOnce.Text = "Resume" Then
        btnIgnoreOnce.Text = "Ignore Once"
    Else
        'Revert the word
        RevertWord()

        'Increment the start index
        intStartIndex = intEndIndex + 1

        'Refresh the data
        txtData.Refresh()
    End If

    'Go to the next
    SpellCheck()
End Sub
```

btnIgnoreAll_Click Event Handler Procedure

The event handler procedure for the Ignore All button begins by adding the word being checked to the list of words to be ignored. Then the word is reverted back to its original state by a call to the RevertWord procedure, after which the starting index is incremented to the next word. The Refresh method is called on the RichTextBoxExtended control and then a call is made to the SpellCheck procedure to check the next word:

```
Private Sub btnIgnoreAll_Click(ByVal sender As System.Object, _
    ByVal e As System.EventArgs) Handles btnIgnoreAll.Click

    'Add the word to the ignore all list
    arrIgnoredWords.Add(strWord)

    'Revert the word
    RevertWord()

    'Increment the start index
    intStartIndex = intEndIndex + 1

    'Refresh the data
    txtData.Refresh()

    'Go to the next
    SpellCheck()
End Sub
```

ChangeWord Procedure

When it has been determined that a word is to be changed, a call is made to the ChangeWord procedure. This procedure begins by finding the end of the current word and setting that position in the intEndIndex variable. Then the word is selected in the `RichTextBoxExtended` control via a call to the `Select` method. Then the `SelectedText` property, which now contains the current word, is set to the replacement word selected by the user from the list of suggested words using the `SelectedItem` property of the `lstSuggestions ListBox`:

```
Private Sub ChangeWord()
    'Find the end of the word
    intEndIndex = FindEndOfWord()

    'Select the word
    txtData.Select(intStartIndex, intEndIndex - intStartIndex)

    'Replace the selected misspelled word with the
    'selected suggested word
    txtData.SelectedText = lstSuggestions.SelectedItem
```

The replacement word could be shorter or longer than the word that it replaced, so you need to find the new ending index of the current word. Therefore, a call to the `FindEndOfWord` function is made again and the return value is set in the `intEndIndex` variable. Then you return the replaced word to its original color and font by calling the `RevertWord` procedure. Finally, increment the starting index using the ending index plus a value of 1 to account for the space character:

```
    'Find the new end of the word
    intEndIndex = FindEndOfWord()

    'Revert the word
    RevertWord()

    'Increment the start index
    intStartIndex = intEndIndex + 1
End Sub
```

btnChange_Click Event Handler Procedure

The `btnChange_Click` procedure is the event handler for the `Change` button and is executed when the user wants to change the currently misspelled word. The first check in this procedure is to ensure that a word has been selected by calling the `IsWordSelected` function. That function merely checks the `ListBox` to ensure that a word has been selected. If not, it displays a message box box to the user, indicating that they must select a word. That function returns a value of `True` if a word has been selected, and a value of `False` if a word has not been selected.

If a replacement word was selected, then a call to the `ChangeWord` procedure is made and the data in the `RichTextBoxExtended` control is refreshed. Then you call the `SpellCheck` procedure to continue checking the rest of the text:

```
Private Sub btnChange_Click(ByVal sender As System.Object, _
    ByVal e As System.EventArgs) Handles btnChange.Click

    'Validate something was selected
    If IsWordSelected() Then
        'Change the word
        ChangeWord()

        'Refresh the data
```

```
            txtData.Refresh()

            'Go to the next
            SpellCheck()
        End If
End Sub
```

btnChangeAll_Click Event Handler Procedure

The btnChangeAll_Click procedure is a little more involved than its btnChange_Click procedure counterpart. This procedure must not only change the current word, but also go through the rest of the text looking for the same word, replacing that word and at the same time not losing track of the current position in the text for the current word.

Given all that this procedure must do, it starts out with a couple of local variable declarations. The first variable is used to save the starting index, and the second variable is used to save the word that is to be replaced.

Next, a quick check is made to ensure that a replacement word was selected, and then the current word is replaced by a call to the ChangeWord procedure. After that, save the current starting index in the intSavedStartIndex variable.

```
Private Sub btnChangeAll_Click(ByVal sender As System.Object, _
    ByVal e As System.EventArgs) Handles btnChangeAll.Click

    'Declare local variables
    Dim intSavedStartIndex As Integer
    Dim strWordtoReplace As String = strWord

    'Validate something was selected
    If IsWordSelected() Then
        'Change the word
        ChangeWord()

        'Save the current starting index
        intSavedStartIndex = intStartIndex
```

Now start a loop to process the rest of the text, looking only for the word that was just replaced. The first line of code inside the While...End While loop is a call to the FindEndOfWord function to find the end of the current word being checked.

Then you extract the word and check it against the word to be replaced. If it is the same word, then you make a call to the ChangeWord procedure. Otherwise, you increment the starting index and start this loop over again.

```
        'Loop through the rest of the words replacing all
        While intStartIndex < txtData.Text.Length
            'Find the end of the word
            intEndIndex = FindEndOfWord()

            'Get the word
            strWord = txtData.Text.Substring(intStartIndex, _
                intEndIndex - intStartIndex)
```

```
                    'Change word if a match was found
                    If strWord = strWordtoReplace Then
                        'Change the word
                        ChangeWord()
                    Else
                        'Increment the start index
                        intStartIndex = intEndIndex + 1
                    End If
                End While
```

Once the `While...End While` loop has completed processing, you must restore the `intStartIndex` variable to its original value when this procedure was first called. Next, refresh the display of the `RichTextBox` to show the replaced words and then invoke the `SpellCheck` process again.

```
                'Restore the starting index for the rest of the spell check
                intStartIndex = intSavedStartIndex

                'Refresh the data
                txtData.Refresh()

                'Go to the next
                SpellCheck()
            End If
        End Sub
```

txtData_KeyUp Event Handler Procedure

The last procedure that I want to cover in this form is the `txtData_KeyUp` procedure. This event handler is fired when the user edits text directly in the SpellCheckDialog form. The user typically does this when a word is identified as being misspelled but there are no suggested replacement words or the replacements words are not applicable. The user would then typically edit the word directly, attempting to correctly spell the misspelled word.

The first thing that happens in this procedure is that you must find the end of the current word. Then you return the word to its original state by calling the `RevertWord` procedure. Next, increment the starting index and change the text in the Ignore Once button to `Resume` so that the user can resume the spell checking of the rest of the text after completing all edits.

```
        Private Sub txtData_KeyUp(ByVal sender As Object, _
            ByVal e As System.Windows.Forms.KeyEventArgs) _
            Handles txtData.KeyUp

            'Find the new end of the word
            intEndIndex = FindEndOfWord()

            'Revert the word
            RevertWord()

            'Increment the start index
            intStartIndex = intEndIndex + 1

            'Change the text on the Ignore Once button
            btnIgnoreOnce.Text = "Resume"
        End Sub
```

The rest of the procedures in this form are simple procedures that need no further code explanation. Review the complete code in this form to ensure that you understand how all the pieces fit together.

Setting Up the Notepad Plus Application

You can set up the Notepad Plus application using the installer or by manually copying the required files to your computer. The first option provides an easy, fast approach to installing the program, whereas the second approach provides greater flexibility over where the files are installed.

Using the Installer

To install the Notepad Plus application, locate the `Chapter 06 - Multi-Threaded Note Pad\Installer` folder on the CD-ROM that came with this book and double-click the `setup.exe` program. You are prompted with the Application Install dialog. Clicking the Install button installs and launches the application. After the installer finishes, your program is ready to be used.

Manual Installation

To manually install the Notepad Plus application, first create a folder on your computer where you want to place the program executable file. Then locate the `Chapter 06 - Multi-Threaded Note Pad\Source` folder on the CD-ROM that came with this book and navigate to the `bin\Release` folder. Copy the following files from the `Release` folder to the folder that you created on your computer:

- ❏ `Microsoft.Office.Interop.Word.dll`
- ❏ `Microsoft.Vbe.Interop.dll`
- ❏ `Notepad Plus.exe`
- ❏ `Office.dll`
- ❏ `RichTextBoxEx.dll`
- ❏ `SortedList.obj`
- ❏ `Spelling.dll`
- ❏ `stdole.dll`

Configuring the Application

No special configuration of the application is required. You can execute the `Notepad Plus.exe` program and start using the application.

If, however, you want to make code changes to the application, you must ensure that you have Microsoft Office 2003 installed along with the Microsoft Office Primary Interop Assemblies. These can be downloaded from the Microsoft Download Center at `microsoft.com/downloads/details .aspx?FamilyId=3C9A983A-AC14-4125-8BA0-D36D67E0F4AD&displaylang=en`. The Interop Assemblies provide .NET applications with the necessary COM interfaces to the Microsoft Office 2003 components (e.g., Word, Excel, Outlook, etc.).

If you are using a different version of Microsoft Office, locate the Interop Assemblies for the version of Microsoft Office that you are using.

Summary

This chapter has introduced and explained several key concepts, the first of which is multi-threading. Version 2.0 of the .NET Framework introduced the `BackgroundWorker` class, which makes it easy for developers to implement multi-threading in their applications. You saw firsthand how easy this is in the `RichTextBoxExtended` control when multiple threads were defined and used.

The next key concept that was introduced was serializing and de-serializing objects to and from disk using the `BinaryFormatter` class. As you studied the code in the `RichTextBoxExtended` class or read through the text, it should have been apparent how important this concept is. It is hoped that you also thought of ways in which this technology might come in handy in your own applications.

Along with the previous two concepts, you learned how to extend an existing control within the .NET Framework to include additional functionality. This was evident with the auto-correct feature that was added to the `RichTextBox` control.

Finally, you learned how to interact with Microsoft Word 2003 by consuming the public methods and interfaces exposed through the Microsoft Office Interop Assemblies. This was evident in the `Spelling` component that tapped into Microsoft Word's rich spell checking features.

It is hoped that this chapter has provided you with more invaluable insight into the .NET Framework and that you have found some new and interesting features that you can implement in your own applications. The concepts introduced in this chapter can go a long way in enhancing and enriching your own applications.

7

Notepad Printing

The .NET Framework has come a long way since its first release in 2001. It has implemented functionality in various classes that make developing applications easier and faster. For example, the My namespace introduced in version 2.0 of the .NET Framework made a lot of common tasks such as accessing application and computer information easier to code and faster.

However, there is one area in which the .NET Framework is still lacking, and that is in providing feature-rich printing functionality. The framework provides classes that enable you to access the Print and Print Preview dialogs, but it lacks the actual classes that perform printing. This task is left up to the developer to implement, and it typically requires complex logic for formatting text on a page and sending it to the printer.

In this chapter I'll cover the implementation of feature-rich printing functionality in the RichTextBoxExtended control. This control has been enhanced with printing functionality that supports printing a document with various fonts and colors. In addition, the control implements this functionality so that all the user of the RichTextBoxExtended control has to do is to invoke the Print method to print the text. This enables a developer to use this control and automatically have the printing functionality already built in.

The main technologies used in this chapter are as follows:

- ❑ Using the PrintDocument, PrintPreviewDialog, and PrintDialog classes
- ❑ Using the WIN32 SendMessage API to format the print text and send it to the printer
- ❑ Support for printing the entire document, the current page, a range of pages, and a selection of text via selections made in the PrintDialog class

Using the Notepad Plus Application

The last chapter covered using the Notepad Plus application, so there's no need to cover that again. If you type a document or open an existing document, you'll be able to explore the printing functionality. To fully explore that functionality, you should open a document with at least three pages of text.

The File menu contains a menu item named Print Preview. Clicking this menu item invokes the code for the `PrintPreviewClass` and displays a Print Preview dialog box, as shown in Figure 7-1. This dialog box enables you to view how your document will look when it is printed; it also enables you to zoom the preview document in or out. Clicking the Print icon on this dialog box automatically sends the entire document to your computer's default printer.

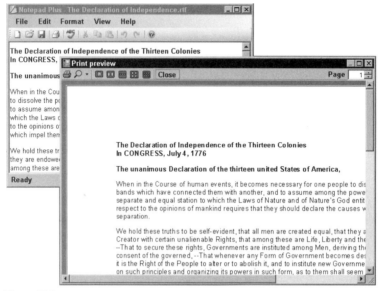

Figure 7-1

If you want to control what text is printed, you can click the Print menu item from the File menu. This opens the Print dialog box shown in Figure 7-2. From here, you can choose which printer to print to if you have more than one printer installed. You can also choose the page range to be printed.

All of the Page Range print options have been implemented in the `RichTextBoxExtended` control. When you select the All option, the entire document will be printed. If you have selected a specific section of text in the document, you can select the Selection option and only the selected text will be printed.

The Current Page option will print the page that your cursor is on. The `RichTextBoxExtended` control automatically keeps track of your cursor position in the control, and printing will occur for the page on which your cursor is located.

You can also choose the Pages option and specify a page range to print. This can be any range within the document, such as pages 1–3 or pages 25–32, depending on how many pages there are in your document and what you want to print.

The final printing option in the Notepad Plus application is the Print icon on the toolbar. Clicking this icon will cause the entire document to be printed to your computer's default printer. This is the standard behavior of most typical Windows applications and has been duplicated in this application.

Now that you've had a brief introduction to the printing functionality in the Notepad Plus application and how to use this new functionality, it's time to explore the design of the application.

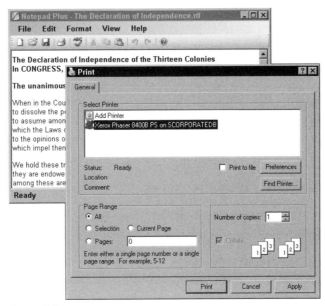

Figure 7-2

Design of the Notepad Plus Application

The design of the Notepad Plus application has been enhanced to implement the required .NET Framework classes required to support printing. These classes can be seen in Figure 7-3 and include the PrintPreviewDialog, PrintDialog, and PrintDocument classes. As you can see from the design, these classes all interact with the RichTextBoxExtended class, providing built-in printing functionality directly in this control.

Because the major design of the Notepad Plus application was covered in the last chapter and remains unchanged, this section only covers the printing enhancements to the RichTextBoxExtended class. The code to implement printing functionality in the Notepad form requires only three lines in total, which merely calls the appropriate printing methods in the RichTextBoxExtended control. I cover that code last in the "Code and Code Explanation" section.

RichTextBoxExtended Class

The printing functionality in the RichTextBoxExtended class has been implemented in three public procedures that enable the consumer of the RichTextBoxExtended control to display the Print Preview dialog box, to display the Print dialog box, and to print the entire document to the computer's default printer. These procedures are listed in Table 7-1.

The remaining procedures and functions in this class are private and support the actual printing of the text in the RichTextBoxExtended control. These procedures and functions are also listed in Table 7-1.

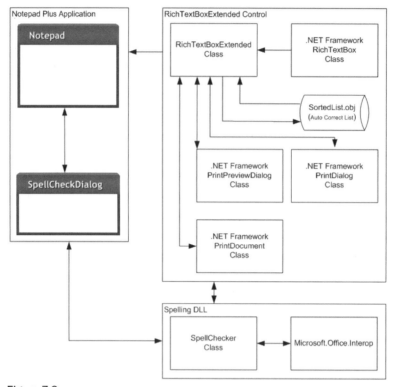

Figure 7-3

Table 7-1: Methods in the RichTextBoxExtended Class

Method	Return Type	Description
Public Sub ShowPrintPreviewDialog()	N/A	Displays the Print Preview dialog box
Public Sub ShowPrintDialog()	N/A	Displays the Print dialog box
Public Sub Print()	N/A	Prints the entire document to the computer's default printer
Private Sub RichTextBoxExtended_MouseDown (ByVal sender As Object, ByVal e As System.Windows.Forms .MouseEventArgs)	N/A	Keeps track of the current character index in the RichTextBoxExtended control
Private Function ConvertInchToTwip(ByVal unitOfMeaure As Integer)	Integer	Converts inches to twips (one twentieth of a point)

Table 7-1: Methods in the RichTextBoxExtended Class *(continued)*

Method	Return Type	Description
`Private Function FormatPrintRange(ByVal printPage As Boolean, ByVal e As PrintPageEventArgs, ByVal charFrom As Integer, ByVal charTo As Integer)`	Integer	Formats a page of contents from the `RichTextBoxExtended` control for printing
`Private Function MorePages()`	Boolean	Returns a value of `True` if there are more pages in the document to be printed; otherwise, returns `False`
`Private Sub RichTextBoxPrintDocument _BeginPrint(ByVal sender As Object, ByVal e As System.Drawing .Printing.PrintEventArgs)`	N/A	Initializes variables used for printing
`Private Sub RichTextBoxPrintDocument _PrintPage(ByVal sender As Object, ByVal e As System.Drawing .Printing.PrintPageEventArgs)`	N/A	Determines what print range was selected, if any, and prints data via a call to the `FormatPrintRange` function
`Private Sub RichTextBoxPrintDocument_EndPrint (ByVal sender As Object, ByVal e As System.Drawing.Printing .PrintEventArgs)`	N/A	Frees cached data from the `RichTextBoxExtended` control after printing

The major printing logic is implemented in two main procedures: `FormatPrintRange` and `RichTextBoxPrintDocument_PrintPage`. While all of the procedures listed in Table 7-1 are explained in the next section, the two procedures just mentioned are where you want to focus your attention.

Code and Code Explanation

In this section you'll learn how a document is actually printed via the procedures and functions listed in Table 7-1. Here is where you will see the details of the procedures and functions and gain an understanding of how the pieces fit and work together.

RichTextBoxExtended Class

As previously mentioned, all of the printing functionality for this application has been implemented in the `RichTextBoxExtended` class. This allows printing functionality to be built into this control out of the box (so to speak) and frees up developers who use this control to focus on other aspects of their application. All the developer has to do is call the appropriate printing methods in this control to have a document printed. No other code needs to be implement in the developer's forms. You can see how this works by looking at the printing methods in the Notepad form, which illustrates how simple this functionality is to implement.

I want to start off with the additional namespace required to support printing. As you might have surmised, it is the System.Drawing.Printing namespace. It is imported in this class after the other namespaces that were already imported in the previous chapter.

```
Imports System.Drawing.Printing
```

Next, a few private variables are used to keep track of a print range, the first and last characters on a page, as well as the current page and current character position on a page. These variables are listed here for reference:

```
'Private variables and objects
Private blnRangeSet As Boolean

...

Private intFirstCharacterOnPage As Integer
Private intLastCharacterOnPage As Integer
Private intSavedFirstCharacter As Integer
Private intCurrentPage As Integer
Private intCurrentCharacterPosition As Integer
```

The key to printing in the .NET Framework is the PrintDocument class. This class provides the events for printing a document and is consumed by the PrintPreviewDialog and PrintDialog classes. However, this class merely provides the events for printing; it does not provide any code for actually printing a document. This is where it is left up to developers to come up with their own code to print a document, and the lack of solid, feature-rich printing examples in the .NET Framework document is probably a frustration for most developers.

Notice that this variable has been declared with the WithEvents keyword. This automatically adds the properties, methods, and events in the Method Name combo box in the IDE and enables you to quickly access these for use in your code.

```
Private WithEvents RichTextBoxPrintDocument As PrintDocument
```

One additional constant is defined that is used with the SendMessage API when sending data to the printer: EM_FORMATRANGE. This constant instructs the SendMessage API to format a range of text for the specified output device (e.g., the printer).

```
Private Const EM_FORMATRANGE As Integer = &H439
```

Several WIN32 structures are required by the SendMessage API when printing. The first of these structures is STRUCT_RECT, which is used to define the margin and page boundaries of a print document. It is also used by the STRUCT_FORMATRANGE structure.

The next of these structures is the STRUCT_CHARRANGE structure; this structure is used to define the character range on a page. It is also used in the STRUCT_FORMATRANGE structure.

The last of the structures is the STRUCT_FORMATRANGE structure. This structure is used to hold all the information about the page to be printed as well as the device context of the printer to which the data is to be sent. This structure is copied to memory and is used by the SendMessage API when printing a page of data.

Notice that all of these structures have been defined using the StructLayoutAttribute class, as indicated by the StructLayout attribute. The common language runtime (CLR) normally controls the physical layout of the data fields of a structure in managed memory. However, when calling unmanaged code (e.g., a WIN32 API) the data structures must be in the layout required by the unmanaged code. Thus, using the Sequential constant from the LayoutKind enumeration forces the CLR to lay out the data members of these structures in the order in which they appear:

```
'Declare WIN32 Structures
<StructLayout(LayoutKind.Sequential)> _
Private Structure STRUCT_RECT
    Public left As Integer
    Public top As Integer
    Public right As Integer
    Public bottom As Integer
End Structure

<StructLayout(LayoutKind.Sequential)> _
Private Structure STRUCT_CHARRANGE
    Public cpMin As Integer
    Public cpMax As Integer
End Structure

<StructLayout(LayoutKind.Sequential)> _
Private Structure STRUCT_FORMATRANGE
    Public hdc As IntPtr
    Public hdcTarget As IntPtr
    Public rc As STRUCT_RECT
    Public rcPage As STRUCT_RECT
    Public chrg As STRUCT_CHARRANGE
End Structure
```

RichTextBoxExtended_MouseDown Event Handler Procedure

The first procedure that I want to cover is the RichTextBoxExtended_MouseDown event handler procedure. This procedure is fired whenever the user clicks the mouse and will get the current character index within the RichTextBoxExtended control. The GetCharIndexFromPosition function retrieves the index of the character nearest to the specified location as specified in the X, Y coordinates that are passed to this function. The value returned is saved in the intCurrentCharacterPosition variable and is used to determine the current page if the user chooses the Current Page option in the Print dialog box:

```
Private Sub RichTextBoxExtended_MouseDown(ByVal sender As Object, _
    ByVal e As System.Windows.Forms.MouseEventArgs) Handles Me.MouseDown

    'Get the current character index in the RichTextBox
    intCurrentCharacterPosition = _
        Me.GetCharIndexFromPosition(New Point(e.X, e.Y))
End Sub
```

ShowPrintPreviewDialog Procedure

The ShowPrintPreviewDialog procedure is a public method implemented in this class that enables developers using the RichTextBoxExtended control to show the Print Preview dialog box (refer to Figure 7-1) without having to write any code of their own. This procedure declares and instantiates a new PrintPreviewDialog class and then instantiates a new instance of the PrintDocument class declared in the RichTextBoxPrintDocument object.

Remember earlier that I mentioned that the PrintPreviewDialog class is one of two classes that consumes the PrintDocument class. The PrintDocument class controls the printing of a document and formats the pages of data, which are then consumed by the PrintPreviewDialog class.

The properties of the PrintPreviewDialog class are set next in the objPrintPreviewDialog object, which shows the Print Preview dialog box by calling the ShowDialog method on the PrintPreviewDialog class. The final line of code will be executed if the user clicks on the Print icon in the Print Preview dialog box:

```
Public Sub ShowPrintPreviewDialog()
    'Declare local objects
    Dim objPrintPreviewDialog As New PrintPreviewDialog

    'Instantiate a new instance of the PrintDocument
    RichTextBoxPrintDocument = New PrintDocument

    'Set PrintPreviewDialog properties
    With objPrintPreviewDialog
        .ClientSize = New Size(600, 400)
        .Document = RichTextBoxPrintDocument
        .Location = New Point(10, 10)
        .UseAntiAlias = True
    End With

    If objPrintPreviewDialog.ShowDialog = _
        Windows.Forms.DialogResult.OK Then
        'Invoke the Print method on the PrintDocument
        RichTextBoxPrintDocument.Print()
    End If
End Sub
```

ShowPrintDialog Procedure

The next public method available in this class is the ShowPrintDialog procedure. The developer using the RichTextBoxExtended control will call this method to display the Print dialog box, which enables the user to both select which printer to print to and select the print range to be printed.

The objPrintDialog object is declared and instantiated using the PrintDialog class. Then a new instance of the PrintDocument class is instantiated in the RichTextBoxPrintDocument object. Next, the properties of the PrintDialog class are set in the objPrintDialog object, which enables the full array of print range options.

Notice that the PrintDocument class declared in the RichTextBoxPrintDocument object is used by the PrintDialog class. Again, the PrintDocument class controls the printing of a document and formats the pages of data that are printed.

The Print dialog box is displayed by calling the ShowDialog method on the PrintDialog class and the next couple of lines of code are executed if the user clicks the Print button in the Print dialog box. These last two lines of code set the printer settings selected by the user in the Print dialog box in the RichTextBoxPrintDocument object and invoke the Print method on the RichTextBoxPrintDocument object:

```
Public Sub ShowPrintDialog()
    'Declare local objects
    Dim objPrintDialog As New PrintDialog

    'Instantiate a new instance of the PrintDocument
    RichTextBoxPrintDocument = New PrintDocument

    'Set the PrintDialog properties
    With objPrintDialog
        .AllowCurrentPage = True
        .AllowPrintToFile = True
        .AllowSelection = True
        .AllowSomePages = True
        .Document = RichTextBoxPrintDocument
        .UseEXDialog = True
    End With

    If objPrintDialog.ShowDialog = DialogResult.OK Then
        'Pass along the selected printer settings
        'to the PrintDocument
        RichTextBoxPrintDocument.PrinterSettings = _
            objPrintDialog.PrinterSettings
        'Invoke the Print method on the PrintDocument
        RichTextBoxPrintDocument.Print()
    End If
End Sub
```

Print Procedure

The last public method available in this class is the Print procedure. This procedure is called when the developer simply wants to enable the entire document to be sent to the default printer without prompting the user to select a printer or print range to be printed. This procedure instantiates a new instance of the PrintDocument class in the RichTextBoxPrintDocument object and then calls the Print method on this object.

This is typically the method that is called when the user clicks the Print icon on the toolbar and is the standard behavior in most Windows applications. When users want more control over what is to be printed or where it is to be printed, they would choose one of the print options in the File menu.

```
Public Sub Print()
    'Instantiate a new instance of the PrintDocument
    RichTextBoxPrintDocument = New PrintDocument

    'Invoke the Print method on the PrintDocument
    RichTextBoxPrintDocument.Print()
End Sub
```

ConvertInchToTwip Function

Now we have arrived at the procedures and functions that do the actual work of printing a document. The first function to be covered is the `ConvertInchToTwip` function. This function converts inches to twips and has been appropriately commented as shown in the following code. The .NET Framework deals with measurements in inches, whereas the WIN32 APIs deal with measurements in twips. Therefore, a function has been created to provide the appropriate conversion when defining the page margins and print area of the document.

To perform the conversion, multiply the `unitOfMeasure` parameter by 14.4 and convert the results into a whole number by using the `ToInt32` method of the `Integer` class. The `ToInt32` method will round the fractional portion of the number to the nearest whole number.

As a side note here, to automatically have a comment block like this inserted into your code, you would type three consecutive apostrophes above the procedure or function declaration. This instructs the IDE to automatically insert the summary, param, returns, and remarks tags in your code. If your procedure or function has parameters, then the `name` attribute of the `param` tag will automatically be populated with the parameter name. All you have to do is insert the appropriate comments in the tags provided in this comment block:

```
''' <summary>
''' Convert between 1/100 of an inch to a twip (1/1440 of an inch).
''' Inches are the unit of measure used by the .NET framework
''' and twips are the unit of measure used by the Win32 APIs
''' </summary>
''' <param name="unitOfMeasure">Value in 1/100 inch</param>
''' <returns>Value in twips</returns>
''' <remarks></remarks>
Private Function ConvertInchToTwip(ByVal unitOfMeasure As Integer) As Integer
    Return Convert.ToInt32(unitOfMeasure * 14.4)
End Function
```

FormatPrintRange Function

The next function is the `FormatPrintRange` function. Again, this function has been appropriately commented for quick reference. This is one of the two main sections of code used for printing. This function formats the text from the `RichTextBoxExtended` control into a printable page; and if the `printPage` parameter is `True`, it actually sends the page to the printer. If the `printPage` parameter is `False`, then this function merely formats a page of text to determine the last character on the page:

```
''' <summary>
''' Format the contents of the RichTextBox for printing
''' </summary>
''' <param name="printPage">If true, the page is formatted and printed.
''' If false, the page is formatted only.</param>
''' <param name="e">The PrintPageEventArgs object from the
''' PrintDocument class PrintPage event</param>
''' <param name="charFrom">Index of first character to be printed</param>
''' <param name="charTo">Index of last character to be printed</param>
''' <returns>Index of last character +1 that printed on the page</returns>
''' <remarks></remarks>
```

The parameters to this function are described in the preceding comments so there is no need to repeat that here. A number of variables and objects are defined in this function, as shown in the code that follows. The first of these is the wParam parameter for the SendMessage API function, which has been defined as an Integer data type. This parameter will be set to a value that determines whether the formatted page is to be actually printed or not. The intLastCharacter variable is used to receive the index of the last character on the formatted page.

Four structures are defined next, which hold the character range of text to be printed, the margins of the page, and the printable page area. The final structure is the stcFormatRange structure, which contains all of the information necessary to print a page of text.

The last two variable declarations are defined as pointers. The first one contains a pointer to the handle of the printer selected or the default printer. The last pointer is used to hold the memory location where the stcFormatRange structure is copied to.

```
Private Function FormatPrintRange(ByVal printPage As Boolean, _
    ByVal e As PrintPageEventArgs, ByVal charFrom As Integer, _
    ByVal charTo As Integer) As Integer

    'Declare variables and objects
    Dim wParam As Integer
    Dim intLastCharacter As Integer
    Dim stcCharRange As STRUCT_CHARRANGE
    Dim stcMarginRect As STRUCT_RECT
    Dim stcPageRect As STRUCT_RECT
    Dim stcFormatRange As STRUCT_FORMATRANGE
    Dim ptrPrinterDeviceContext As IntPtr
    Dim lParam As IntPtr
```

The print range is set in the stcCharRange structure, which contains the starting and ending characters in the print range. Next, the page margins are set in the stcMarginRect structure and the values of the printer margins are converted from inches to twips before being set in the structure. The page margins come from the PrinterSettings property of the RichTextBoxPrintDocument object, which is associated with either the selected printer or the default printer.

The stcPageRect structure is set to the printable page boundaries. This data comes from the PageBounds property of the RichTextBoxPrintDocument object and is converted from inches to twips before being set in the structure. Note that although the PageBounds property defines the printable area of a page, most printers cannot print to the defined edges of the physical page contained in this property.

```
'Specify which characters to print
stcCharRange.cpMin = charFrom
stcCharRange.cpMax = charTo

'Specify the area inside page margins
stcMarginRect.top = ConvertInchToTwip(e.MarginBounds.Top)
stcMarginRect.bottom = ConvertInchToTwip(e.MarginBounds.Bottom)
stcMarginRect.left = ConvertInchToTwip(e.MarginBounds.Left)
stcMarginRect.right = ConvertInchToTwip(e.MarginBounds.Right)

'Specify the page area
stcPageRect.top = ConvertInchToTwip(e.PageBounds.Top)
```

```
stcPageRect.bottom = ConvertInchToTwip(e.PageBounds.Bottom)
stcPageRect.left = ConvertInchToTwip(e.PageBounds.Left)
stcPageRect.right = ConvertInchToTwip(e.PageBounds.Right)
```

The `GetHdc` method of the `Graphics` class gets the handle to the device context associated with the `Graphics` object contained in the `RichTextBoxPrintDocument` object. The device context in this instance is a printer but could be any graphics device supported by the `Graphics` class, such as a control or a form. The handle to the printer is set in the `ptrPrinterDeviceContext` object.

Next, the `stcFormatRange` structure is populated with all the information about a printable page. This includes the character range to be printed, the handle to the printer, the target device, and the page margins and printable page area:

```
'Get device context of the selected printer
ptrPrinterDeviceContext = e.Graphics.GetHdc()

'Fill in the FORMATRANGE structure
stcFormatRange.chrg = stcCharRange
stcFormatRange.hdc = ptrPrinterDeviceContext
stcFormatRange.hdcTarget = ptrPrinterDeviceContext
stcFormatRange.rc = stcMarginRect
stcFormatRange.rcPage = stcPageRect
```

The `wParam` variable is set based on the value passed in the `printPage` parameter. If this page is to be formatted merely in order to determine the last printable character, then the `printPage` parameter will contain a value of `False`. If the page is to actually be printed, then the `printPage` parameter will contain a value of `True`.

The `stcFormatRange` is now ready to be copied to memory in preparation for the call to the `SendMessage` API. Before copying the `stcFormatRange` structure to memory, however, you must first allocate the appropriate amount of memory based on the size of the structure.

This is done via the `AllocCoTaskMem` method of the `Marshal` class. The `Marshal` class is a .NET Framework class that is used for allocating unmanaged memory and copying unmanaged memory blocks. The `AllocCoTaskMem` method allocates the requested memory and returns a pointer to that memory. The parameter to the `AllocCoTaskMem` method is the size in bytes of the memory to be allocated. In order to determine the size of the memory needed, a call is made to the `SizeOf` method to get the size of the `stcFormatRange` structure, in bytes.

Finally, once the appropriate amount of memory has been allocated and a pointer to the memory has been returned in the `lParam` variable, you need to actually copy the `stcFormatRange` structure to memory. This is done via a call to the `StructureToPtr` method. This method accepts three parameters: the data to be copied to memory, the pointer to the block of memory, and a `Boolean` value indicating whether to clear the existing data in the memory block before copying the new data:

```
'Zero means format the page, One means print the page
If printPage Then
    wParam = 1
Else
    wParam = 0
End If
```

```
'Allocate memory for the FORMATRANGE struct and
'copy the contents of the struct to this memory
lParam = Marshal.AllocCoTaskMem(Marshal.SizeOf(stcFormatRange))
Marshal.StructureToPtr(stcFormatRange, lParam, True)
```

Once the `stcFormatRange` structure has been copied to memory, it's time to call the `SendMessage` API to perform the actual printing, if required. You pass the `SendMessage` API the handle of the `RichTextBox`, the `EM_FORMATRANGE` constant that tells the `SendMessage` API which function it should perform, the `wParam` parameter, telling the `SendMessage` API whether or not to physically print the page, and the `lParam` pointer to the block of memory containing the data for the page. The return value from the `SendMessage` API will be the last character +1 that was printed on the page.

After printing the page, free the allocated memory by calling the `FreeCoTaskMem` method and passing it the pointer to the block of memory to be freed. Next, release the handle to the printer by calling the `ReleaseHdc` method on the `Graphics` object and pass it the pointer to the handle for the printer. Finally, you return the last character +1 that was printed on the current page:

```
'Send the Win32 message to format the range
intLastCharacter = SendMessage(Me.Handle, EM_FORMATRANGE, wParam, lParam)

'Free allocated memory
Marshal.FreeCoTaskMem(lParam)

'Release the device context
e.Graphics.ReleaseHdc(ptrPrinterDeviceContext)

Return intLastCharacter
End Function
```

MorePages Function

The `MorePages` function returns a `Boolean` value indicating whether there are more pages to be printed. This function examines the `intFirstCharacterOnPage` variable, which contains the first character on the page, and compares that value to the `TextLength` property of the `RichTextBox` control. The `intFirstCharacterOnPage` variable is incremented each time a page is printed and is set to the index of the next character to be printed on the subsequent page:

```
Private Function MorePages() As Boolean
    'Are there more pages...
    If intFirstCharacterOnPage < Me.TextLength Then
        Return True
    Else
        Return False
    End If
End Function
```

RichTextBoxPrintDocument_BeginPrint Event Handler Procedure

The next and last three procedures to be covered are the event handlers for the `PrintDocument` class, which is defined in the `RichTextBoxPrintDocument` object. The first of these event handlers is the `RichTextBoxPrintDocument_BeginPrint` procedure. This procedure is fired before any printing takes place and is only fired once. This is the perfect place to initialize the variables that will be used during the printing operation. The variables listed in the following code are self-explanatory and are simply set to default values based on their data types:

```
Private Sub RichTextBoxPrintDocument_BeginPrint(ByVal sender As Object, _
    ByVal e As System.Drawing.Printing.PrintEventArgs) _
    Handles RichTextBoxPrintDocument.BeginPrint

    'Initializes print variables
    intFirstCharacterOnPage = 0
    intLastCharacterOnPage = 0
    intCurrentPage = 0
    blnRangeSet = False
End Sub
```

RichTextBoxPrintDocument_PrintPage Event Handler Procedure

The next event handler of the `RichTextBoxPrintDocument` object is the `RichTextBoxPrintDocument_PrintPage` procedure. This is the other main section of code used for printing. I have added a comment at the beginning of this procedure because it is noteworthy and can save you a lot of time troubleshooting blank pages. Whenever this event is fired, a blank page is automatically created. It is up to you to put something on this page before sending it to the printer. If you do not and this procedure is called again, a blank page will be printed.

Thus, the `blnPagePrinted` variable is defined at the top of this procedure and has a default value of `False`. A `Do While...Loop` has been defined and the code inside this loop will execute while the `blnPagePrinted` variable is `False`. This procedure is only called when the user actually requests something to be printed, so there's no need to worry about branching into this procedure unnecessarily.

```
Private Sub RichTextBoxPrintDocument_PrintPage(ByVal sender As Object, _
    ByVal e As System.Drawing.Printing.PrintPageEventArgs) _
    Handles RichTextBoxPrintDocument.PrintPage

    'A blank page is automatically created when this event is fired.
    'Therefore, we need to stay in this event until a page of data
    'is printed, otherwise we'll end up printing blank pages.

    Dim blnPagePrinted As Boolean = False

    Do While Not blnPagePrinted
```

A `Select...Case` statement has been defined to select the appropriate `PrintRange` enumeration from the `PrintRange` property of the `PrintSettings` property of the `PrintDocument` class defined in the `RichTextBoxPrintDocument` object. The `PrintRange` property is set to the print range option chosen in the Print dialog box or has a default value of `AllPages` if the Print dialog box was not displayed.

The first `Case` statement handles the `AllPages` constant of the `PrintRange` enumeration. The code inside this `Case` statement prints all pages in a document. The first thing that happens inside this `Case` statement is a call to the `FormatPrintRange` function to print the first page. The first character on the next page is set in the `intFirstCharacterOnPage` variable and then the `HasMorePages` property of the `PrintPageEventArgs` is set by a call to the `MorePages` function. Then the `blnPagePrinted` variable is set to `True` so you can exit the `Do While...Loop` statement block:

```
'Find the range to print
Select Case RichTextBoxPrintDocument.PrinterSettings.PrintRange
    Case PrintRange.AllPages
        'Print the current page and get the index of the first
        'character on the next page
        intFirstCharacterOnPage = FormatPrintRange(True, e, _
            intFirstCharacterOnPage, Me.TextLength)
        'See if there are more pages to print
        e.HasMorePages = MorePages()
        'Turn the page printed flag on
        blnPagePrinted = True
```

The `Case` statement for the `CurrentPage` constant of the `PrintRange` enumeration handles printing the current page. There's a lot going on inside this `Case` statement, as you need to determine the current page by determining on what page the cursor resides.

The first thing that happens in this `Case` statement is a call to the `FormatPrintRange` function to get the first character on the next page without actually printing the current page. Therefore, a value of `False` has been passed to this function and the first character on the next page is set in the `intLastCharacterOnPage` variable. Then a check is made to determine whether the current character position contained in the `intCurrentCharacterPosition` variable is greater than or equal to the first character on the page, which is contained in the `intFirstCharacterOnPage` variable, and whether the current character position is less than the value contained in the `intLastCharacterOnPage` variable. If this logic is true, then a call is made to the `FormatPrintRange` function to print the current page.

Next, the `HasMorePages` property is set to `False` because you have already printed the current page. Then the `blnPagePrinted` variable is set to `True` to exit the `Do While...Loop` statement block.

If the current character position is not on the current page, then the code in the `Else` block is executed and you increment the `intFirstCharacterOnPage` variable using the value that was set in the `intLastCharacterOnPage` variable. Then you set the `HasMorePages` property according to the value returned by the `MorePages` function:

```
Case PrintRange.CurrentPage
    'Get the last character on the page without
    'printing the page
    intLastCharacterOnPage = FormatPrintRange(False, e, _
        intFirstCharacterOnPage, Me.TextLength)
    'If the current character position is in the range
    'of the current page...
    If intCurrentCharacterPosition >= intFirstCharacterOnPage _
        And intCurrentCharacterPosition < _
        intLastCharacterOnPage Then
        'Print the current page
        FormatPrintRange(True, e, intFirstCharacterOnPage, _
            Me.TextLength)
        'Set the HasMorePages property to false as we have
        'already printed the current page
        e.HasMorePages = False
```

```
            'Turn the page printed flag on
            blnPagePrinted = True
        Else
            'Reset the first character to the next page
            intFirstCharacterOnPage = intLastCharacterOnPage
            'See if there are more pages to print
            e.HasMorePages = MorePages()
        End If
```

The Case statement that handles printing a selection of text is fairly straightforward. First a check is made to determine whether the range has been set. If it hasn't been set, then the code inside the first If...Then block is executed. Here you want to set the first character on the page by using the SelectionStart property of the RichTextBox control. This property returns the starting character index of the first high-lighted character. Then you set the last character on the page using the SelectionLength property of the RichTextBox control. This property returns the length of the selected text. Finally, you set the blnRangeSet variable to True so this block of code is not executed again.

Next, print the range of selected text by calling the FormatPrintRange function, passing it the range of the selected text. The first character on the next page is returned in the intFirstCharacterOnPage variable and then a check is made to determine whether this value is greater than or equal to the value contained in the intLastCharacterOnPage variable. If the intFirstCharacterOnPage variable is not greater than or equal to the intLastCharacterOnPage variable, then there are no more pages to be printed and the HasMorePages property is set to False. Otherwise, it is set to True. Regardless of whether or not the HasMorePages property is True or False, the blnPagePrinted variable is set to True so you can exit the Do While...Loop statement block:

```
        Case PrintRange.Selection
            If Not blnRangeSet Then
                'Set the first and last character in the print range
                intFirstCharacterOnPage = Me.SelectionStart
                intLastCharacterOnPage = _
                    Me.SelectionStart + Me.SelectionLength
                blnRangeSet = True
            End If
            'Print only the selected text
            intFirstCharacterOnPage = FormatPrintRange(True, e, _
                intFirstCharacterOnPage, intLastCharacterOnPage)
            If intFirstCharacterOnPage >= intLastCharacterOnPage Then
                'Set the HasMorePages property to false as we have
                'already printed the selected text
                e.HasMorePages = False
            Else
                'Set the HasMorePages property to true as there is
                'more text to be printed
                e.HasMorePages = True
            End If
            'Turn the page printed flag on
            blnPagePrinted = True
```

This last Case statement is used when a range of pages are to be printed. The first thing that you want to do here is save the first character on the page in the intSavedFirstCharacter variable. Then make a call to the FormatPrintRange function, passing it a value of False because you actually don't want to print the current page. Next, increment the current page counter variable and then check the current page count against the range of pages specified in the `FromPage` and `ToPage` properties of the `PrinterSettings` property of the `RichTextBoxPrintDocument` object.

If the current page contained in the `intCurrentPage` variable is greater than or equal to the `FromPage` property and is less than or equal to the `ToPage` property, then the `intFirstCharacterOnPage` variable is set using the `intSavedFirstCharacter` variable. Then a call is made to the `FormatPrintRange` function to have the current page printed and the `blnPagePrinted` variable is set to `True`.

If the current page number equals the `ToPage` property, then set the `HasMorePages` property to `False`. Otherwise, there are more pages in the range to be printed and you set the `HasMorePages` property according the value returned from the `MorePages` function.

```
Case PrintRange.SomePages
    'Save the first character
    intSavedFirstCharacter = intFirstCharacterOnPage
    'Determine the print range of the page
    intFirstCharacterOnPage = FormatPrintRange(False, e, _
        intFirstCharacterOnPage, Me.TextLength)
    'Increment the page count
    intCurrentPage += 1
    'If the current page is in the range...
    If intCurrentPage >= _
        RichTextBoxPrintDocument.PrinterSettings.FromPage _
        And intCurrentPage <= _
        RichTextBoxPrintDocument.PrinterSettings.ToPage Then
        'Reset the first character on the page and print the page
        intFirstCharacterOnPage = intSavedFirstCharacter
        intFirstCharacterOnPage = FormatPrintRange(True, e, _
            intFirstCharacterOnPage, Me.TextLength)
        'Turn the page printed flag on
        blnPagePrinted = True
    End If
    If intCurrentPage = _
        RichTextBoxPrintDocument.PrinterSettings.ToPage Then
        'If this was the last page then set the
        'HasMorePages property to false
        e.HasMorePages = False
    Else
        'Set the HasMorePages property to true as there is
        'more pages to be printed
        e.HasMorePages = MorePages()
    End If
    End Select
    Loop
End Sub
```

RichTextBoxPrintDocument_EndPrint Event Handler Procedure

The last event handler for the `RichTextBoxPrintDocument` object and the last procedure to be covered is the `RichTextBoxPrintDocument_EndPrint` procedure. This procedure is executed only once when a document has completed printing (e.g., the `HasMorePages` property has been set to `False`).

During the printing process, the RichTextBox control will have cached the data, so another call to the SendMessage API is made to free the cached data. This is done by using the EM_FORMATRANGE constant and a value of 0 for the Message parameter and a Null pointer for the lParam parameter. This call effectively clears the cache held by the RichTextBox control:

```
Private Sub RichTextBoxPrintDocument_EndPrint(ByVal sender As Object, _
    ByVal e As System.Drawing.Printing.PrintEventArgs) _
    Handles RichTextBoxPrintDocument.EndPrint

    'Free cached data from RichTextBox after printing
    Dim lParam As New IntPtr(0)
    SendMessage(Me.Handle, EM_FORMATRANGE, 0, lParam)
End Sub
```

Notepad Form

As mentioned earlier, the Notepad form requires only three lines of code to implement printing functionality. This makes the job of the developer using the RichTextBoxExtended control easy, as it should be.

The Print button on the toolbar will cause the entire document to be printed to the computer's default printer. The PrintToolStripButton_Click event handler procedure simply calls the Print method on the RichTextBoxExtended control, which has been named txtData in the form:

```
Private Sub PrintToolStripButton_Click(ByVal sender As Object, _
    ByVal e As System.EventArgs) Handles PrintToolStripButton.Click

    txtData.Print()
End Sub
```

This next event handler procedure is for the Print Preview menu item in the File menu. Here you simply call the ShowPrintPreviewDialog method in the RichTextBoxExtended control to have the Print Preview dialog box displayed, as shown earlier in Figure 7-1.

```
Private Sub PrintPreviewToolStripMenuItem_Click(ByVal sender As Object, _
    ByVal e As System.EventArgs) Handles PrintPreviewToolStripMenuItem.Click

    txtData.ShowPrintPreviewDialog()
End Sub
```

The final printing event handler procedure in the Notepad form is the PrintToolStripMenuItem_Click procedure. This is the event handler procedure for the Print menu item in the File menu. This code calls the ShowPrintDialog method in the RichTextBoxExtended control to display the Print dialog box shown in Figure 7-2.

```
Private Sub PrintToolStripMenuItem_Click(ByVal sender As Object, _
    ByVal e As System.EventArgs) Handles PrintToolStripMenuItem.Click

    txtData.ShowPrintDialog()
End Sub
```

Setting Up the Notepad Plus Application

Setup of the Notepad Plus application was covered in the last chapter but is reproduced here so you don't have to flip back to look at it. You have two options for setting up the Notepad Plus application: using the installer or manually copying the required files to your computer. The first option provides an easy, fast approach to installing the program, whereas the second approach provides greater flexibility over where the files are installed.

Using the Installer

To install the Notepad Plus application, locate the `Chapter 07 -Notepad Printing\Installer` folder on the CD-ROM that came with this book and double-click the `setup.exe` program. You will be prompted with the Application Install dialog. Clicking the Install button will install and launch the application. Once the installer has installed your program, it is ready to be used.

Manual Installation

To manually install the Notepad Plus application, first create a folder on your computer where you want to place the program executable file. Then locate the `Chapter 07 -Notepad Printing\Source` folder on the CD-ROM that came with this book and navigate to the `bin\Release` folder. Copy the following files from the `Release` folder to the folder that you created on your computer:

- ❑ `Microsoft.Office.Interop.Word.dll`
- ❑ `Microsoft.Vbe.Interop.dll`
- ❑ `Notepad Plus.exe`
- ❑ `Office.dll`
- ❑ `RichTextBoxEx.dll`
- ❑ `SortedList.obj`
- ❑ `Spelling.dll`
- ❑ `stdole.dll`

Configuring the Application

No special configuration of the application is required. You can execute the `Notepad Plus.exe` program and start using the application.

If, however, you want to edit the application, you need to ensure that you have Microsoft Office 2003 installed along with the Microsoft Office Primary Interop Assemblies. These can be downloaded from the Microsoft Download Center at `microsoft.com/downloads/details.aspx?FamilyId=3C9A983A-AC14-4125-8BA0-D36D67E0F4AD&displaylang=en`. The Interop Assemblies provide .NET applications with the necessary COM interfaces to the Microsoft Office 2003 components (e.g., Word, Excel, Outlook, etc.).

If you are using a different version of Microsoft Office, you need to locate the Interop Assemblies for the version of Microsoft Office that you are using.

Using the Printing Functionality in Your Own Programs

The printing code that was covered in the `RichTextBoxExtended` class can be used in your own applications. This code could be placed in the form code that uses a `TextBox` control or a `RichTextBox` control.

You can even place this code in a separate class that can be used with any `TextBox` or `RichTextBox` control. If this is the route that you decide to take, you need to declare an object of the appropriate type (`TextBox` or `RichTextBox`) in the class and pass the constructor of the class the `TextBox` or `RichTextBox` that contains the data to be printed. You would then set your object to the object that was passed in your class.

Summary

This chapter has struck a balance between using the .NET Framework classes and the `SendMessage` API to implement feature-rich printing in the Notepad Plus application and more specifically in the `RichTextBoxExtended` class and control. The functionality provided in this application not only provides the flexibility to select what is to be printed, but also implements rich printing, enabling you to print a document that contains multiple fonts and colors without losing the formatting applied to the document.

The code for the `PrintPreviewDialog` and `PrintDialog` classes was very simple and straightforward. The code for the `PrintDocument` class, however, was more involved. The `PrintDocument` class is at the heart of printing in the .NET Framework by automatically providing the properties, methods, and events that control printing a document.

You saw firsthand, however, that this class merely provides the shell for printing implementation. It is up to you to provide the actual code to perform printing, which was implemented in the `FormatPrintRange` function. This function formatted the structures required to represent a printed page, copied those structures to memory, and then called the `SendMessage` API to perform the actual printing.

It is hoped that this chapter has provided you with more valuable insight into how printing is implemented in the .NET Framework and that you have gained a better understanding of how to use the powerful `SendMessage` API. It is also hoped that you have identified a use for some of this code in your own applications in order to provide printing functionality.

8

Data Binding

If you read the title for this chapter and thought to yourself, not another chapter on data binding using the wizards and strongly typed datasets, you could not have been farther from the truth. The data wizards in the Visual Studio .NET Integrated Development Environment (IDE) are ideal for creating applications that use data binding and strongly typed datasets, but these types of interfaces do not lend themselves well to extensibility and changing business requirements.

This chapter takes a different approach to data binding: binding various data sources to commonly used controls in code. This approach provides several key benefits, such as control over when your data sources are populated, when controls are bound, control over refreshing or even changing a control's data source, and an application that allows for changing business requirements and business rules.

This chapter focuses on data binding using the following data sources: `DataSet`, `DataView`, `DataTable`, XML, `ArrayList`, and user-defined business objects. Using these data sources, data binding is discussed and demonstrated using the following controls: `ComboBox`, `ListBox`, `DataGridView`, and `ListView`. Anyone who has used the `ListView` control before knows that it does not natively support data binding. This chapter extends this control to support data binding through code.

The main technologies covered in this chapter are as follows:

❑ Using the `XmlTextWriter` class to generate XML

❑ Using the `MemoryStream` class to pass data between classes

❑ Using a user-defined business object as a data source

❑ Extending the `ListView` control to provide the `DataSource`, `DisplayMember`, and `ValueMember` properties

Using the Data Binding Application

The Data Binding application is merely a sample application that demonstrates data binding to the ComboBox, ListBox, DataGridView, and ListView controls using various data sources. When the application is first started, it displays the controls mentioned previously unbound and a choice of data sources that can be bound to the controls, as shown in Figure 8-1. The data sources demonstrated in this application are the common data sources that you are most likely to use in real-world applications. This is especially true of the DataSet, DataView, XML, and Business Object data sources shown in Figure 8-1.

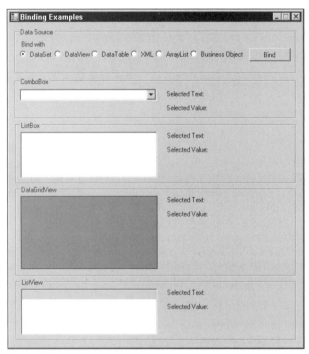

Figure 8-1

Once you select a data source and click the Bind button, the data is generated using the appropriate data source and bound to the controls as shown in Figure 8-2. In this example, the controls are bound to a DataSet object that contains only two fields: ID and Name. Although the DataSet can contain as many fields as needed for your application, the ComboBox and ListBox typically only have one or two fields from the DataSet bound to it. This is typically the data that is displayed to the user and the key to the data in the DataSet or database if the data was retrieved from a database.

In this example, the Name field from the data source is displayed to the user while the ID field from the data source is used to identify the user selected in the control. Figure 8-2 demonstrates the selected text and selected values from the various controls, as shown in the labels next to each control.

The ComboBox and ListBox natively support the displaying of only one bound field of data, as shown in Figure 8-2. The ListView control has also been extended to duplicate this functionality, also demonstrated in Figure 8-2. However, notice the default display of the DataGridView control. It natively displays all fields of data that are contained in the bound data source.

The ComboBox, ListBox, and extended ListView controls all provide the DisplayMember property to specify which field in the data source should be used to display data to the user, while the ValueMember property is used to set the field in the data source that contains the primary key of each row of data.

The DataGridView control does not provide any corresponding properties to control which field in the data source to use to display, as its default behavior is to display all fields in the bound data source. This behavior can also be duplicated in the extended ListView control by not setting the DisplayMember and ValueMember properties, as demonstrated later.

The DataView and DataTable data sources are similar to the DataSet in behavior and design because a DataSet contains a collection of DataTable objects and a DataView contains a single DataTable object. When binding these data sources to the controls in this sample application, you'll see the same display of data as shown in Figure 8-2.

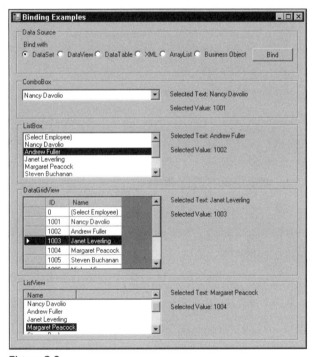

Figure 8-2

When using XML as a data source, the easiest way to bind the XML to the controls is to load the XML into a DataSet object and then bind the DataSet to the controls. Because a DataSet object is nothing more than XML behind the scenes anyway, it provides the necessary methods for reading and writing XML data, which makes it an excellent medium for using XML in your applications.

The example shown in Figure 8-3 generates an XML document with three fields (HexValue, SystemColorName, and RGBValue) and then loads the XML document into a DataSet object and binds the DataSet object to the controls. Notice that the only data you see in the ComboBox, ListBox, and ListView controls is data from the SystemColorName field. The DataGridView, however, displays all fields in the DataSet that was loaded from an XML document.

This example was designed to demonstrate an important point about data binding with XML: It does not matter how many fields are contained in your XML document. The ComboBox, ListBox, and ListView controls display only the data from the field that is set in the DisplayMember property. Therefore, your XML document can contain any number of fields, as can your DataSet, DataView, and DataTable.

When you actually view the code for this example, you will see how easy it is to use XML data as a data source. This code is covered in detail in the "Code and Code Explanation" section and demonstrates how to generate an XML document using the XmlTextWriter class. Although this example generates the XML in code, it can just as easily be read from disk or passed from another application.

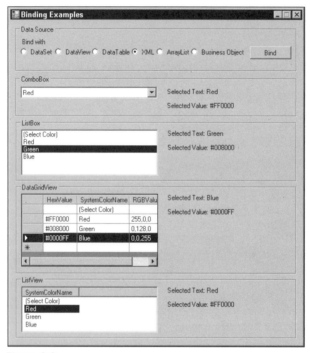

Figure 8-3

The next data binding example demonstrates binding an ArrayList object to the controls, as shown in Figure 8-4. Notice the message box shown in this example relating to data binding with the DataGridView control. Even though the ArrayList object contains a list of string values, only the length of the strings is displayed in the DataGridView (see Figure 8-4).

You can, however, coerce the DataGridView control to display the actual string values from an ArrayList, as shown in Figure 8-5. This involves creating a separate class to hold the string data, one that has a property that returns a String data type. Then you can add the class to the ArrayList as an object and when the ArrayList is bound to the DataGridView control, the actual string values from the object are displayed.

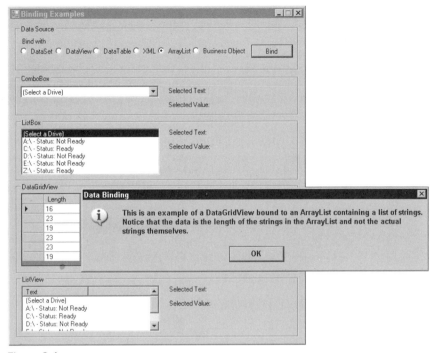

Figure 8-4

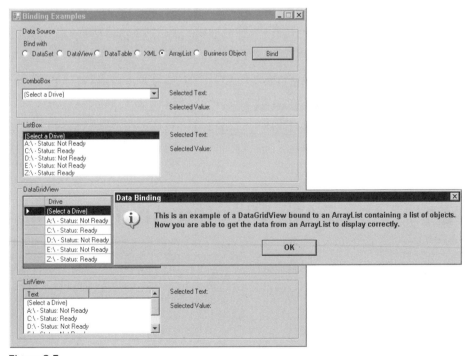

Figure 8-5

The final data binding example demonstrated in the Data Binding application uses a user-defined business object, as shown in Figure 8-6. This business object returns a list of customers and their contacts, although only the customers are displayed in the `ComboBox` and `ListBox` controls.

Your business object can contain any number of methods that return data, and those methods can return data as a `DataSet`, `DataView`, `DataTable`, XML, or an `ArrayList`. The business object used in this example returns the customer list as a `DataTable`, and this `DataTable` object contains the CustomerID, CompanyName, ContactName, and ContactTitle fields.

You know that the `DataGridView` will automatically display all of the fields in the data source that it is bound to. In this example, the extended `ListView` control does not have the `DisplayMember` and `ValueMember` properties set, so it also displays all of the fields in the data source to which it is bound, as shown in Figure 8-6.

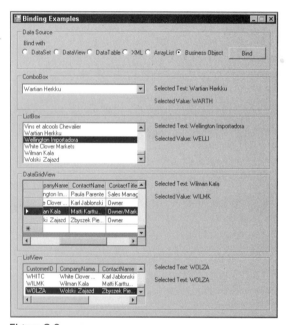

Figure 8-6

Design of the Data Binding Application

Now that you've had an overview of how this sample Data Binding application works, it's time to look at the design of the application. The code that performs the actual data binding is all contained in the Binding Examples form, so the main design focus of this application is the user-defined business object named `Customers`, the `ListViewExtended` control, and the classes used to generate and return the sample data used in this application. Figure 8-7 details how all these components fit together.

Notice that the `ListViewExtended` control has been designed in the same manner as the `RichTextBoxExtended` control discussed in Chapter 6. The `Customers.dll` is the user-defined business object for this application and is a separate component from the application. The `ControlData`, `Generate`, and `DriveInfo` classes are part of the Data Binding application and are used to generate the data that is bound to the controls.

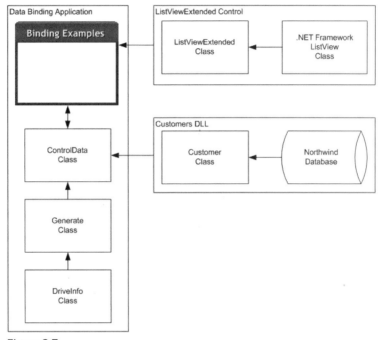

Figure 8-7

ListViewExtended Class

As previously mentioned, the `ListViewExtended` class extends the `ListView` control by providing the necessary properties and methods to support data binding in the same manner as the `ComboBox` and `ListBox` classes. Therefore, it has three main properties that are used for data binding support: `DataSource`, `DisplayMember`, and `ValueMember`. These public properties and the private methods necessary to support data binding are described in Table 8-1.

The `ListViewExtended` control has been built to support data binding through code only. However, with a little work, it can be further extended to support data binding at design time within the Visual Studio IDE.

Table 8-1: Properties and Methods for Supporting Data Binding

Property/Method	Return Type	Description
`Public Sub New()`	N/A	Changes the default properties of the `ListView` control
`Public Property DataSource()`	`Object`	Sets or returns the data source used for data binding

Continued

Table 8-1: Properties and Methods for Supporting Data Binding *(continued)*

Property/Method	Return Type	Description
`Public Property DisplayMember()`	String	Sets or returns the field in the data source that is used to display data to the user
`Public Property ValueMember()`	String	Sets or returns the field in the data source that is used to indicate the key for the selected data-bound item
`Private Sub BindDataSource()`	N/A	Determines the type of data source in use and binds it to an `IList` interface
`Private Sub AddColumnHeaders()`	N/A	Determines the type of data source in use and calls the appropriate overloaded `AddColumnHeaders` method
`Private Sub AddColumnHeaders(ByVal dataView As DataView)`	N/A	Adds column headers from a `DataView` data source
`Private Sub AddColumnHeaders(ByVal list As IList)`	N/A	Adds column headers from all other data sources
`Private Sub BindData()`	N/A	Builds a `ListViewItem` object and adds it to the `Items` collection
`Private Function GetItemData(ByVal objDataRow As Object, ByVal itemName As String)`	String	Gets the data from the specified column in the data row and returns it as a string

When you look at the `ListViewExtended` control in the ListViewEx project in the Visual Studio 2005 IDE, you'll notice that it does not have a UI as you might expect. When designing your own controls, you are presented with a designer on which you can draw other controls to create a composite control.

However, when extending an existing control, you merely want to enhance the functionality of that control. Therefore, you create a class, inherit the control in question, and then add your own code to enhance the control.

Customer Class

The `Customer` class exists in the `Customers.dll`, which is a component separate from the Data Binding application. This class reads data from the Northwind Access database and returns a customer list with associated data. This class is simplistic in design and is used for illustrative purposes only. Your real-world business classes and components will contain other methods that implement the required business logic for which your component was designed.

The constructor and properties for the `Customer` class are described in Table 8-2. As previously mentioned, this class has been designed for illustrative purposes only, so the code in this class has been kept to a minimum.

Table 8-2: Properties and Methods of the Customer Class

Property/Method	Return Type	Description
`Public Sub New()`	N/A	Instantiates the `OleDbConnection` object
`Protected Overridable Sub Dispose(ByVal disposing As Boolean)`	N/A	Disposes of the `OleDbConnection` object
`Public ReadOnly Property CustomerListBindingProperties()`	SortedList	Used for self-discovery by the caller and returns a list containing the `DisplayMember`, `ValueMember`, and `Table Name` available in the `CustomerList` property
`Public ReadOnly Property CustomerList(ByVal firstRowData As String)`	DataTable	Reads data from the Northwind database and returns a customer list

DriveInfo Class

The `DriveInfo` class is used to demonstrate how to get strings from an `ArrayList` to display in the `DataGridView` control. This class contains a constructor and a read-only `String` property, as shown in Table 8-3.

Table 8-3: Properties and Methods of the DriveInfo Class

Property/Method	Return Type	Description
`Public Sub New(ByVal driveName As String)`	N/A	Sets the drive name passed to this constructor in a private variable
`Public ReadOnly Property Drive()`	String	Returns the drive information contained in a private variable

Generate Class

Here's where the real fun starts. The `Generate` class is used to generate data for the `ControlData` class in various formats. Most of the data generated in a class is derived from static data defined in `String` arrays in this class and is used to generate data in various formats, such as a `DataSet`, `ArrayList`, and XML. Table 8-4 describes the methods in this class.

Table 8-4: Methods of the Generate Class

Method	Return Type	Description
`Public Function DataSet()`	`DataSet`	Generates a `DataSet` populated with static data contained in a `String` array
`Public Function DataView()`	`DataView`	Returns a `DataView` by calling the `DataSet` method
`Public Function DataTable()`	`DataTable`	Returns a `DataTable` by calling the `DataSet` method
`Public Function ArrayListOfStrings() As ArrayList`	`ArrayList`	Generates an `ArrayList` of `Strings` using data from the `Drives` collection on your computer
`Public Function ArrayListOfObjects() As ArrayList`	`ArrayList`	Generates an `ArrayList` of `DriveInfo` objects using data from the `Drives` collection on your computer
`Public Function XML()`	`MemoryStream`	Generates an XML document from static data contained in three `String` arrays and returns the XML document as a `MemoryStream`

ControlData Class

The `ControlData` class is a generic class that is used as the data source for data binding in the Binding Examples form. To that end, this class has five overloaded constructors and four public properties. These constructors and properties are described in Table 8-5.

Table 8-5: Methods and Properties of the ControlData Class

Property/Method	Return Type	Description
`Public Sub New(ByVal dataSet As DataSet)`	N/A	Instantiates this class to return a `DataSet` as the data source
`Public Sub New(ByVal dataView As DataView)`	N/A	Instantiates this class to return a `DataView` as the data source
`Public Sub New(ByVal dataTable As DataTable)`	N/A	Instantiates this class to return a `DataTable` as the data source
`Public Sub New(ByVal arrayList As ArrayList)`	N/A	Instantiates this class to return an `ArrayList` as the data source

Table 8-5: Methods and Properties of the ControlData Class *(continued)*

Property/Method	Return Type	Description
`Public Sub New(ByVal xml As MemoryStream)`	N/A	Instantiates this class to return the XML input as a `DataSet` as the data source
`Public ReadOnly Property DataSource()`	`Object`	Returns the appropriate typed data source that this class was instantiated with as an `Object`
`Public ReadOnly Property DisplayMember()`	`String`	Returns the field name in the data source that should be used to display data in a control
`Public ReadOnly Property ValueMember()`	`String`	Returns the field name in the data source that should be used as a key to identify a row of data in the data source
`Public ReadOnly Property DataTableName()`	`String`	Returns the table name of the `DataTable` in a `DataSet`

Code and Code Explanation

This section explains the code from the previous classes in more detail and demonstrates they all fit together. You'll also get a chance to take a look at the code in the Binding Examples form as it relates to using these classes to bind data to the controls.

ListViewExtended Class

I want to start the code explanation with the `ListViewExtended` class, as this control has been enhanced to support data binding at runtime. Before I go into any code details for this class, I want to make it perfectly clear that this control has been enhanced to support runtime data binding only. The framework has been laid to support design-time data binding within the IDE, and with some work and testing you'll be able to enhance this control further if you need to support design-time data binding.

The code in this class is based on the article "Creating a Data Bound ListView Control" written by Rockford Lhotka in August 2002. I took some of the key concepts that I learned from that article and applied it to this class. Not all of the functionality mentioned in that article has been implemented in this class because some of it did not relate to the data binding demonstrations designed for this chapter.

This class begins by importing the `System.ComponentModel` namespace. This namespace is needed to provide access to various classes that support design-time properties within the IDE and the `IListSource` interface. Let's take a look at the beginning part of this class as shown in the following code fragment.

You can see the `Imports` statement that imports the `System.ComponentModel` namespace. You can also see that this class inherits the `ListView` class because that is the class being extended. Next are the declarations of the private variables and objects that are used throughout the rest of the class.

The `intIndex` variable is used as an index to loop through collections of column and data items. The `strDisplayMember` and `strValueMember` variables are used to save the values that the user sets in the `DisplayMember` and `ValueMember` properties. The `objDataSource` object is used to save the data source that is set in the `DataSource` property. The last three objects are used in various procedures in this class to add data to the control.

```
Imports System.ComponentModel

Public Class ListViewExtended
    Inherits ListView

        'Private variables and objects
        Private intIndex As Integer

        Private strDisplayMember As String
        Private strValueMember As String

        Private objDataSource As Object

        Private objUnderlyingDataSource As IList

        Private objColumnHeader As ColumnHeader

        Private objListViewItem As ListViewItem
```

New Constructor

The constructor for this class overrides some of the default properties for the `ListView` control and sets them to support typical data binding that you see in the `DataGridView` control. First, you override the `View` property, which by default is set to `LargeIcon`. Next, you override the `FullRowSelect` property to allow the full row of data to be selected when the user clicks on any column in a row of data. Finally, you override the `MultiSelect` property, setting it to `False` to allow only a single row of data to be selected at any given time:

```
Public Sub New()
    'Override default ListView properties
    Me.View = Windows.Forms.View.Details
    Me.FullRowSelect = True
    Me.MultiSelect = False
End Sub
```

DataSource Property

Now it's time to implement the properties that support data binding. The first of these properties is the `DataSource` property. Attributes from the `System.ComponentModel` namespace have been specified for this property, supported by the Properties window and shown in that window.

The first of these attributes is `Category`. The properties of a control are categorized in the Properties window, where you can view the properties of a control by category or in alphabetical order. Here you specify that this property belongs to the `Data` category.

Next is the `RefreshProperties` attribute, which instructs the Properties window to refresh itself when the value of this property changes. This is the typical behavior of design-time controls when setting the DataSource property. Typically, once the DataSource property for a control is set, the Properties window refreshes itself and the DataMember property is populated with the available members of the DataSource property.

The AttributeProvider attribute is next. It provides the UI type editor for this property. The AttributeProvider accepts the type of interface that it should provide as input. Specifying the IListSource interface causes this property to provide the UI type editor (see Figure 8-8). This is the UI type editor that you typically see for the DataSource property of other controls such as the ComboBox, ListBox, and DataGridView controls.

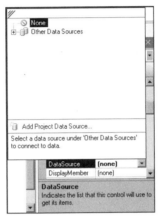

Figure 8-8

The Description attribute merely provides a property description, which is displayed at the bottom of the Properties window (refer to Figure 8-8). It's always a good idea to provide a description for your properties just in case their purpose is not clear from their name.

This property returns the data source. It also sets it, as indicated by the Get and Set statements. The Set statement contains a few lines of code, starting with the clearing of the strDisplayMember and strValueMember variables. Whenever the DataSource property is changed, you need to clear the strDisplayMember and strValueMember variables as shown here in case they were previously set.

Next, save the data source being set in the objDataSource object. Notice in the variable declarations previously discussed that the objDataSource object is actually defined as an Object data type because you want to support a variety of different data sources.

Now a call is made to the BindDataSource procedure to determine the type of data source being set and to set that data source in the objUnderlyingDataSource object by converting the data source to the appropriate type. You'll see this procedure in detail shortly.

Next, a call is made to the AddColumnHeaders procedure, which adds the column headers to the ListView Columns collection. Then a call is made to the BindData procedure to add the data from the data source to the ListView control. You'll see both of these procedures in detail shortly.

```
<Category("Data"), _
RefreshProperties(RefreshProperties.Repaint), _
```

```
            AttributeProvider(GetType(IListSource)), _
            Description("Indicates the list that this control will use to " & _
            "get its items.")> _
            Public Property DataSource() As Object
              Get
                  Return objDataSource
              End Get
              Set(ByVal value As Object)
                  'Clear any existing DisplayMember and ValueMember
                  strDisplayMember = Nothing
                  strValueMember = Nothing
                  'Set the DataSource and then bind it
                  objDataSource = value
                  BindDataSource()
                  AddColumnHeaders()
                  BindData()
              End Set
           End Property
       End Property
```

DisplayMember Property

The `DisplayMember` property is next. This property specifies the column name in the data source that should be displayed in the `ListView` control. Again, attributes have been provided for this property to support design-time editing. The `Category` and `Description` attributes have already been discussed, leaving the two new attributes to be covered.

The `Editor` attribute specifies the UI type editor to be used for this property to support changes to the property. The `DataMemberListEditor` editor used in this property is the standard UI type editor that you typically see for the `DisplayMember` property of the `ComboBox` and `ListBox` controls and is shown in Figure 8-9.

The `DefaultValue` attribute sets a default value for this property. When you view this property in the Properties window, as shown in Figure 8-9, it has a default value of `(none)` specified, indicating that this property has not yet been set.

The `Set` statement for this property saves the value passed in the `strDisplayMember` variable and then makes a call to the `BindDataSource`, `AddColumnHeaders`, and `BindData` procedures. These three procedures are called in order from the `DataSource`, `DisplayMember`, and `ValueMember` properties, as you will not know in which order these properties are set at runtime.

```
        <Category("Data"), _
        Editor("System.Windows.Forms.Design.DataMemberListEditor," & _
        "System.Design", GetType(System.Drawing.Design.UITypeEditor)), _
        Description("Indicates the property to display for the items in " & _
        "this control."), _
        DefaultValue("(none)")> _
        Public Property DisplayMember() As String
            Get
                Return strDisplayMember
            End Get
            Set(ByVal value As String)
                strDisplayMember = value
```

```
            BindDataSource()
            AddColumnHeaders()
            BindData()
        End Set
    End Property
```

Figure 8-9

ValueMember Property

The last property in this class is the ValueMember property. As before, the Category and Description attributes have been supplied. Additionally, the Editor attribute has also been supplied using the same editor that was used in the DisplayMember property. This duplicates the editor shown in the ValueMember property of the ComboBox and ListBox controls.

The Set statement for this property saves the value passed in the strValueMember variable. Like the DisplayMember and DataSource properties, this property also calls the BindDataSource, AddColumnHeaders, and BindData procedures to bind the data source, add the column headers, and populate the ListView control with the data contained in the data source:

```
    <Category("Data"), _
    Editor("System.Windows.Forms.Design.DataMemberListEditor," & _
    "System.Design", GetType(System.Drawing.Design.UITypeEditor)), _
    Description("Indicates the property to use as the actual value for " & _
    "the items in the control.")> _
Public Property ValueMember() As String
    Get
        Return strValueMember
    End Get
    Set(ByVal value As String)
        strValueMember = value
        BindDataSource()
        AddColumnHeaders()
        BindData()
    End Set
End Property
```

BindDataSource Procedure

Any object that provides the `IList` or `IListSource` interface can be bound to a control. However, you do not work directly with the `IListSource` interface but with the `IList` interface. Therefore, you need to get an `IList` interface from any data source that provides the `IListSource` interface, which is done by calling the `GetList` method on that data source.

The `objUnderlyingDataSource` object is defined using the `IList` interface. Thus, the `BindDataSource` procedure needs to determine what type of interface the data source in use provides and then it converts the interface from the data source to the appropriate type in the `objUnderlyingDataSource` object. Remember that the data source is specified as an `Object` data type, so you must specifically convert the interface provided by the data source using the `CType` function.

You first make a check to determine whether the type of object contained in the `objDataSource` object is a `DataSet`. If it is, then you set the `objUnderlyingDataSource` object to the `IList` interface from the `DataTable` in the `DataSet` by calling the `GetList` method on the `DataTable` contained in the `DataSet`.

If the data source is not a `DataSet`, then the next check is to determine whether the data source provides the `IListSource` interface, which is contained in the `ElseIf` line of code that follows. If it is, then you call the `GetList` method in the data source after converting the `objDataSource` object to an `IListSource` interface.

Finally, if neither of the previous checks is `true`, then the data source must contain the `IList` interface and you merely set the `objUnderlyingDataSource` object to the `IList` interface contained in the data source by converting it to an `IList` interface using the `CType` function:

```
Private Sub BindDataSource()
    'Get the underlying data source type
    If TypeOf objDataSource Is DataSet Then
        objUnderlyingDataSource = CType(objDataSource.Tables(0), _
            IListSource).GetList
    ElseIf TypeOf objDataSource Is IListSource Then
        objUnderlyingDataSource = CType(objDataSource, IListSource).GetList
    Else
        objUnderlyingDataSource = CType(objDataSource, IList)
    End If
End Sub
```

AddColumnHeaders Procedure

The `AddColumnHeaders` procedure is an overloaded procedure that determines what type of interface the `objUnderlyingDataSource` object provides and calls the appropriate overloaded `AddColumnHeaders` procedure to add the column headers to the `Columns` collection of the `ListView` control.

You start by clearing the existing `Columns` collection in case it has been previously set. Because this procedure is also called by the `DisplayMember` and `ValueMember` properties, you must check whether the data source has been set; this is done in the second line of code here. If the data source was not previously set, you exit this procedure, as there is nothing to do.

If the interface provided in the `objUnderlyingDataSource` object is a `DataView`, then you can call the first overloaded `AddColumnHeaders` procedure, passing it the data source converted to a `DataView`.

Remember that the `objUnderlyingDataSource` object is defined as an `IList` interface, so you must specifically convert it using the `CType` function.

If the interface provided in the `objUnderlyingDataSource` object is not a `DataView`, then you call the second overloaded `AddColumnHeaders` procedure. That procedure sets the column name to one of two values: `Value` or `Text`. You'll see that procedure in detail shortly.

```
Private Sub AddColumnHeaders()
    'Clear the current collection
    Me.Columns.Clear()

    'Exit if the underlying data source is nothing
    If IsNothing(objUnderlyingDataSource) Then
        Exit Sub
    End If

    'Determine the underlying data source and call the appropriate method
    If TypeOf objUnderlyingDataSource Is DataView Then
        AddColumnHeaders(CType(objUnderlyingDataSource, DataView))
    Else
        AddColumnHeaders(objUnderlyingDataSource)
    End If
End Sub
```

First Overloaded AddColumnHeaders Procedure

The first overloaded `AddColumnHeaders` procedure uses a `DataView` object to add the columns to the `Columns` collection of the `ListView` control. This procedure starts by checking the `strDisplayMember` variable. If this variable has been set, then this procedure adds only a single column to the `Columns` collection using the value specified in that variable. This is the value that would be set using the `DisplayMember` property.

If the `strDisplayMember` variable has not been set, then this procedure loops through the columns contained in the `DataView` and adds each column to the `Columns` collection in the `ListView` control. The first thing that happens inside in the `For...Next` loop is instantiating an object as a new `ColumnHeader` class. Then, using the `Caption` property from the column contained in the `DataView` `Columns` collection, you set the `Text` property of the column to be added. The `Caption` property contains the display name of the column.

Next, set the `Name` property of the new column using the `ColumnName` property of the column in the `DataView`. This is typically the column name that came from the database if the data was retrieved from a database.

Finally, you add the new column to the `Columns` collection in the `ListView` control. The `For...Next` loop will loop through the `Columns` collection in the `DataView` and add each column to the `Columns` collection in the `ListView` control:

```
Private Sub AddColumnHeaders(ByVal dataView As DataView)
    If Not IsNothing(strDisplayMember) Then
        'Add only the column header requested
        Me.Columns.Add(strDisplayMember)
    Else
        'Add all columns contained in the DataView
```

```
        For intIndex = 0 To dataView.Table.Columns.Count - 1
            'Instantiate a new ColumnHeader
            objColumnHeader = New ColumnHeader
            'Set the ColumnHeader properties
            objColumnHeader.Text = _
                dataView.Table.Columns(intIndex).Caption
            objColumnHeader.Name = _
                dataView.Table.Columns(intIndex).ColumnName
            'Add the ColumnHeader to the Columns collection
            Me.Columns.Add(objColumnHeader)
        Next
    End If
End Sub
```

Second Overloaded AddColumnHeaders Procedure

The second overloaded `AddColumnHeaders` procedure is more generic and deterministic. This procedure accepts its input as an `IList` interface and thus must determine what type of data is being passed in a column in order to determine what text should be set in the column name.

Again, the first thing that happens in this procedure is to determine whether the `strDisplayMember` variable has been set. If it has, then you add only one column to the `Columns` collection and use the value that was set in this variable.

If the `strDisplayMember` variable was not set, then you get the first item in the list. The `IList` interface in treated like a one-dimensional array, so the `Item` property returns the actual data in the interface and no column name. Therefore, you take the first item in the interface and examine its data type.

The first step in this process is to set the item in the `objItem` object, which has been defined as an `Object` data type. Then you test this object to determine whether it contains a primitive data type using the `IsPrimitive` property of the `GetType` method of the `Object` class. The `IsPrimitive` property returns a `Boolean` value indicating whether the value contained in the object is a primitive data type. Primitive data types are numeric data types such as `Integer`, `Byte`, `Single`, and `Double`. They are also data types that store numeric values behind the scenes, such as `Boolean` and `Char`.

If the value of the data contained in the `objItem` object is a primitive data type, then the column header is set to `Value`. This indicates to the end user who sees this column header in the `ListView` control that the data displayed is numeric data, which would be obvious from the data displayed.

If the data type of the data in the `objItem` object is not a primitive data type, then a check is made to determine whether the type of data in the object is a string. This is done by using the `TypeOf` operator, comparing the type of data in the `objItem` to the `String` class. If this comparison checks out, the column header in the `ListView` control is set to `Text` indicating that the data in the `ListView` control is string data. If either of these checks fails, the column header is set to an empty string, and a blank column header is displayed:

```
    Private Sub AddColumnHeaders(ByVal list As IList)
        If Not IsNothing(strDisplayMember) Then
            'Add only the column header requested
            Me.Columns.Add(strDisplayMember)
        Else
            If list.Count > 0 Then
```

```
            'Get the first item from the list
            Dim objItem As Object = list.Item(0)

            If objItem.GetType.IsPrimitive Then

                'Add the column header to the Columns collection
                Me.Columns.Add("Value")

            ElseIf TypeOf objItem Is String Then

                'Add the column header to the Columns collection
                Me.Columns.Add("Text")

            Else

                'Add the column header to the Columns collection
                Me.Columns.Add(String.Empty)

            End If
        End If
    End If
End Sub
```

BindData Procedure

Now comes the fun part — adding data to the ListView control. This functionality has been separated into two procedures. The first and main procedure is the BindData procedure, which is called from the DataSource, DisplayMember, and ValueMember properties. This procedure loops through the rows and columns of data in the data source and adds the data to a ListViewItem object. A call is made to the GetItemData function to actually get the data for a specific row and column and return it as a String value.

This procedure starts by clearing the Items collection in case it contains data that was previously loaded. The Items collection of the ListView control contains a collection of ListViewItem objects, which represents a row of data in the ListView control.

The next check is for the objUnderlyingDataSource object. If this object has not been set, then you exit this procedure, as there is nothing to do. The final check ensures that you actually have some columns in the ListView control; you can't add data if you haven't added any columns. Here you check the Count property of the Columns collection; if it is equal to 0, you exit this procedure.

```
    Private Sub BindData()
        'Clear the current collection
        Me.Items.Clear()

        'Exit if the underlying data source is nothing
        If IsNothing(objUnderlyingDataSource) Then
            Exit Sub
        End If

        'Exit if there are no columns
        If Me.Columns.Count = 0 Then
            Exit Sub
        End If
```

You now loop through the rows of data in the data source, adding each row of data to a `ListViewItem` object and then adding that object to the `Items` collection. Begin by setting up a `For...Next` loop using the `Count` property of the `objUnderlyingDataSource` object. Remember that the `Count` property provides the actual number of rows in the `objUnderlyingDataSource` object but the starting index is `0`, so you use `Count -1` in the `For` statement of the `For...Next` loop.

The first thing that happens inside this loop is instantiating a new instance of the `ListViewItem` class in the `objListViewItem` object. Next, an `If...Then...Else` statement block is set up and then a check is made against the `strDisplayMember` variable; if it has been set, then you only add data for this one column.

Inside the `If...Then...Else` statement block, set the `Text` property of the `objListViewItem` object using the data from the column specified by the `strDisplayMember` variable. A call is made to the `GetItemData` function to retrieve the data for this row and column.

Next, check whether the `strValueMember` variable has been set. If it has, then set the `Tag` property of the `objListViewItem` object using the data from this column in the data source. Again a call is made to the `GetItemData` function to get the data for this row and column.

The `Tag` property can contain any object that you want to associate with a row of data. Here you use the `strValueMember` property, which typically contains a column of data to associate with this row. In most cases this is the key of the column of data from a database that uniquely identifies this particular row of data.

```
'Add the rows of data to the Items collection
For intIndex = 0 To objUnderlyingDataSource.Count - 1

    'Instantiate a new instance of the ListViewItem class
    objListViewItem = New ListViewItem

    If Not IsNothing(strDisplayMember) Then

        'Load the data for the DisplayMember
        objListViewItem.Text = _
            GetItemData(objUnderlyingDataSource.Item(intIndex), _
            strDisplayMember).ToString

        If Not IsNothing(strValueMember) Then
            'Load the data for the ValueMember
            objListViewItem.Tag = _
                GetItemData(objUnderlyingDataSource.Item(intIndex), _
                strValueMember).ToString()
        End If
```

The `Else` block of the `If...Then...Else` statement block is executed if the `DisplayMember` property was not set. This causes all columns of data in the data source to be displayed in the `ListView` control.

Because a `ListView` control can display its data in a variety of ways (e.g., Tile, Large Icons, Small Icons, List, and Detail), the `ListViewItem` property has a default property called `Text`. This is the data that is displayed in each of the views above, and in the case of the Detail view it is the first column of data displayed. In the Detail view, each subsequent column is actually a sub-item of the `ListViewItem` object.

Therefore, set the `Text` property of the `objListViewItem` object using the first column in the data source. Next, loop through the remaining columns in the data source and add the data for each of those columns as sub-items to the `SubItems` collection of the `objListViewItem` object.

```
        Else

            'Add the first column of data as the Item
            objListViewItem.Text = _
                GetItemData(objUnderlyingDataSource.Item(intIndex), _
                    Me.Columns(0).Name).ToString

            'Add the remaining columns of data as the SubItems
            For intColumn As Integer = 1 To Me.Columns.Count - 1
                objListViewItem.SubItems.Add( _
                    GetItemData(objUnderlyingDataSource.Item(intIndex), _
                    Me.Columns(intColumn).Name))
            Next

        End If
```

Once the `objListViewItem` object has been built, it is added to the `Items` collection of the `ListView` control. The previous process is repeated for each row of data contained in the data source.

```
            'Add the objListViewItem object to the Items collection
            Items.Add(objListViewItem)
        Next
    End Sub
```

GetItemData Function

The last procedure in this class is the `GetItemData` function. This function accepts a data row from the data source and the name of the column of data from which this function should retrieve and return the data.

The first check in this function is a check to see whether the `itemName` parameter is set to `Nothing`. If it is, then it returns an empty string. If the `itemName` parameter contains data, then the remaining code performs a series of checks against the data row passed to this function to determine what type of data it contains:

```
    Private Function GetItemData(ByVal dataRow As Object, _
        ByVal itemName As String) As String

        If IsNothing(itemName) Then
            'Return an empty string
            Return String.Empty
```

The first check of the `dataRow` parameter is to see whether this object is a `DataRowView` object. If it is, then a `Try...Catch` block is set up and you attempt to return the column of data using the `itemName` parameter. If the `itemName` parameter is not a valid column name, then an argument exception is thrown and is handled by the `Catch` block. In this case, you simply return an empty string. An argument exception would be thrown if the user supplied a column name in the `DisplayMember` or `ValueMember` properties that did not actually exist in the data source.

```
ElseIf TypeOf dataRow Is DataRowView Then
    'Get the item from the DataRowView
    Try
        Return CType(dataRow, DataRowView).Item(itemName).ToString
    Catch ArgumentExceptionErr As ArgumentException
        Return String.Empty
    End Try
```

The next check of the `dataRow` parameter is to see whether the data row contains a primitive data type. Remember that a primitive data type is any data type that returns a numeric value. If the data row is a primitive data type, then it only contains one column and the value is returned as a string value by using the `ToString` method of the object contained in the `dataRow` parameter:

```
ElseIf dataRow.GetType.IsPrimitive Then
    'Get the primitive value
    Return dataRow.ToString
```

The final check of the `dataRow` parameter is to see whether the data row contains a `String` data type. If the data row is a `String` data type, then the one and only column of data is returned as a string value again by calling the `ToString` method on the data row that was passed to this function as an `Object` data type:

```
ElseIf TypeOf dataRow Is String Then
    'Get the string
    Return dataRow.ToString
```

If all of the preceding checks fail for the `dataRow` parameter, then you do not know what it is and simply return an empty string from this function:

```
Else
    'Default if nothing was found
    Return String.Empty
End If
End Function
```

Customer Class

The `Customer` class is contained in the `Customers.dll` and provides the Data Binding application with a user-defined business object that supplies data for data binding in the form of a `DataTable`. This class provides two properties: `CustomerList` and `CustomerListBindingProperties`. The `CustomerList` property reads customer data from the Customers table in the Northwind database and returns the data as a `DataTable`. The `CustomerListBindingProperties` property returns a `SortedList` containing the data binding properties for the `CustomerList` property.

CustomerList Property

Let's take a look at the `CustomerList` property first. This is a read-only property that returns customer data in this simple user-defined business object. In a real-world business object, this property would typically enable a user to add customers as well as read customers from a database.

This property accepts a string parameter that the caller can provide and inserts a row at the beginning of the `DataTable`. This is typically useful when this property is used to bind data in a `ComboBox` control and can provide some initial instructions to the end user, such as "Select a Customer." When this property is being bound to a `ListBox` control, you can pass an empty string to this property and no extra row is inserted into the `DataTable`.

The `OleDbConnection` object is instantiated in the constructor for this class and is disposed of in the `Dispose` method for this class. Therefore, when this property is called, all you need to do is instantiate an `OleDbDataAdapter` object that will be used to fill a `DataSet`. You can see in the following code that the `objDataAdapter` object is instantiated with the `select` command and the `objConnection` object. Next, a new instance of the `DataSet` class is set in the `objDataSet` object and the `Fill` method is called on the `objDataAdapter` object to populate the `DataSet` with customer data. Then dispose of the `objDataAdapter` object, as you are done with it.

```
Public ReadOnly Property CustomerList(ByVal firstRowData As String) _
    As DataTable

    Get
        'Declare and instantiate a new OleDbDataAdapter
        Dim objDataAdapter As New OleDbDataAdapter( _
            "Select CustomerID, CompanyName, ContactName, ContactTitle " & _
            "From Customers Order By CompanyName", objConnection)

        'Populate the customer list
        Dim objDataSet As New DataSet
        objDataAdapter.Fill(objDataSet, "Customers")

        'Cleanup
        objDataAdapter.Dispose()
        objDataAdapter = Nothing
```

Now check the `firstRowData` parameter to ensure that it is not equal to an empty string. If it is not, then you want to insert a new row of data in the Customers table in the `objDataSet` object. You do this by first declaring a new `DataRow` in the `objDataRow` object and then initializing this object by calling the `NewRow` method on the `DataTable`. This sets the `objDataRow` object with a new blank data row containing the same schema information contained in the `DataTable`.

Because the primary data elements in this `DataTable` are the `CustomerID` and `CompanyName` fields, those are the only fields that you set in the data row. You set the `CustomerID` field to a value of `0` and the `CompanyName` field to the value passed in the `firstDataRow` parameter. Then you insert the new data row at the beginning of the `DataTable` by calling the `InsertAt` method on the `Rows` collection and specify the index at which the new row should be inserted.

Finally, return the `DataTable` to the caller by specifying the table in the `DataSet` that contains the data. In this case, the `DataSet` only contains one table, but your business logic could have populated a `DataSet` with multiple tables.

```
        'Add first row data if requested
        If firstRowData <> String.Empty Then
            Dim objDataRow As DataRow
            objDataRow = objDataSet.Tables("Customers").NewRow
```

```
                    objDataRow.Item("CustomerID") = 0
                    objDataRow.Item("CompanyName") = firstRowData
                    objDataSet.Tables("Customers").Rows.InsertAt(objDataRow, 0)
            End If

            'Return the DataTable
            Return objDataSet.Tables("Customers")
        End Get
    End Property
```

CustomerListBindingProperties Property

The `CustomerListBindingProperties` property is sort of a binding helper property that provides the key binding information needed for the `DataTable` returned from the `CustomerList` property. Here you return a `SortedList` object containing the key data binding elements as well as the table name of the `DataTable` returned from the `CustomerList` property.

All of this information could automatically be discovered through examination of the `DataTable` returned from the `CustomerList` property but it would take a few lines of code to do so. Here you provide this key information in an easy-to-use format.

The code in this property starts off by instantiating a new `SortedList` object using the property name of this property because this is the data type that this property returns. Then you simply add the key elements to the list in the next three lines of code.

The first item to be added is the `DisplayMember`, which contains the field name in the `DataTable` that would be set in the `DisplayMember` property of the control to which you are binding data. The `ValueMember` item contains the field name in the `DataTable` that would be set in the `ValueMember` property of the control that you are binding. Finally, the `TableName` item is merely informational and not required, but it does help to make code more readable.

```
    Public ReadOnly Property CustomerListBindingProperties() As SortedList
        Get
            'Instantiate the SortedList
            CustomerListBindingProperties = New SortedList

            'Add the properties
            CustomerListBindingProperties.Add("DisplayMember", "CompanyName")
            CustomerListBindingProperties.Add("TableName", "Customers")
            CustomerListBindingProperties.Add("ValueMember", "CustomerID")
        End Get
    End Property
```

DriveInfo Class

The `DriveInfo` class is a simple class that provides a read-only property that returns a `String` data type. This class is used to demonstrate how to get string values to display properly in a `DataGridView` control when binding this control to an `Array` or `ArrayList`.

The constructor for this class accepts the string data as input and sets this string data in a private variable. The `Drive` property is a read-only property that returns this information as a `String` data type.

When the `DataGridView` is bound to an `Array` or `ArrayList` containing a collection of `DriveInfo` objects, it detects that this class returns a `String` property and binds the control to this list. Thus, the data contained in this object automatically displays correctly, as shown in Figure 8-5 earlier in this chapter.

```
Public Class DriveInfo
    'Private variables
    Private strDrive As String

    'Constructor
    Public Sub New(ByVal driveName As String)
        strDrive = driveName
    End Sub

    'Read only property
    Public ReadOnly Property Drive() As String
        Get
            Return strDrive
        End Get
    End Property
End Class
```

Generate Class

As previously mentioned, the `Generate` class is used to generate static data in various formats that is used in the Data Binding application. While most of the data used in this class is static, this class does serve a useful purpose: It exposes you to the code used to programmatically create a `DataSet`, `DataTable`, `DataView`, `ArrayList`, and `XML` data.

Let's start by taking a look at the variables used in this class. You'll notice in the following code that all but one of the variables defined in this class contain static data. These variables are used as the source of data for most of the methods in this class.

```
Public Class Generate
    'Private variables and objects
    Private intIndex As Integer
    Private intIDs() As String = {1001, 1002, 1003, 1004, _
        1005, 1006, 1007, 1008, 1009}

    Private strNames() As String = {"Nancy Davolio", "Andrew Fuller", _
        "Janet Leverling", "Margaret Peacock", "Steven Buchanan", _
        "Michael Suyama", "Robert King", "Laura Callahan", "Anne Dodsworth"}
    Private strHexValues() As String = {"", "#FF0000", "#008000", "#0000FF"}
    Private strColorNames() As String = {"(Select Color)", "Red", "Green", "Blue"}
    Private strRGBValues() As String = {"", "255,0,0", "0,128,0", "0,0,255"}
```

DataSet Function

The first method in this class is the `DataSet` function, which creates and returns a `DataSet` object. A `DataSet` object contains at least one `DataTable`, and the `DataTable` object typically contains at least one `DataRow` object. Therefore, these are the first three objects that you see declared in this function.

Next, you instantiate the `objDataSet` object as a new `DataSet` class and then create a new `DataTable` in the `objDataTable` object by calling the `Add` method on the `Tables` collection in the `objDataSet` object. Notice that you pass the table name to the Add method so that your table is created with a table name of Employees. It should also be noted that you do not have to specify a name for the DataTable being created. You can create a new DataTable with no name at all.

```
Public Function DataSet() As DataSet
    'Declare local objects
    Dim objDataSet As DataSet
    Dim objDataTable As DataTable
    Dim objDataRow As DataRow

    'Instantiate a new DataSet
    objDataSet = New DataSet

    'Create a DataTable
    objDataTable = objDataSet.Tables.Add("Employees")
```

You now have both a DataSet and DataTable object. These are two separate objects at this point but they have an automatic relationship. The DataTable does not currently have any columns or data rows. The next two lines of code add two new columns to your objDataTable object.

You accomplish this by calling the Add method on the Columns collection and pass the Add method the name of the column to add and the data type of the column. As you can see, the ID column is added as an Integer data type, while the Name column is added as a String data type.

As a side note, the Integer data type is a Visual Basic.NET data type that maps to the .NET Framework System.Int32 data type. Several data types were carried over from Visual Basic 6.0 to the new Visual Basic .NET language when .NET was first introduced and are automatically mapped to their .NET Framework equivalents. This was done in an effort to make the Visual Basic developer's transition to Visual Basic.NET programming easier. These two data types are equivalent and can be used interchangeably.

Once the columns have been added to the DataTable, you instantiate the objDataRow object by calling the NewRow method on the DataTable in the objDataSet object. A new DataRow object is created in the objDataRow object with the columns that you just added to the objDataTable object. All you have to do is set the data in these columns in the objDataRow object.

This is done by accessing the Item property of the DataRow object, specifying the column name of the Item, and setting the appropriate values for each column according to the data type that was specified when, the column was created. As you can see in the following code, you set the ID column to an Integer value and the Name column to a String value. Then you add this new DataRow to the Rows collection in the Employees table in the DataSet by calling the Add method on the Rows collection, passing it the objDataRow object.

```
'Add the DataColumns to the table
objDataTable.Columns.Add("ID", Type.GetType("System.Int32"))
objDataTable.Columns.Add("Name", Type.GetType("System.String"))

'Instantiate a datarow object from the DataSet
objDataRow = objDataSet.Tables("Employees").NewRow

'Set the values in the DataRow
objDataRow.Item("ID") = 0
```

```
            objDataRow.Item("Name") = "(Select Employee)"

            'Add the DataRow to the DataSet
            objDataSet.Tables("Employees").Rows.Add(objDataRow)
```

You set the first row of data in a similar manner to how you did it in the `CustomerList` property of the `Customer` class. Now you want to loop through the data contained in the `intIDs` and `strNames` variables creating new `DataRow` objects and adding them to the `Rows` collection of the `Employees` table.

In the `For...Next` loop, instantiate a new `objDataRow` object by calling the `NewRow` method on the `Employees` table and then set the values in the `ID` and `Name` columns from the `intIDs` and `strNames` variables. Next, add the new row of data to the `Employees` table by calling the `Add` method on the `Rows` collection, passing it the `objDataRow` object.

```
        For intIndex = 0 To 8
            'Instantiate a datarow object from the DataSet
            objDataRow = objDataSet.Tables("Employees").NewRow

            'Set the values in the DataRow
            objDataRow.Item("ID") = intIDs(intIndex)
            objDataRow.Item("Name") = strNames(intIndex)

            'Add the DataRow to the DataSet
            objDataSet.Tables("Employees").Rows.Add(objDataRow)
        Next
```

At this point you have constructed an entire `DataSet` object, including a new `DataTable` object with columns and rows, programmatically using static data. All that's left to do now is to return the `DataSet` to the caller, which is done in the last line of code here:

```
        'Return the DataSet
        Return objDataSet
    End Function
```

DataView Function

The next method in the `Generate` class is the `DataView` function. As you might have guessed, this function returns a `DataView` object. Because a `DataView` is derived from a `DataTable` in a `DataSet`, the code in this method couldn't be simpler. All you need to do is instantiate a new instance of the `DataView` class, passing it the `DataTable` from a `DataSet` object.

Because the `DataSet` method in this class creates a `DataTable`, you can simply call that method and specify the `Employees` table, passing that data to the constructor for the `DataView` class. Finally, just to make things interesting, sort the `DataView` using the `Name` column, sorting the data in ascending order:

```
    Public Function DataView() As DataView
        'Instantiate a new DataView with the Employees table
        DataView = New DataView(DataSet.Tables("Employees"))
        'Sort the DataView by the Name column in ascending order
        DataView.Sort = "Name Asc"
    End Function
```

DataTable Function

Creating the `DataTable` function is even easier that the `DataView` function. Here all you need to do is return a `DataTable`, so you call the `DataSet` function and specify the table name in the `Return` statement:

```
Public Function DataTable() As DataTable
    'Return the Employees DataTable
    Return DataSet.Tables("Employees")
End Function
```

ArrayListOfStrings Function

Now things start to get interesting again. The next two methods in this class return an `ArrayList` object, and the data returned by these two methods are the only dynamically generated data in this class.

The `ArrayListOfStrings` function returns an `ArrayList` created using string values. This function starts by instantiating a new instance of the `ArrayList` class. Then you add a static value as the first item. Again, this first item provides a little instruction to the end user when this `ArrayList` is bound to a `ComboBox` control and the first item is set as the selected item.

```
Public Function ArrayListOfStrings() As ArrayList
    'Instantiate a new ArrayList
    ArrayListOfStrings = New ArrayList

    'Add the first item to the ArrayList
    ArrayListOfStrings.Add("(Select a Drive)")
```

You want to use the `Drives` property of the `FileSystem` class to add each drive on the user's computer and its status to the `ArrayList`. The `Drives` property returns a collection of `DriveInfo` classes, and you can extract the drive name and its status using the `Name` and `IsReady` properties of this class, as shown in the following code:

```
    'Loop through the drives on the local computer
    'and add each drive and its status to the ArrayList
    For Each objDriveInfo As IO.DriveInfo In My.Computer.FileSystem.Drives
        If objDriveInfo.IsReady Then
            ArrayListOfStrings.Add(objDriveInfo.Name & " - Status: Ready")
        Else
            ArrayListOfStrings.Add(objDriveInfo.Name & " - Status: Not Ready")
        End If
    Next
End Function
```

ArrayListOfObjects Function

The `ArrayListOfObjects` function operates in a similar manner as the `ArrayListOfStrings` function in that it returns an `ArrayList` containing drive information on the user's computer. Where this function differs is that it uses the user-defined `DriveInfo` class, adding the drive information obtained from the `IO.DriveInfo` class and then adding the user-defined `DriveInfo` class to the `ArrayList`:

```
Public Function ArrayListOfObjects() As ArrayList
    'Instantiate a new ArrayList
    ArrayListOfObjects = New ArrayList
```

```
                'Add the first item to the ArrayList
                ArrayListOfObjects.Add(New DriveInfo("(Select a Drive)"))

                'Loop through the drives on the local computer
                'and add each drive and its status to the ArrayList
                For Each objDriveInfo As IO.DriveInfo In My.Computer.FileSystem.Drives
                    If objDriveInfo.IsReady Then
                        ArrayListOfObjects.Add(New DriveInfo(objDriveInfo.Name & _
                            " - Status: Ready"))
                    Else
                        ArrayListOfObjects.Add(New DriveInfo(objDriveInfo.Name & _
                            " - Status: Not Ready"))
                    End If
                Next
            End Function
```

XML Function

The final method in the `Generate` class is the `XML` function. However, this function does not return an `XmlDocument` class as you would expect. Instead, it returns the XML data as a `MemoryStream` object. The design decision behind this is that this allows the `ControlData` class to read the XML data contained in the `MemoryStream` object directly into a `DataSet` object via the `ReadXml` method of the `DataSet` object without having to save the XML data to the hard drive and read that data from the hard drive into the `DataSet` object.

This function starts by instantiating a new `MemoryStream` object and an `XmlTextWriter` object. The `objMemoryStream` object will be used to return the data in the memory stream, and the `objXmlTextWriter` object will be used to generate the XML data. Notice that the constructor for the `XmlTextWriter` class accepts the `objMemoryStream` object as input along with the type of encoding to use. The `UTF8` (Unicode Transformation Format) encoding format is the standard encoding format used with XML, as it supports Unicode data, enabling you to have special characters in the XML data.

```
        Public Function XML() As MemoryStream
            'Declare and instantiate a MemoryStream and XmlTextWriter objects
            Dim objMemoryStream As New MemoryStream
            Dim objXmlTextWriter As New XmlTextWriter(objMemoryStream, Encoding.UTF8)
```

The `WriteStartDocument` method of the `objXmlTextWriter` object writes the XML declaration of an XML document. The declaration produced by this method looks as follows: `<?xml version="1.0" standalone="yes"?>`.

Next, start the root element of the XML document by calling the `WriteStartElement` method. This method accepts the element name to write. You must call the `WriteEndElement` method for each starting element that you write calling the `WriteStartElement` method.

```
        'Begin the XML document
        objXmlTextWriter.WriteStartDocument()

        'Write the root element
        objXmlTextWriter.WriteStartElement("Colors")
```

Now set up a `For...Next` loop to process the system colors in the array variables that were defined at the top of this class. Notice that you are writing three different child elements under the `<Color>` element: `<HexValue>`, `<SystemColorName>`, and `<RGBValue>`. This is to demonstrate that it does matter how many elements are contained in your XML document; you bind only the element names that you need in your controls. In the binding examples shown in Figure 8-3, the `<HexValue>` and `<SystemColorName>` elements were bound to the `ComboBox`, `ListBox`, and `ListView` controls. The `DataGridView` control accepts the data source and data table, so all columns in the XML document are displayed in that control.

You write the `<Color>` element out by calling the `WriteStartElement` method on the `objXMLTextWriter` object and then write the child elements and their values using the `WriteElementString` method. This method writes the element and the element value. Notice that when using the `WriteElementString` method there is no corresponding end method that you need to call. This method writes the element, the value for the element, and the closing element tag all in one method call.

```
For intIndex = 0 To 3
    'Write the Color element
    objXmlTextWriter.WriteStartElement("Color")
    objXmlTextWriter.WriteElementString("HexValue", strHexValues(intIndex))
    objXmlTextWriter.WriteElementString("SystemColorName", _
        strColorNames(intIndex))
    objXmlTextWriter.WriteElementString("RGBValue", strRGBValues(intIndex))
    'End the Color element
    objXmlTextWriter.WriteEndElement()
Next
```

After processing the loop, you write the ending `</Colors>` element by calling the `WriteEndElement` method and then close the XML document by calling the `WriteEndDocument` method. Then you flush the buffer on the `objXmlTextWriter` object and reposition the `objMemoryStream` object back to the beginning of the stream in preparation for reading by the procedure that called this method:

```
    'End the root element and document
    objXmlTextWriter.WriteEndElement()
    objXmlTextWriter.WriteEndDocument()

    'Flush the buffer to the MemoryStream and reset
    'the position of the MemoryStream to the beginning
    'of the XML document
    objXmlTextWriter.Flush()
    objMemoryStream.Position = 0

    Return objMemoryStream
End Function
```

ControlData Class

The last class to cover before getting to the code in the Binding Examples form is the `ControlData` class. This class is a generic class that is used as the data source for data binding in the Binding Examples form. It contains five overloaded constructors for accepting input data in the following formats:

❑ DataSet

❑ DataView

- ❏ DataTable
- ❏ ArrayList
- ❏ XML

This class provides three properties that are used for data binding the controls shown in Figure 8-1: DataSource, DisplayMember, and ValueMember. An additional property is provided to support data binding the DataGridView control to a DataTable and is called DataTableName.

Let's start with the class design. This class was designed to be used as a source of data and therefore implements the IDisposable interface, as shown in the following code. This enables the class to clean up the resources it uses and to be used in a Using...End Using statement block.

There are very few variables and objects defined in this class. strDisplayMember and strValueMember are used to save the column names in the data source that will be bound to the DisplayMember and ValueMember properties of the ComboBox, ListBox, and ListView controls. The strDataTableName variable is used to save the table name of a DataTable. Each of these variables is returned in their corresponding properties.

The objDataSource object is defined as an Object data type and will contain the data source for this class. This will be the data source that is bound to the DataSource property of the ComboBox, ListBox, ListView, and DataGridView controls:

```
Public Class ControlData
    Implements IDisposable

    'Private variables and objects
    Private strDisplayMember As String
    Private strValueMember As String
    Private strDataTableName As String

    Private objDataSource As Object
```

Constructor That Accepts a DataSet

The first constructor for this class accepts a DataSet as input. Therefore, when this class is instantiated, a DataSet object is passed to this constructor and sets this class up to work with a DataSet. The DataSet is saved in the objDataSource object, the second column name is saved in the strDisplayMember variable, and the first column name is saved in the strValueMember variable.

This constructor assumes and requires that your DataSet have at least two columns. If you wanted to use the same column for the DisplayMember and ValueMember properties, then you would need to write an overloaded constructor that accepts a DataSet and the name of the column to set in the strDisplayMember and strValueMember properties. This holds true for all constructors in this class.

```
    Public Sub New(ByVal dataSet As DataSet)
        'Save the input parameters
        objDataSource = dataSet
        strDisplayMember = dataSet.Tables(0).Columns.Item(1).ColumnName
        strValueMember = dataSet.Tables(0).Columns.Item(0).ColumnName
    End Sub
```

Constructor That Accepts a DataView

The next constructor for this class accepts a DataView as input. Again the input parameter, the DataView object, is set in the objDataSource object, the second column name in the DataView is set in the strDisplayMember variable, and the first column name in the DataView is set in the strValueMember variable:

```
Public Sub New(ByVal dataView As DataView)
    'Save the input parameters
    objDataSource = dataView
    strDisplayMember = dataView.Table.Columns.Item(1).ColumnName
    strValueMember = dataView.Table.Columns.Item(0).ColumnName
End Sub
```

Constructor That Accepts a DataTable

The third constructor for this class accepts a DataTable as its input parameter. Like the previous two constructors, it is assumed that the DataTable contains at least two columns. The second column name is set in the strDisplayMember variable, and the first column name is set in the strValueMember variable:

```
Public Sub New(ByVal dataTable As DataTable)
    'Save the input parameters
    objDataSource = dataTable
    strDisplayMember = dataTable.Columns.Item(1).ColumnName
    strValueMember = dataTable.Columns.Item(0).ColumnName
End Sub
```

Constructor That Accepts an ArrayList

The next constructor accepts an ArrayList as its input parameter. An ArrayList only contains one column of data; therefore, the strDisplayMember and strValueMember variables are set to empty strings:

```
Public Sub New(ByVal arrayList As ArrayList)
    'Save the input parameters
    objDataSource = arrayList
    strDisplayMember = String.Empty
    strValueMember = String.Empty
End Sub
```

Constructor That Accepts a MemoryStream

The final constructor for this class accepts the XML document through a MemoryStream. The XML document will actually be loaded into a DataSet object because a DataSet is nothing more than XML behind the scenes. This enables you to work with an XML document very easily when performing data binding on your controls.

As shown in the second line of code, the DataSet object reads the XML from the MemoryStream via the ReadXml method of the DataSet object. The ReadXml method is an overloaded method that accepts a variety of XML input. The MemoryStream object is very easy to work with and provides a clean method for loading the XML into a DataSet.

Once the DataSet has been loaded with the XML document, it is saved in the objDataSource object. As before, this constructor assumes that the DataSet contains at least two columns of data; and the second column name is set in the `strDisplayMember` variable and the first column name is set in the `strValueMember` variable:

```
Public Sub New(ByVal xml As MemoryStream)
    'Declare and instantiate a DataSet object
    Dim objDataSet As New DataSet
    'Read the XML from the MemoryStream
    objDataSet.ReadXml(xml)
    'Save the input
    objDataSource = objDataSet
    strDisplayMember = objDataSet.Tables(0).Columns.Item(1).ColumnName
    strValueMember = objDataSet.Tables(0).Columns.Item(0).ColumnName
End Sub
```

Read-Only Properties

The four read-only properties are shown in the code that follows. The `DataSource` property returns its output as an `Object` data type because the constructors for this class accept a variety of input data types. If the data type of the `objDataSource` object is a `DataSet`, then the table name of the first table in the `DataSet` is set in the `strDataTableName` variable, which is returned in the last property shown here.

The `DisplayMember` property returns the `strDisplayMember` variable as a `String` data type and the `ValueMember` property returns the `strValueMember` variable as a `String` data type. These first three properties correspond to the `DataSource`, `DisplayMember`, and `ValueMember` properties of the `ComboBox`, `ListBox`, and `ListView` controls; therefore, when using this class as a data source for these controls, these properties are set to their counterparts in those controls.

The `DataGridView` control contains the `DataSource` property but does not contain the `DisplayMember` or `ValueMember` properties. It does, however, contain the `DataMember` property, which is set to the table name of the table in the data source. Therefore, the last property shown here is named `DataTableName` in order to more clearly identify its purpose:

```
Public ReadOnly Property DataSource() As Object
    Get
        If TypeOf objDataSource Is DataSet Then
            strDataTableName = objDataSource.Tables(0).TableName
        End If

        Return objDataSource
    End Get
End Property

Public ReadOnly Property DisplayMember() As String
    Get
        Return strDisplayMember
    End Get
End Property

Public ReadOnly Property ValueMember() As String
    Get
        Return strValueMember
    End Get
End Property

Public ReadOnly Property DataTableName() As String
```

```
        Get
            Return strDataTableName
        End Get
    End Property
```

Binding Examples Form

The Binding Examples form contains one main procedure that handles binding data to the controls, and four procedures to handle the selection of data in the four controls: ComboBox, ListBox, DataGridView, and ListView.

The form class has some basic variables and objects that are used throughout the form. The blnLoading variable is used in the event handler for the SelectedIndexChanged event for the ComboBox and ListBox control and in the event handler for the RowEnter event for the DataGridView control. You'll see how this is used in those event handlers later in this section.

The SelectedText and SelectedValue constants are String constants that are set in the event handlers for the controls when an item is selected in those controls. Again, you'll see how this is implemented later in this section.

The objGenerate object is used when binding data to the controls. You'll see how this object is used next.

```
    'Private variables and objects
    Private blnLoading As Boolean

    Private Const SelectedText As String = "Selected Text: "
    Private Const SelectedValue As String = "Selected Value: "

    Private objGenerate As New Generate
```

btnBind_Click Procedure

The btnBind_Click procedure is the event handler procedure for the Click event of the Bind button on the form and is where all the data binding takes place. This procedure starts off by setting the blnLoading variable to True; you'll see its purpose later in the SelectedIndexChanged event and RowEnter event handlers. Next, you clear all the labels on the form, setting them to the constants that were defined in the preceding code:

```
    Private Sub btnBind_Click(ByVal sender As Object, _
        ByVal e As System.EventArgs) Handles btnBind.Click

        'Turn on loading flag
        blnLoading = True

        'Clear the labels
        lblComboBoxSelectedText.Text = SelectedText
        lblComboBoxSelectedValue.Text = SelectedValue
        lblListBoxSelectedText.Text = SelectedText
        lblListBoxSelectedValue.Text = SelectedValue
        lblDataGridViewSelectedText.Text = SelectedText
        lblDataGridViewSelectedValue.Text = SelectedValue
        lblListViewSelectedText.Text = SelectedText
        lblListViewSelectedValue.Text = SelectedValue
```

Binding a DataSet in the btnBind_Click Procedure

Using a `Select...Case` statement, you determine which radio button on the form has been checked and then perform the appropriate data binding based on the selected radio button. The first radio button performs data binding for a `DataSet` and is appropriately commented in the code that follows.

The first control to be bound is the `ComboBox` control. The `ControlData` class is declared and instantiated in a `Using...End Using` statement block. Notice that you also use the `Generate` class to generate a `DataSet` object and pass it to the constructor of the `ControlData` class.

Then, using a `With...End With` statement block, you set the data binding properties of the `ComboBox` control. Set the `DataSource` property using the `objControlData` object, setting it to the `DataTable` contained in the `DataSet`.

The `DataSet` class implements the `IListSource` interface, which, if you recall from the `ListViewExtended` class, does not provide the data that you need. You need the object that implements the `IList` interface, which is the `DataTable` contained in the `DataSet`.

The `DisplayMember` and `ValueMember` properties are set using their counterparts from the `ControlData` class. Remember that these properties in the `ControlData` class return the column names in the `DataTable` to which these properties will bind in the `DataTable`.

```
'Bind the ComboBox based on the selected option
Select Case True
    Case optComboBoxDataSet.Checked
        '************************************************
        'Bind a DataSet
        '************************************************

        Using objControlData As New ControlData(objGenerate.DataSet)
            'Bind to a ComboBox
            With cboBinding
                .DataSource = objControlData.DataSource.Tables( _
                    objControlData.DataTableName)
                .DisplayMember = objControlData.DisplayMember
                .ValueMember = objControlData.ValueMember
            End With
        End Using
```

The next control that is bound is the `ListBox` control. As before, go through the same steps by implementing the binding code in a `Using...End Using` block. Declare and instantiate a new instance of the `ControlData` class and pass the constructor a `DataSet` object generated by the `Generate` class.

Again, the `DataSource` property is set to the `DataTable` within the `DataSet` object to ensure proper data binding to the data. The `DisplayMember` and `ValueMember` properties are set using the column names returned in their corresponding properties in the `ControlData` class:

```
Using objControlData As New ControlData(objGenerate.DataSet)
    'Bind to a ListBox
    With lstBinding
        .DataSource = objControlData.DataSource.Tables( _
            objControlData.DataTableName)
```

```
                .DisplayMember = objControlData.DisplayMember
                .ValueMember = objControlData.ValueMember
            End With
        End Using
```

You start the data binding process for the `DataGridView` in the same manner as the previous two controls by declaring and instantiating a new instance of the `ControlData` class and using the `Generate` class to generate a `DataSet`.

The difference lies in the properties of the `DataGridView` control that are bound. The `DataSource` property can and does expect a complete `DataSet` object to be bound to it. However, recall that the `DataGridView` control does not implement a `DisplayMember` and `ValueMember` property but does implement the `DataMember` property. This property expects the table name of the `DataTable` in the `DataSet` that it should use. The code in the `DataGridView` control examines the columns in the `DataTable` in the `DataSet` and binds all columns to the control.

The final two lines of code shown here are merely for aesthetic purposes. The `AutoResizeColumns` method automatically resizes the columns in the `DataGridView` control based on the length of data in the columns. The `SelectionMode` property enables the full row select feature so that clicking on any column in a row of data causes the entire row to be selected:

```
            Using objControlData As New ControlData(objGenerate.DataSet)
                'Bind to a DataGridView
                With dgvBinding
                    .DataSource = objControlData.DataSource
                    .DataMember = objControlData.DataTableName
                    .AutoResizeColumns()
                    .SelectionMode = DataGridViewSelectionMode.FullRowSelect
                End With
            End Using
```

The last control in this `Case` statement to be bound to a `DataSet` is the `ListViewExtended` control. This `ListView` control has been extended to provide the `DataSource`, `DisplayMember`, and `ValueMember` properties that can be bound at runtime, as shown in the code that follows. These properties are set to their corresponding properties in the `ControlData` class.

Note that the `DataSource` property is bound directly to the `DataSet` and not to the `DataTable` contained in the `DataSet`. This is because code has been written in the `ListViewExtended` class to handle various data sources and to automatically determine the appropriate data type of the data source.

The final line of code in the `With...End With` statement is the `AutoResizeColumns` method. This method accepts a constant from the `ColumnHeaderAutoResizeStyle` enumeration, indicating the type of auto resizing that it should perform. The code here specifies that the `AutoResizeColumns` method should resize the columns based on the width of their content. The other two options are to resize the columns based on the size of the content in the column header and to clear the resized columns back to their default widths:

```
            Using objControlData As New ControlData(objGenerate.DataSet)
                'Bind to a ListView
                With lvwBinding
                    .DataSource = objControlData.DataSource
```

```
            .DisplayMember = objControlData.DisplayMember
            .ValueMember = objControlData.ValueMember
            .AutoResizeColumns( _
                ColumnHeaderAutoResizeStyle.ColumnContent)
        End With
    End Using
```

Binding a DataView in the btnBind_Click Procedure

The next Case statement binds a DataView to the controls and has been appropriately commented in the code that follows. All of the code in this procedure uses the same format: The ControlData class is used in a Using...End Using block of code and the Generate class is used to generate the input for the appropriate constructor within the ControlData class. Then the various controls on the form are bound to the data in a With...End With block of code.

In the last Case statement you bound the DataSource property of the ComboBox to the DataTable in the DataSet. However, notice that the following code uses the DataView directly and does not specify a DataTable. That is because a DataSet can contain one or more DataTables, whereas a DataView is a view based on the contents of a single DataTable. The DataSource, DisplayMember, and ValueMember properties of the ComboBox control are bound to their counterparts in the ControlData class.

```
Case optComboBoxDataView.Checked
    '**********************************************
    'Bind a DataView that was sorted
    '**********************************************

    Using objControlData As New ControlData(objGenerate.DataView)
        'Bind to a ComboBox
        With cboBinding
            .DataSource = objControlData.DataSource
            .DisplayMember = objControlData.DisplayMember
            .ValueMember = objControlData.ValueMember
        End With
    End Using
```

The ListBox control is also bound directly to the DataView, as indicated by the following code. Likewise, the DataSource, DisplayMember, and ValueMember properties are bound to their counterparts in the ControlData class.

```
    Using objControlData As New ControlData(objGenerate.DataView)
        'Bind to a ListBox
        With lstBinding
            .DataSource = objControlData.DataSource
            .DisplayMember = objControlData.DisplayMember
            .ValueMember = objControlData.ValueMember
        End With
    End Using
```

The code for the DataGridView control is slightly different from the code that was used when binding this control to a DataSet. The DataSource property in the following code specifies the DataView and does not contain the DataMember property. When you bound this control to a DataSet, you had to let the control know which table in the DataSet to use by specifying the table name in the DataMember property. Here you simply bind the `DataView` to the `DataSource` property and do not specify the `DataMember` property, as a `DataView` only has a single `DataTable`.

You still call the `AutoResizeColumns` method to automatically resize the columns, and set the `SelectionMode` property to select a full row when the user clicks on a column in a row of data. These properties can be set at design time, but I thought it would be interesting for you to see these properties set at runtime.

```
Using objControlData As New ControlData(objGenerate.DataView)
    'Bind to a DataGridView
    With dgvBinding
        .DataSource = objControlData.DataSource
        .AutoResizeColumns()
        .SelectionMode = DataGridViewSelectionMode.FullRowSelect
    End With
End Using
```

The `ListViewExtended` control is bound in the same manner as it was when binding it to a `DataSet`. You just set the `DataSource` property to the `DataSource` property in the `ControlData` class and then set the `DisplayMember` and `ValueMember` properties to their counterparts in the `ControlData` class. As before, you call the `AutoResizeColumns` method to automatically resize the column data.

```
Using objControlData As New ControlData(objGenerate.DataView)
    'Bind to a ListView
    With lvwBinding
        .DataSource = objControlData.DataSource
        .DisplayMember = objControlData.DisplayMember
        .ValueMember = objControlData.ValueMember
        .AutoResizeColumns( _
            ColumnHeaderAutoResizeStyle.ColumnContent)
    End With
End Using
```

Binding a DataTable in the btnBind_Click Procedure

The next `Case` statement binds the controls to a `DataTable`. All of the code in this section is very straightforward and simply binds the `DataSource`, `DisplayMember`, and `ValueMember` properties of the controls to their corresponding properties in the `ControlData` class:

```
Case optComboBoxDataTable.Checked
    '***********************************************
    'Bind a DataTable
    '***********************************************

    Using objControlData As New ControlData(objGenerate.DataTable)
        'Bind to a ComboBox
        With cboBinding
            .DataSource = objControlData.DataSource
            .DisplayMember = objControlData.DisplayMember
            .ValueMember = objControlData.ValueMember
        End With
    End Using
```

```
                Using objControlData As New ControlData(objGenerate.DataTable)
                    'Bind to a ListBox
                    With lstBinding
                        .DataSource = objControlData.DataSource
                        .DisplayMember = objControlData.DisplayMember
                        .ValueMember = objControlData.ValueMember
                    End With
                End Using

                Using objControlData As New ControlData(objGenerate.DataTable)
                    'Bind to a DataGridView
                    With dgvBinding
                        .DataSource = objControlData.DataSource
                        .AutoResizeColumns()
                        .SelectionMode = DataGridViewSelectionMode.FullRowSelect
                    End With
                End Using

                Using objControlData As New ControlData(objGenerate.DataTable)
                    'Bind to a ListView
                    With lvwBinding
                        .DataSource = objControlData.DataSource
                        .DisplayMember = objControlData.DisplayMember
                        .ValueMember = objControlData.ValueMember
                        .AutoResizeColumns( _
                            ColumnHeaderAutoResizeStyle.ColumnContent)
                    End With
                End Using
```

Binding XML in the btnBind_Click Procedure

The code in this next Case statement mimics the code that was used to bind the controls to a DataSet. Remember that while the ControlData class reads XML data, it converts that data into a DataSet. Thus, the code here mimics the code needed when binding to a DataSet:

```
            Case optComboBoxXML.Checked
                '************************************************
                'Bind an XML Document
                '************************************************

                Using objControlData As New ControlData(objGenerate.XML)
                    'Bind to a ComboBox
                    With cboBinding
                        .DataSource = objControlData.DataSource.Tables( _
                            objControlData.DataTableName)
                        .DisplayMember = objControlData.DisplayMember
                        .ValueMember = objControlData.ValueMember
                    End With
                End Using

                Using objControlData As New ControlData(objGenerate.XML)
                    'Bind to a ListBox
                    With lstBinding
                        .DataSource = objControlData.DataSource.Tables( _
```

```
                        objControlData.DataTableName)
                    .DisplayMember = objControlData.DisplayMember
                    .ValueMember = objControlData.ValueMember
            End With
        End Using

        Using objControlData As New ControlData(objGenerate.XML)
            'Bind to a DataGridView
            With dgvBinding
                .DataSource = objControlData.DataSource
                .DataMember = objControlData.DataTableName
                .AutoResizeColumns()
                .SelectionMode = DataGridViewSelectionMode.FullRowSelect
            End With
        End Using

        Using objControlData As New ControlData(objGenerate.XML)
            'Bind to a ListView
            With lvwBinding
                .DataSource = objControlData.DataSource.Tables( _
                    objControlData.DataTableName)
                .DisplayMember = objControlData.DisplayMember
                .ValueMember = objControlData.ValueMember
                .AutoResizeColumns( _
                    ColumnHeaderAutoResizeStyle.ColumnContent)
            End With
        End Using
```

Binding an ArrayList in the btnBind_Click Procedure

This is where things start to get really interesting. Remember that an `ArrayList` contains only one column of data; therefore, you do not set the `DisplayMember` or `ValueMember` properties on the controls. These properties are used to specify the column in a `DataTable` that the control should use to display data. Because an `ArrayList` does not have named columns, these properties are omitted from the code, as you'll see when you examine the following example.

The code for the `ComboBox`, `ListBox`, and `ListViewExtended` controls are all the same. You use the `Generate` class to generate an array of strings in an `ArrayList` and bind the `DataSource` property in the `ControlData` class to the `DataSource` property of these controls:

```
        Case optComboBoxArrayList.Checked
            '***********************************************
            'Bind an ArrayList
            '***********************************************

            Using objControlData As New ControlData( _
                objGenerate.ArrayListOfStrings)
                'Bind to a ComboBox
                With cboBinding
                    .DataSource = objControlData.DataSource
                End With
            End Using

            Using objControlData As New ControlData( _
                objGenerate.ArrayListOfStrings)
```

```
            'Bind to a ListBox
            With lstBinding
                .DataSource = objControlData.DataSource
            End With
        End Using

        Using objControlData As New ControlData( _
            objGenerate.ArrayListOfStrings)
            'Bind to a ListView
            With lvwBinding
                .DataSource = objControlData.DataSource
                .AutoResizeColumns( _
                    ColumnHeaderAutoResizeStyle.ColumnContent)
            End With
        End Using
```

If you refer back to Figure 8-4 for a moment, you'll notice that the DataGridView control displays the length of the strings contained in the ArrayList and not the actual data itself. The following code shows that the Generate class has been called to generate an ArrayList of strings, as it was for the controls in the previous section of code.

Although the Visual Studio 2005 documentation states that a DataGridView control can be bound to an Array or ArrayList of strings, you'll quickly discover that the data does not display correctly, as demonstrated in this example. A message dialog box is displayed after the control is bound, with the appropriate message about the binding of this control to an array of string values. This pauses the execution of the code so you can see this behavior before moving on to a workaround for this problem.

```
        Using objControlData As New ControlData( _
            objGenerate.ArrayListOfStrings)
            'Bind to a DataGridView
            With dgvBinding
                .DataSource = objControlData.DataSource
                .AutoResizeColumns()
                .SelectionMode = DataGridViewSelectionMode.FullRowSelect
            End With

            MessageBox.Show("This is an example of a DataGridView " & _
                "bound to an ArrayList containing a list of strings." & _
                ControlChars.CrLf & "Notice that the data is the " & _
                "length of the strings in the ArrayList and not the " & _
                "actual" & ControlChars.CrLf & "strings themselves.", _
                My.Application.Info.Title, MessageBoxButtons.OK, _
                MessageBoxIcon.Information)
        End Using
```

If you refer back to Figure 8-5 for a moment, you'll notice that the data in the DataGridView control is displayed in the same manner as it is for the other controls, displaying the data contained in the ArrayList. This is because of the ArrayListOfObjects method in the Generate class. Remember that this method adds the DriveInfo class to the ArrayList, and the DriveInfo class implements a read-only property that returns a String data type.

The DataGridView control is "smart" enough to recognize the object in the ArrayList and that it implements a property that returns a String value. Interestingly enough, if you were to create a class that returned a `Double` data type in a property and added a collection of that class to an `ArrayList` and bound that `ArrayList` to the `DataGridView` control, it would display the actual values returned from the property in that class.

As before, a message box dialog box is used with the appropriate message to pause the code. This enables you to view the data in the `DataGridView` control and compare it to the other controls, while at the same time you are informed about what is happening in the code.

```
Using objControlData As New ControlData( _
    objGenerate.ArrayListOfObjects)
    With dgvBinding
        .DataSource = objControlData.DataSource
        .AutoResizeColumns()
        .SelectionMode = DataGridViewSelectionMode.FullRowSelect
    End With

    MessageBox.Show("This is an example of a DataGridView " & _
        "bound to an ArrayList containing a list of objects." & _
        ControlChars.CrLf & "Now you are able to get the " & _
        "data from an ArrayList to display correctly.", _
        My.Application.Info.Title, MessageBoxButtons.OK, _
        MessageBoxIcon.Information)
End Using
```

Binding a Business Object in the btnBind_Click Procedure

This last `Case` statement binds a user-defined business object to the controls. Remember that the `Customer` class in this business object implements the `CustomerList` property, which accepts an input parameter that enables you to specify a value that should be inserted before the first row of data, and that this property returns a `DataTable` object.

Notice in this first section of code that binds the business object to the `ComboBox` that you are passing a string of the data that you want inserted before the first row of data. This provides some instructions to users when they see the `ComboBox` that they need to select a customer.

Recall that the `Customer` class provides the `CustomerListBindingProperties` property, which returns a `SortedList` of data that describes the bindings for the `CustomerList` property. The `DisplayMember` and `ValueMember` properties use this data to specify the columns in the `DataTable` returned from the `CustomerList` property that the `ComboBox` should use.

The `SortedList` data type contains a key/value pair of objects. In this case, the key and value are defined as `String` data types, but they could contain any data that you wanted. A key exists in the `SortedList` named `DisplayMember`, which returns the column name in the `DataSet` that contains the data that should be displayed via the `DisplayMember` property. The key named `ValueMember` in the `SortedList` contains the column name in the `DataSet` that should be used for the `ValueMember` property. Each of these items is accessed through the `Item` property of the `SortedList` specifying the key name and returning the value from the `Item` for the specified key.

```
Case optComboBoxBusinessObject.Checked
    '************************************************
    'Bind a Business Object
    '************************************************
```

```
Using objCustomer As New Customers.Customer
    'Bind to a ComboBox
    With cboBinding
        .DataSource = objCustomer.CustomerList("(Select Customer)")
        .DisplayMember = _
            objCustomer.CustomerListBindingProperties.Item( _
            "DisplayMember").ToString
        .ValueMember = _
            objCustomer.CustomerListBindingProperties.Item( _
            "ValueMember").ToString
    End With
End Using
```

The `ListBox` uses the same key/value pairs from the `CustomerListBindingProperties` property for the `DisplayMember` and `ValueMember` properties as the `ComboBox`. The call to the `CustomerList` property in this code passes an empty string, which indicates that you do not want a value inserted before the first row of data. When the `ListBox` is bound to the `DataTable`, it displays the column specified in the `DisplayMember` property:

```
Using objCustomer As New Customers.Customer
    'Bind to a ListBox
    With lstBinding
        .DataSource = objCustomer.CustomerList(String.Empty)
        .DisplayMember = _
            objCustomer.CustomerListBindingProperties.Item( _
            "DisplayMember").ToString
        .ValueMember = _
            objCustomer.CustomerListBindingProperties.Item( _
            "ValueMember").ToString
    End With
End Using
```

Because you are binding the `DataGridView` control to a `DataTable` object, you do not have to set the `DataMember` property. Therefore, it has been omitted. Here you bind the `DataSource` property to the `DataTable` returned from the `CustomerList` property in the `Customer` class of the business object:

```
Using objCustomer As New Customers.Customer
    'Bind to a DataGridView
    With dgvBinding
        .DataSource = objCustomer.CustomerList(String.Empty)
        .AutoResizeColumns()
        .SelectionMode = DataGridViewSelectionMode.FullRowSelect
    End With
End Using
```

The final section of code in this procedure binds the data returned from the `CustomerList` property to the `DataSource` property of the `ListViewExtended` control. Notice that the `DisplayMember` and `ValueMember` properties have been commented out in the following code. The commented code is included so you can see how this control can be bound to specific columns of data from the `CustomerList` property.

By commenting out these two properties, the `ListViewExtended` control displays all columns of data contained in the `DataTable` returned from the `CustomerList` property, as shown in Figure 8-6. This demonstrates the dual functionality in the `AddColumnHeaders` and `BindData` procedures of the `ListViewExtended` class.

The final line of code in this procedure turns off the `blnLoading` flag. You'll see how this flag is used in the next section of code.

```
Using objCustomer As New Customers.Customer
    'Bind to a ListView
    With lvwBinding
        .DataSource = objCustomer.CustomerList(String.Empty)
        '.DisplayMember = _
        '    objCustomer.CustomerListBindingProperties.Item( _
        '    "DisplayMember").ToString
        '.ValueMember = _
        '    objCustomer.CustomerListBindingProperties.Item( _
        '    "ValueMember").ToString
        .AutoResizeColumns( _
            ColumnHeaderAutoResizeStyle.ColumnContent)
    End With
End Using

End Select

'Turn off the loading flag
blnLoading = False
End Sub
```

cboBinding_SelectedIndexChanged Event Handler Procedure

You are almost finished with the code examination. This section covers the event handler procedures for the `ComboBox`, `ListBox`, `DataGridView`, and `ListViewExtended` controls. These event handler procedures are executed when you select a row of data in these controls.

The `SelectedIndexChanged` event is fired when you select an entry in the `ComboBox` control, which causes the selected index value to be changed to the row of data selected. The first thing that happens in this procedure is a check of the `blnLoading` flag. If this flag has a value of `True`, then you exit this procedure, as the control is being loaded.

If you comment out this section of code and set a breakpoint on the `Try` statement and then bind the controls on the form, you'll notice that this event is fired twice: once when the `DataSource` property of the `ComboBox` is set and once when the `DisplayMember` property is set. The selected index of the `ComboBox` is changed during the loading of this control, so the `SelectedIndexChanged` event is fired. By including this flag, you can test for a loading event and exit the procedure, as there is nothing to do.

Notice that a `Try...Catch` block has been added to this procedure. When the `ComboBox` is bound to a data source that contains a `DataTable`, the `SelectedItem` property contains a `DataRowView` object. Therefore, in order to access the selected item text, you must access the second column in the `DataRowView` object using the `Item` property of the `SelectedItem` property of the `ComboBox` control.

When the `ComboBox` control is bound to an `ArrayList`, there is only one column of data, and trying to access a specific item using the `Item` property of the `SelectedItem` property will cause a `MissingMemberException` exception to be thrown. The `Catch` block is set to handle this exception and then to access the `SelectedItem` property, which at this point contains the actual text of the selected item.

The value returned from either the specific item in the `Item` property or the `SelectItem` property will be concatenated to the `SelectedText` constant and set in the `lblComboBoxSelectedText` label on the form. The last line of code concatenates the selected value of the row of data selected in the `ComboBox` to the `SelectedValue` constant and sets that text in the `lblComboBoxSelectedValue` label on the form. The `SelectedValue` property always returns the selected value as specified in the `ValueMember` property regardless of the data source that was used when binding this control.

```
Private Sub cboBinding_SelectedIndexChanged(ByVal sender As Object, _
    ByVal e As System.EventArgs) Handles cboBinding.SelectedIndexChanged

    'Exit if the ComboBox is being bound
    If blnLoading Then
        Exit Sub
    End If

    'Display the selected text and value
    Try
        lblComboBoxSelectedText.Text = _
            SelectedText & cboBinding.SelectedItem.Item(1)
    Catch MissingMemberExceptionErr As MissingMemberException
        lblComboBoxSelectedText.Text = _
            SelectedText & cboBinding.SelectedItem
    End Try
    lblComboBoxSelectedValue.Text = _
        SelectedValue & cboBinding.SelectedValue
End Sub
```

lstBinding_SelectedIndexChanged Event Handler Procedure

The `ListBox` control operates in the same manner as the `ComboBox` and therefore contains identical code:

```
Private Sub lstBinding_SelectedIndexChanged(ByVal sender As Object, _
    ByVal e As System.EventArgs) Handles lstBinding.SelectedIndexChanged

    'Exit if the ListBox is being bound
    If blnLoading Then
        Exit Sub
    End If

    'Display the selected text and value
    Try
        lblListBoxSelectedText.Text = _
            SelectedText & lstBinding.SelectedItem.Item(1)
    Catch MissingMemberExceptionErr As MissingMemberException
        lblListBoxSelectedText.Text = _
            SelectedText & lstBinding.SelectedItem
    End Try
    lblListBoxSelectedValue.Text = _
        SelectedValue & lstBinding.SelectedValue
End Sub
```

dgvBinding_RowEnter Event Handler Procedure

Just a quick note about the `DataGridView`: The `DataGridView` contains rows and columns, and the point where a row and column intersects is called a *cell*. You can access a column via the `Columns` collection, a row via the `Rows` collection, and a cell via the `Item` property.

The `DataGridView` does not have a `SelectedIndexChanged` event but a `RowEnter` event, as shown in the next section of code. The `RowEnter` event is fired when the `DataGridView` is loaded but does not cause an error like the `ComboBox` and `ListBox` controls. Instead, it merely selects the first row of data in control. To be consistent with the other controls and to prevent the first item from being automatically selected, the check for the `blnLoading` flag has also been added to this event handler procedure.

When you click on any cell in a row, this `RowEnter` event handler procedure is executed. You'll want to display the same text from the `DataGridView` that is displayed in the `ComboBox`, `ListBox`, and `ListViewExtended` controls in the `lblDataGridViewSelectedText` label. Therefore, you need to check the column count of the `Columns` collection to ensure that it is greater than 1. If it is, then you display the data from the second column in the `lblDataGridViewSelectedText` label. You access the data for a specific cell via the `Item` collection, passing it the zero-based index of the column and the row index. The row index of the selected row is available from the `DataGridViewCellEventArgs`, as shown in the following code.

The selected data from the `DataGridView` that is displayed in the `lblDataGridViewSelectedValue` on the form is always taken from the first column in the `DataGridView` control. In the binding examples demonstrated in this program, the first column of data is always the key to the row of data.

```
Private Sub dgvBinding_RowEnter(ByVal sender As Object, _
    ByVal e As System.Windows.Forms.DataGridViewCellEventArgs) _
    Handles dgvBinding.RowEnter

    'Exit if the DataGridView is being bound
    If blnLoading Then
        Exit Sub
    End If

    'Display the selected text and value
    If dgvBinding.Columns.Count > 1 Then
        lblDataGridViewSelectedText.Text = _
            SelectedText & dgvBinding.Item(1, e.RowIndex).Value
    Else
        lblDataGridViewSelectedText.Text = _
            SelectedValue & dgvBinding.Item(0, e.RowIndex).Value
    End If
    lblDataGridViewSelectedValue.Text = _
        SelectedValue & dgvBinding.Item(0, e.RowIndex).Value
End Sub
```

lvwBinding_SelectedIndexChanged Event Handler Procedure

When code was added to the `ListViewExtended` class to perform data binding, no code was added to automatically raise the `SelectedIndexChanged` event during the data binding process. Therefore, no check is needed for the `blnLoading` flag in this event handler for the `ListViewExtended` control.

The `ListView` control exhibits an odd behavior that is different from the `ComboBox` and `ListBox` controls. When an item is selected in the `ListView` control, the `SelectedIndexChanged` event is fired and the `SelectedItems` property contains the item that was selected. When you select another item in the `ListView` control, the `SelectedIndexChanged` is fired again but this time the `SelectedItems` property does not contain any data. Then the `SelectedIndexChanged` event is immediately fired again with the selected data in the `SelectedItems` property.

To overcome this odd behavior, you have to add code to check the `Count` property of the `SelectedItems` property to ensure that it has a value greater than 0, indicating that the `SelectedItems` property actually contains some data. You can see this check in the following code.

The data that is displayed in the `lblListViewSelectedText` label on the form always comes from the `Text` property of the `Item` property, which gets its data from the column in the data source that was specified in the `DisplayMember` property. The data that is displayed in the `lblListViewSelectedValue` label on the form comes from the `Tag` property of the `Item` property, which gets its data from the column in the data source that was specified in the `ValueMember` property. If the `ValueMember` property of the `ListViewExtended` control is not set, then the `Tag` property contains a value of `Nothing`. In this case, you simply use the data contained in the `Text` property.

```
Private Sub lvwBinding_SelectedIndexChanged(ByVal sender As Object, _
    ByVal e As System.EventArgs) Handles lvwBinding.SelectedIndexChanged

If lvwBinding.SelectedItems.Count > 0 Then
    'Display the selected text and value
    lblListViewSelectedText.Text = _
        SelectedText & lvwBinding.SelectedItems.Item(0).Text
    If IsNothing(lvwBinding.SelectedItems.Item(0).Tag) Then
        lblListViewSelectedValue.Text = _
            SelectedText & lvwBinding.SelectedItems.Item(0).Text
    Else
        lblListViewSelectedValue.Text = _
            SelectedValue & lvwBinding.SelectedItems.Item(0).Tag
    End If
End If
End Sub
```

Setting Up the Data Binding Application

Setup of the Data Binding application can be covered in one of two ways: using the installer or manually copying the required files to your computer. The first option provides an easy, fast approach to installing the program, whereas the second approach provides greater flexibility over where the files are installed.

Using the Installer

To install the Data Binding application, locate the `Chapter 08 - Data Binding\Installer` folder on the CD-ROM that came with this book and double-click the `setup.exe` program. You will be prompted with the Application Install dialog. Clicking the Install button will install and launch the application. Once the installer has installed your program, it is ready to be used.

Manual Installation

To manually install the Data Binding application, first create a folder on your computer where you want to place the program executable files. Then locate the `Chapter 08 - Data Binding\Source` folder on the CD-ROM that came with this book and navigate to the `bin\Release` folder. Copy the following files from the `Release` folder to the folder that you created on your computer:

❏   `Customers.dll`

❏   `Data Binding.exe`

❏   `ListViewEx.dll`

❏   `Northwind.mdb`

Configuring the Application

No special configuration of the application is required. You can execute the `Data Binding.exe` program and start using the application.

Summary

This chapter has touched on a lot of different areas related to data binding in the `ComboBox`, `ListBox`, `DataGridView`, and `ListView` controls. The first of these was extending the `ListView` control. When you examined the code for this extended control, you saw how the `IListSource` and `IList` interfaces were used in various data sources. When the functionality was implemented to build column headers and populate this control with data, you got a firsthand look at how to deal with the various interfaces provided by the different data sources that were set in the `DataSource` property.

Although the `ListViewExtended` control did not provide the code to implement design-time data binding, it did provide the appropriate attributes for the `DataSource`, `DisplayMember`, and `ValueMember` properties. You saw what attributes were required to provide the appropriate UI type editors for each of these properties.

The code in the `Generate` class provided a glimpse into creating a `DataSet`, `DataTable`, and `DataView` through code. It also demonstrated how to create an XML document using the `XmlTextWriter` and the `MemoryStream` classes. You learned how to create an `ArrayList` of strings and an `ArrayList` of objects, which demonstrated how string values are displayed in the `DataGridView` control when binding this data source to that control.

The code in the Binding Examples form was perhaps the highlight of this chapter. It demonstrated how runtime data binding is performed on the `ComboBox`, `ListBox`, `DataGridView`, and `ListViewExtended` controls. You saw what properties were used in data binding and how binding the various data sources to these controls affected them. This was especially true in the display of data in these controls as well as the code demonstrated in the `SelectedIndexChanged` and `RowEnter` event handlers for each of these controls.

It is hoped that you have learned something new in this chapter about binding data to your controls at runtime. You should understand how this can help your applications adapt to changing business needs and be more flexible in the data that they support. Runtime data binding provides more flexibility over design-time bound controls that are bound to strongly typed datasets, as your data source can change, whereas your UI does not necessarily have to.

Database Image Manager

A lot of Windows and Web applications rely on the use of images to spruce up their user interface and to convey visual information to the user. It is not uncommon for multiple applications within an organization to share the same images, such as a company logo image or tag line image. Keeping these images in a common central repository is key to ensuring that all applications display the same image, thereby achieving a uniform look. Media storage preferences vary from organization to organization: Some use a common shared folder on the network, others a database, or even a source control system.

This chapter explores storing and managing images in a database, particularly a SQL Server 2005 Express database. Therefore, a requirement for this chapter is that the target computer must have SQL Server 2005 Express installed on it. The Database Image Manager application provides its own SQL Server 2005 Express database and automatically attaches the database in SQL Server Express.

This application enables you to add, update, and delete images in a database. The user interface (UI) for this application enables you to view thumbnail images of all images contained in the database, select an image for editing, resize the image, and then update the image in the database.

The main technologies used in this chapter are as follows:

- ❑ Using SQL Server 2005 Express to attach a database
- ❑ Using the `SqlConnection`, `SqlCommand`, and `SqlDataReader` objects to manage images in the database
- ❑ Using the `Bitmap`, `Image`, `Graphics`, and `MemoryStream` classes to manipulate images
- ❑ Creating of a `Thumbnail` user-control to display image thumbnails in the UI

Using the Database Image Manager Application

When you first start the Database Image Manager application, you'll see three messages in the main part of the application. The first of these messages, shown in Figure 9-1, indicates that the application is attaching the images database in SQL Server Express. This process may take a few seconds the first time the application starts.

Once the images database has been attached in SQL Server Express, the next message that you see is the message indicating that the application is loading the images from the database. If one or more images are found, the first image is automatically selected and displayed in the main area of the application. If no images are found, then a message indicating that is displayed.

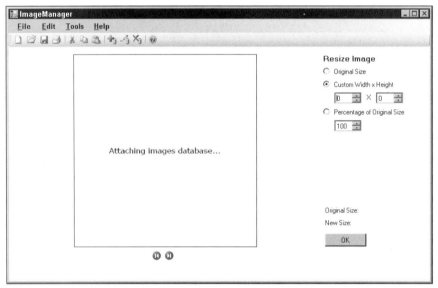

Figure 9-1

To add a new image, you must first find and open an image from a drive on your computer using the Open dialog. To invoke the Open dialog, you can either click the Open icon on the toolbar or click the File menu and select the Open menu item. The Open dialog shown in Figure 9-2 is displayed and as you can see, this application supports Bitmap, JPEG, and GIF images.

After you select an image in the Open dialog and click the Open button, the image is displayed in the Database Image Manager application, as shown in Figure 9-3. The image shown in Figure 9-3 has been resized, as indicated on the right-hand side of the window.

The image that you select and open is displayed full size; this application enables you to resize the image before adding it to the database. This is particularly useful when you want to display images in a Web application and want most, if not all, of the images to be the same size. This application enables you to resize images smaller or larger than the image that you initially open.

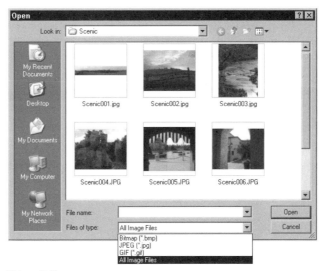

Figure 9-2

Figure 9-3

After you have resized the image, if so desired, you need to add the image to the database. This is done by clicking the Add Image icon on the toolbar (the icon with the green plus sign and database). When the image has been added to the database, the application clears the thumbnail collection and rebuilds it as shown in the Figure 9-4. If this is the first image added to the database, the first `Thumbnail` control is automatically selected, as shown in Figure 9-4.

The Thumbnail control shown at the bottom of Figure 9-4 is a custom user control built for this application. It displays a thumbnail of the image along with the image name that is stored in the database. It also maintains other information about the image behind the scenes, such as the image key, which is the key to the row of data in the database containing this image.

Figure 9-4

A Thumbnail control is added to the collection for each image that you add to the database, as shown in Figure 9-5. As the number of controls grows beyond the visible limit of the UI, a horizontal scroll bar is automatically displayed, as shown in Figure 9-5.

The selected Thumbnail control has a blue border displayed around it. You can select any Thumbnail control by clicking it, and you can navigate from one Thumbnail control to the next by clicking the Previous and Next icons shown in the middle of the application.

To edit an image, click the Thumbnail control of the image to be edited, resize the image appropriately, and then click the Update Image icon on the toolbar (the icon with the pencil and database) to update the image in the database.

To delete an image from the database, click the Thumbnail control of the image to be deleted and then click the Delete Image icon on the toolbar (the icon with the red X and database). The image is deleted from the database and the collection of Thumbnail controls is rebuilt to remove the deleted image.

Using the application is straightforward and provides a means to maintain a collection of images in a single repository that can be accessed from a variety of applications. The database used in this application is a SQL Server 2005 database that can be attached to any edition of SQL Server 2005. SQL Server 2005 Express is used in this application to provide ease of use and to enable this application to be used on any machine that has SQL Server 2005 Express edition installed on it.

Figure 9-5

Design of the Database Image Manager Application

The main design of this application is centered on the DBImages class and the DBImage class as well as the Thumbnail control. The DBImages class contains the code necessary to attach the images database to SQL Server Express, as well as the code to add, update, delete, and retrieve images from the database. The DBImage class is used to contain the details of a single image read from the database.

The Thumbnail control is a user control that represents a thumbnail of the image, as was shown in Figure 9-6. A collection of the Thumbnail controls is added to the ImageManager form, as also shown in Figure 9-6.

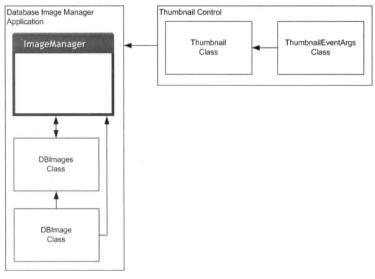

Figure 9-6

DBImages Class

DBImages is the database images class — the class that attaches the images database to SQL Server Express, and the class that adds, updates, deletes, and retrieves images from the database. All database functionality contained in the entire application is consolidated in this class.

Because this class manages database resources — for example, SqlConnection, SqlCommand, and SqlDataReader — it implements the IDisposable interface so that the SQL resources can be properly disposed of via the Dispose method of this class. Table 9-1 lists the methods available in this class.

Table 9-1: Methods in the DBImages Class

Method	Return Type	Description
Public Sub New()	N/A	Instantiates the SqlConnection object, which attaches the database to SQL Server Express
Protected Overridable Sub Dispose(ByVal disposing As Boolean)	N/A	Disposes of the SqlConnection object used in this class
Public Function GetImages()	DBImage()	Retrieves all images in the database and returns them as an array of DBImage classes

Table 9-1: Methods in the DBImages Class *(continued)*

Method	Return Type	Description
`Public Sub AddImage(ByVal imageName As String, ByVal image As Image, ByVal imageWidth As Integer, ByVal imageHeight As Integer, ByVal imagePixelFormat As Imaging.PixelFormat)`	N/A	Adds an image to the database
`Public Sub UpdateImage(ByVal imageKey As Guid, ByVal imageName As String, ByVal image As Image, ByVal imageWidth As Integer, ByVal imageHeight As Integer, ByVal imagePixelFormat As Imaging.PixelFormat)`	N/A	Updates an image in the database
`Public Sub DeleteImage(ByVal imageKey As Guid)`	N/A	Deletes an image from the database

DBImage Class

The DBImage class is used to hold information about a single image read from the database. This class is used in the ImageManager form to set the properties of the Thumbnail control before adding the Thumbnail control to the form. The properties and methods of the DBImage class are listed in Table 9-2.

Table 9-2: Properties and Methods of DBImage

Property/Method	Return Type	Description
`Public Sub New(ByVal imageIndex As Integer, ByVal imageName As String, ByVal imageKey As Guid, ByVal image As Image)`	N/A	Constructor for this class, which sets the private variables using the parameters passed to the constructor. The properties of this class return data from the private variable.
`Public ReadOnly Property ImageIndex()`	Integer	Returns the zero-based index of this image from the DBImages() array
`Public ReadOnly Property ImageName()`	String	Returns the name of the image
`Public ReadOnly Property ImageKey()`	Guid	Returns the database key of this image
`Public ReadOnly Property Image()`	Image	Returns the image

ThumbnailEventArgs Class

The `ThumbnailEventArgs` class is used to contain information about the selected image and is populated and returned in the `ImageSelected` event for the `Thumbnail` class. This class contains a single constructor and one public field, as shown in Table 9-3.

Table 9-3: Methods and Fields of the ThumbnailEventArgs Class

Method/Field	Return Type	Description
Public Sub New(ByVal imageSelected As String)	N/A	Sets the `ImageName` field
Public ImageName	String	Returns the name of the selected image

Thumbnail Class

The `Thumbnail` class contains the code for the `Thumbnail` user control. This class contains several properties and methods that provide for the interaction of the user with this control and the form hosting this control. Table 9-4 lists these properties and methods.

Table 9-4: Properties and Methods of the Thumbnail Class

Property/Method	Return Type	Description
Public Property Image()	Image	Sets or returns the image for this control
Public Overrides Property Text()	String	Sets or returns the image name displayed in this control
Public Property Key()	String	Sets or returns the key for the image displayed in this control
Public Property Index()	Integer	Set or returns the index of this control as contained in a collection
Public Property Selected()	Boolean	Selects the control or returns a value indicating whether the control is selected
Public Sub ClearBorder()	N/A	Clears the selected border around the control
Private Sub ClickEvent()	N/A	Sets this control as selected and raises the `ImageSelected` event
Private Sub Thumbnail_Click(ByVal sender As Object, ByVal e As System.EventArgs) Handles Me.Click	N/A	Handles the click event for the actual control and calls the internal `ClickEvent` method

Table 9-4: Properties and Methods of the Thumbnail Class (*continued*)

Property/Method	Return Type	Description
`Private Sub lblImageName_Click(ByVal sender As Object, ByVal e As System.EventArgs) Handles lblImageName.Click`	N/A	Handles the click event of the label on the control and calls the internal `ClickEvent` method
`Private Sub picImage_Click(ByVal sender As Object, ByVal e As System.EventArgs) Handles picImage.Click`	N/A	Handles the click event of the image on this control and calls the internal `ClickEvent` method

ImageManager Class

The `ImageManager` class is the class for the ImageManager form. There are several procedures in this class but only the key procedures are listed in Table 9-5. These and the other procedures are covered in detail in the "Code and Code Explanation" section coming up next.

Table 9-5: Properties and Methods of the ImageManager Class

Property/Method	Return Type	Description
`Private Sub ImageSelected(ByVal sender As Object, ByVal e As ImagePlaceHolder.ThumbnailEventArgs)`	N/A	Event handler for the `ImageSelected` event of the `Thumbnail` control
`Private Sub picPrevious_Click (ByVal sender As Object, ByVal e As System.EventArgs) Handles picPrevious.Click`	N/A	Navigates to the previous `Thumbnail` control
`Private Sub picNext_Click(ByVal sender As Object, ByVal e As System.EventArgs) Handles picNext.Click`	N/A	Navigates to the next `Thumbnail` control
`Private Sub OpenToolStripMenuItem_Click(ByVal sender As Object, ByVal e As System.EventArgs) Handles OpenToolStripMenuItem.Click`	N/A	Opens an image from disk and displays it in the ImageManager form

Continued

Table 9-5: Properties and Methods of the ImageManager Class *(continued)*

Property/Method	Return Type	Description
`Private Sub AddImageToolStripButton_Click(ByVal sender As Object, ByVal e As System.EventArgs) Handles AddImageToolStripButton.Click`	N/A	Calls the `DBImages.AddImage` method to add a new image
`Private Sub UpdateImageToolStripButton_Click(ByVal sender As Object, ByVal e As System.EventArgs) Handles UpdateImageToolStripButton.Click`	N/A	Calls the `DBImages.UpdateImage` method to update an existing image
`Private Sub DeleteImageToolStripButton_Click(ByVal sender As Object, ByVal e As System.EventArgs) Handles DeleteImageToolStripButton.Click`	N/A	Calls the `DBImages.DeleteImage` method to delete an existing image
`Private Sub LoadDatabaseImages()`	N/A	Gets an array of `DBImage` classes, creates a new `Thumbnail` control, and adds it to the form's control collection
`Private Sub btnOK_Click(ByVal sender As System.Object, ByVal e As System.EventArgs) Handles btnOK.Click`	N/A	Resizes the displayed image based on the `Resize` Image properties displayed on the ImageManager form

Code and Code Explanation

This section examines the details of the properties and methods just highlighted for the various classes. You'll get to see how all the pieces fit together to form the complete application and gain an understanding about how the various classes interact with the ImageManager form.

DBImages Class

The sole purpose of the DBImages class is to provide support for attaching the ImagesDB database to SQL Server Express and managing the images in the database. The ImagesDB database is part of the project files for this application and is copied to `bin\Debug\Database` when running in debug mode or `bin\Release\Database` when running the release version of the application. I'll explain how that works shortly.

The design of the database is very simplistic as shown in Figure 9-7. The ImagesDB database contains one table: Images. Within this table are three columns named ImageKey, ImageName, and ImagePicture.

The ImageKey column maintains the key for this image and is defined as a `Uniqueidentifier` data type in SQL Server, correlating to a `Guid` structure in the .NET Framework. The ImageName column is defined as a `Varchar(100)` data type, which correlates to a `String` data type in the .NET Framework and can contain a maximum of 100 characters. A `Varchar` data type in SQL Server will only use the number of characters contained in the image name. For example, if the image name is only 30 characters long, then only 30 characters will be stored in the database, thus allowing for efficient use of disk storage. A value of 100 was chosen for a maximum value because realistically an image name should not exceed that length.

The ImagePicture column is defined as an `Image` data type, which just happens to correlate to an `Image` data type in the .NET Framework. However, getting an image into and out of the database requires sending and receiving the image in an array of `Bytes`. I'll go into this shortly.

Four stored procedures exist to support inserting an image, updating an image, deleting an image, and retrieving all images contained in the database. The input parameters for these stored procedures are shown in Figure 9-7.

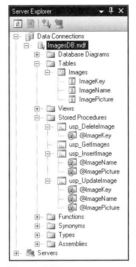

Figure 9-7

The `DBImages` class imports two namespaces, as shown in the following code. The `System.Data`
`.SqlClient` namespace supports the database classes — namely, `SqlConnection`, `SqlCommand`, and `SqlDataReader`. The `System.IO` namespace supports the `MemoryStream` class, which is used to read and write the bytes of an image to and from memory.

```
Imports System.Data.SqlClient
Imports System.IO
```

This class implements the `IDisposable` interface, as previously mentioned. This enables you to add code to the `Dispose` method in this class to call the `Dispose` method on the `objSqlConnection` object, which allows that object to free the resources that it is holding with SQL Server Express.

```
Public Class DBImages
    Implements IDisposable
```

Several private variables and objects are defined at the class level, as these variables and objects are used by several methods in this class. The first of these is the `bytImageBuffer(0)` Byte array. This Byte array contains an array of bytes of the image to be sent to SQL Server Express when inserting an image and is set to the bytes of an image returned from SQL Server Express.

The `objMemoryStream`, `objBitmap`, `objImage`, and `objGraphics` objects are all used in conjunction with the `bytImageBuffer(0)` Byte array to convert an image from bytes to an actual image and from an image to bytes.

The last three objects shown here provide support for interacting with SQL Server Express. The `objConnection` object establishes and maintains a connection with the database in SQL Server Express, while the `objCommand` object is used to execute the stored procedures in the database. The `objDataReader` object is used to read all images from the database.

```
'Private variables and objects
Private bytImageBuffer(0) As Byte

Private objMemoryStream As MemoryStream

Private objBitmap As Bitmap
Private objImage As Image
Private objGraphics As Graphics

Private objConnection As SqlConnection
Private objCommand As SqlCommand
Private objDataReader As SqlDataReader
```

The connection string used in the constructor for this class is stored as an application setting in the `app.config` file named `DBConnectionString` and should look like the following code:

```
Data Source=.\SQLEXPRESS;AttachDbFilename=|DataDirectory|\Databases\
ImagesDB.mdf;Integrated Security=True;User Instance=True;
```

However, a known problem exists when using the preceding connection string from within the Visual Studio 2005 IDE. The Microsoft Knowledge Base Article 908038 (`http://support.microsoft.com/kb/908038/en-us`) discusses this issue and a workaround. Basically, you receive the following error when using the aforementioned connection string:

```
An attempt to attach an auto-named database for file DriveLetter:\
FullPathName\ImagesDB.mdf failed. A database with the same name exists,
or specified file cannot be opened, or it is located on UNC share.
```

To get around this problem, you need to forgo using the `DataDirectory` keyword of the `AttachDbFilename` property. The `DataDirectory` keyword is used by SQL Server Express to expand the path of the current executing program. However, when running in the Visual Studio IDE, the currently executing program is the Visual Studio IDE program, `Devenv.exe`. Thus, the path of this program is used in the `DataDirectory` keyword and not the path to your executable.

Given the known problems, you need to specify the full path name to the database instead of using the `DataDirectory` keyword. The following connection string provides the full path name, and your connection string should be modified using the appropriate path to your executable:

```
Data Source=.\SQLEXPRESS;AttachDbFilename=C:\Books\Visual Basic 2005 Instant Results\
Chapter 9\Database Image Manager\bin\Debug\Database\ImagesDB.mdf;Integrated
Security=True;User Instance=True;
```

The `Data Source` property in the connection string provides the name of the SQL Server to be used. In this case, SQL Server Express is installed as a named instance called `SQLEXPRESS`. You specify a named instance of the SQL Server using a period (.), followed by a blackslash (\ ), followed by the named instance of the SQL Server installation.

The `AttachedDbFilename` property instructs SQL Server Express to dynamically attach the specified database for the user running the program. If that user does not have admin privileges to SQL Server Express, temporary admin privileges are granted to the executing program.

The `Integrated Security` property is set to `True`. This specifies that the user's Windows credentials will be used when connecting to the database.

The `User Instance` property specifies how SQL Server Express attaches the database specified. When this property is set to `True`, SQL Server Express redirects the connection from the default SQL Server Express instance to a runtime-initiated instance running under the account of the caller.

New Constructor

The constructor for this class instantiates a new connection with SQL Server Express and attaches the ImagesDB database. As previously mentioned, the connection string is stored as an application setting in the `app.config` file named `DBConnectionString`.

Just to ensure everything is working properly, the connection is opened in the `Try` portion of the `Try...Catch...Finally` statement block and closed in the `Finally` block of this statement. Any error from SQL Server Express is handled in the `Catch` block and returned to the caller.

```
    Public Sub New()
        Try
            'Instantiate the database connection and attach the database
            objConnection = New SqlConnection(My.Settings.DBConnectionString)

            'Open the database to verify our connection
            objConnection.Open()

        Catch SqlExceptionErr As SqlException
            Throw New Exception(SqlExceptionErr.Message)
        Finally
            If Not IsNothing(objConnection) Then
                objConnection.Close()
            End If
        End Try
    End Sub
```

New Constructor

The `Dispose` method for this class is the standard `Dispose` method created when implementing the `IDisposable` interface, and code has been added to close the database connection and to call the `Dispose` method on the `objConnection` object. This allows the `objConnection` object to dispose of any resources that are held against SQL Server Express.

```
Protected Overridable Sub Dispose(ByVal disposing As Boolean)
    If Not Me.disposedValue Then
        If disposing Then

        End If

        'Clean up
        If Not IsNothing(objConnection) Then
            objConnection.Close()
            objConnection.Dispose()
        End If
    End If
    Me.disposedValue = True
End Sub
```

GetImages Function

The `GetImages` function gets all images from the database and returns those images in an array of `DBImage` classes. This function starts out with the declaration of the `intIndex` variable and the `objDBImage()` array. The `intIndex` variable is used to keep track of the index when creating the `objDBImage()` array, which is used to hold an array of `DBImage` classes.

The rest of the code in this function is contained in a `Try...Catch...Finally` statement block to handle any database errors that might occur. The first thing that happens inside the `Try` block is opening the database connection.

Next, you need to instantiate the `SqlCommand` in the `objCommand` object, setting it to the stored procedure that you want to execute and passing it the `objConnection` object. You set the `CommandType` property of the `objCommand` object to the `StoredProcedure` constant of the `CommandType` enumeration to indicate the type of command that you want to execute. Then you call the `ExecuteReader` method on the `objCommand` object to execute the stored procedure. The `ExecuteReader` method executes the stored procedure and returns a `SqlDataReader`, which is set in your `objDataReader` object.

```
Public Function GetImages() As DBImage()
    'Declare local variables and objects
    Dim intIndex As Integer = -1
    Dim objDBImage() As DBImage

    Try
        'Open the connection
        objConnection.Open()

        'Instantiate the SqlCommand object
        objCommand = New SqlCommand("usp_GetImages", objConnection)
```

```
objCommand.CommandType = CommandType.StoredProcedure

'Read the images
objDataReader = objCommand.ExecuteReader
```

Using the `HasRows` property of the `SqlDataReader` set in your `objDataReader` object, you determine whether the `SqlDataReader` contains any rows of data. If it does, then you set up a `While...End While` loop to process the data.

Inside the `While...End While` loop you increment the `intIndex` variable and then redimension the `objDBImage()` array using the `intIndex` variable to specify how large to redimension the array. Notice the `Preserve` keyword. When redimensioning an array you must specify the `Preserve` keyword in order to retain the existing data in the array; otherwise, all existing data will be cleared.

```
If objDataReader.HasRows Then

    'Process all images
    While objDataReader.Read

        'Increment the image index
        intIndex += 1

        'Increment the DBImage array
        ReDim Preserve objDBImage(intIndex)
```

You clear any existing data in the `bytImageBuffer` Byte array by calling the `Clear` method on the `Array` class. Then you load the image data into the `bytImageBuffer` Byte array by setting it to the `Byte` array contained in the `ImagePicture` Item of the `objDataReader` object.

> *When an image is returned from SQL Server, it is returned in a `Byte` array; and when you send an image to SQL Server, you must send it as a `Byte` array.*

To get the image from the `Byte` array into the `objImage` object, load the `Byte` array into memory so you can use the `FromStream` method of the `Image` class to read the image data from a stream. This is done by instantiating a new instance of the `MemoryStream` class in the `objMemoryStream` object, passing the constructor of the `MemoryStream` class the `Byte` array containing your image data and passing a value of `True` for the `Writable` parameter of the constructor. The `Writeable` parameter sets the `CanWrite` property of the `MemoryStream` class to the value it receives and indicates whether this `MemoryStream` supports writing data. The next line of code writes the data from the `bytImageBuffer` Byte array into memory.

Now you can read the image data into your `objImage` object using the `FromStream` method of the `Image` class, passing that method the `objMemoryStream` object. Once that has been completed, close the `MemoryStream` in your `objMemoryStream` object and dispose of it by calling the `Dispose` method.

Now you set a new instance of the `DBImage` class in the `objDBImage` object, passing the constructor of the `DBImage` class the required parameters. The first of these parameters is the `imageIndex` parameter, indicating the index of this image in the `objDBImage` array. Next, you pass the name of the image using the `ImageName` Item from the `objDataReader` object and the image key contained in the `ImageKey` Item of the `objDataReader` object. The final parameter is the actual image, which is contained in the `objImage` object.

You then start the loop over, processing the next row of data returned by the objDataReader object to get the next image.

```
'Get the image
Array.Clear(bytImageBuffer, 0, bytImageBuffer.Length)
bytImageBuffer = objDataReader.Item("ImagePicture")
objMemoryStream = New MemoryStream(bytImageBuffer, True)
objMemoryStream.Write(bytImageBuffer, 0, bytImageBuffer.Length)
objImage = Image.FromStream(objMemoryStream)
objMemoryStream.Close()
objMemoryStream.Dispose()

'Add a new DBImage class to the collection
objDBImage(intIndex) = New DBImage(intIndex, _
        objDataReader.Item("ImageName"), _
        objDataReader.Item("ImageKey"), objImage)

End While

End If
```

Regardless of whether the objDataReader object contained any data, it is still open and you need to close it and dispose of it. This is done in the next two lines of code by calling the Close and Dispose methods on this object.

The Catch block handles any type of database error returned and simply returns that error to the caller. Notice that the Catch block has been set to catch a SqlException error instead of a generic Exception error. In most cases, this provides more information that is relevant to the processing taking place in this function.

The Finally block checks to ensure that the objConnection object was instantiated and closes the database connection if it was. If the objConnection object was not instantiated, then this object is set to Nothing.

The last line of code here returns the objDBImage array. This array is either set to a collection of DBImage objects or has a value of Nothing if no images are found in the database:

```
'Clean up
objDataReader.Close()
objCommand.Dispose()

Catch SqlExceptionErr As SqlException
    Throw New Exception(SqlExceptionErr.Message)
Finally
    If Not IsNothing(objConnection) Then
        objConnection.Close()
    End If
End Try

'Return the collection
Return objDBImage
End Function
```

AddImage Procedure

The `AddImage` procedure adds a new image of the specified size to the database. This procedure has several input parameters that provide the necessary data to appropriately resize the image before adding it to the database. When an image is passed to this procedure, the original image size is passed. If you resize the image in the ImageManager form, the displayed image is resized but the original image size is maintained and sent to this procedure. This is the reason for the input parameters that specify the desired image size and pixel format.

Everything in this procedure is encapsulated in a `Try...Catch...Finally` statement block. This helps ensure that you can properly catch and handle any database errors that might occur as a result of trying to insert a new image.

> When you try to access and load the image passed to this procedure into a `Byte` array, you receive the `A generic error occurred in GDI+` error message. This error is a known issue covered by Microsoft Knowledge Base Article 814675 (`http://support.microsoft.com/?id=814675`), which provides a workaround for this problem. Basically, you need to create a copy of the original image and work with the copy.

To avoid the error mentioned, create a new instance of the `Bitmap` class in the `objBitmap` object, passing the constructor of the `Bitmap` class the size and format of the image to be created. Notice that the parameters that you pass to the `Bitmap` constructor are the same parameters passed to this procedure. At this point you have a bitmap of the appropriate size and pixel format.

Next, you need to instantiate a new instance of the `Graphics` class in the `objGraphics` object, creating a graphic in this object by calling the `FromImage` method in the `Graphics` class. You convert the image in the `Bitmap` class to an `Image` data type.

At this point, your `objGraphics` object contains a blank graphic of the appropriate size and pixel format but does not contain an actual picture. The `DrawImage` method draws an image using the `Graphics` class at the specified coordinates and of the appropriate size. You pass the `DrawImage` method the source image that should be used to draw from, the X, Y coordinates of your drawing surface, and the width and height of your destination image. The `DrawImage` method draws the image in the `objBitmap` object that is referenced in the `objGraphics` object.

Now you must take the image in the `objBitmap` object and load it in the `objImage` object. You do this by setting the `objImage` object to the image contained in the `objBitmap` object by calling the `FromHbitmap` method on the `Image` class. This creates a `Bitmap` image in the `objImage` object from the handle of the `objBitmap` object.

```
Public Sub AddImage(ByVal imageName As String, ByVal image As Image, _
    ByVal imageWidth As Integer, ByVal imageHeight As Integer, _
    ByVal imagePixelFormat As Imaging.PixelFormat)

    Try
        'To prevent the "A generic error occurred in GDI+" error message,
        'we must create a copy of the image because GDI+ has locked the
        'original image
        objBitmap = New Bitmap(imageWidth, imageHeight, imagePixelFormat)
        objGraphics = _
            Graphics.FromImage(CType(objBitmap, System.Drawing.Image))
        objGraphics.DrawImage(image, 0, 0, imageWidth, imageHeight)
        objImage = System.Drawing.Image.FromHbitmap(objBitmap.GetHbitmap())
```

255

Now the objImage object contains your image formatted as a Bitmap. You want to convert that image to a JPEG format before loading it into the database because a JPEG image is smaller than a bitmap image. You must also convert the image to a Byte array. This is all done using the MemoryStream class. The objMemoryStream object is declared and instantiated in a Using...End Using statement block of code. Inside this block of code you save the image contained in the objImage object to the MemoryStream and specify the format in which you want the image saved. Then you convert the data contained in the MemoryStream to a Byte array in the bytImageBuffer variable by calling the ToArray method in the objMemoryStream object:

```
'Load the Byte buffer with the image
Using objMemoryStream As New MemoryStream
    objImage.Save(objMemoryStream, _
        System.Drawing.Imaging.ImageFormat.Jpeg)
    bytImageBuffer = objMemoryStream.ToArray
End Using
```

You are now ready to insert this image into the database, so you open your database connection in the next line of code. Then you instantiate the objCommand object using the SqlCommand class, passing the constructor for that class the stored procedure name to execute and the objConnection object. You then set the CommandType property of the objCommand object to the StoredProcedure constant of the CommandType enumeration to indicate the type of command that you want to execute.

Next, you need to add the stored procedure parameters to the Parameters collection in the objCommand object. The first parameter to be added is for the image name. You call the Add method of the Parameters collection, passing it the parameter name in the stored procedure, the SQL Server data type contained in the SqlDbType enumeration, and the size of the data type. Then you set the Value of the parameter to the imageName parameter passed to this procedure.

Repeat this process for the actual image but you don't have to specify a size for the data type, as it will automatically be determined. Set the Value property of the parameter to the bytImageBuffer Byte array containing the image data.

After the parameters have been added to the Parameters collection, you can insert the image into the database by calling the ExecuteNonQuery method in the objCommand object. This method executes a query that does not return any results, such as a SQL Select statement.

```
'Open the database connection
objConnection.Open()

'Instantiate the SqlCommand object
objCommand = New SqlCommand("usp_InsertImage", objConnection)
objCommand.CommandType = CommandType.StoredProcedure

'Add the parameters and set their values
objCommand.Parameters.Add("@ImageName", _
    SqlDbType.VarChar, 100).Value = imageName
objCommand.Parameters.Add("@ImagePicture", _
    SqlDbType.Image).Value = bytImageBuffer

'Execute the query
objCommand.ExecuteNonQuery()
```

The `Catch` block handles any errors that might occur and the `Finally` block disposes of the `objCommand` object and closes the database connection:

```
Catch SqlExceptionErr As SqlException
    Throw New Exception(SqlExceptionErr.Message)
Finally
    'Clean up
    If Not IsNothing(objCommand) Then
        objCommand.Dispose()
    End If
    objConnection.Close()
End Try
End Sub
```

UpdateImage Procedure

The `UpdateImage` procedure operates in an identical manner to the `AddImage` procedure. There is one additional parameter for this procedure: the `imageKey` parameter. This is the `Guid` of the image in the database. It enables the `usp_UpdateImage` stored procedure to know which image to update:

```
Public Sub UpdateImage(ByVal imageKey As Guid, ByVal imageName As String, _
    ByVal image As Image, ByVal imageWidth As Integer, _
    ByVal imageHeight As Integer, ByVal imagePixelFormat As _
    Imaging.PixelFormat)
```

This procedure also starts with the code wrapped in a `Try...Catch...Finally` block to handle any database errors that may occur. Then you must copy the image passed to this procedure to a `Bitmap` and then copy the `Bitmap` to an `Image` data type. Next, place the `Image` data type into memory via the `MemoryStream` class and then convert the image into an array of `Bytes`. This section of code is identical to the code in the `AddImage` procedure and could be wrapped in a separate procedure if so desired.

```
Try
    'To prevent the "A generic error occurred in GDI+" error message,
    'we must create a copy of the image because GDI+ has locked the
    'original image
    objBitmap = New Bitmap(imageWidth, imageHeight, imagePixelFormat)
    objGraphics = _
        Graphics.FromImage(CType(objBitmap, System.Drawing.Image))
    objGraphics.DrawImage(image, 0, 0, imageWidth, imageHeight)
    objImage = System.Drawing.Image.FromHbitmap(objBitmap.GetHbitmap())

    'Load the Byte buffer with the image
    Using objMemoryStream As New MemoryStream
        objImage.Save(objMemoryStream, _
            System.Drawing.Imaging.ImageFormat.Jpeg)
        bytImageBuffer = objMemoryStream.ToArray
    End Using
```

Next, the database connection is opened and the `objCommand` object is instantiated and set to the stored procedure to be executed along with the `objConnection` object. Then the `CommandType` property is set to the `StoredProcedure` constant from the `CommandType` enumeration.

Now the parameters are added to the `Parameters` collection. The last two parameters you saw in the `AddImage` procedure and are identical here. The first parameter is new and contains the key to the

257

image to be updated. If you'll recall from the discussion about the database earlier, the `ImageKey` column is defined as a `UniqueIdentifier` data type in SQL Server and correlates to a `Guid` data type in the .NET Framework.

After the parameters have been added to the `Parameters` collection, the stored procedure is executed via a call to the `ExecuteNonQuery` method of the `objCommand` object. Remember that this method executes a command that does not return rows of data. This command does, however, return the number of rows affected by the command as an `Integer` value. Because you are updating only one row of data, there is no need to capture the number of rows affected by the command, as you know it is only one row.

```
'Open the database connection
objConnection.Open()

'Instantiate the SqlCommand object
objCommand = New SqlCommand("usp_UpdateImage", objConnection)
objCommand.CommandType = CommandType.StoredProcedure

'Add the parameters and set their values
objCommand.Parameters.Add("@ImageKey", _
    SqlDbType.UniqueIdentifier).Value = imageKey
objCommand.Parameters.Add("@ImageName", _
    SqlDbType.VarChar, 100).Value = imageName
objCommand.Parameters.Add("@ImagePicture", _
    SqlDbType.Image).Value = bytImageBuffer

'Execute the query
objCommand.ExecuteNonQuery()
```

This procedure wraps up with the `Catch` and `Finally` blocks of code. Again the `Catch` block handles any `SqlException` error that might be thrown and returns that error to the caller. The `Finally` block performs cleanup by disposing of the `objCommand` object and closing the database connection:

```
Catch SqlExceptionErr As SqlException
    Throw New Exception(SqlExceptionErr.Message)
Finally
    'Clean up
    If Not IsNothing(objCommand) Then
        objCommand.Dispose()
    End If
    objConnection.Close()
End Try
End Sub
```

DeleteImage Procedure

The last procedure in this class is the `DeleteImage` procedure. This procedure is very simple and the only input parameter required for it is the key of the image to be deleted. Once again, the code is wrapped in a `Try...Catch...Finally` statement block to handle any database errors that might occur.

This procedure starts by opening the database connection and then instantiating a new instance of the `SqlCommand` class in the `objCommand` object. You pass the constructor for the `SqlCommand` class the stored procedure to be executed and the `objConnection` object.

You add only one parameter to the `Parameters` collection in the next line of code. Then you execute the stored procedure via a call to the `ExecuteNonQuery` method in the `objCommand` object.

The `Catch` and `Finally` blocks of code handle any `SqlException` error that might be thrown and perform cleanup by disposing of the `objCommand` object and closing the database connection.

```
Public Sub DeleteImage(ByVal imageKey As Guid)
    Try
        'Open the database connection
        objConnection.Open()

        'Instantiate the SqlCommand object
        objCommand = New SqlCommand("usp_DeleteImage", objConnection)
        objCommand.CommandType = CommandType.StoredProcedure

        'Add the parameters and set their values
        objCommand.Parameters.Add("@ImageKey", _
            SqlDbType.UniqueIdentifier).Value = imageKey

        'Execute the query
        objCommand.ExecuteNonQuery()

    Catch SqlExceptionErr As SqlException
        Throw New Exception(SqlExceptionErr.Message)
    Finally
        If Not IsNothing(objCommand) Then
            objCommand.Dispose()
        End If
        objConnection.Close()
    End Try
End Sub
```

DBImage Class

The `DBImage` class is really just a placeholder for a collection of image data returned from the `GetImages` method in the `DBImages` class. You'll see how this class is really used when you examine the code in the ImageManager form.

This class starts with the declaration of some private variables and objects. These variables and objects are set in the constructor of the class, which you examine next. The properties of this class are read-only properties that use the values stored in these variables and objects and return them to the caller of those properties.

```
'Private variables and objects
Private intImageIndex As Integer
Private strImageName As String
Private gudImageKey As Guid
Private objImage As Image
```

New Constructor

The constructor for this class accepts four parameters that correspond to the variables and objects defined earlier. The code in the constructor sets these variables and objects to the values passed in these parameters.

```
Public Sub New(ByVal imageIndex As Integer, ByVal imageName As String, _
    ByVal imageKey As Guid, ByVal image As Image)

    intImageIndex = imageIndex
    strImageName = imageName
    gudImageKey = imageKey
    objImage = image
End Sub
```

Read-Only Properties

This class contains four read-only properties that correspond to the four private variables and objects defined earlier. The property names are self-explanatory and return the values from the private variables and objects defined in the preceding code.

```
Public ReadOnly Property ImageIndex() As Integer
    Get
        Return intImageIndex
    End Get
End Property

Public ReadOnly Property ImageName() As String
    Get
        Return strImageName
    End Get
End Property

Public ReadOnly Property ImageKey() As Guid
    Get
        Return gudImageKey
    End Get
End Property

Public ReadOnly Property Image() As Image
    Get
        Return objImage
    End Get
End Property
```

ThumbnailEventArgs Class

The `Thumbnail` user control provides the `ImageSelected` event. This event is fired when the `Thumbnail` control is selected by the user. It is necessary to pass data from the `Thumbnail` control that has been selected to the host of that control, which in this case would be the `ImageManager` form. Therefore, the `ThumbnailEventArgs` class has been designed to provide that medium of passing data.

The `ThumbnailEventArgs` class inherits the `EventArgs` class as its base class, thus providing this class with all the methods and fields available in that class. The `EventArgs` class, and any class derived from it, is used to pass state information from a control to the event handler for that event, which is exactly what this class does.

```
Public Class ThumbnailEventArgs
    Inherits EventArgs
```

This class contains one public field and one constructor that sets that field. When this class is instantiated in the `Thumbnail` control, it is passed the name of the image selected. This information will then be available to this control's host, which implements the `ImageSelected` event.

Other public fields can be defined and populated via the constructor should you see the need for that information to be passed to the host of the `Thumbnail` control.

```
Public ImageName As String

Public Sub New(ByVal imageSelected As String)
    ImageName = imageSelected
End Sub
```

Thumbnail Class

The designer for the `Thumbnail` user control is very simple. It contains a `PictureBox` control that is visible in the control, as shown in Figure 9-8, and contains the thumbnail image of the image that is set in this control. This `PictureBox` control has its `BorderStyle` property set to `FixedSingle`. There is a `Label` control beneath the `PictureBox` control that is not visible in Figure 9-8, as it has its `Text` property cleared. When set in the control, this `Label` contains the name of the image. Four other `Label` controls around the border of this control are set to the color blue when this control is selected.

Figure 9-8

The `Thumbnail` class, the class for this user control, starts off with the declaration of three private variables. The `blnSelected` variable is used to hold a `Boolean` value indicating whether or not this control has its `Selected` state set to `True`. The `intIndex` variable is used indicate the index of this control within a collection of other `Thumbnail` controls, and the `strImageKey` is used to hold the key for the image associated with this control. Notice that this last variable has been defined as a `String` data type. This enables this control to be used by other applications that may not necessarily use a `Guid` data type for the image key or may not even implement an image key.

```
'Private variables
Private blnSelected As Boolean = False
Private intIndex As Integer
Private strImageKey As String = String.Empty
```

ImageSelected Event

The ImageSelected event provides a standard procedure with parameters, just like the Click event for a Button control. To that end, you must declare a Delegate procedure defining the parameters for that procedure. The sender is defined as the first parameter and is the sender who sends this event. The e parameter is defined as the ThumbnailEventArgs class and thus provides the ImageName field to the implementer of the ImageSelected event. Next, you declare the ImageSelected event as the ImageSelectedEventHandler delegate.

When this control is placed on a form, the ImageSelected event is listed in the Method Name combo box in the IDE when the control is selected in the Class Name combo box; and when the developer selects the ImageSelected event from the list in the Method Name combo box, an ImageSelected procedure with the parameters defined in this delegate is automatically inserted into the code.

However, this is not how it will be used in your implementation, as all of the Thumbnail controls are dynamically added to the ImageManager form. A generic event handler procedure with the same parameters defined in the delegate is defined in the ImageManager form class, as you'll see when you get to that code.

```
'Event handler delegate for the ImageSelected event
Delegate Sub ImageSelectedEventHandler(ByVal sender As Object, _
    ByVal e As ThumbnailEventArgs)

'Public ImageSelected event
Public Event ImageSelected As ImageSelectedEventHandler
```

Image and Text Properties

Several properties have been defined for the Thumbnail control to enable you to set the data for the control and to query that data when needed. The first of these properties is the Image property, and as you might have guessed, this property enables you to set the image that is displayed in this control, as well as to retrieve the image set.

The next property is the Text property. This is the image name that is displayed in the label beneath the image in the property, as shown earlier in Figures 9-4 and 9-5. You might think that this property should be called something else, such as "Image Name." However, in keeping with the naming standards of controls within the .NET Framework, this property has been named Text, as it displays text in the control that is visible to the end user.

```
'Image property
Public Property Image() As Image
    Get
        Return picImage.Image
    End Get
    Set(ByVal value As Image)
        picImage.Image = value
    End Set
End Property

'Image name property
Public Overrides Property Text() As String
    Get
```

```
        Return lblImageName.Text
    End Get
    Set(ByVal value As String)
        lblImageName.Text = value
    End Set
End Property
```

Key and Index Properties

The next couple of properties are the Key and Index properties. The Key property enables you to set and read the key for this image. This would be the key in the database that defines the row of data for this image. As previously mentioned, in order to keep this control generic, the Key property has been defined as a String data type. You'll see how to convert a Guid structure to a String and convert a String back into a Guid structure in the ImageManager form.

The Index property has been implemented as a means for developers to keep track of this particular instance of the control when there is an array of Thumbnail controls hosted in a form. You would set the index of this control within the array, enabling you to access the control by its index within the array.

```
'Image key property
Public Property Key() As String
    Get
        Return strImageKey
    End Get
    Set(ByVal value As String)
        strImageKey = value
    End Set
End Property

'Image index property
Public Property Index() As Integer
    Get
        Return intIndex
    End Get
    Set(ByVal value As Integer)
        intIndex = value
    End Set
End Property
```

Selected Property

The final property is the Selected property. You can set this control as selected or choose to leave it unselected. When this control is selected, its borders are set to a blue color. Notice that the Set statement of this property calls one of two methods depending on whether this property is set to True or False. These methods are discussed next.

```
'Selected property
Public Property Selected() As Boolean
    Get
        Return blnSelected
    End Get
    Set(ByVal value As Boolean)
        blnSelected = value
```

```
                        If Not blnSelected Then
                            ClearBorder()
                        Else
                            ClickEvent()
                        End If
                End Set
            End Property
```

ClearBorder Procedure

The ClearBorder procedure sets the color of the labels around the border of the control using the Transparent member from the Color structure, which then indicates that this control is no longer selected. The Transparent member of the Color structure is set to the BackColor property of the labels using the same color defined in the BackColor property of the parent control, which in this case is the designer surface of the Thumbnail control:

```
        Private Sub ClearBorder()
            lblBorderTop.BackColor = Color.Transparent
            lblBorderBottom.BackColor = Color.Transparent
            lblBorderLeft.BackColor = Color.Transparent
            lblBorderRight.BackColor = Color.Transparent
        End Sub
```

ClickEvent Procedure

The ClickEvent procedure is called when this control is selected, either through the Selected property or when the user clicks on this control. This procedure loops through the Controls collection of the parent control and clears any other existing Thumbnail controls. This is performed in a For Each...Next loop. You define the objControl object as an Object data type in the loop and use the Controls collection of the Parent property. The Parent property is the control that is hosting this control, which in your application is the ImageManager form.

Next, a check is made to determine whether the control returned from the Controls collection is a Thumbnail control. This is done using the TypeOf operator, which compares an object reference to the data type that you specified. Here you use the control returned in the objControl object and compare it against the Thumbnail data type, which is the Thumbnail control. If a match is made, you set the Selected property to False, causing that control to clear its borders.

The BackColor property of the border labels then have their color set to blue using the Blue member of the Color structure. This causes the control to have a highlighted border indicating that this is the control selected.

This procedure is called when the Selected property is set and when the user clicks on the control. Therefore, because you do not know in which instance this procedure was called, it's a safe bet to just set the blnSelected flag to True because this control is now active.

Finally, you raise the ImageSelected event so the implementer of this control can perform any actions necessary when this control is selected. Notice that you pass the Me keyword as the sender parameter of the ImageSelected event. The Me keyword refers to the Thumbnail class. You then instantiate and pass a new reference of the ThumbnailEventArgs class, passing the constructor for that class the Text property of this control:

```
Private Sub ClickEvent()
    'Clear the border of existing Thumbnail controls in the parent control
    For Each objControl As Object In Parent.Controls
        If TypeOf objControl Is Thumbnail Then
            objControl.Selected = False
        End If
    Next

    'Highlight this controls border as selected
    lblBorderTop.BackColor = Color.Blue
    lblBorderBottom.BackColor = Color.Blue
    lblBorderLeft.BackColor = Color.Blue
    lblBorderRight.BackColor = Color.Blue

    'Set the selected flag to true
    blnSelected = True

    'Set the selected image name and raise an event
    RaiseEvent ImageSelected(Me, New ThumbnailEventArgs(Me.Text))
End Sub
```

Click Event Handler Procedures

The next three procedures handle the Click event for the controls that make up your Thumbnail control. If the user clicks the designer surface of the Thumbnail control, the image on the Thumbnail control, or the label beneath the image of the Thumbnail control, one of these events is fired. The code in each of these event handlers merely calls the ClickEvent procedure just discussed.

If you implemented only the Click event for the image on your control, then a user would be forced to click only the image of the control to select the control. Having these event handlers in place enables a user to click any part of the control to select it. This provides a better UI experience by allowing the user to click anywhere on the control in order to select it.

```
Private Sub Thumbnail_Click(ByVal sender As Object, _
    ByVal e As System.EventArgs) Handles Me.Click
    ClickEvent()
End Sub

Private Sub lblImageName_Click(ByVal sender As Object, _
    ByVal e As System.EventArgs) Handles lblImageName.Click
    ClickEvent()
End Sub

Private Sub picImage_Click(ByVal sender As Object, _
    ByVal e As System.EventArgs) Handles picImage.Click
    ClickEvent()
End Sub
```

ImageManager Class

Before you jump into the code for the `ImageManager` class, take a look at the ImageManager form in the designer for a moment, which is shown in Figure 9-9. Notice the blank area at the bottom of the form. This blank area actually contains a `FlowLayoutPanel` control, which is the control to which you will be dynamically adding the `Thumbnail` controls.

The `FlowLayoutPanel` control can display controls added to it in either a horizontal or vertical direction. In our case, it has been set to display its controls in a horizontal direction. Additionally, this control automatically left-aligns the controls added to it and can either wrap the controls or clip their display. This control has been set to clip the display of the controls and to automatically provide a scroll bar when the number of controls exceeds the displayable area of this control. This was demonstrated earlier in Figure 9-5.

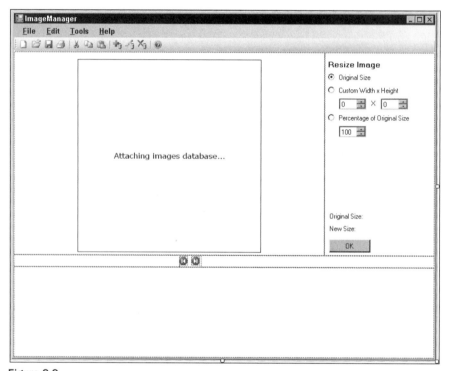

Figure 9-9

ImageManager_Load Event Handler Procedure

The `Load` event for the form first shows the form and then refreshes its display, as indicated in the first two lines of the following code. The reason for this is to have the form displayed so the user can see the message shown in the designer in Figure 9-9 indicating that the images database is being attached. This provides the user with an indication as to what is happening as the form loads.

Next, the `DBImages` class is instantiated in the `objDBImages` object, which has been declared at the class level. Then a call is made to the `LoadDatabaseImages` procedure. This code is wrapped in a `Try...Catch` block to handle any errors that may occur while attaching the images database or reading the images from the database.

```
Private Sub ImageManager_Load(ByVal sender As System.Object, _
    ByVal e As System.EventArgs) Handles MyBase.Load

    'Show and refresh the form before performing the load events
    Me.Show()
    Me.Refresh()

    Try
        'Instantiate the DBImages class
        objDBImages = New DBImages

        'Load the database images
        LoadDatabaseImages()
    Catch ExceptionErr As Exception
        MessageBox.Show(ExceptionErr.Message, My.Application.Info.Title, _
            MessageBoxButtons.OK, MessageBoxIcon.Error)
    End Try
End Sub
```

LoadDatabaseImages Procedure

The LoadDatabaseImages procedure has its code also wrapped in a Try...Catch block to handle any database errors that might occur. This procedure is called when the form initially loads and whenever an image is added, updated, or deleted. To that end, the first thing that happens in this procedure is to clear any existing Thumbnail controls in the FlowLayoutPanel control, which is aptly named flpThumbnails. You do this by calling the Clear method on the Controls collection.

Next, you want to indicate to the user that you are loading the database images, so set the Image property of the PictureBox control to the Loading_Images image in your resource file. You then resize the PictureBox back to its original size in case it previously displayed a large image, and then refresh the form so the user is able to view the new message.

Now declare the objDBImageCollection() object as an array of the DBImage class and set it by calling the GetImages method in the DBImages class defined in your objDBImages object. Then declare the objDBImage as a DBImage class, which enables you to access a single image in the objDBImageCollection() object array:

```
Private Sub LoadDatabaseImages()
    Try
        'Clear all previous controls
        flpThumbnails.Controls.Clear()

        'Change images
        picPreview.Image = My.Resources.Loading_Images
        picPreview.Size = New Size(338, 342)
        Me.Refresh()

        'Get the images
        Dim objDBImageCollection() As DBImage = objDBImages.GetImages
        Dim objDBImage As DBImage
```

Remember that the GetImages method in the DBImages class returns either an array of the DBImage class or a value of Nothing. To that end, you first check the objDBImageCollection object array to ensure that it does not contain a value of Nothing. Then you set up a For Each...Next loop to process each DBImage class in the objDBImageCollection object array.

The first thing that happens inside this loop is the instantiation of a new instance of the Thumbnail control in the objThumbnail object, which was defined at the class level. Then you proceed to set the various properties of the Thumbnail control using the properties provided in the DBImage class. Once that has been completed, add the new Thumbnail control to the FlowLayoutPanel control by calling the Add method on the Controls collection.

Since you are dynamically adding these controls, you do not have access to the ImageSelected event for each of these controls within the IDE. Therefore, you have to add an event handler for the ImageSelected event in code. A generic procedure named ImageSelected has been defined with the same parameters as the ImageSelectedEventHandler delegate in the Thumbnail class. I'll cover that procedure next.

To add an event handler, call the AddHandler statement, passing it the event to handle and the address of the event handler procedure. The AddressOf operator creates a function delegate using the procedure that you specify; in this case, the procedure is ImageSelected:

```
If Not IsNothing(objDBImageCollection) Then

    'Process the collection of images
    For Each objDBImage In objDBImageCollection

        'Instantiate a new instance of the Thumbnail class
        objThumbnail = New Thumbnail

        'Set the properties of the control
        objThumbnail.Image = objDBImage.Image
        objThumbnail.Text = objDBImage.ImageName
        objThumbnail.Key = objDBImage.ImageKey.ToString
        objThumbnail.Index = objDBImage.ImageIndex

        'Add the control to the FlowLayoutPanel
        flpThumbnails.Controls.Add(objThumbnail)

        'Add the event handler for the control
        AddHandler objThumbnail.ImageSelected, AddressOf ImageSelected

    Next
```

If the objDBImageCollection object array had a value of Nothing, then the code in the Else block of your If...Then...Else statement block is executed. Here you set the Image property of the PictureBox to the No_Images image in your resource file. That image displays a message that no images were found in the database. Again, resize the PictureBox control back to its original size and then refresh the form.

The Catch block displays any errors that might have occurred while reading or loading the images in the Thumbnail controls. A message box dialog box is displayed with appropriate information about the error that occurred.

```
    Else
```

```
                        'Change images
                        picPreview.Image = My.Resources.No_Images
                        picPreview.Size = New Size(338, 342)
                        Me.Refresh()

                End If

        Catch ExceptionErr As Exception
                MessageBox.Show(ExceptionErr.Message, My.Application.Info.Title, _
                        MessageBoxButtons.OK, MessageBoxIcon.Error)
        End Try
```

Now do a little housekeeping to keep track of the number of Thumbnail controls, if any, that you have, and to automatically select the first control in the collection. Start by setting the number of Thumbnail controls in the FlowLayoutPanel control in the intControlCount variable using the Count property of the Controls collection.

The intControlIndex variable keeps track of the currently selected Thumbnail control. If this variable contains a value greater than zero, then a Thumbnail control was previously selected and you need to ensure that it was not the last control and deleted. The next line of code compares the intControlIndex variable to the number of controls contained in the intControlCount variable minus 1 because the intControlIndex variable contains the zero-based index of the selected control. If the intControlIndex is greater than the number of controls, then you reset it to the first control, which is zero.

The last section of code here first checks the number of Thumbnail controls, as contained in the intControlCount variable. If the number of controls is greater than zero, then set the Selected property to True for the specific Thumbnail control. To do this, you must convert the control contained in the Controls collection of the FlowLayoutPanel to a Thumbnail control because the Controls collection contains a collection of Objects.

Using the DirectCast keyword, you can cast the specific Object contained in the Controls collection to a Thumbnail control. Notice that you access the specific control in the Controls collection using the intControlIndex variable. After the Object has been cast to a Thumbnail control, you can access the Selected property and set it to True.

```
            'Get the number of controls
            intControlCount = flpThumbnails.Controls.Count

            'If the control index was previous set...
            If intControlIndex > 0 Then

                    'If the control index is greater then the number of controls...
                    If intControlIndex > intControlCount - 1 Then
                        'Set the control index to the first item
                        intControlIndex = 0
                    End If

            End If

            'Select the first control if any exist
            If intControlCount > 0 Then
```

```
                DirectCast(flpThumbnails.Controls(intControlIndex), _
                    Thumbnail).Selected = True
            End If

        End Sub
```

ImageSelected Event Handler Procedure

The `ImageSelected` procedure is the generic event handler for the `ImageSelected` event of the `Thumbnail` control. Remember that you added an event handler for the `Thumbnail` control that was added to the `FlowLayoutPanel` control that pointed to this procedure. Also notice that this procedure contains the same methods as the `ImageSelectedEventHandler` delegate in the `Thumbnail` class.

The first thing to do in this procedure is set the `Image` property of the `PictureBox` in the ImageManager form using the `Image` property of the `sender` input parameter, which is the `Thumbnail` control that raised the `ImageSelected` event.

Next, resize the `PictureBox` using the size of the image contained in the `Thumbnail` control. Even though the displayed picture in the `Thumbnail` control is set to 133 × 123 pixels, the actual image retains its original size. Therefore, using the `Image` property of the `PictureBox` control in the `Thumbnail` control, set the `Size` property of the `PictureBox` in the ImageManager form.

Now set the `intControlIndex` variable to the index of the selected `Thumbnail` control, as contained in the `Index` property of the `sender` parameter. A call is then made to the `SetSizingControls` procedure, passing it a reference to the `Image` property of the `Thumbnail` control.

```
        Private Sub ImageSelected(ByVal sender As Object, _
            ByVal e As ThumbnailEventArgs)

            'Display the selected image and get the control index
            picPreview.Image = sender.Image
            picPreview.Size = New Size(sender.Image.Width, sender.Image.Height)
            intControlIndex = sender.Index

            'Set the properties of the sizing controls
            SetSizingControls(sender.Image)
        End Sub
```

SetSizingControls Procedure

The `SetSizingControls` procedure sets the values in the Resize Image section in the right-hand portion of the ImageManager form (refer to Figure 9-9). The `lblOriginalSize` Label control contains the original size of the image and is set according to the `Width` and `Height` of the image passed to this procedure. The `lblNewSize` Label control is then set to the same measurements using the `Text` property of the `lblOriginalSize` label.

Next, the `NumericUpDown` controls for the width and height of an image have their `Maximum` property set to two times the current image width and height. This means you can resize the current image to twice its current size. The `Value` property of these controls is set to the current width and height of the image.

Finally, the `NumericUpDown` control for the percentage of an image's size is set to a value of `100`, indicating that the image is displayed at 100 percent of its current size. Then set the focus to the Option button control for the original size:

```
Private Sub SetSizingControls(ByVal imageSource As Image)
    'Display the original size and set the sizing ComboBoxes
    lblOriginalSize.Text = imageSource.Width.ToString & _
        " x " & imageSource.Height.ToString & " pixels"
    lblNewSize.Text = lblOriginalSize.Text

    nudWidth.Maximum = (imageSource.Width * 2)
    nudWidth.Value = imageSource.Width
    nudHeight.Maximum = (imageSource.Height * 2)
    nudHeight.Value = imageSource.Height

    nudPercentage.Value = 100

    optOriginalSize.Focus()
End Sub
```

picPrevious_Click and picNext_Click Event Handler Procedures

The Previous and Next images on the ImageManager form enable the user to navigate to the previous and next `Thumbnail` control. The previous image that is displayed is named `picPrevious` and the event handler for the `Click` event is shown below. The first thing that happens in this procedure is a check to ensure that the `intControlIndex` variable is greater than zero. If it is, then you decrement that variable by one and set the `Selected` property of the `Thumbnail` control to `True`. Remember that you must convert the control in the `Controls` collection of the `FlowLayoutPanel` control to a `Thumbnail` control in order to access its `Selected` property using the `DirectCast` keyword.

Once the appropriate `Thumbnail` control has its `Selected` property set to `True`, you want to ensure that the control is visible within the `FlowLayoutPanel` control. This is done by calling the `ScrollControlIntoView` method on the `FlowLayoutPanel` control. This method accepts the control within the `FlowLayoutPanel` that should be scrolled into view.

The `Click` event handler for the next image operates in a similar manner. However, here you want to first check to ensure that the `intControlIndex` variable is less than the value contained in the `intControlCount` variable, minus 1 to account for the zero-based index of the `intControlIndex` variable:

```
Private Sub picPrevious_Click(ByVal sender As Object, _
    ByVal e As System.EventArgs) Handles picPrevious.Click

    If intControlIndex > 0 Then
        'Decrement the control index
        intControlIndex -= 1
        'Set the control's Selected property
        DirectCast(flpThumbnails.Controls(intControlIndex), _
            Thumbnail).Selected = True
        'Scroll the control in the FlowLayoutPanel into view
        flpThumbnails.ScrollControlIntoView(DirectCast( _
            flpThumbnails.Controls(intControlIndex), Thumbnail))
    End If
End Sub
```

```
        Private Sub picNext_Click(ByVal sender As Object, _
            ByVal e As System.EventArgs) Handles picNext.Click

            If intControlIndex < intControlCount - 1 Then
                'Increment the control index
                intControlIndex += 1
                'Set the control's Selected property
                DirectCast(flpThumbnails.Controls(intControlIndex), _
                    Thumbnail).Selected = True
                'Scroll the control in the FlowLayoutPanel into view
                flpThumbnails.ScrollControlIntoView(DirectCast( _
                    flpThumbnails.Controls(intControlIndex), Thumbnail))
            End If
        End Sub
```

OpenToolStripMenuItem_Click Event Handler Procedure

When the user clicks the Open button on the toolbar or clicks the Open menu item under the File menu, the `OpenToolStripMenuItem_Click` procedure is executed. This is the procedure that displays the Open File dialog box. The first thing you do here is declare the `objOpenFileDialog` object and set it to a new instance of the `OpenFileDialog` class.

Then you set the properties of this object, starting with the `Filter` property. This property sets the filter that is seen in the Files Of Type combo box in the dialog shown in Figure 9-2. This application supports Bitmap, JPEG, and GIF images, so each of these file types has an entry in the `Filter` property. The final filter is one that displays all image files and has been appropriately named.

The `FilterIndex` property indicates which filter should be initially displayed. The `intFilterIndex` variable has an initial value of 4 indicating the last filter, but if another filter was chosen, then this will be the filter applied the next time this dialog is shown. Finally, set the `Title` property to `Open`. This is the value that is displayed on the title bar of the dialog box.

```
        Private Sub OpenToolStripMenuItem_Click(ByVal sender As Object, _
            ByVal e As System.EventArgs) Handles OpenToolStripMenuItem.Click

            'Declare local variables
            Dim objOpenFileDialog As New OpenFileDialog

            'Set the OpenFileDialog properties
            With objOpenFileDialog
                .Filter = "Bitmap (*.bmp)|*.bmp|JPEG (*.jpg)|*.jpg|" & _
                    "GIF (*.gif)|*.gif|All Image Files|*.bmp;*.jpg;*.gif"
                .FilterIndex = intFilterIndex
                .Title = "Open"
            End With
```

At this point, the Open File dialog box is shown and you wait for a dialog result. If the dialog result returned from the Open File dialog box is OK, then you proceed with the code inside the If . . . Then statement block.

First check the `Count` property of the `Controls` collection in the `FlowLayoutPanel` control. If that property returns a value greater than zero, then you have one or more `Thumbnail` controls. With this being the case, set the `Selected` property of the currently selected `Thumbnail` control to `False`, which is done in the next line of code. This prevents the Update Image and Delete Image buttons on the toolbar from updating or deleting an image that is not selected.

```
'Show the dialog and open the file if appropriate
If objOpenFileDialog.ShowDialog = Windows.Forms.DialogResult.OK Then
    Try
        'Clear the selected Thumbnail control
        If flpThumbnails.Controls.Count > 0 Then
            DirectCast(flpThumbnails.Controls(intControlIndex), _
                Thumbnail).Selected = False
        End If
```

Now you want to instantiate a new instance of the `FileStream` class in your `objFileStream` object, passing the constructor for the `FileStream` class the `FileName` property of the Open File dialog box along with the file mode and file access requested for this file. Then load the image into the `objImage` object and dispose of the `objFileStream` object.

```
'Instaniate the FileStream to load the image
objFileStream = New FileStream(objOpenFileDialog.FileName, _
    FileMode.Open, FileAccess.Read)

'Load the image into an Image object so we can
'determine the proper size
objImage = Image.FromStream(objFileStream)

'Close the file stream and dispose of it
objFileStream.Close()
objFileStream.Dispose()
```

Set the `Image` property of the `PictureBox` control to the image that you just loaded into the `objImage` object and then set the `Size` property of the `PictureBox` control to the width and height of the image as contained in the `Width` and `Height` properties of the `objImage` object.

You want to save the filename by setting the `strImageName` variable to the filename contained in the `FileName` property of the Open File dialog box. The `FileName` property contains the full path and file name, so you extract just the filename using the `SubString` method.

Next, save the filter index that was selected in the Open File dialog box in the `intFilterIndex` variable. Remember that this is set at the beginning of this procedure, so if the user chooses to open another file, then the Files Of Type combo box is automatically set to the same value that the user chose this time, if any.

Now call the `SetSizingControls` procedure, passing it the `objImage` object so the image sizes can be set in the Resize Image section of the ImageManager form. The `Catch` block handles any errors that might occur opening and reading the selected image file.

```
'Load the image into the PictureBox control and
'resize it accordingly
picPreview.Image = objImage
picPreview.Size = New Size(objImage.Width, objImage.Height)
```

```
                      'Save the file name
                      strImageName = objOpenFileDialog.FileName.Substring( _
                          objOpenFileDialog.FileName.LastIndexOf("\") + 1)

                      'Save the filter index
                      intFilterIndex = objOpenFileDialog.FilterIndex

                      'Set the properties of the sizing controls
                      SetSizingControls(objImage)

                  Catch ExceptionErr As Exception
                      MessageBox.Show(ExceptionErr.Message, My.Application.Info.Title, _
                          MessageBoxButtons.OK, MessageBoxIcon.Error)
                  End Try
              End If
      End Sub
```

AddImageToolStripButton_Click Event Handler Procedure

The `AddImageToolStripButton_Click` procedure is the event handler for the Add Image button on the toolbar. The code in this procedure is wrapped in a `Try...Catch...Finally` block. The first check in the `Try` block is to check the length of the `strImageName` variable; if it equals 0, then you exit the procedure because no image has been opened and thus there is nothing to add.

If an image has been opened, then you call the `AddImage` method in the `DBImages` class, passing it the name of the image as contained in the `strImageName` variable, the image contained in the `PictureBox` control on the ImageManager form, the width and height of the image, and the pixel format of the image. The last three parameters are derived from the `PictureBox` control on the form.

After the image has been added, call the `LoadDatabaseImages` procedure to refresh the list of `Thumbnail` controls in the `FlowLayoutPanel` control. The `Catch` block handles any errors that might arise when adding the image and the `Finally` block clears the image name in the `strImageName` variable:

```
      Private Sub AddImageToolStripButton_Click(ByVal sender As Object, _
          ByVal e As System.EventArgs) Handles AddImageToolStripButton.Click

          Try
              'Exit if the file name is not set
              If strImageName.Length = 0 Then
                  Exit Sub
              End If

              'Add the image to the database
              objDBImages.AddImage(strImageName, picPreview.Image, _
                  picPreview.Width, picPreview.Height, picPreview.Image.PixelFormat)

              'Reload the list of images
              LoadDatabaseImages()

          Catch ExceptionErr As Exception
              MessageBox.Show(ExceptionErr.Message, My.Application.Info.Title, _
                  MessageBoxButtons.OK, MessageBoxIcon.Error)
```

```
        Finally
            'Clear the file name
            strImageName = String.Empty        .
        End Try
    End Sub
```

UpdateImageToolStripButton_Click Event Handler Procedure

The `UpdateImageToolStripButton_Click` procedure is the event handler for the `Click` event of the
Update Image button on the toolbar. This procedure has its code wrapped in a `Try...Catch` block to
handle any database errors that might occur when updating an image.

There are two checks at the beginning of this procedure. The first check ensures that the `intControlCount`
variable is not equal to `0`, indicating that there are no `Thumbnail` controls. The next check is one for the
`Selected` property of the `Thumbnail` control indicated by the `intControlIndex` variable; if it is set to
`False`, you exit the procedure:

```
    Private Sub UpdateImageToolStripButton_Click(ByVal sender As Object, _
        ByVal e As System.EventArgs) Handles UpdateImageToolStripButton.Click

        Try
            'Exit if there are no Thumbnail controls
            If intControlCount = 0 Then
                Exit Sub
            End If

            'Exit if the Thumbnail control is not selected
            If Not DirectCast(flpThumbnails.Controls(intControlIndex), _
                Thumbnail).Selected Then
                Exit Sub
            End If
```

If everything checks out, then you update the selected image in the database. Call the `UpdateImage`
method in the `DBImages` class, passing it the key of the selected image by accessing the `Key` property of the
selected image and converting it to a `Guid` structure. Remember that the `Key` property in the `Thumbnail`
control was defined as a `String` data type to keep it generic, so you must convert that `String` value into a
`Guid` structure. The constructor for the `Guid` structure accepts a `Guid` formatted as a `String` and returns
a `Guid` structure with the `String` converted to a `Guid`.

The remaining parameters of the `UpdateImage` method are the same as the `AddImage` method and
you get that information from the `PictureBox` control on the form. After the image has been updated
in the database, call the `LoadDatabaseImages` procedure to update the `Thumbnail` controls in the
`FlowLayoutPanel` control.

```
            'Update the image in the database
            objDBImages.UpdateImage(New Guid(DirectCast( _
                flpThumbnails.Controls(intControlIndex), Thumbnail).Key), _
                DirectCast(flpThumbnails.Controls(intControlIndex), _
                Thumbnail).Text, picPreview.Image, picPreview.Width, _
                picPreview.Height, picPreview.Image.PixelFormat)

            'Reload the list of images
```

```
        LoadDatabaseImages()

    Catch ExceptionErr As Exception
        MessageBox.Show(ExceptionErr.Message, My.Application.Info.Title, _
            MessageBoxButtons.OK, MessageBoxIcon.Error)
    End Try
End Sub
```

DeleteImageToolStripButton_Click Event Handler Procedure

The `DeleteImageToolStripButton_Click` procedure is the event handler for the `Click` event of the Delete Image button on the toolbar. This procedure also has its code wrapped in a `Try...Catch` block to handle any possible database errors. The code in the `Try` block starts in the same manner as it did in the `UpdateImageToolStripButton_Click` procedure, to ensure that you have at least one `Thumbnail` control and that the `Thumbnail` control pointed to by the `intControlIndex` variable has its `Selected` property set to `True`. If neither of these conditions is true, then you exit this procedure.

The `DeleteImage` method in the `DBImages` class accepts only one parameter: the key of the image to be deleted. As before, extract the key of the selected image from the `Key` property of the `Thumbnail` control and convert that `String` value to a `Guid` structure. After the image has been deleted, call the `LoadDatabaseImages` procedure to reload the collection of `Thumbnail` controls in the `FlowLayoutPanel` control:

```
Private Sub DeleteImageToolStripButton_Click(ByVal sender As Object, _
    ByVal e As System.EventArgs) Handles DeleteImageToolStripButton.Click

    Try
        'Exit if there are no Thumbnail controls
        If intControlCount = 0 Then
            Exit Sub
        End If

        'Exit if the Thumbnail control is not selected
        If Not DirectCast(flpThumbnails.Controls(intControlIndex), _
            Thumbnail).Selected Then
            Exit Sub
        End If

        'Delete the image in the database
        objDBImages.DeleteImage(New Guid(DirectCast( _
            flpThumbnails.Controls(intControlIndex), Thumbnail).Key))

        'Reload the list of images
        LoadDatabaseImages()

    Catch ExceptionErr As Exception
        MessageBox.Show(ExceptionErr.Message, My.Application.Info.Title, _
            MessageBoxButtons.OK, MessageBoxIcon.Error)
    End Try
End Sub
```

Setting Up the Database Image Manager Application

Setup of the Database Image Manager application can be performed using the installer or by manually copying the required files to your computer. The first option provides an easy, fast approach to installing the program, whereas the second approach provides greater flexibility over where the files are installed.

Using the Installer

To install the Data Binding application, locate the `Chapter 09 - Database Image Manager\Installer` folder on the CD-ROM that came with this book and double-click the `setup.exe` program. You are prompted with the Application Install dialog. Clicking the Install button installs and launches the application. Once the installer is finished, your program is ready to be used.

Manual Installation

To manually install the Data Binding application, first create a folder on your computer where you want to place the program executable files. Then locate the `Chapter 09 - Database Image Manager\Source` folder on the CD-ROM that came with this book and navigate to the `bin\Release` folder. Copy the following files from the `Release` folder to the folder that you created on your computer. Notice that the last two files are placed in a subfolder to which you are copying the files:

- ❑   `Database Image Manager.exe`
- ❑   `Database Image Manager.exe.config`
- ❑   `ImagePlaceHolder.dll`
- ❑   `Database\ImagesDB.mdf`
- ❑   `Database\ImagesDB_log.ldf`

Configuring the Application

Before running the application you need to edit the `Database Image Manager.exe.config` file to set the path to the `ImageDB.mdf` database file. This will be the path to where you copied the file when using the manual installation method.

If you used the installer to install the application and you run into problems having the file attached when the application starts, you can edit the `Database Image Manager.exe.config` file to set the path to the location where the `ImageDB.mdf` database file was installed.

Summary

This chapter has taken a look at using SQL Server Express to automatically attach a SQL Server database when your application starts. This enables you to take advantage of the power of SQL Server and to distribute a SQL Server database with your application. The only drawback to this approach is that you must ensure that SQL Server Express is installed on the target machine where your application is installed. If you are using the installer, this is not a problem. If you are manually copying the files to the target computer, then you must ensure that SQL Server Express is already installed on that machine.

This chapter showed you firsthand how you can create a user control that provides a rich set of features for displaying images. You also learned how that control can declare and raise an event when the user selects it. In addition to seeing how the `Thumbnail` user control was put together, you also saw how to dynamically instantiate this control through code and add it to the ImageManager form.

A lot of work was done with images in this application, as that is what it was designed for. To that end, you should have a better understanding of the `Image` class and how to work with the `MemoryStream` class and a `Byte` array to get image data into and out of the database. You also got experience working with the `Image` class when setting the properties of the `Thumbnail` control, reading the `Image` property of the selected `Thumbnail` control, and setting the `PictureBox` control to the selected image.

10

Custom Controls

I believe the TextBox control is one of the most powerful and versatile controls in the Toolbox. This control can be used for data entry such as names and addresses, enabling you to set the width of the TextBox to the approximate size of the data to be entered. You can also bind the TextBox to data from a DataSet to display data from your database. Set one property on a TextBox control and it can be used for passwords, preventing the password from being seen or copied. Set a different property on this control and the TextBox becomes a big multi-line text editor.

However, for all of its power and flexibility, the TextBox control still lacks some basic properties that would enhance the user experience and make the developer's job easier. These are properties that prevent the user from entering numeric data in a name field, for example, or that require numeric data and disallow character data in a phone number field. These are basic data entry tasks, and properties like these would greatly enhance this already versatile control.

Another simple and basic feature lacking in the TextBox control is the ToolTip property. Why should a developer be forced to drag another control to the designer surface of a form just to implement a ToolTip property? This is a very basic property that enhances the user's experience with any application.

The Custom Controls application in this chapter extends the TextBox control to provide some of these basic features, and other helpful features, and then demonstrates their usefulness and functionality. This application implements nine new properties for the TextBox control and overloads an existing property to enhance, it making it more useful. The existence of these new properties reduces the amount of code that you, as a developer, have to write to support a rich user experience when using the TextBox control.

The main technologies covered in this chapter are as follows:

❑ Using the CategoryAttribute, DescriptionAttribute, and DefaultAttribute classes to categorize, describe, and assign values to properties

❑ Using the ToolTip class to provide built-in tooltip functionality for a TextBox control

❑ Overloading an existing property to enhance its functionality

Using the Custom Controls Application

The Custom Controls application is a simple application to demonstrate the functionality of the new properties implemented in the `TextBoxExtended` control. The `TextBoxExtended` control inherits the `TextBox` class and then extends it by providing new properties and overloading the `CharacterCasing` property to enhance its functionality.

When you first start the application, the screen's fields are blank, as shown in Figure 10-1. Each of the new and enhanced properties has been divided into separate groups, as indicated by the `GroupBox` controls shown in the figure. Every `TextBox` control on this form is actually a `TextBoxExtended` control, whose properties are set accordingly to demonstrate the functionality of the new properties. The labels above the `TextBoxExtended` controls indicate the property being demonstrated by the `TextBoxExtended` control, and the labels contain the value of the property where applicable.

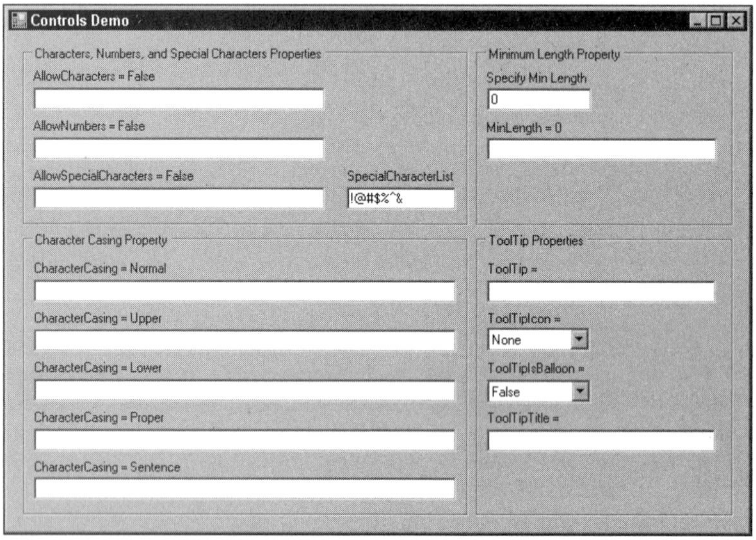

Figure 10-1

The first `GroupBox` demonstrates characters, numbers, and special characters, as indicated by the `Text` property of the `GroupBox`. Four new properties have been added to the `TextBoxExtended` control in this area, as indicated by the labels above the `TextBoxExtended` controls. The `AllowCharacters` property is a `Boolean` property that indicates whether alpha characters are allowed to be entered. This property is an idea property to set to `False` when you need to enter an all-numeric phone number or zip code or if you need to enter numbers and special characters.

When set to `False`, the `AllowNumbers` property disallows any numbers from being entered into the `TextBoxExtended` control. This would be an ideal property to set for a name field or for other fields where all character data is expected.

The `AllowSpecialCharacters` property works in conjunction with the `SpecialCharacterList` property. The `SpecialCharacterList` property is a `Char` array of special characters. When setting this property through the Properties window, the Char Collection Editor is displayed, as shown in

Figure 10-2. This allows you to enter any number of special characters that should be excluded when the AllowSpecialCharacters property is set False.

When the AllowSpecialCharacters property is set False, it only looks at the list of special characters in the SpecialCharacterList for special characters to block from being entered. If a special character that is not in this list is entered, then the special character is allowed. These two properties work great for only allowing certain special characters in a password field.

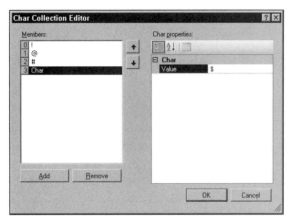

Figure 10-2

The CharacterCasing property overloads the default CharacterCasing property of the TextBox class. The default implementation of this property contains the Normal, Upper, and Lower constants from the CharacterCasing enumeration. The overloaded implementation of this property adds two new constants: Proper and Sentence. Figure 10-3 demonstrates the various constants available in this property.

When the CharacterCasing property is set to Normal, you get what you type. In other words, you have to provide your own uppercase and lowercase characters. When this property is set to Upper, all characters that you enter are forced to uppercase, as demonstrated in Figure 10-3. When this property is set to Lower, all characters that are entered are forced to lowercase.

The new Proper constant of the CharacterCasing property automatically capitalizes the first letter of each word, as demonstrated in Figure 10-3. The new Sentence constant of this property automatically capitalizes the first letter of the first word after a period and the first letter entered into the TextBoxExtended control, as demonstrated in Figure 10-3.

The MinLength property is another ideal property to be used with passwords, as it forces a minimum length in a TextBoxExtended control. Figure 10-3 shows that the property has been set to a value of 7, as indicated by the value in the TextBoxExtended control with the label Specify Min Length. This TextBoxExtended control is used to dynamically set the MinLength property of the TextBoxExtended control beneath it.

Figure 10-4 illustrates that when you try to leave the TextBoxExtended control without entering the minimum number of characters, you receive a warning message indicating as much. This works even if you try to tab out of the `TextBoxExtended` control or you click on another control with your mouse. This functionality forces the user to enter a minimum number of characters.

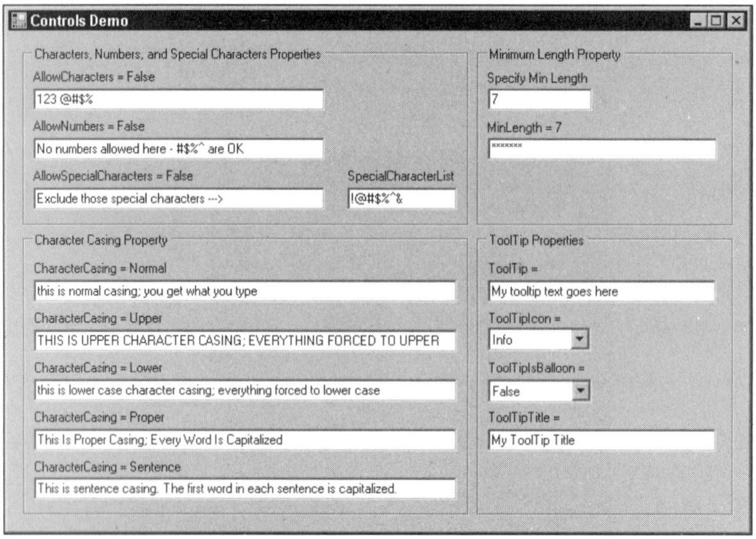

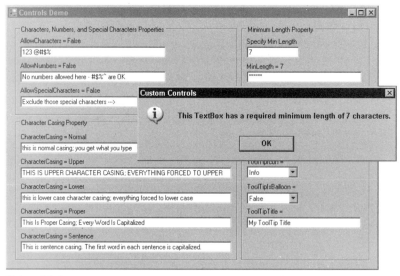

Figure 10-3

The message displayed is automatically generated and there is nothing that you need to do to implement this functionality. The length specified in the message is dynamically built based on the value specified in the `MinLength` property. When the `Minlength` property is set to a value of `0`, which is the default, no checking on the length of input is performed.

Figure 10-4

The last set of properties to discuss are the properties displayed in the ToolTip Properties GroupBox, as shown in Figure 10-5. These properties all work together, although the only one required to display a tooltip is the ToolTip property itself. This is the text of the tooltip, and when this property contains text, a tooltip will be displayed in the control. The remaining three properties shown merely enhance the appearance of your tooltip.

The ToolTipIcon property has four options: None, Info, Warning, and Error. When this property is set to None, no icon is displayed on the tooltip. When set to one of the other values, the appropriate icon is displayed on the tooltip, as indicated in Figure 10-5.

You can use the ToolTipTitle property to specify a title for your tooltip, enabling you to dress it up as shown in Figure 10-5. It also provides additional information. This property works like the ToolTip property in that if no text is specified, then it will not be displayed in your tooltip.

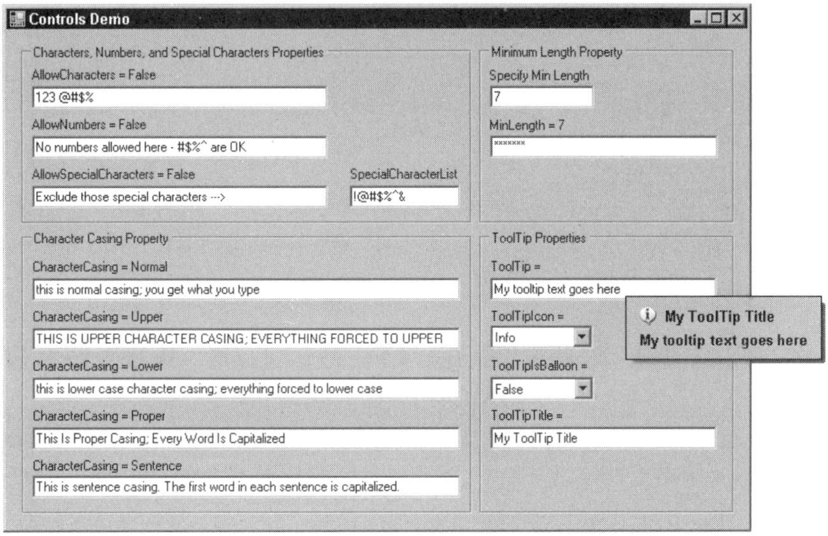

Figure 10-5

The Windows XP operating system introduced a lot of user interface enhancements, such as the balloon tooltip shown in Figure 10-6. This provides an alternative to the standard tooltip shown in Figure 10-5 and helps provide a more interesting look for your application.

The balloon tooltip provides one additional feature. If you look closely at Figure 10-5 and Figure 10-6, you'll notice that the balloon tooltip points directly to the control that it is for. The tooltip shown in Figure 10-5 could be for either the TextBoxExtended control or the combo box beneath it, as it really isn't clear after hovering your mouse over a particular control in order to have the tooltip appear.

All four of these ToolTip properties have been built into the TextBoxExtended control, providing a more versatile control. It also enables you to choose the style of tooltip for your application or even to mix the styles between two different TextBoxExtended controls on the same form.

Now that you've had an overview of how the Custom Controls application works, spend a few minutes trying it yourself before moving on to the design discussion, which is covered next. If you need help installing or executing this application, see the "Setting Up the Custom Controls Application" section at the end of this chapter.

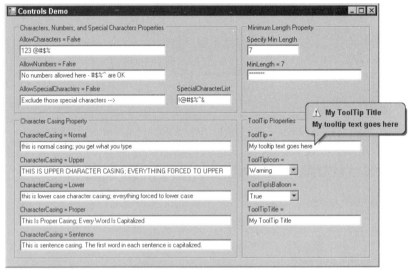

Figure 10-6

Design of the Custom Controls Application

The design of the Custom Controls application couldn't be simpler. It contains one form and one user control, the TextBoxExtended control. Figure 10-7 illustrates this simple design and shows how the pieces fit together. As you can see in the design, the TextBoxExtended control inherits the TextBox class in the .NET Framework.

The TextBoxExtended control is a separate project in the solution and when you build that project, the TextBoxExtended control is automatically added to the Toolbox in the IDE in its own group named after the project — in this case, TextBoxEx. When building a user control that extends an existing .NET Framework control, you have no control interface as you did with the Thumbnail control in the previous chapter.

In fact, the steps you take to create an extended control are similar to creating a user control. First you create a new project using the Windows Control Library project template and then delete the user control that is automatically added. Then you add a new class to the project and inherit the control that you want to extend in the new class using the Inherits statement. You'll see the details of this shortly when I discuss the code in detail.

TextBoxExtended Class

The TextBoxExtended class extends the TextBox class from the .NET Framework, adding the new properties previously discussed and demonstrated. It also overloads the CharacterCasing property, enhancing its functionality. Table 10-1 lists the properties and methods available in this class.

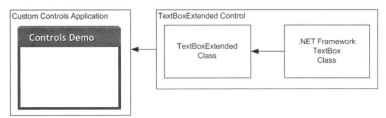

Figure 10-7

Table 10-1: Properties and Methods of the TextBoxExtended Class

Property/Method	Return Type	Description
Public Property AllowCharacters()	Boolean	Indicates whether the control accepts character data
Public Property AllowNumbers()	Boolean	Indicates whether the control accepts numeric data
Public Property AllowSpecialCharacters()	Boolean	Indicates whether the control accepts special characters. If False, the SpecialCharacterList property must specify which special characters to exclude
Public Property SpecialCharacterList()	Char()	A list of special characters to exclude when the AllowSpecialCharacter property is set to False
Public Property MinLength()	Integer	Specifies the minimum number of characters that should be entered into the edit control
Public Overloads Property CharacterCasing()	OverloadsCharacterCasing	Indicates whether all characters should left alone or converted to another case
Public Property ToolTip()	String	Determines the tooltip displayed when the mouse hovers over the control
Public Property ToolTipIcon()	ToolTipIcon	Determines the icon that is shown on the tooltip

Continued

Table 10-1: Properties and Methods of the TextBoxExtended Class *(continued)*

Property/Method	Return Type	Description
`Public Property ToolTipIsBalloon()`	Boolean	Indicates whether the tooltip takes on a balloon form
`Public Property ToolTipTitle()`	String	Determines the title of the tooltip
`Private Sub TextBoxExtended_KeyPress(By Val sender As Object, ByVal e As System.Windows.Forms .KeyPressEventArgs)`	N/A	Implements code to act on the properties described previously
`Private Sub TextBoxExtended_KeyUp(ByVal sender As Object, ByVal e As System.Windows.Forms .KeyEventArgs)`	N/A	Implements code to fix the CTRL+A shortcut key
`Private Sub TextBoxExtended_Validating( ByVal sender As Object, ByVal e As System.ComponentModel .CancelEventArgs)`	N/A	Implements code to validate the number of characters entered into the control based on the `MinLength` property

Controls Demo Form

The Controls Demo form contains very little code and none that is critical to the design or operation of the application. The code merely supports the UI, enabling you to test the functionality of the properties. It is covered in detail in the next section.

Code and Code Explanation

This section describes the code in the `TextBoxExtended` class in detail and explains how it implements the properties listed in Table 10-1. You'll also get to see how the code in the Controls Demo form supports the UI by dynamically setting some of these properties through code.

TextBoxExtended Class

This class starts off by importing the `System.ComponentModel` namespace. This namespace is needed to provide access to the `CategoryAttribute`, `DescriptionAttribute`, and `DefaultAttribute` classes that provide the attributes for a property. These are the attributes that are displayed in the

Properties window within the IDE. Let's take a look at the beginning part of this class, shown in the code fragment that follows.

The `Imports` statement imports the `System.ComponentModel` namespace. You can also see that this class inherits the `TextBox` class, as that is the class you are extending. Once you inherit an existing class from the .NET Framework, you gain access to all of the properties and methods exposed by that class. Depending on how the property or method is implemented in the base class, you may be able to override or overload the property or method. You'll see this in practice shortly with the `CharacterCasing` property.

```
Imports System.ComponentModel


Public Class TextBoxExtended
    Inherits TextBox
```

Several variables and objects have been defined at the class level. All of these variables and objects are defined as `Private` because they are used internally to keep track of the various property values. In other words, when a developer changes the value of a property in the IDE, that value is stored in one of these variables.

The `TextBoxToolTip` object instantiates a new instance of the `ToolTip` class and this object is what provides the various `ToolTip` properties shown in Figures 10-5 and 10-6. This object enables you to provide the tooltip functionality for this extended control.

```
    'Private variables
    Private blnAllowCharacters As Boolean = True
    Private blnAllowNumbers As Boolean = True
    Private blnAllowSpecialCharacters As Boolean = True
    Private blnSpaceEntered As Boolean = False
    Private blnPeriodEntered As Boolean = False

    Private intMinLength As Integer = 0
    Private intCharacterCasing As Integer = 0

    Private chrSpecialCharacterList() As Char
    Private chrCharacter As Char

    Private TextBoxToolTip As New ToolTip
```

AllowCharacters Property

The first property that you want to take a look at is the `AllowCharacters` property, which is shown in the following code. The `Category` attribute defines the category in the Properties window in which this control should be placed. Because this property affects the behavior of the `TextBox`, this category has been set to `Behavior`.

After you have created a property, the Properties window displays the `Category` and `Default Value` properties for this property code, as shown in Figure 10-8. You can manually add the `Category` attribute to your property code or choose an appropriate category from the list in the Properties window, which causes the `Category` attribute to be automatically added to your code for that property.

The `Description` attribute provides a description for this property. When you click on a property in the Properties window, the description provided is displayed at the bottom of the window. The description should be fairly short and to the point, describing the basic functionality of the property. The description shown in Figure 10-9 is for the CaracterCasing property, and you can see how this type of description would be important to the developer using your control and how important it is that you provide this description in the Description attribute.

The last attribute that has been defined for this property is the DefaultValue attribute. This attribute, as its name implies, provides an initial default value that is displayed in the Properties window at design time. This attribute can also be manually specified in your code as shown in the following code fragment or you can set this attribute using the Properties window shown in Figure 10-8, which causes the IDE to automatically add the attribute to your code.

```
<Category("Behavior"), _
Description("Indicates whether or not the control accepts character data."), _
DefaultValue(True)> _
Public Property AllowCharacters() As Boolean
    Get
        Return blnAllowCharacters
    End Get
    Set(ByVal value As Boolean)
        blnAllowCharacters = value
    End Set
End Property
```

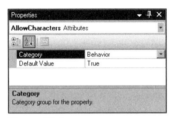

Figure 10-8

AllowNumbers Property

The next property to be covered is the AllowNumbers property. Like the AllowCharacters property, this property also returns a Boolean value. When this property is set to True, numbers are allowed to be entered into the TextBoxExtended control; when set to False, numbers are not allowed to be entered into the control.

Again the Category, Description, and DefaultValue attributes have been specified for this property. The Category attribute provides the category in the Properties window under which this property is listed, the Description attribute provides a brief description of what this property is used for, and the DefaultValue attribute provides the initial setting for this property.

```
<Category("Behavior"), _
Description("Indicates whether or not the control accepts numeric data."), _
DefaultValue(True)> _
Public Property AllowNumbers() As Boolean
    Get
        Return blnAllowNumbers
    End Get
```

```
        Set(ByVal value As Boolean)
            blnAllowNumbers = value
        End Set
    End Property
```

AllowSpecialCharacters Property

The `AllowSpecialCharacters` property works in conjunction with the `SpecialCharacterList` property. When this property is set to `False`, the code in this class examines each special character entered and compares it to the list of special characters contained in the `SpecialCharacterList` property. If a match is found, then that special character will not be allowed to be entered into the control.

The `Description` attribute for this property is a bit wordy, but it's necessary to convey how this property works in conjunction with another property. As before, keep the description brief when possible because there is a minimal amount of space in the Properties window to display the description for a property.

```
    <Category("Behavior"), _
    Description("Indicates whether or not the control accepts special " & _
    "characters. If False, the SpecialCharacterList property must specify " & _
    "which special characters to exclude."), _
    DefaultValue(True)> _
    Public Property AllowSpecialCharacters() As Boolean
        Get
            Return blnAllowSpecialCharacters
        End Get
        Set(ByVal value As Boolean)
            blnAllowSpecialCharacters = value
        End Set
    End Property
```

SpecialCharacterList Property

The `SpecialCharacterList` property contains a `Char` array of special characters. When adding special characters to this property at design time, the IDE displays the Char Collection Editor, as shown previously in Figure 10-2. This enables you to enter each special character as a `Char` data type, and the editor then converts these special characters into a `Char` array. When you examine the code for the Controls Demo form, you'll see how to set this property at runtime using a `String` data type, converting it to a `Char` array.

Again, this property contains the `Category`, `Description`, and `DefaultValue` attributes. Notice that the `DefaultValue` attribute has been set to an empty string, as it is nearly impossible to determine what special characters your application's users want to exclude, and it is best not to provide the wrong default value to the majority of developers who are implementing this control. A good rule of thumb is, when in doubt leave it blank.

```
    <Category("Behavior"), _
    Description("A list of special characters to exclude when the " & _
    "AllowSpecialCharacter property is set to False."), _
    DefaultValue("")> _
    Public Property SpecialCharacterList() As Char()
        Get
            Return chrSpecialCharacterList
        End Get
```

```
            Set(ByVal value As Char())
                chrSpecialCharacterList = value
            End Set
      End Property
```

MinLength Property

The MinLength property specifies the minimum number of characters that must be entered into the control. A value of 0 has been specified in the DefaultValue attribute, which essentially bypasses processing of the checks for this property.

This property was demonstrated in Figure 10-4 and is an ideal property to be used with password fields to force a minimum-length password. Used in conjunction with the MaxLength property, you can require a password with a minimum and maximum length without writing a single line of code.

```
      <Category("Behavior"), _
      Description("Specifies the minimum number of characters that should " & _
      "be entered into the edit control."), _
      DefaultValue(0)> _
      Public Property MinLength() As Integer
          Get
                Return intMinLength
          End Get
          Set(ByVal value As Integer)
                intMinLength = value
          End Set
      End Property
```

CharacterCasing Property

Before looking at the CharacterCasing property, you need to examine the enumeration used with this property. The OverloadsCharacterCasing enumeration provides the values in the drop-down list of the CharacterCasing property, as demonstrated in Figure 10-9.

The Normal, Upper, and Lower constants in this enumeration correspond to the same values as the Normal, Upper, and Lower constants in the CharacterCasing enumeration. You'll see why this is important in a minute. The remaining two constants are the new constants added to the CharacterCasing property (see Figure 10-9).

```
      Public Enum OverloadsCharacterCasing
          Normal = 0
          Upper = 1
          Lower = 2
          Proper = 3
          Sentence = 4
      End Enum
```

The Category, Description, and DefaultValue attributes in the CharacterCasing property contain the same values specified in the CharacterCasing property in the base class. Because you are merely augmenting the functionality of this property, you do not want to change any of these attributes specified in the property in the base class. However, you must still provide these attributes for this property in order to have the property displayed in the correct category, have a description, and provide the correct default value.

Note that the value contained in the `DefaultValue` attribute specifies the `Normal` constant from the `OverloadsCharacterCasing` enumeration. This is because this property sets and returns a constant from this enumeration, as shown in the `Property` statement in the code that follows.

The `CharacterCasing` property has been defined with the `Overloads` keyword, as this property overloads an existing property in the base class. Some properties in the base class are defined with the `NotOverridable` keyword, which means that you cannot override them. You can, however, overload them, and this is exactly what you are doing here.

In the `Set` statement block of this property, you check the value being set in this property in a `Select...Case` statement block. If the value being set is the `Normal`, `Upper`, or `Lower` constant, then you merely pass that information onto the `CharacterCasing` property in the base class. The reason for this is that the base class has already implemented the code to convert the characters entered in the control to all uppercase characters when this property is set to `Upper`. Likewise, it already has the code implemented to convert the characters entered into the control to all lowercase when the `Lower` constant has been specified. You do not want to reinvent the wheel, so you merely set the `CharacterCasing` property in the base class and let the base class handle the conversion of characters.

```
<Category("Behavior"), _
Description("Indicates if all characters should left alone or " & _
"converted to another case."), _
DefaultValue(OverloadsCharacterCasing.Normal)> _
Public Overloads Property CharacterCasing() As OverloadsCharacterCasing
    Get
        Return intCharacterCasing
    End Get
    Set(ByVal value As OverloadsCharacterCasing)
        Select Case value
            Case OverloadsCharacterCasing.Normal
                MyBase.CharacterCasing = Windows.Forms.CharacterCasing.Normal
            Case OverloadsCharacterCasing.Upper
                MyBase.CharacterCasing = Windows.Forms.CharacterCasing.Upper
            Case OverloadsCharacterCasing.Lower
                MyBase.CharacterCasing = Windows.Forms.CharacterCasing.Lower
        End Select
        intCharacterCasing = value
    End Set
End Property
```

Figure 10-9

ToolTip Property

The `ToolTip` property gets or sets the tooltip for your control. Notice that in the code for this property the values are being set and read from the `TextBoxToolTip` object, which was declared and instantiated as a `ToolTip` class at the beginning of this class.

When setting the `ToolTip` for this control you must call the `SetToolTip` method on the `TextBoxToolTip` object and pass it the control that the `ToolTip` is for and the `ToolTip` string. Using the `Me` keyword, you reference this instance of the `TextBoxExtended` control as the control parameter. The value set in this property is passed as the `ToolTip` parameter to the `SetToolTip` method.

To return the `ToolTip` that has already been set, you call the `GetToopTip` method of the `TextBoxToolTip` object and pass it the control that you want the tooltip for; again you use the `Me` keyword to reference this control. This method returns a string containing the tooltip, and you merely return that information to the caller.

```
<Category("Misc"), _
Description("Determines the ToolTip shown when the mouse " & _
"hovers over the control."), _
DefaultValue("")> _
Public Property ToolTip() As String
    Get
        Return TextBoxToolTip.GetToolTip(Me)
    End Get
    Set(ByVal value As String)
        TextBoxToolTip.SetToolTip(Me, value)
    End Set
End Property
```

ToolTipIcon Property

The `ToolTipIcon` property implements the `ToolTipIcon` property from the `ToolTip` class, which is declared in the `TextBoxToolTip` object. Notice that this property sets and returns the `ToolTipIcon` from the `TextBoxToolTip` object.

You can see in Figure 10-10 how this functionality works. By implementing this property as the same property in another class, you automatically gain access to its design and functionality. Figure 10-10 shows how you automatically get the constants from the `ToolTipIcon` enumeration displayed in a drop-down list. You did not have to write any code for this; you merely implemented the `ToolTipIcon` property from the `ToolTip` class in your property. This provides an excellent means of code reuse and reduces the amount of code that you have to write to implement such a property.

```
<Category("Misc"), _
Description("Determines the icon that is shown on the ToolTip."), _
DefaultValue(ToolTipIcon.None)> _
Public Property ToolTipIcon() As ToolTipIcon
    Get
        Return TextBoxToolTip.ToolTipIcon
    End Get
    Set(ByVal value As ToolTipIcon)
        TextBoxToolTip.ToolTipIcon = value
    End Set
End Property
```

Figure 10-10

ToolTipIsBalloon Property

The `ToolTipIsBallon` property works in the same manner as the `ToolTipIcon` property although this property does not have the same name as the property that it implements in the `ToolTip` class. Notice that this property has been appropriately named to keep all the tooltip-related properties grouped together in the Properties window, as shown earlier in Figure 10-10.

This property implements the `IsBalloon` property from the `ToolTip` class defined in your `TextBoxToolTip` object. That property expects a `Boolean` value, so this property has also been defined to set and return a `Boolean` value. When this property is set, it sets the `IsBalloon` property in the `TextBoxToolTip` object, and when this property returns the value that has been set, it returns the `Boolean` value from the `IsBalloon` property in the `TextBoxToolTip` object.

```
<Category("Misc"), _
Description("Indicates whether the ToolTip will take on a balloon form."), _
DefaultValue(False)> _
Public Property ToolTipIsBalloon() As Boolean
    Get
        Return TextBoxToolTip.IsBalloon
    End Get
    Set(ByVal value As Boolean)
        TextBoxToolTip.IsBalloon = value
    End Set
End Property
```

ToolTipTitle Property

The last property to be covered is the `ToolTipTitle` property. This property also implements the same named property in the `ToolTip` class contained in your `TextBoxToolTip` object. When this property is being set, it sets its counterpart property in the `TextBoxToolTip` object, and when this property returns the value that has been set, it returns the value from the `ToolTipTitle` property in the `TextBoxToolTip` object.

```
<Category("Misc"), _
Description("Determines the title of the ToolTip."), _
DefaultValue("")> _
```

```
Public Property ToolTipTitle() As String
    Get
        Return TextBoxToolTip.ToolTipTitle
    End Get
    Set(ByVal value As String)
        TextBoxToolTip.ToolTipTitle = value
    End Set
End Property
```

Note one final thing about these four tooltip-related properties. Each has the same `Category`, `Description`, and `DefaultValue` attributes as its counterpart in the `ToolTip` class. This helps provide consistency for these properties for the developer using this control and using the `ToolTip` class for another control.

Key Events

Before diving into the code that supports these properties, I want to take a minute to discuss the order of key events. These are the events that occur when a user types a character in the `TextBoxExtended` control. The order of events is as follows: `KeyDown`, `KeyPress`, `KeyUp`.

The `KeyDown` event occurs when a key is pressed, and the `KeyPress` event occurs immediately after the `KeyDown` event. The `KeyUp` event occurs once when the user releases the key that was pressed. Both the `KeyDown` and `KeyPress` events are fired in succession if a user presses a key and holds it down. These events are fired to process each repeating character for the key. The `KeyUp` event is executed only once — as soon as the key is released.

The `KeyDown` and `KeyUp` events are passed the `KeyEventArgs` class, which provides data for the `KeyDown` and `KeyUp` events. The `KeyPress` event is passed the `KeyPressEventArgs` class, which provides a different set of data specific to the `KeyPress` event.

The `KeyEventArgs` class provides information about key combinations, such as when a control key is pressed. This would be the Shift key, Ctrl key, Alt key, and so on. It also provides information about the actual key that was pressed. For example, if the a key was pressed, you can query information about the key, such as which key it is and the `Integer` value that represents the key. Note that the key data that is returned in this class is a value from the `Keys` enumeration and only contains uppercase keys; thus, both a lowercase a and an uppercase A are the same in the `Keys` enumeration.

The `KeyPressEventArgs` class provides a `Char` data type of the key that was pressed. If the key pressed was a lowercase a, then the `KeyChar` value returned from this class contains the lowercase a. If the key pressed was an uppercase A, then the `KeyChar` value returned contains the uppercase A.

Knowing how these events work, the order in which they are fired, and the data available to these events helps you determine in which event you should place your code. Given that you want to stop certain keys from being entered into the control based on various properties, the `KeyPress` event is the logical event handler to implement your code. This way you are able to trap the key being pressed even if the user continues to hold the key down, and you can discern between uppercase and lowercase letters.

To that end, the event handler procedure for the `KeyPress` event is shown next. This is where you implement the code for the properties that you are handling.

TextBoxExtended_KeyPress Event Handler Procedure

The first property that you want to check for is the `AllowCharacters` property. Remember that when this property is set, it saves the value in the `blnAllowCharacters` variable. A lot of developers would simply query the property in the `If...Then` statement, writing their statement as follows: `If Not AllowCharacters Then`. This causes a lot of extra code to be unnecessarily executed as control branches from this procedure to the code in the property. All you need to do is query the `blnAllowCharacters` variable directly in your `If...Then` statement. This is more efficient and no branching to another procedure takes place.

If the `AllowCharacters` property has been set to `True`, then the `blnAllowCharacters` variable contains a value of `True` and you execute the code inside the `If...Then` statement. Using the `Char` structure, you can test whether the key pressed is an alpha character by calling the `IsLetter` method in the `Char` structure. You pass the `IsLetter` method the `Char` data type to be tested, which is provided to you in the `KeyChar` property of the `KeyPressEventArgs` class. The `IsLetter` method returns a `True` or `False` `Boolean` value indicating whether the key pressed is an alpha character.

If the `IsLetter` method returns a value of `True`, then you want to prevent this alpha character from being entered into the `TextBoxExtended` control. The `KeyPressEventArgs` class provides the `Handled` property. The `Handled` property gets or sets a `Boolean` value that indicates whether the `KeyPress` event is handled by the control. This property has a default value of `False`, indicating that the control has not handled the `KeyPress` event, and thus sends the key that was pressed to the operating system for processing. By setting the `Handled` property to `True`, you prevent the key from being processed by the operating system and thus prevent it from being displayed in the control.

```
Private Sub TextBoxExtended_KeyPress(ByVal sender As Object, _
    ByVal e As System.Windows.Forms.KeyPressEventArgs) Handles Me.KeyPress

    'If not allowing characters...
    If Not blnAllowCharacters Then
        'Check the key character entered
        If Char.IsLetter(e.KeyChar) Then
            'Stop the character from being entered
            e.Handled = True
        End If
    End If
```

Next, check the `AllowNumbers` property. When this property is set, it sets the value that it receives in the `blnAllowNumbers` variable. Therefore, use that variable in your `If...Then` statement.

If you are not allowing numbers, you need to make two checks. The first check uses the `IsNumber` method of the `Char` structure. This method checks a character to determine whether it is a number in the range of `0` through `9`. This check would be enough for most applications but in an effort to be thorough, I have also included the check for radix-10 digits by calling the `IsDigit` method. This method checks a Unicode character to determine whether it is a radix-10 digit.

If either of these checks returns a value of `True`, then you set the `Handled` property of the `KeyPressEventArgs` class to `True`. Again, this prevents the character from being processed by the operating system, thereby preventing it from being displayed in the control.

```
    'If not allowing numbers...
    If Not blnAllowNumbers Then
        'Check the key character entered
```

```
            If Char.IsNumber(e.KeyChar) Or Char.IsDigit(e.KeyChar) Then
                'Stop the character from being entered
                e.Handled = True
            End If
        End If
    End If
```

The check for special characters is next and this little bit of logic is more involved. If you'll recall the discussion earlier about the `AllowSpecialCharacters` property, this works in conjunction with the `SpecialCharacterList` property. Thus, the code that follows requires checking the character entered against all the special characters contained in the `SpecialCharacterList` property.

This section of code starts by querying the `blnAllowSpecialCharacters` variable; if it is not `True`, then you proceed with the next line of code. A `For Each...Next` loop has been set up to process all characters in the `chrSpecialCharacterList` Char array. The `chrCharacter` variable has been defined as a `Char` data type in order to access each `Char` data type in the `chrSpecialCharacterList` Char array.

Inside the `For Each...Next` loop, you compare the character contained in the `chrCharacter` variable against the character contained in the `KeyChar` property of the `KeyPressEventArgs` class passed as the e input parameter to this procedure. If these two characters are equal, you set the `Handled` property to `True` and then exit the loop. If these two characters do not match, then you process the next character contained in the `chrSpecialCharacterList` Char array.

```
            'If not allowing special characters...
            If Not blnAllowSpecialCharacters Then
                'Loop through the special character list
                For Each chrCharacter In chrSpecialCharacterList
                    If chrCharacter = e.KeyChar Then
                        'Stop the character from being entered
                        e.Handled = True
                        'Exit the loop as a match was found
                        Exit For
                    End If
                Next
            End If
```

The next section of code handles the `CharacterCasing` property. Using a `Select...Case` statement, you provide a `Case` statement for each constant in the `OverloadsCharacterCasing` enumeration, comparing it to the value contained in the `intCharacterCasing` variable.

The `CharacterCasing` property overloads the `CharacterCasing` property in the base class. Remember that the base class has already implemented code to convert the characters entered in the control to all uppercase or all lowercase depending on the value set in this property. Therefore, the first part of this code checks the `Normal`, `Upper`, and `Lower` constants from the `OverloadsCharacterCasing` enumeration and does nothing if one of these constants has been specified in the `CharacterCasing` property. This lets the base class handle conversion of those characters if necessary.

When the `Normal` constant has been set, you do not want to make any changes to the characters entered, so a comment has been added to that effect. When the `Upper` or `Lower` constant has been specified, you still do not want to do anything; the base class will take care of it because your `CharacterCasing` property set the same value in the base class' `CharacterCasing` property. Therefore, the appropriate comment has been added to each of these `Case` statements as well.

```
'Set the case of the character
Select Case intCharacterCasing
    Case OverloadsCharacterCasing.Normal
        'Do nothing
    Case OverloadsCharacterCasing.Upper
        'Do nothing - let the base class handle it
    Case OverloadsCharacterCasing.Lower
        'Do nothing - let the base class handle it
```

The `Proper` constant is the constant that you added to the `CharacterCasing` property to enhance this property. Therefore, you must provide the code to handle the conversion of characters when required. The `blnSpaceEntered` variable is used to determine whether a space character has been entered prior to the current character. There is a check for a space character later in this procedure that sets this variable.

You want to convert the current character only if a space character was entered prior to this character or if this is the first character being entered into the control. The `If...Then` statement in the following code queries the `blnSpaceEntered` variable and checks the `Length` property of the `Text` property of this control for a value of `0`. If either of these conditions are `true`, then you proceed with the code inside the `If...Then` statement.

You cannot change the character entered to uppercase and let it be processed by the operating system. You have to convert the character entered to uppercase and then append it to the `Text` property of the control, which is done in the next line of code. You then set the `Handled` property to `True` to prevent the operating system from processing the character.

Finally, you must manually reposition the cursor within the control, as this is something the operating system would have automatically handled had it processed the character. To do this, set the `SelectionStart` property of the control to the `Length` property of the `Text` property. The `SelectionStart` property sets the starting point for text to be selected in the control. You use this property to your advantage to reposition the cursor so the user can continue typing.

```
Case OverloadsCharacterCasing.Proper
    If blnSpaceEntered Or Me.Text.Length = 0 Then
        'Add the character to the Text property
        Me.Text &= Char.ToUpper(e.KeyChar)
        'Set the Handled property to True to
        'prevent the operating system from processing it
        e.Handled = True
        'Reposition the cursor back to the end of the text
        Me.SelectionStart = Me.Text.Length
    End If
```

When the `CharacterCasing` property has been set using the `Sentence` constant from the `OverloadsCharacterCasing` enumeration, you want to convert the first character of the first word of each sentence to uppercase. The assumptions here are that a sentence starts with the first word entered in the control and that the next sentence starts after a period and a space.

Given these assumptions, you must look for either the first character entered or both a period and a space. The If...Then statement first examines the Length property of the Text property of the control. If the Length property is equal to 0, then this is the first character being entered and you convert the character to an uppercase character.

If the Length property is greater than 0, then the next check is for both a period and space using the Boolean variables blnPeriod and blnSpace. If both of these variables are set to True, then you convert the character to an uppercase character.

The logic to convert the character is the same as that for the previous Case statement. You convert the character entered to uppercase and then append it to the Text property of the control. Then you set the Handled property to True to prevent the operating system from processing the character, and then reposition the cursor within the control by setting the SelectionStart property using the Length property of the Text property of the control.

After you have converted the character to uppercase, you must turn off the period flag by setting the blnPeriodEntered variable to a value of False. You'll see how this variable is set to True in the next segment of code discussed.

```
Case OverloadsCharacterCasing.Sentence
    'If this is the first character...
    If Me.Text.Length = 0 Or _
        (blnPeriodEntered And blnSpaceEntered) Then
        'Add the character to the Text property
        Me.Text &= Char.ToUpper(e.KeyChar)
        'Set the Handled property to True to
        'prevent the operating system from processing it
        e.Handled = True
        'Reposition the cursor back to the end of the text
        Me.SelectionStart = Me.Text.Length
        'Turn off the period flag
        blnPeriodEntered = False
    End If
End Select
```

The blnSpaceEntered variable is set in the next check when the character entered is a white space character, as determined by the IsWhiteSpace method of the Char structure. This method categorizes the space character, line separator character, and paragraph separator character as white space and returns True if any of these characters are entered. This method also recognizes linefeed, newline, and carriage return characters as white-space characters. Thus, if the control has the MultiLine property set to True, then it would also take those characters into consideration.

The reason for having this check for a space character at the end of this procedure is that this check sets the blnSpaceEntered variable to True or False based on the value returned from the IsWhiteSpace method. For example, if a space character were entered, then the blnSpaceEntered variable would be set to True.

When the next character is processed, the logic for the CharacterCasing property is executed, and if processing was for either the Proper or Sentence constants, then this variable would come into play having already been set to True. Then, after processing the character and converting it to uppercase as required by the previous logic, this variable would be set to False.

The check for a period is made in the last section of code. Here you use the `CompareTo` method of the `Char` structure to compare the character entered against a period. Remember that the `KeyChar` is a property returned from the `KeyPressEventArgs` class, and this property is returned as a `Char` structure; therefore, you have access to the methods and fields of the `Char` structure through the `KeyChar` property.

The `CompareTo` method compares two characters and returns an `Integer` value indicating their relevance. The first value is contained in the `KeyChar` property itself and the second value is passed to the `CompareTo` method; in this case, you pass a period.

When the `Integer` value returned is less than zero, a negative number, this indicates that the instance (the value contained in the `KeyChar` property) is less than the value (the character you pass). A return value of zero indicates that the instance and value are equal, which is what you are looking for in your code. Finally, a return value greater than zero indicates that the instance is greater than the value passed to the `CompareTo` method.

If the character entered is a period, then the `blnPeriodEntered` variable is set to a value of `True`. Notice that this section of code does not set the value to `False` when the character is not a period. This is because when you are looking for the end of a sentence, the space character should follow the period. Therefore, you do not want to reset this variable here. It is reset in the `Case` statement above to process the code for the `Sentence` constant of the `OverloadsCharacterCasing` enumeration.

```
        'Track the space key
        If Char.IsWhiteSpace(e.KeyChar) Then
            blnSpaceEntered = True
        Else
            blnSpaceEntered = False
        End If

        'Track the period key
        If e.KeyChar.CompareTo("."c) = 0 Then
            blnPeriodEntered = True
        End If
    End Sub
```

TextBoxExtended_KeyUp Event Handler Procedure

The next procedure contains a fix for what I consider to be a bug in the `TextBox` control. By default, the shortcut keys are enabled for the control, thus allowing the shortcuts Ctrl+Z, Ctrl+X, Ctrl+C, and Ctrl+V for the undo, cut, copy, and paste commands, respectively. Every other Windows application supports Ctrl+A for the select all command, even the Visual Studio IDE. Why this basic shortcut key is not implemented in this control is unclear, but the following procedure fixes this behavior.

The `KeyUp` event is where you need to implement this shortcut, as you want all text in the control selected when you release the shortcut keys. The `KeyEventArgs` class is passed to the `KeyUp` event handler and this class provides properties to detect if a modifier key (Alt, Ctrl, Shift) was also pressed in combination with another key.

The following code queries the `Control` property of the `KeyEventArgs` class, which returns a `Boolean` value indicating whether the Ctrl key was pressed. In addition, you query the `KeyCode` property to see whether it equals the `A` key from the `Keys` enumeration, as shown in the following code. If both of these tests are `true`, then you select all the text in the control.

To select all the text in the control, set the SelectionStart property to 0, which indicates that the selection of text starts with the first character. This property uses a zero-based index to specify the offset of the characters in the control. You then set the SelectionLength property to the Length property of the Text property. The SelectionLength property selects the number of characters specified in this property, starting with the character specified in the SelectionStart property.

```
Private Sub TextBoxExtended_KeyUp(ByVal sender As Object, _
    ByVal e As System.Windows.Forms.KeyEventArgs) Handles Me.KeyUp

    'Fix CTRL+A shortcut key to select all text
    If e.Control And e.KeyCode = Keys.A Then
        Me.SelectionStart = 0
        Me.SelectionLength = Me.Text.Length
    End If
End Sub
```

TextBoxExtended_Validating Event Handler Procedure

The last procedure in the TextBoxExtended class is the TextBoxExtended_Validating procedure. This procedure is the event handler for the Validating event. The Validating event is fired when the current control loses focus but before focus is set to the next control. You can cancel the Validating event, thereby rendering the control as invalidated and thus preventing another control from receiving focus.

The code in this procedure checks the value of the intMinLength variable. If you'll recall, this variable is set by the MinLength property. If the value in this variable is greater than 0, then you want to validate the Length property of the Text property to ensure that the user has entered the minimum number of characters, which is done in the next line of code.

If the Length property of the Text property is less than the value contained in the intMinLength variable, then you cancel the Validating event, which effectively invalidates the control, preventing focus from moving to another control. You then display a message box dialog box indicating that the minimum number of characters has not been entered and specify that minimum requirement, as contained in the intMinLength variable.

```
Private Sub TextBoxExtended_Validating(ByVal sender As Object, _
    ByVal e As System.ComponentModel.CancelEventArgs) Handles Me.Validating

    'Validate the minimum length
    If intMinLength > 0 Then
        If Me.Text.Length < intMinLength Then
            e.Cancel = True
            MessageBox.Show("This TextBox has a required minimum length " & _
                "of " & intMinLength.ToString & " characters.", _
                My.Application.Info.Title, MessageBoxButtons.OK, _
                MessageBoxIcon.Information)
        End If
    End If
End Sub
```

Controls Demo Class

The Controls Demo class is the class for the Controls Demo form. It contains a minimum amount of code so this section covers the code in its entirety. The code in this class provides for setting some of the properties dynamically based on the values that you enter in the form at runtime.

Controls_Demo_Load Event Handler Procedure

Let's start with the code in the form's Load event. The txtSpecialCharacterList TextBoxExtended control contains some special characters that were set in the Text property at design time. When the form loads, you want to take the characters entered here and set them in the SpecialCharacterList property of the txtAllowSpecialCharacters TextBoxExtended control.

This is done by taking the String value returned by the Text property and calling the ToCharArray method on the String class. This method copies the characters in the String, converts them to a Char array, and returns a Char array data type. This Char array is then set in the SpecialCharacterList property of the txtAllowSpecialCharacters control.

The last two lines of code here set the SelectedIndex property of the two ComboBox controls on the form to specify the default value of the ToolTip icon and the ToolTip balloon.

```
Private Sub Controls_Demo_Load(ByVal sender As System.Object, _
    ByVal e As System.EventArgs) Handles MyBase.Load

    'Set default values
    txtAllowSpecialCharacters.SpecialCharacterList = _
        txtSpecialCharacterList.Text.ToCharArray

    cboToolTipIcon.SelectedIndex = 0
    cboToolTipIsBalloon.SelectedIndex = 1
End Sub
```

txtSpecialCharacterList_LostFocus Event Handler Procedure

As you are running the Custom Controls application, you can change the special characters contained in the TextBoxExtended control below the label that reads SpecialCharacterList. When this control loses focus, the special characters that you entered are converted into a Char array and set in the SpecialCharacterList property of the txtAllowSpecialCharacters control. The code in the following txtSpecialCharacterList_LostFocus procedure demonstrates this.

This enables you to change the list of special characters and then test this new list in the txtAllowSpecialCharacters control. You can keep changing the list and then perform another test to get a solid grasp of how this property works in conjunction with the AllowSpecialCharacters property.

```
Private Sub txtSpecialCharacterList_LostFocus(ByVal sender As Object, _
    ByVal e As System.EventArgs) Handles txtSpecialCharacterList.LostFocus
    'Reload the SpecialCharacterList property of the
    'txtAllowSpecialCharacters TextBoxExtended control
    txtAllowSpecialCharacters.SpecialCharacterList = _
        txtSpecialCharacterList.Text.ToCharArray
End Sub
```

txtSpecifyMinLength_LostFocus Event Handler Procedure

The next procedure handles the LostFocus event for the TextBoxExtended control with the label Specify Min Length. This control enables you to specify the minimum length that will be required in the TextBoxExtended control with the label MinLength = 0.

This procedure takes the value that you entered in the control and converts it to an Integer data type and sets it in the MinLength property of the txtMinLength control. It then changes the label above this control to read MinLength = and the value that you specify.

This enables you to test the MinLength property using various lengths and to test the behavior of this property when you try to navigate to another control without entering the minimum number of characters. Remember that trying to navigate away from this control either by tabbing or clicking another control with the mouse causes the Validating event to be fired, and a check is performed on the length of the characters that you entered against the MinLength property.

```
Private Sub txtSpecifyMinLength_LostFocus(ByVal sender As Object, _
    ByVal e As System.EventArgs) Handles txtSpecifyMinLength.LostFocus

    'Reset the MinLength property of the txtMinLength TextBoxExtended control
    txtMinLength.MinLength = CType(txtSpecifyMinLength.Text, Integer)
    lblMinLength.Text = "MinLength = " & txtSpecifyMinLength.Text
End Sub
```

txtToolTip_LostFocus Event Handler Procedure

The txtToolTip_LostFocus procedure is the event handler for the LostFocus event of the TextBoxExtended control with the label ToolTip =. This procedure will set the ToolTip property of this control and the control with the label ToolTipTitle =. This enables you to test the tooltip that you set on two different TextBoxExtended controls. As you can see in the following code, the ToolTip property is set using the Text property of the txtToolTip TextBoxExtended control:

```
Private Sub txtToolTip_LostFocus(ByVal sender As Object, _
    ByVal e As System.EventArgs) Handles txtToolTip.LostFocus

    'Set the ToolTip property of the two TextBoxExtended controls
    'in this GroupBox
    txtToolTip.ToolTip = txtToolTip.Text
    txtToolTipTitle.ToolTip = txtToolTip.Text
End Sub
```

txtToolTipTitle_LostFocus Event Handler Procedure

When you set a ToolTip title in the TextBoxExtended control with the label ToolTipTitle = and then navigate to another control, the ToolTipTitle property is set in this control and the TextBoxExtended control with the label ToolTip =. Again, this enables you to test the ToolTip title on two different TextBoxExtended controls.

```
Private Sub txtToolTipTitle_LostFocus(ByVal sender As Object, _
    ByVal e As System.EventArgs) Handles txtToolTipTitle.LostFocus
```

```
                'Set the ToolTipTitle property of the two TextBoxExtended controls
                'in this GroupBox
                txtToolTip.ToolTipTitle = txtToolTipTitle.Text
                txtToolTipTitle.ToolTipTitle = txtToolTipTitle.Text
        End Sub
```

cboToolTipIcon_SelectedIndexChanged Event Handler Procedure

The ComboBox with the label ToolTipIcon = contains a list of available ToolTip icons that are displayed in the ToolTipIcon property. When you make a selection in this ComboBox, the SelectedIndexChanged event is fired and the following code is executed. Using this ComboBox, you can set the ToolTip icon that is displayed in the tooltip in the txtToolTip and txtToolTipTitle controls. Using a Select...Case statement, the text of the selected entry is found and then the corresponding ToolTipIcon property is set in the txtToolTip and txtToolTipTitle controls.

```
        Private Sub cboToolTipIcon_SelectedIndexChanged(ByVal sender As Object, _
            ByVal e As System.EventArgs) Handles cboToolTipIcon.SelectedIndexChanged

            'Set the ToolTipIcon property based on the selected icon
            Select Case cboToolTipIcon.Text
                Case "None"
                    txtToolTip.ToolTipIcon = ToolTipIcon.None
                    txtToolTipTitle.ToolTipIcon = ToolTipIcon.None
                Case "Info"
                    txtToolTip.ToolTipIcon = ToolTipIcon.Info
                    txtToolTipTitle.ToolTipIcon = ToolTipIcon.Info
                Case "Warning"
                    txtToolTip.ToolTipIcon = ToolTipIcon.Warning
                    txtToolTipTitle.ToolTipIcon = ToolTipIcon.Warning
                Case "Error"
                    txtToolTip.ToolTipIcon = ToolTipIcon.Error
                    txtToolTipTitle.ToolTipIcon = ToolTipIcon.Error
            End Select
        End Sub
```

cboToolTipIsBalloon_SelectedIndexChanged Event Handler Procedure

The last code procedure in this form class is the cboToolTipIsBalloon_SelectedIndexChanged procedure. This is the event handler for the SelectedIndexChanged event of the ComboBox control with the label ToolTipIsBalloon =. When you select an entry in this ComboBox, the ToolTipIsBalloon property is set on the txtToolTip and txtToolTipTitle controls using the value specified in this ComboBox.

```
        Private Sub cboToolTipIsBalloon_SelectedIndexChanged( _
            ByVal sender As Object, ByVal e As System.EventArgs) _
            Handles cboToolTipIsBalloon.SelectedIndexChanged

            'Turn the ToolTipIsBalloon property on or off
            txtToolTip.ToolTipIsBalloon = CType(cboToolTipIsBalloon.Text, Boolean)
            txtToolTipTitle.ToolTipIsBalloon = CType(cboToolTipIsBalloon.Text, Boolean)
        End Sub
```

Setting Up the Custom Controls Application

You have two options for setting up the Custom Controls application: use the installer or manually copy the required files to your computer. The first option provides an easy, fast approach to installing the application, whereas the second method provides more control over where the application is placed.

Using the Installer

To install the Custom Controls application, locate the `Chapter 10 - Custom Controls\Installer` folder on the CD-ROM that came with this book and double-click the `setup.exe` program. You will be prompted with the Application Install dialog. Clicking the Install button will install and launch the application. Once the installer has installed your program, it is ready to be used.

Manual Installation

To manually install the Custom Controls application, first create a folder on your computer where you want to place the program executable files. Then locate the `Chapter 10 - Custom Controls\Source` folder on the CD-ROM that came with this book and navigate to the `bin\Release` folder. Copy the following files from the `Release` folder to the folder that you created on your computer:

- ❑ `Custom Controls.exe`
- ❑ `TextBoxEx.dll`

Configuring the Application

No configuration is needed. Simply run the application and start experimenting with the properties that were added to the `TextBoxExtended` control.

Summary

While this chapter was fairly short and the amount of code added to the `TextBoxExtended` class was minimal, the functionality implemented goes a long way in simplifying your life as a developer. The properties that are implemented in this control eliminate the need for you to constantly write the same code to implement this functionality yourself. Now, all you need to do is set a property on the control at design time or at runtime and the functionality will automatically be implemented.

Whenever an existing control in the .NET Framework has been extended throughout this book, the `CategoryAttribute`, `DescriptionAttribute`, and `DefaultAttribute` classes were used to provide the appropriate information for design-time support in the Properties window. This chapter showed you the importance of this, especially when implementing properties that affect the way a control behaves and in providing miscellaneous support, as with the `ToolTip` properties.

Adding a property to the correct category is essential, as is providing a description of the property that appropriately describes its purpose. You also saw how setting the appropriate default value can affect the developer implementing this control. Always remember that if you are in doubt about the default value that should be set, then you should set it to an empty string or 0 if the property implements a numerical value.

New in this chapter was the code for a property that overloaded an existing property, as demonstrated with the `CharacterCasing` property. Here you took an existing property of the `TextBox` control and enhanced it while still taking advantage of the code in the base class. You saw firsthand how you can provide code for the enhanced portion of the property and how to let the base class execute its code for its implementation of the property.

Providing ToolTip functionality for the `TextBoxExtended` control was covered through the implementation of an object that was defined as a `ToolTip` class. This allowed you to implement various tooltip properties that used the `ToolTip` object and in turn provided built-in tooltip functionality for the `TextBoxExtended` control.

Index